PRESIDENTIAL DEBATES

Presidential Debates

Risky Business on the Campaign Trail

Third Edition

ALAN SCHROEDER

 Columbia University Press   *New York*

Columbia University Press
Publishers Since 1893
New York   Chichester, West Sussex

cup.columbia.edu

Library of Congress Cataloging-in-Publication Data

Names: Schroeder, Alan, 1954– author.
Title: Presidential debates : risky business on the campaign trail /
Alan Schroeder.
Description: Third edition. | New York : Columbia University Press, [2016] |
Includes bibliographical references and index. | Description based on print version
record and CIP data provided by publisher; resource not viewed.
Identifiers: LCCN 2015050152 (print) | LCCN 2015043873 (e-book) |
ISBN 9780231541503 (e-book) | ISBN 9780231170567 (cloth : alk. paper) |
ISBN 9780231170574 (pbk. : alk. paper)
Subjects: LCSH: Campaign debates—United States. |
Television in politics—United States. | Presidents—United States—Election.
Classification: LCC JF2112.D43 (print) | LCC JF2112.D43 S37 2016 (e-book) |
DDC 324.7/30973—dc23
LC record available at http://lccn.loc.gov/2015050152

♾️

Columbia University Press books are printed on permanent and durable
acid-free paper.
Printed in the United States of America

c 10 9 8 7 6 5 4 3 2 1
p 10 9 8 7 6 5 4 3 2 1

COVER IMAGE: Photo by Doug Pensinger/ © Getty Images
COVER DESIGN: Milenda Nan Ok Lee

This book is dedicated to
Carl Schroeder, Jennifer Schroeder Dahlen,
Kirsten Schroeder Larkin, and Dan Hammons

CONTENTS

Introduction: The First Presidential Debate **1**

Part I: Anticipation

1 / The Predebate Debate **15**
2 / Predebate Strategy **51**
3 / Candidate Preparation **92**
4 / Predebate News Coverage **114**

Part II: Execution

5 / The Debaters **149**
6 / The Questioners **205**
7 / The Productions **240**

Part III: Reaction

8 / Social Media and Real-Time Reactions **275**
9 / Postdebate News Coverage **291**
10 / Debates and Voters **325**

Conclusion: The Globalization of an American Tradition **339**

Schedule of Televised Presidential and
Vice Presidential Debates, 1960–2012 **347**
Notes **351**
Selected Bibliography **399**
Index **405**

PRESIDENTIAL DEBATES

I should say the most important thing about the business of government and politics is not to bore the people.
—Richard Nixon to Jack Paar, *Tonight Show*, August 25, 1960

INTRODUCTION

The First Presidential Debate

September 26, 1960. At exactly 7:30 P.M., a shiny Oldsmobile carrying Vice President Richard M. Nixon pulled into an interior drive at the CBS broadcast facility in downtown Chicago. As with other details surrounding the first presidential debate in history, the timing of Nixon's arrival at this skating rink–turned–television station had been meticulously plotted. Like dueling divas, Nixon and his opponent, John F. Kennedy, would reach the studio a comfortable quarter hour apart.

For Richard Nixon, the evening began almost as unpromisingly as it would end. Stepping out of the backseat of the car, he banged his knee sharply and painfully against the door; bystanders waiting to greet him saw the color drain from his face. Just two weeks earlier, the vice president had concluded twelve days of hospitalization for a knee infection caused by a similar mishap with a car door. Almost immediately after his release, Nixon had bounded back onto the campaign trail, hoping to make up for lost time with a grueling schedule of cross-country travel. Now, heading into the most critical media event of his life, he looked exhausted, underweight, and wan—"better suited for going to a funeral, perhaps his own, than to a debate," in the view of journalist David Halberstam.[1]

At the WBBM loading dock, Nixon quickly composed himself and started through a high-powered receiving line. Gathered to greet this first of the star debaters were the titans of American broadcasting: fierce competitors like William Paley of CBS, Robert Sarnoff of NBC, and Leonard Goldenson of ABC, momentarily allied in their patronage of the 1960 debates. Working the line, Nixon came to Oliver Treyz, the president of ABC News, who greeted the candidate by asking what no one else had dared: "How do you feel?"

At a dinner commemorating the debate twenty-five years later, Treyz would recall the moment: "I asked the question because he looked ill. And he said, 'Not so well. I have a temperature of a hundred and two degrees.'" When Nixon pulled from his pocket the bottle of Terramycin he was taking, Treyz asked if he wished to cancel. Nixon declined, saying he did not want to be seen as a coward.[2]

Poor physical health and a freshly injured knee were only the beginning of Richard Nixon's troubles. For weeks, a more vexing problem had been brewing: a lack of appreciation by campaign decision makers for the momentousness of the occasion. "Nixon knew the power of television very well," said Ted Rogers, Nixon's television adviser, "but I don't think the people around him did." According to Rogers, Kennedy's staff handled their candidate as a thoroughbred, while Nixon's treated theirs like a mule, "working him to death."[3] Nixon had turned down an invitation from debate producer-director Don Hewitt for a preproduction meeting; Kennedy used his session to grill the director about staging details. As Hewitt saw it, for Nixon the debate was "just another campaign appearance."[4]

To prepare for the broadcast, Vice President Nixon studied briefing books by himself, dismissing suggestions that he rehearse with aides. Senator Kennedy, by contrast, brought an entourage to Chicago two days ahead of schedule, and spent much of the weekend holed up in a hotel suite practicing his responses out loud. In the hours immediately before broadcast, members of Kennedy's campaign team were still lobbing questions at him.

Fifteen minutes after Nixon's arrival at WBBM, the network executives reassembled to greet the man who would emerge as the evening's undisputed champion. Unlike his Republican counterpart, John F. Kennedy arrived fit, rested, and ready. Weeks of open-air campaigning around the country had left Kennedy bronzed. Journalist Howard K. Smith, who moderated the first debate, would compare JFK to an "athlete come to receive his wreath of laurel." Said Nixon's adviser Rogers, "When he came in the studio I thought he was Cochise, he was so tan."[5]

As Kennedy strode down the long corridor linking the driveway to Studio One, Nixon was already on the debate set, posing for cameramen with an air of jocularity that would quickly evaporate. "Have you ever had a picture printed yet?" Nixon teased one of the photographers, getting a laugh from the group: "You're always taking them, I never see them printed." Kennedy's entrance into the studio a few moments later immediately siphoned attention away from Nixon. "I assume you two guys know each other," Hewitt cracked, as the rivals extended their hands in greeting. The cameramen clamored for shots of the pair shaking hands; over and over they obliged, their chitchat muffled by the snap of flash bulbs.

"You get that tan the way I do?" Nixon asked Kennedy, prefiguring postdebate interest in the candidates' appearance. "Riding around in open cars? It's the wind, you know, not the sun." Though Kennedy's answer is not recorded, it is apparent from the question that the vice president was struck by how well his opponent looked. Did Nixon sense that his own posthospital pallor was no match for Kennedy's summer glow? For weeks, television consultant Rogers had urged Nixon to use a sun lamp. Like most of Rogers's advice, the recommendation went unheeded.

After shooing away the photographers, Don Hewitt ushered Kennedy and Nixon to their seats on the debate set for a quick orientation. Footage of this meeting shows Nixon casting his glance at a monitor offscreen, uncomfortably shifting positions in his chair, seeming to pass in and out of a daze. Kennedy, who does not deign to look at Nixon, occupies his side of the studio set with the casual presumption of a lion in his den.[6]

To both debaters, Hewitt offered the services of CBS's top makeup artist, imported from New York for the occasion. When Kennedy said no, Nixon quickly followed suit, in a show of machismo that proved to be a serious blunder. "What I tried to explain to Dick," Rogers later recalled, "was he has a certain characteristic of his skin where it's almost transparent. And it was a very nice thought to say 'I don't want any makeup,' but he really needed it in order to have what we would call even an acceptable television picture."[7]

Nixon himself knew this. Two weeks before the first debate, he spoke of the cosmetic peculiarities of his skin in a television interview with Walter Cronkite: "I can shave within 30 seconds before I go on television and still have a beard, unless we put some powder on, as we have done today."[8] Instead of giving Nixon a proper predebate makeup job, an aide slathered Nixon's face with an over-the-counter cosmetic called "Lazy Shave," the same product the vice president had worn in his "kitchen debate" with Nikita Khrushchev a year earlier. Meanwhile, unknown to Nixon, Kennedy got a touch-up from his own people.

In the technical checks that followed, each debater took a final opportunity to sit before the lens for last-minute adjustments. Kennedy's advisers examined the shade of their man's dark suit to make sure an appropriate contrast would be achieved on camera, and a staff person was dispatched back to the hotel for a blue shirt, which the senator donned for the broadcast. Another handler had brought along a pair of long socks, in case regular socks looked too short when the candidates were shown sitting on the set.

If JFK's tech check was obsessive, the other side's was fatalistic. Alarmed by Nixon's on-screen appearance, Hewitt asked Ted Rogers if he approved of the way his debater looked. Although Rogers pronounced himself "satisfied"[9]—*resigned* might have been a better word—Hewitt felt concerned enough to press the matter with his boss at CBS, Frank Stanton. Stanton again asked Rogers if the shots of Nixon were acceptable, and again Rogers said yes.

Exacerbating his misfortune, Nixon had selected a light gray suit which, according to CBS News president Sig Mickelson, "blended into the background and, if anything, exaggerated his pale appearance."[10] At the Republicans' insistence, stagehands repainted the gray backdrop several times in the hours before the debate, but each new coat dried lighter than Nixon's people had anticipated. As air time approached, the backdrop was still moist from the latest application.

With less than half an hour to go, both candidates retired to their dressing rooms.

In Hyannis Port, Massachusetts, Jacqueline Kennedy, six months pregnant with her second child, was hosting a debate-watching party. About thirty people had gathered in the Kennedys' summer home on Nantucket Sound, where the guest list included Jackie's sister, Lee Radziwill; Harvard professors Archibald Cox and Arthur Schlesinger Jr. and their wives; Democratic committeewomen from around New England; and last but not least, about a dozen journalists.

Jackie Kennedy's "Listening Party," as the newspapers anachronistically termed it, offers further evidence of how differently the two political camps regarded the debate. While the wife of the Democratic candidate used the occasion for public relations, Pat Nixon spent a quiet evening watching at home with her two daughters in Washington, out of sight of reporters until the next day, when she would be enlisted for damage control.

The Boston press breathlessly reported every detail of Jacqueline Kennedy's party on this cool Cape Cod evening: the coffee and pastries in the dining room; the lemon-yellow couch where the hostess perched next to Professor Cox; two-and-a-half-year-old Caroline sleeping upstairs; Jackie's pearl necklace and coral-colored, silk maternity dress. Sensitive to recent press reports about her expensive wardrobe, Mrs. Kennedy assured reporters that the outfit had been sewn by a local seamstress.

Jacqueline Kennedy had rented a sixteen-inch portable television set for the debate. "I own one in Washington," she told her guests, "but we don't have one here. I guess I'll have to break down and buy one." A *Boston Globe* photo showed the television set incongruously situated atop a piece of antique furniture identified as an "early American Governor Winthrop desk."[11]

As the program drew nearer, Jacqueline confessed to being nervous. "I'm not apprehensive," she said in the debutante voice the whole country would soon recognize. "But I'm always nervous before he speaks. I must say I have no reason to be." With partygoers scattered around the room in chairs and on the floor, the moment approached. Mrs. Kennedy herself clicked on the set, took a deep breath, and sat down to watch.

"The candidates need no introduction," began moderator Howard K. Smith. And for the next hour the country's first televised presidential debate unfolded, attracting the largest audience that had ever assembled for a political event. An estimated 70 million Americans watched on television, while several million more listened on radio.[12]

The issues Kennedy and Nixon addressed were familiar to anyone following the news in 1960: communism and national security; labor and farm problems; the candidates' leadership experience. Though the substance of their remarks would account for most of the ink in the next day's papers, it was the debaters' personal characteristics that resonated most strongly with the viewers. "Within hours," wrote David Halberstam, "no one could recall anything that was said, only what they looked liked, what they felt like."[13]

In his landmark book *The Making of the President*, campaign chronicler Theodore White famously limned the contrast between performers: Kennedy "calm and nerveless in appearance," Nixon "tense, almost frightened, at turns glowering and, occasionally, haggard-looking to the point of sickness." For Richard Nixon, White concluded, "everything that could have gone wrong that night went wrong."[14] Media historian Erik Barnouw noted that Kennedy's "air of confidence" came across not only in his statements and gestures, but more crucially during the cutaway reaction shots: "A glimpse of the listening Kennedy showed him attentive, alert, with a suggestion of a smile on his lips. A Nixon glimpse showed him haggard; the lines on his face seemed like gashes and gave a fearful look."[15]

What viewers at home could not know was that these same images were igniting a parallel debate in the control room of WBBM, where the issue was not public policy but visual aesthetics. Candidate cutaways had been a flashpoint in the lengthy and contentious predebate negotiations between the campaigns and the networks, but no firm guidelines had emerged as to how the program would be shot. By prior agreement, the candidates' television representatives sat in the control room during the program: Ted Rogers for Nixon and, for Kennedy, a former WBBM producer named Bill Wilson. With the debate under way, Wilson chided Hewitt that he "owed" Kennedy more reaction shots.

"What do you mean?" Hewitt asked. "I've cut away from Kennedy more than I've cut away from Nixon."

But the reaction shots Wilson wanted were of Nixon. The two advisers got into a heated argument with each other and with Hewitt, each side demanding more reactions of the other's candidate, each keeping a running count of the cutaways. Hewitt was hollering at them both to stop interfering with his work, which, as he saw it, was to serve as a surrogate for people watching in their living rooms. "I didn't try to catch the candidates in a grimace," Hewitt later explained. "I listened to the comments and tried to anticipate the public—to switch to a reaction shot when I thought viewers would expect one."[16] Although Nixon's close-up cutaways would loom larger in the national perception than Kennedy's, postdebate tallies showed eleven reactions of Kennedy running a total of 118 seconds, compared with nine of Nixon totaling 85 seconds.

The potency of these images may unintentionally have been enhanced by improvements in television technology. The day before the debate, CBS engineers outfitted the studio cameras with new tubes that delivered a sharper-than-normal picture. "This was unfortunate for Nixon," CBS's Mickelson concluded. "The cameras exaggerated his paleness and heavy beard, but it was a break for Kennedy, who looked robust and healthy. As the cameras had exaggerated Nixon's apparent ill health, they likewise enhanced Kennedy's rugged vitality."[17] An additional visual factor must be considered: as black and white broadcasts, the debates exuded a documentary crispness that verged on the hyperreal. Especially when compared with debates from later, color-television years, the debates in 1960 offer the clarity and punch of a *Life* magazine photo essay come to life.

Beyond production considerations, an eleventh-hour phone call from running mate Henry Cabot Lodge apparently helped steer Nixon onto the wrong tactical course. Lodge, who had debated Kennedy in their senatorial race in 1952, advised Nixon to take the high road and "erase the assassin image" that had dogged him throughout his political career.[18] And so it was that Richard Nixon adopted a posture of conciliation, even deference, toward his fellow debater. "The things that Senator Kennedy has said many of us can agree with," Nixon declared in his opening statement. "I can subscribe completely to the spirit that Senator Kennedy has expressed tonight."[19] At one point, the Republican nominee chose to forgo a response altogether, passing up the opportunity to rebut his opponent's remarks.

"Thank you, gentlemen. This hour has gone by all too quickly." With this coda from Howard K. Smith, the historic encounter drew to a close. In Texas, Henry Cabot Lodge, the running mate who had counseled gentility in his predebate phone call to Nixon, was heard to say, "That son of a bitch just cost us the election."[20]

Before leaving the studio, Kennedy and Nixon posed for a final round of photographs, making small talk about travel schedules and weather as the shutters clicked away. Afterward, JFK told an aide that whenever a photographer prepared to snap, Nixon "would put a stern expression on his face and start jabbing his finger into my chest, so he would look as if he was laying down the law to me about foreign policy or communism. Nice fellow."[21]

Outside the television station, a crowd of 2,500 political enthusiasts had gathered in the street. Asked by a reporter to estimate the ratio of Democrats to Republicans, a Chicago policeman quipped, "I'd say it's about twenty-five hundred to zero."[22] As Nixon slipped out the back, Kennedy triumphantly emerged at the main entrance of the building to greet his supporters. "When it was all over," Don Hewitt said, "a man walked out of this studio president of the United States. He didn't have to wait till election day."[23]

In what history records as the first example of postdebate spin, Jacqueline Kennedy turned to her guests at program's end and exclaimed, "I think my husband was brilliant."

For most of the hour, Mrs. Kennedy had watched the debate "almost immobile," as one observer put it, though she did get up several times to adjust the picture on the temperamental television set. Others in the highly partisan Kennedy living room broke into laughter when Nixon misspoke and declared, "It's our responsibility that we get rid of the farmer," before correcting himself and saying, "the surpluses." The hostess concealed her reaction to this verbal slip behind a "Mona Lisa–kind of smile."[24]

Fifteen minutes after the debate ended, the phone rang at the Kennedy home in Hyannis Port: the senator was on the line. Jacqueline took the call upstairs, away from the guests, and reappeared a few minutes later. Her husband had asked about the listening party, she said; otherwise their conversation remained private. One of the reporters present wrote that after the call Mrs. Kennedy was "as flushed with happiness and suppressed excitement as a schoolgirl."[25]

The first indication that the debate had not gone Richard Nixon's way came from longtime secretary Rose Mary Woods, a woman he counted among his most honest critics. Shortly after the broadcast, Woods told Nixon about a phone call from her parents in Ohio, who had watched the program and wondered if the vice president was feeling well. When the debate aired in California, Nixon's own mother phoned with the same question. And so the reaction went. "I recognized the basic mistake I had made," Nixon would write in *Six Crises*. "I had concentrated too much on substance and not enough on appearance. I should have remembered that 'a picture is worth a thousand words.' "[26]

Indeed. In the days that followed, the thousands of words printed about the first Kennedy–Nixon debate would be no match for the pictures that had seared themselves into the nation's consciousness. Pat Nixon, flying to her husband's side the next day, gamely told a reporter, "He looked wonderful on my TV set." Nixon himself assured interviewers that despite a weight loss, he felt fine. Press secretary Herbert Klein lamented that "the fault obviously was television," while other Republicans voiced public displeasure with their candidate's kid-gloves approach to his opponent.[27]

JFK, on the other hand, reaped an immediate windfall. Theodore White described the change in the crowds that turned out for Kennedy the next day in northern Ohio: "Overnight, they seethed with enthusiasm and multiplied in numbers, as if the sight of him, in their homes on the video box, had given him a 'star quality' reserved only for television and movie idols." *Time* magazine wrote that before the debate, reporters had amused themselves by counting "jumpers" in the crowds—women who hopped up and down to get a better look at Kennedy: "Now they noted 'double jumpers' [jumpers with babies in their arms]. By week's end they even spotted a few 'leapers' who reached prodigious heights."[28]

Although the mythology surrounding the first Kennedy–Nixon broadcast would greatly amplify in the years to follow, the moral of the story has never varied: presidential debates are best apprehended as *television shows*, governed not by the rules of rhetoric or politics but by the demands of their host medium. The values of debates are the values of television: celebrity, visuals, conflict, and hype. On every level, Kennedy and his team perceived this, while Nixon and his did not.

After Chicago, campaigns would have no choice but to school themselves in the subtleties of visual persuasion, and eagerly have they taken to the task. "It didn't matter whether the televised debate had been decisive in Kennedy's victory," wrote social critic Todd Gitlin. "What mattered was that the management of television was one factor that candidates believed they could control. The time of the professional media consultant had arrived."[29]

Yet the steamroller nature of live television supersedes the campaigns' tireless attempts to minimize risk. Spontaneity is the overriding determinant of presidential debates, and a major reason, perhaps *the* major reason, audiences continue to watch in such staggering numbers. "Modern debates are the political version of the Indianapolis Speedway," according to political scientist Nelson Polsby. "What we're all there for—the journalists, the political pundits, the public—is to see somebody crack up in flames."[30]

Presidential Debates: Risky Business on the Campaign Trail will take the reader on a backstage tour through the fractious world of presidential debates, where the perils are enormous and the precautions illusory. We will meet the cast of characters in the behind-the-scenes drama: the debaters, who perform under unimaginable pressure before the largest audiences of their careers; advisers, who strive to protect their candidates by whatever means necessary; journalists and commentators, who interpret the events; moderators and questioners, who serve as supporting players; debate sponsors and production crews, who navigate a minefield of politics and egos to bring the programs to air; and viewers, the ostensible beneficiaries of the exercise, whose once passive role is being reshaped by interactive digital media.

We will approach presidential debates as the campaigns and media do, following a chronology of anticipation, execution, and reaction. By definition, the live telecast overshadows all else; but as the experience of 1960 shows, debates are also profoundly influenced by what happens before and after the fact—in the campaign, in the media, in the body politic. Thus, our exploration begins with the predebate period, when rules are hammered out, candidates prepped, and expectations set; moves to the debates themselves and the real-time responses they engender; and ends in the postdebate aftermath, when first impressions solidify into conventional wisdom.

The images of John F. Kennedy and Richard M. Nixon that filled the airwaves on September 26, 1960 can be read as harbingers of change. A revolutionary programming genre burst forth that night in Chicago, one that fundamentally realigned both politics and the media in America. In the decades since Kennedy–Nixon, televised debates have lost none of their fascination for the press and the public, and none of their terror for candidates. Choreographed and unscripted, contrived and authentic, debates straddle the fault line between artifice and reality—like everything else on television, only more so. With their clashing co-stars, enormous stakes, and "must-see" status, presidential debates are nothing so much as television writ large.

PART I / ANTICIPATION

1 / THE PREDEBATE DEBATE

A few weeks after losing the election in 1960, Richard Nixon went sailing off the coast of Florida with a group of associates that included a trusted adviser named Leonard Hall. As David Halberstam recounted in an essay in 1976 on the Kennedy–Nixon debates, "There were just a few old friends around and they all went out on a boat. Finally, Hall asked the question he had always wanted to ask—Why did you decide to debate? For a long time Nixon simply looked up at the sky, his eyes closed, his face drawn and tense. And Hall waited, but there was never an answer."[1]

In retrospect, the participation of Richard Nixon in the debates in 1960 qualifies as one of the great political miscalculations in campaign history. Even at the time, the vice president seemed to be acting against his instincts. Early in the race, Nixon assured his handlers that debates with Kennedy were out of the question. "In 1946 a damn fool incumbent named Jerry Voorhis debated a young lawyer and it cost him the election," he reminded staffers, citing his own experience.[2] Nixon obviously understood what later front-runners and incumbents would come to regard as gospel: debates favor the challenger.

In the summer of 1960 John F. Kennedy, by far the lesser-known contender, immediately accepted the invitation of the broadcast networks for a series of televised debates. A few days later, over the objections of President Eisenhower and Republican advisers, Richard Nixon followed suit. Press secretary Herbert G. Klein recalled that his "mouth dropped open" when Nixon announced at a news conference in Chicago that he would debate JFK; senior campaign aides had not been notified. "I could attribute his reversal only to the fact that he did not want his manhood sullied by appearing as if he were afraid to win such an encounter," Klein wrote.[3] According to Nixon's biographer Earl Mazo, "The vice president could find no way of rejecting the television network offers."[4]

By the end of the Kennedy–Nixon series, provocative new lessons about television and politics had come into focus; on the future of presidential debates, however, opinion split down the middle. The more optimistic observers saw debates as inevitable. Walter Lippmann predicted that "from now on it will be impossible for any candidate . . . to avoid this kind of confrontation with his opponent." Others, like Eisenhower's press secretary James Hagerty, reached a different conclusion: "You can bet your bottom dollar that no incumbent president will ever engage in any such debate or joint appearance in the future."[5]

As it happened, the pessimists came closer to the mark than the optimists, and another sixteen years would pass before candidates for the White House again agreed to debate. It is interesting to note that before his assassination, President Kennedy had verbally committed to a second round of appearances in 1964. Furthermore, according to Republican nominee Barry Goldwater, Kennedy and Goldwater had seriously discussed a plan to barnstorm the country together in a series of matches. "We even talked about using the same airplane and doing it the old-fashioned way—get out on the stump and debate," Goldwater reported.[6]

But the election of 1964 rolled around with an unanticipated Democratic nominee. Lyndon Johnson, nobody's idea of a glittering television personality, gave campaign debates a wide berth as the incumbent president. In 1968 and 1972, once-burned Richard Nixon likewise refused to meet his opponents for a joint appearance. "The 1960 Great Debates had taught him a bitter lesson," wrote the authors of a Twentieth Century Fund study of presidential debates. "He would take no more chances with programs that might show him in an unfavorable light, literally or figuratively."[7]

Both Nixon and Johnson hid behind a legal technicality that blocked the television networks from airing candidate forums: Section 315 of the Communications Act, which granted all participants in a race, even those on the fringe, "equal opportunities" to television time. Broadcasters had been lobbying against this restriction since the 1950s. Their original hope in sponsoring the Kennedy–Nixon debates was to rid themselves of Section 315, but Congress agreed only to a temporary suspension for the campaign of 1960.

In 1975, in the so-called Aspen ruling, the Federal Communications Commission finally exempted debates from the equal access requirement. Incumbent president Gerald Ford, badly trailing Jimmy Carter in the polls, departed from his acceptance speech during the Republican convention in 1976 and challenged his opponent to a face-to-face television debate. Using one live media event to advance another, Ford declared, "The American people have the right to know where both of us stand."[8] Carter quickly signaled his acceptance, and in each election since, presidential debates have occurred in one form or another.

Gerald Ford resurrected the institution of presidential debates not out of a sense of civic duty but for political advantage. "The Ford campaign needed something dramatic," said Republican adviser Michael Duval. "We needed something that would cause the country to reserve its judgment. The debates seemed to be the answer."[9] As this remark indicates, the decision to meet one's opponent comes down to self-interest. General election debates hinge on the assumption that the presidential nominees will see fit to take part, but in fact only tradition and political pressure require them to do so. As veteran CBS news producer Lane Venardos put it, "The candidates have all the high cards, including the ultimate high card—whether to participate."[10]

From Richard Nixon to Barack Obama, the ambivalence of politicians toward engaging in live debates is not difficult to comprehend. Even for battle-scarred presidential nominees accustomed to the relentless scrutiny of cameras, the perils can be enormous. "In no other mode of presentation," wrote communications scholar Walter Fisher, "does the candidate risk or reveal so much of his character."[11] Debaters understand that the lens will magnify their every word, gesture, and facial expression, not just for the duration of the broadcast but for the ages.

Ford and Carter managed to revive the debate tradition because as competitors, they were fairly evenly matched. In subsequent elections, a different dynamic took hold: the campaign in the lead—the one with the most to lose—sought either to shirk debates or to participate on the most favorable of terms. Only in recent cycles, with the electorate closely divided, have both sides approached their participation in debates on a more or less equal footing.

DEBATES IN DOUBT

In 1980, disagreement over the inclusion of independent John Anderson gave President Jimmy Carter and challenger Ronald Reagan a pretext for cutting short that year's debate series. Only two matches would take place: an inconsequential meeting in late September between Reagan and Anderson that Carter boycotted, and a climactic debate with Carter and Reagan one week before the election.

Carter's refusal to join Reagan and Anderson in a three-way debate irked the sponsoring League of Women Voters, which retaliated by announcing its intention to place an empty chair onstage at the Baltimore Convention Center as a reminder of the candidate's absence. Editorial cartoonist Pat Oliphant sketched this as a baby's high chair, while Johnny Carson wondered in his *Tonight Show* monologue, "Suppose the chair wins?"[12] Under pressure from Democrats and the White House, the league eventually withdrew its threat, and no extraneous furniture materialized on the Reagan-Anderson set.

At least in the short term, Carter sustained little damage by skipping the debate. "Despite some predictions to the contrary," said the *Christian Science Monitor*, "no widespread, high-intensity wave of criticism against the president has emerged."[13] Instead, the media found a new narrative thread: the will-they-or-won't-they possibility of a two-way Carter–Reagan encounter. Publicly both candidates maintained a posture of favorability, but in private neither side could muster much enthusiasm for a debate.

Although Carter dismissed Reagan as his intellectual inferior, other Democrats were understandably apprehensive about the former California governor's performing prowess. Carter at first sought a schedule of multiple debates, hoping that "over a more extended period of time, [Reagan] and I would have to get down to specific issues, where my knowledge of foreign and domestic affairs would give me an edge."[14] Like Nixon before him, Carter mistakenly assumed that substance would prevail over image.

By the time the two campaigns agreed to debate, only a single appearance could be scheduled before Election Day. "If we're going to debate him," said Carter's pollster Patrick Caddell, a staunch opponent of any face-to-face meeting with Reagan, "it's damn important that we get rules that increase the possibility that he'll say something dumb or screw up." Caddell drafted a strategy memorandum a week before the debate that warned of the dangers ahead, cautioning that "the risks far outweigh the possible advantages."[15]

Reagan's handlers had reasons of their own to fear a debate. The Republican candidate had made a number of ill-advised statements during speeches and press conferences. According to Reagan's aide Michael Deaver, "It was particularly the international subjects that we felt we would have a problem with."[16] Among the strongest dissenters was pollster Richard Wirthlin, whose data indicated that Reagan could be elected without debating. "One of the keys to winning a campaign is that you deal with those things you can control," Wirthlin said, "and, quite frankly, a debate is a game of roulette. There's no telling which way that marble will bounce."[17]

What turned the tide for Reagan was the white-tie Alfred E. Smith political banquet in New York City, attended by both presidential candidates in mid-October. Concerned that Carter would use his platform to issue an impromptu debate challenge, Reagan's people armed their man with a 400-word acceptance speech. When Carter failed to mention the subject, Reagan instead delivered a program of self-deprecating jokes that sharply contrasted with the humorless tone of the incumbent. In the view of columnists Rowland Evans and Robert Novak, "genial Ron" bested "uptight Jimmy" in this, their only joint appearance of the campaign other than the debate.[18] The next morning the die was cast. After listening to his aides weigh the pros and cons, Reagan said, "Well, everything considered, I feel I should debate. If I'm going to fill the shoes of Carter, I should be willing to meet him face-to-face."[19]

In the end, after one of the most successful debate performances in history, Reagan knew he had made the right call. Just as Richard Nixon got scorched by the heat of JFK's stardom, so did Carter find himself singed by the superior media presence of the former Hollywood actor. Asked afterward if he had been nervous sharing the stage with the president of the United States, Reagan gave a response that put the matter in perspective: "Not at all. I've been on the same stage with John Wayne."[20] Beneath the humor lay a simple truth: in television debates, star power carries the day.

If presidential debates can be said to have a savior, the honor goes to Ronald Reagan. By agreeing to appear with Walter Mondale in 1984, then-president Reagan shored up campaign debates as a permanent institution. The popular incumbent stood so far ahead in the polls that he most likely could have survived the fallout from not participating that year, a course many advisers recommended. William F. Buckley Jr. wrote that if he were Reagan, he would not debate: "I'd say, 'Let's get it straight: Debates between presidential contenders should be restricted to debates between men who have not served as president. Men who have served should be judged by what they have done.' "[21]

Why, then, did Reagan debate? According to Deaver, "I think he believed in debates. I think he just decided, in fact I can hear him saying, you have to debate, people expect it now, it's become part of our system."[22] Furthermore, Reagan had reason to be confident. As the "Great Communicator," he approached the event with five decades of experience at the microphone and an undefeated track record as a political debater.

At the first 1984 debate in Louisville, Ronald Reagan would turn in the worst performance of his long career, appearing disengaged, disjointed, and discombobulated against Walter Mondale, an opponent whom voters and the press had largely written off. Not since Richard Nixon had a presidential debater stepped off the stage so battered. That such misfortune could befall a speaker of Reagan's stature proves the riskiness of debate participation. If a star performer like Ronald Reagan can stumble, what tribulations await a candidate of lesser powers?

THE DEBATE INSTITUTION TAKES SHAPE

By 1988 debates had more than ever become a public expectation. That year negotiators for incumbent Vice President George H. W. Bush played hardball at the bargaining table, giving the Democratic campaign of Michael Dukakis a take-it-or-leave-it offer: two presidential debates and one vice presidential match in the standard press conference format.

Bush, no fan of presidential debates, emerged unscathed; even a maladroit performance by running mate Dan Quayle did not adversely affect Republican prospects.

Four years later, in 1992, when foot-dragging by Bush's campaign cast doubt on the debates, the price of nonparticipation had gone up. The case of George Bush presents an object lesson for any candidate seeking to shirk what the press and the public now consider a presidential aspirant's obligation to debate. In September 1992 the chief executive of the land found himself being chased around America by chickens—more accurately, humans in chicken costumes, offering themselves as metaphors for Bush's reluctance to debate Bill Clinton.

The phenomenon began with a single freelance protester in East Lansing, Michigan, a city that had been selected to host the season's first debate. When stalling by Bush's campaign caused the event to be canceled, Clinton showed up anyway, as did the prototype "Chicken George." Television stations in Lansing jumped on the story, airing video of the costumed demonstrator on their evening newscasts. Inspired by this example, Clinton's "counter-events" forces set up an operation called "Get on TV," and soon a veritable flock of imitators around the country started turning up at Bush's rallies and on television.

When President Bush took to addressing the chickens personally, Clinton's people knew they had scored a hit. One of the more bizarre vignettes of the presidential campaign in 1992 featured George Bush squabbling with a giant fowl during a whistle-stop tour of the Midwest. The protester's sign—"Chicken George Won't Debate"—caught the president's eye and precipitated this classic example of Bush-speak: "You talking about the draft-record chicken or you talking about the chicken in the Arkansas River? Which one are you talking about? Which one? Get out of here. Maybe it's the draft? Is that what's bothering you?"[23] Inevitably the exchange made the newscasts: the leader of the most powerful country on earth having it out with an anonymous citizen in a poultry outfit.

However goofy, the "Chicken George" episode in 1992 shows the pressures facing presidential candidates as they ponder the pros and cons of debate participation. George Bush discovered that even the appearance of hesitation was enough to give the opposition a toehold. The news media, unable to resist any story that combines conflict with visuals, eagerly played its role in the drama, promoting the perception that the president did not want to debate. Eventually Bush's high command concluded that they had no choice but to commit.

In a backhanded way, the Republican delays may have served a positive purpose. By waiting until late in the game to fix a schedule, negotiators were forced to bunch up the debates on the few available dates that remained, creating a tournament-like sequence of four telecasts within nine days. The unforeseen result was to build audience interest from one program to the next, a trend further enhanced by the introduction of experimental formats.

The series in 1992 brought another important innovation: the first and, to date, only three-person debates. When Ross Perot reentered the presidential race in early October, representatives for Clinton and Bush were applying the finishing touches to their two-man debate agreement. With approval from the sponsoring Commission on Presidential Debates (CPD), the campaigns quickly expanded the cast of characters to include the picturesque Texan and his running mate, Admiral James B. Stockdale. Although the Reform Party candidates were given no say in the negotiations, the invitation delighted Perot. "Basically, they resurrected him by letting him in the debates," said Perot's adviser Dan Routman.[24]

In 1996 Bob Dole's campaign struggled to avoid another round of three-person debates, touching off a brief controversy over whether Perot merited an invitation. Applying the debate commission's criteria for inclusion—"evidence of national organization, signs of national newsworthiness and competitiveness, and indicators of national public enthusiasm or concern"—an advisory committee deemed Ross Perot ineligible. With Perot excluded, negotiators for Bill Clinton and Bob Dole quickly resolved their differences. In view of Clinton's formidable skills as a television performer, for the first time, debates were not viewed as inherently risky for the incumbent.

PRESIDENTIAL DEBATES AS AN EXPECTATION

In a hastily arranged news conference the Sunday before Labor Day in 2000, after several weeks of stalling, George W. Bush announced that he was willing to participate in three debates with Vice President Al

Gore. But the announcement carried with it a dramatic challenge to precedent: only one of the events would be produced by the CPD, despite its history as sponsor of every presidential and vice presidential match since 1988. According to Bush's plan, the two remaining debates would take place on NBC's *Meet the Press* and CNN's *Larry King Live*, and would run for sixty minutes instead of the usual ninety.

Almost before the words had left Bush's mouth, the proposal began to fizzle, illustrating the degree to which candidates endanger themselves when they tamper with the institution of presidential debates. Gore, having previously agreed to the debate commission's plan, immediately rejected the Republicans' offer. "What's wrong with the commission debates?" he asked. "Is it that so many people are watching?"[25] Rival networks declared that they would not carry NBC and CNN's programs, and editorial pages around the country denounced Bush's attempt to subvert the established procedure for debating. "Gore looked magnanimous," wrote Republican strategist Karl Rove. "Bush came off looking weak and manipulative."[26] In the view of Bush's aide Stuart Stevens, "We might just as well have gone to church and refuse to stand up when everyone else did."[27]

Bush's counteroffer reinforced the perception that the governor of Texas, like his father before him, was debate-averse. Press accounts revisited Bush's history as a gubernatorial debater, particularly his race in 1998, in which he insisted on scheduling that year's one debate on a Friday night in October, when many Texans were attending high school football games, and in El Paso, a city remote from the state's media spotlight. Other stories speculated about the effect of Bush's proposal on viewership. Bill Carter in the *New York Times* wrote, "If the presidential debates were held on the networks and days chosen by George W. Bush, they would almost surely be seen by the fewest number of people ever to have watched them."[28]

Less than two weeks after Bush's Labor Day weekend announcement, the Republicans abandoned their quest to dictate terms. In the face of mounting criticism, Bush's campaign accepted the original proposal that the CPD had announced months earlier, including dates, times, and locations. In the opinion of debate commissioner Paul Kirk, George W. Bush "didn't want to fall into the trap that his father fell into with the 'chicken man' in 1992. As a first impression, as a non-incumbent, to be looking like he wasn't enthusiastic about debating, I think the political pressures were probably too much."[29]

As in the two previous cycles, debate sponsors in 2000 faced the issue of whether to include third-party candidates—in this case, the principal players were Ralph Nader of the Green Party and Patrick Buchanan of the Reform Party. To avoid the problems of previous years, the CPD laid out its standard for inclusion well in advance of the fall election season: in order to qualify, potential participants would need to demonstrate national poll standings of at least 15 percent, based on an average of several media surveys. Despite complaints from critics and a lawsuit from Ralph Nader, the debates in 2000 proceeded with only the major party nominees. In every election since, the 15 percent test has meant two-person presidential debates.

In 2004 incumbent George W. Bush carefully avoided the protracted "debate over debates" that had dogged his campaign four years earlier. Even so, Democrats sought to bolster the lingering perception that Bush was a reluctant debater. Shortly after clinching the Democratic nomination in 2004, Senator John Kerry traveled to Quincy, Illinois, a stop on the Lincoln–Douglas circuit of 1858, and challenged his rival to a series of monthly debates throughout the general election campaign. Late in the summer Kerry upped the ante by proposing weekly meetings. Predictably, Bush declined both offers, though in an August interview on CNN he took pains to assure voters that "there will be debates. I don't think you have to worry about that."[30]

After floating the possibility of participating in only two joint appearances instead of the debate commission's proposed three, Bush's campaign eventually accepted the original slate of three presidential debates and one vice presidential match. Could Bush have gotten away with fewer debates? Historical precedent for such a timetable did exist. Incumbents Ronald Reagan in 1984 and Bill Clinton in 1996 both agreed to only two debates, and paid no apparent price. Yet these presidents enjoyed a substantial lead over their challengers. Given George W. Bush's shakier support, not to mention his record of ambivalence toward debates, it was politically necessary for him to avoid the sense that he was ducking his opponent.

As it happened, after weak showings in the first two debates, the third encounter with John Kerry ended up handing Bush a much-needed opportunity to set things right. Negotiator James Baker, in persuading Bush to accept three debates, had told him, "I remember times when I was darn glad my candidate had another debate to make up for a poor performance in an earlier one." In this case Baker's words proved prophetic. However, Baker admitted that the decision might just as easily have backfired: "You never know in advance how these things will turn out. I thought our bargain was a good one, and it certainly worked out well this time, but it could have bitten us in the tail."[31]

CHALLENGES, THREATS, AND ALTERNATIVES

On September 24, 2008, against the backdrop of a rapidly deteriorating economic situation, Republican presidential candidate John McCain unexpectedly announced that he was suspending his campaign in order to return to Washington and confront the crisis. As part of his plan, McCain recommended postponement of the first presidential debate, scheduled for two days later in Oxford, Mississippi.

The purpose of McCain's action was unclear: in what way would suspending his campaign and delaying the debate restore calm to a shaky American economy? Both the debate commission and the University of Mississippi, which was hosting the event, expressed their desire for the debate to proceed. But it was the response from Obama's campaign that mattered, and the candidate and his staff wasted no time staking out a pro-debate position. "This is exactly the time when the American people need to hear from the person who, in approximately 40 days, will be responsible for dealing with this mess," Barack Obama said at an impromptu news conference in Florida. In a not-so-subtle dig at his opponent, he added that it would be "part of the president's job to deal with more than one thing at once." (On *Saturday Night Live*, Seth Myers would joke that Obama's debate attendance marked "the first time in history that a black man was more eager to go to Mississippi than a white one.")[32]

McCain's debate negotiator Senator Lindsey Graham told reporters that the Republican nominee would not debate "unless there is an agreement that would provide a solution" to the financial crisis. Graham further suggested that absent a bailout deal, McCain's campaign would seek to hold the first presidential debate in lieu of the vice presidential debate.[33] That debate, scheduled for the following week, had drawn enormous advance interest for its inclusion of Sarah Palin, a candidate then in the spotlight for her disastrous series of interviews with network news anchors. To skeptics, any suggestion of canceling or postponing the vice presidential debate smelled like a ploy to sweep Palin off the chessboard, safely out of harm's way.

The day after McCain's surprise announcement, both presidential candidates attended a bipartisan meeting at the White House that amounted to little more than a photo op. "As a matter of political appearances, the day's events succeeded most of all in raising questions about precisely why Mr. McCain had called for postponing the first debate," noted the *New York Times*. Meanwhile, a poll by the Associated Press showed overwhelming public desire for the debate to happen: 60 percent in favor, 22 percent against, with the remainder undecided.[34]

The night before the debate, Barack Obama headed to Mississippi, uncertain whether the event was on or off. The next morning, McCain's campaign announced via press release that John McCain would attend after all, bailout agreement or no bailout agreement. At the debate site in Oxford, debate commission officials received the news through a phone call from the Secret Service after McCain's plane departed Washington.[35] Less than ten hours remained before the candidates' opening statements.

Throughout the drama, McCain and his team had been getting an earful behind the scenes, not least from high-profile Mississippi Republicans like Governor Haley Barbour and former senator Trent Lott. The state and its flagship university had invested millions of dollars in the debate, viewing the event as an opportunity to showcase how far Ole Miss had come in the fifty years since its forced racial integration. With the eyes of the world on Oxford, a debate featuring the first African American presidential nominee deepened the historical resonance. "That part was just pure luck," said Obama's debate adviser Ron Klain, "that we weren't in a Democratic state with a Democratic governor, that we were in a state with a Republican governor who had been chairman of the Republican National Committee, whose Republican credentials could not be assailed, who said this debate should go forward. That put McCain in a tough spot."[36]

Apart from interfering with both candidates' debate prep at a crucial moment, what effect did McCain's threatened action have? To most observers, the suspension reinforced an existing perception of the Republican nominee as reckless—even McCain's campaign officials would later describe the move as a mistake. In the words of David Plouffe, campaign manager for Obama, "We looked strong, confident, and steady. McCain looked erratic and a bit desperate."[37]

Ironically, it was the Republican nominee who for months had been demanding more debates. In June McCain formally challenged Obama to a series of ten televised town meetings to take place at locations around the country throughout the summer. In a letter to his opponent, McCain said he hoped to avoid "the regimented trappings, rules, and spectacle of formal debates" in favor of "the higher level of discourse that Americans clearly would prefer." Publicly Obama feigned interest, telling reporters, "I think that's a great idea," but in reality, the candidate and his advisers saw little to be gained.[38]

Under pressure to accept McCain's challenge, Obama's campaign came back with a counterproposal: a single town hall meeting over the Fourth of July weekend; a debate in August devoted to international issues; and the three traditional debates after Labor Day. Rejecting this offer as insufficient, McCain continued to push for a roster of weekly town halls, until talks between the campaigns fell apart.

Obama and McCain did share billing at two events before the fall debates, albeit in back-to-back interviews, not simultaneously. In September both attended the ServiceNation Summit at Columbia University, a televised forum on the theme of public service. The more interesting joint appearance, unprecedented in American presidential campaigns, was an August event at the Saddleback megachurch in California, where each candidate responded to questions from celebrity preacher Rick Warren. As Jim Rutenberg noted in the *New York Times*, "It has taken a man of God, perhaps, to do what nobody else has been able to do since the general election season began: get Barack Obama and John McCain together on the same stage before their party conventions later this summer."[39]

Despite a viewing audience of only 5.5 million, Saddleback generated extensive media coverage. Journalists treated the event as a mini–presidential debate, declaring a winner (McCain) and loser (Obama), isolating key moments for replay (a thirty-six-second onstage hug as the candidates crossed paths between interviews), and analyzing perceived errors. Asked by Warren at what point a baby could be considered to have human rights, Obama dismissed the topic as "above my pay grade." Asked to define *rich*, McCain set the amount at $5 million—nearly twenty times what Obama had said when answering the same question.

In both 2008 and 2012, various attempts were made to stage alternatives to the traditional presidential debates. After the debate commission turned down a bid from New Orleans to host a 2008 debate, community leaders tried unsuccessfully to produce their own event with help from Google and YouTube. Rick Warren of Saddleback Church, hoping to duplicate his earlier triumph, invited Obama and Mitt Romney to a forum in 2012; neither accepted. The Spanish-language television network Univision also sought its own Obama–Romney debate, settling instead on individual interviews.

THE RITUAL OF DEBATE NEGOTIATIONS

Even in years when both sides want to debate, the ritual known as the "debate over debates" can play out as a kind of promotional trailer for the main event to come. Like the debates themselves, preproduction negotiations have boasted winners and losers, surprise moves and tactical blunders, high stakes and colorful characters. Victories have been won not just on the battlefield of television but also at the bargaining table. It is generally believed that Kennedy's team won the negotiations in 1960; Republicans and Democrats more or less tied in 1976; Reagan's handlers triumphed in 1980 and again in 1984; Bush's took the talks in 1988; and Clinton's staff prevailed in 1992 and 1996. Miscalculations by strategists for George W. Bush gave Al Gore an advantage in 2000, but in 2004 Bush's negotiators got most of what they wanted in exchange for three debates with John Kerry.

As the debate commission becomes more proactive in announcing sites, dates, formats, and moderators in advance of campaign negotiations, the momentousness of these bargaining sessions diminishes. The wheeling and dealing in 2008 and 2012 revolved around relatively arcane points of format and staging: response times, lecterns versus tables, whether there would be opening and closing statements. By the time negotiators began their horse-trading, most of the critical decisions had already been rendered.

Campaign professionals in Washington routinely complain about the clout the debate commission has amassed in its three decades of existence. Campaign apparatchiks make no secret of their desire to seize the reins and produce presidential debates on their own terms; after the election of 2012, they joined forces to propose changes that challenged the commission's authority.[40] Co-chair of this bipartisan Annenberg Working Group on Presidential Campaign Debate Reforms was Democratic consultant Anita Dunn. According to Dunn, the commission sets up debates "in locales that the nominees would never go to in their right minds if they had any choice, on a schedule that's not done in consultation with anyone, with moderators that are not done in consultation with anybody. It's not a process that serves the campaigns or the candidates all that well."[41]

With so much riding on the outcome, it is easy to understand why candidates and their surrogates crave input into predebate decision making. "A debate negotiator's client, frankly, is his candidate, not the press and not some abstract ideal of how presidential debates should be conducted," said Republican politico James Baker. "The goal of the negotiator is to try to win a format and rules that play to his candidate's strengths and minimize his weaknesses."[42]

As early as 1960, it became apparent that the sponsoring organizations—the stagers of the event and payers of the bills—could and would be relegated to a secondary role. The "Great Debates" of 1960 may have been the brainchild of ABC, CBS, and NBC, but when it came to setting terms, these powerful institutions got foreclosed. Negotiating sessions for the Kennedy–Nixon debates started off with all parties at the table, but in their second meeting, the handlers asked the broadcasters to leave the room. "When we came back in again," recalled CBS's Mickelson, "they laid down the pattern for the debates."[43]

Until the debate commission took over key programmatic decisions, the campaigns would hammer out an agreement that suited their own purposes, which they then handed to the sponsoring institution as a done deal. "It is to the everlasting credit of the television networks that the debate programs were presented in the 1960 campaign, but the evidence is overwhelming that they relinquished essential control of the programs to do so," observed debate scholars Herbert Seltz and Richard Yoakam shortly after the Kennedy–Nixon events.[44] The same charge can be made against the League of Women Voters, sponsors of the debates in 1976, 1980, and 1984. The CPD, which has produced every debate since 1988, started off in a similarly weak position vis-à-vis the campaigns, but time and experience have considerably enhanced its leverage.

After Kennedy–Nixon, debate negotiations between presidential campaign staffs grew more convoluted. The debates in 1960 left political handlers with a heightened sensitivity to the volatile nature of live television; in every debate since, the objective has been to install an invisible safety net that keeps the tightrope artists from crashing to the ground. Campaigns engage in what can best be described as a mix of talent management and preventive damage control, doing whatever they can to stabilize an inherently combustible production situation for the leading players.

As Ford and Carter prepared to resume the debate tradition in 1976, strategists for both candidates looked to the series in 1960 for inspiration. In a planning memo, an adviser to Carter expressed admiration for the squabbles of Carter's predecessors: "The constant bickering between the candidates' staffs and with the production crews about studio temperature, candidate facilities, furniture, sets, lights, etc., serves an important purpose: It tells the opposition that you do not trust them and that you are tough enough not to be walked over."[45] In this quote can be discerned the prevailing philosophy that has guided debate negotiations from 1960 forward: never give an inch.

Jody Powell, who as press secretary to Carter participated in the talks in 1976 and 1980, called debate negotiations a process of "bluff and counterbluff, scheming, conniving, and hard-nosed horse trading." According to Powell, the bargaining sessions offer campaign professionals "the opportunity, so rare in political contests, to sit down face-to-face with your adversaries. It is a chance to take their measure, assess their intelligence and flappability."[46] This comment suggests a reason besides candidate protection that campaigns so reliably indulge in prede-bate negotiations: they enjoy checking out their opponents eyeball to eyeball.

One of the opponents Powell was checking out in 1976 would emerge as a legend in presidential debate bargaining: James Baker, who as the Republicans' lead negotiator in the 1980s crafted highly favorable rules for Ronald Reagan and George H. W. Bush. Among other negotiating triumphs, Baker is credited with scheduling the last-minute Carter–Reagan debate in 1980 and whittling down the Reagan–Mondale series in 1984 to two presidential matches. In the lopsided negotiations in 1988, Baker's team got essentially everything it wanted; the Democrats' consolation prize was an elevated podium for the shorter Michael Dukakis.

So persuasive was Baker's negotiating rhetoric that it boomeranged back at the Republicans in the "Baker-less" talks of 1992 and 1996. Mickey Kantor, lead debate negotiator for Bill Clinton, reiterated many of Baker's hardline positions, even some of the same language, in iron-ing out agreements with his counterparts. Like Baker, Kantor got most of what he was seeking, especially in 1996 against Bob Dole's rookie ne-gotiating team. Already disadvantaged by low poll standings, Dole's representatives compounded their trouble by introducing a number of irrelevant issues, at one point asking if the live audience could be made to abide by a dress code.

As the naiveté of Dole's negotiators demonstrates, these talks have be-come too highly specialized to be left to neophytes. Debate negotiations are a blood sport, played under arcane rules by a cast of experienced Washington insiders, drawn from the elite ranks of political strate-gists, media consultants, and high-dollar law firms. Predebate bargain-ing sessions may be conducted between individuals or involve several people per campaign, each with a particular area of expertise. Out of sight, but never out of mind, are the candidates, whose degree of in-volvement varies.

Debate negotiations have become a game that players on both sides relish. As Karl Rove put it at a Harvard postmortem after the election of 2000, "If you can't argue over how many you're going to have, and when you're going to have them, and where you're going to have them, you're left debating important things like how tall the chair is." Rove described the talks of 2000 as "an endless back and forth about all kinds of things. I think one of the big issues was whether they would wear lavaliere mics. They'd never had lavaliere mics before, and this was a demand of the Gore campaign, and because the Gore campaign demanded it, we were obviously against it."[47]

Another participant in the Harvard postmortem, Gore's media adviser Robert Shrum, confirmed Rove's recollection about the lavaliere microphones. "We always had to come up with a list of things we were going to demand, that we could give away in return for them giving away some things," Shrum said, adding, "To say we're going to change that is to say that we're going to change human nature."[48]

THE MEMORANDUM OF UNDERSTANDING

A byproduct of each cycle's predebate negotiations is the quasi-legal document called a memorandum of understanding, or memorandum of agreement, that addresses every conceivable point of scheduling, format, and staging. Employing courtroom language to codify the rules of engagement, the memos are written and signed by representatives of the campaigns—but not by debate sponsors (the Commission on Presidential Debates), producers (whichever pool network is assigned with staging and transmitting the production), or moderators. Without all stakeholders on board, debate memos offer little more than a theoretical security blanket to the campaigns that draft them.

Predebate memoranda of understanding have been misinterpreted by critics who see in them evidence of collusion between the two major political parties and the CPD. But the commission, by its own design, is not a signatory. And in practice—which is to say during the live events themselves—predebate contracts tend to go up in smoke anyway. Media critic Jay Rosen perceptively diagnosed the situation in 2012, describing a precarious distribution of power among campaigns, sponsors, and moderators (he might have added the television networks that bring the program to air). "No one is fully in charge," Rosen concluded. "But this is too scary for such high stakes. So rules are invented."[49]

With so much of the decision making now in the hands of the debate commission, recent memoranda of understanding have come to reflect wishful thinking by the campaigns. Because matters of scheduling, site selection, format, and moderator have already been settled, the memos represent tinkering around the margins. According to co-commissioner Frank Fahrenkopf, "75 to 80 percent of what's in their agreement, they've just taken from what we do anyway."[50]

The forerunner of modern debate contracts was an informal memo in 1960 from Kennedy's press secretary Pierre Salinger to Nixon's press secretary Herbert Klein. This document, just over a page long, dealt only with press logistics and the method of choosing journalists as questioners for the Kennedy–Nixon panels. A more substantial debate contract came into being in 1984, when Reagan's and Mondale's campaigns drew up and signed a three-page document covering the rudiments of debate production.

Four years later a Republican adviser named Robert Goodwin drafted the first comprehensive predebate memorandum of understanding. Goodwin had cut his teeth as an aide to George Bush in the primary debates of 1980, and then served as Bush's on-site negotiator in the vice presidential match of 1984 with Geraldine Ferraro. Out of these experiences he devised a detailed production agreement that would serve as a template for later rounds of presidential debates.

What began as a sixteen-page contract in 1988 ballooned to thirty-seven pages in 1992, when untested formats and the presence of a third participant complicated the proceedings. Clay Mulford, counsel for Perot's campaign, remembered being astonished when he read that year's agreement. Said Mulford, "It was like the Internal Revenue code."[51] The documents anticipate every contingency, from what form of address the debaters will use with each other to where the candidates' spouses will sit in the audience.

The language of the contract betrays the mutual suspicion that exists between opposing presidential campaigns. Among the particulars of the memorandum of understanding of 1992: "All other candidates and their representatives shall vacate the debate site while another candidate has his private production and technical briefing and walk-through" and "No candidate shall have any staff member in the wings or backstage later than five minutes after the debate has begun nor sooner than five minutes before the debate concludes."[52] Clearly each side is on guard for the unanticipated competitive stunt.

Representatives of Bill Clinton and Bob Dole signed a relatively modest eleven-page document in 1996, its brevity a reflection of the negotiators' unequal standing. Apparently, when one side dictates terms, prolixity vanishes, because four years later the more evenly matched Bush–Gore campaigns hashed out a memorandum of understanding thirty-one pages in length. A thirty-two-page contract would emerge from the Bush–Kerry negotiations in the closely contested race of 2004, one page longer than the Obama–McCain memo in 2008. For 2012 the contract ran only twenty-one pages.

To observers of presidential debates, the memorandum of understanding of 2004 is of particular interest. First, it is the only agreement to be publicly released by the campaigns in advance of the debates. Upon finalizing a deal in mid-September, Bush's and Kerry's teams jointly posted the document on their websites, a departure from the norm that caught official Washington by surprise. Even the debate commission first saw the document by reading it online. Although bits and pieces of previous debate contracts had found their way into news stories over the years, standard practice on both sides was to keep the memo hush-hush, lest the campaigns' obsessive attention to detail appear overly petty.

The second unusual element of the contract of 2004 was a demand, pushed for by Bush's negotiators, that sponsors and moderators of the debates become signatories to the document. The CPD refused, as did the moderators. According to debate commissioner Paul Kirk, "The commission is not an agent of the two political parties. It's a freestanding, nonpartisan, educational entity that is guided by its own mission and not by what a particular set of candidates may say in a particular election cycle."[53] With only days remaining before the first scheduled debate, the campaigns had little alternative but to drop the demand.

In 2008 the handlers went back to their traditional practice of keeping the memorandum of understanding under wraps, though enterprising reporters did manage to pry loose a few details. In 2012 reporter Mark Halperin scooped the competition by obtaining and posting that year's contract on the *Time* magazine website. Halperin broke the story the day before the town hall debate, inspiring a last-minute flurry of media coverage about the absurdity of trying to preordain an hour and a half of live television.

Although it is understandable why campaigns might wish to downplay their written agreements, voters and journalists are ill-served by hidden debate rules. Writing after the town hall debate of 2008, Aaron Zelinksy of the *Presidential Debate Blog* lamented the secrecy that shrouded that year's memo. "Without knowledge of the memorandum," he said, "watching the presidential debate is like seeing a baseball game without foul lines or base paths: The general idea is to round the bases, but we don't have any idea about the critical rules of the game."[54]

THE DEBATE OVER SCHEDULING

In his vice presidential match in 1976, Bob Dole claimed there were three presidential debates that year because Jimmy Carter "has three positions on everything." Though the quip was intended for laughs, it does get at a serious point of disputation in debate negotiations: scheduling. Mindful of the lessons of the past, campaign strategists attach talismanic significance to the issue of timing—an issue the debate commission has essentially taken out of their hands.

Conventional wisdom about the scheduling of presidential debates coalesces around several points. First, whoever is ahead wants fewer debates; whoever is behind wants more. Second, candidates in the lead will insist on as much distance as possible between the final debate and Election Day, in case time is needed to rebound from a disaster. Third, the busy autumn sports schedule must be navigated in choosing debate days, lest the public be tempted to watch something else. And finally, once announced, debates tend to freeze a campaign, as candidates go into rehearsal hibernation and voters wait to assess the performers side by side.

The "freeze" theory was first promulgated by James Baker, who in 1980 worked the principle to his advantage by scheduling the single eleventh-hour debate between Ronald Reagan and Jimmy Carter one week before the election. "They do freeze a campaign," Baker says, "but they also have the ability to move the numbers. So the front-runner is always going to be more hesitant to extend the period of time for the debates, and the number of debates, and even the fact of debates."[55]

In 1980 this campaign paralysis hardened Reagan's lead at a critical point in the race. "After the debate was agreed to," wrote Reagan's biographer Lou Cannon, "press coverage and the candidates' speeches became virtually perfunctory, with everyone waiting for the big event. The beneficiary was Reagan."[56] In postmortems of the race of 1980, Carter's campaign officials admitted they had been outfoxed. "That late debate was the worst thing that happened to us in the campaign," one of Carter's aides told Jack Germond and Jules Witcover. "When we wanted to debate Reagan, I think they very smartly suckered us into the late debate."[57]

The schedule might have been even worse for Carter. Baker's initial proposal called for a debate on November 3, the night before the election, "when most voters are making up their minds," as Baker told reporters. Predictably Carter's camp nixed this idea. Jody Powell said a debate so late in the season "would leave no time for anybody to be called for misstatements, contradictions, or inaccuracies," a not-so-subtle hint that Reagan played loose with his facts.[58]

Negotiating for Reagan in 1984, Baker won the reverse concession, denying Walter Mondale's wish for a debate close to Election Day. Baker told the *Washington Post* his side preferred an earlier encounter so as to avoid "undue impact on voters' decision."[59] At the bargaining table for George Bush in 1988, Baker got an even better deal: the last debate of the season took place more than three weeks before the election. "Though Baker did this out of concern for his own man, it's also better for the country," concluded journalist Elizabeth Drew.[60] Drew, like other observers, feared that a debate too close to the vote could have dangerous electoral repercussions.

In 1992, after the "Chicken George" issue forced Bush's hand, Republicans offered Clinton's campaign a counterproposal: four debates to be televised on the last four Sundays of the campaign. The final debate would air November 1, two days before the election. As it turned out, an even more revolutionary timetable fell into place: three presidential debates and a vice presidential match held in rapid succession between October 11 and October 19.

The compressed sequence fulfilled the prophecy of Hollywood producer Harry Thomason, a debate negotiator for Bill Clinton, who predicted the schedule would play out like a television miniseries.[61] "Americans everywhere are wild about the drama," wrote David Von Drehle in the *Washington Post* during the debates in 1992. "All day, they speculated with the urgent palaver of a klatch of soap-opera fans. What would happen next?"[62] High ratings affirmed the series' popularity. But audience enthusiasm was not shared by the campaigns, and 1992 remains the only year in which presidential debates have unfolded on such a tight timetable.

In 1996, Democratic negotiators won a schedule that deliberately slotted the second and last Clinton–Dole debate against a baseball play-off game. After the election, Roger Simon asked Clinton's aide George Stephanopoulos why the president's team had insisted on competing with a major athletic event. Stephanopoulos's reply is a classic of self-serving election-year reasoning: "We didn't *want* people watching the debates. We wanted the debates to be a metaphor for the campaign. And we didn't want people to concentrate on the campaign."[63]

For George W. Bush in 2000, the ideal schedule involved debates as early and as far apart as possible, though in the end the Republican campaign won neither concession. "We thought the debates were crammed too closely together," said Bush's adviser Karl Rove. "I don't think it served any of the candidates to have these debates jammed up against each other so much." Rove pointed out that candidates lose several days of campaigning for each debate they take part in. He also complained that the schedule was dictated by televised sporting events: "This question about timing particularly bothers me because it's not what is in the best interest of the American voter, and what can be done to give the candidates a reasonable chance to prepare, talk and defend, but how do we accommodate ourselves to the networks." As things turned out, the later-than-desired timing of the debates in 2000 worked to Bush's advantage—"ironically enough," Rove said—by giving the candidate a bump in the polls closer to Election Day.[64]

Four years later the Bush campaign offered no resistance to the debate commission's timetable, but they did insist on reversing the order of subject matter for the first and third debates. Instead of leading with domestic issues, as the commission had originally proposed, James Baker got Kerry's negotiators to agree to foreign policy as the opening topic. "The viewing audience is always larger," Baker said, "and we thought foreign would be our strength in the aftermath of 9/11 and the president's role in that."[65] Once again, advance considerations did not align with the reality of live television: Bush had his worst showing before the largest number of viewers, on a topic that represented his supposed strength.

A similar switch of topic areas occurred in 2008, when Obama's and McCain's campaigns jointly agreed that foreign policy, not domestic issues, should come first. "Both in 2004 and 2008 the Republicans had the view that their candidate was better on international affairs and foreign policy, that the first debate was more important, and therefore they wanted that topic first," said Democratic strategist Ron Klain. "And both times we had the view that our candidate was underrated on these issues, that our candidate would beat expectations on these issues, and that we would rather lead with this topic where we were being underappreciated."[66]

Debate timing is quirky; it can either help or hurt a candidate. Weak performances by George W. Bush in 2004 were offset by a gap of three weeks between the final debate and Election Day, granting the incumbent president sufficient time to recover. "For debates to have maximum impact, they need to be closer to the election itself," said Robert Shrum of Kerry's campaign. "Unfortunately, the Kerry advantage in the debates couldn't quite be carried all the way to November 2. If it had, I think we would have won the election."[67] Shrum's comment reflects a political reality of presidential debates: most challengers want them later; most incumbents want them sooner.

The length of time between debates can also matter. In 2012, after Barack Obama badly fumbled his first debate with Mitt Romney, nearly two weeks passed before the rematch. This exacerbated the fallout from Obama's poor showing, and raised the stakes for the vice presidential debate, which fell in between. A more compressed schedule might have hastened the president's comeback.

Beyond the usual scheduling factors, a new consideration looms over the debate calendar: early voting. In 2008 and 2012 around 30 percent of American voters cast their ballots prior to Election Day. About two-thirds of the states now permit some version of early voting, ranging from forty-five days in advance to the weekend prior. Additionally, national party conventions are being held earlier in the summer; by Labor

Day the general election campaign is well under way. Clearly these shifts in the electoral calendar have implications for the timing of presidential debates.

Finally, it should be noted that not all debate scheduling has been driven by practical concerns. In 1984 Nancy Reagan's personal stargazer offered her input into the timing and location of that year's matches. Astrologer Joan Quigley would claim responsibility for President Reagan's stumbling performance in Louisville on October 7, calling the selection her "one important error the entire seven years I did the Reagans' astrology."[68] White House aide Michael Deaver confirmed that he routinely ran important dates on the political calendar past Quigley, "but if she had called back and said, 'My God, all the stars in the sky are coming together at that time,' there wasn't anything I could do."[69]

How many debates are too many? The most debates in any year were the four between Kennedy and Nixon in 1960; 1980 offered the fewest, one between Reagan and Carter, another between Reagan and Anderson. Never has more than a single vice presidential debate taken place in a given year; no vice presidential matches at all were held in 1960 or 1980, though consideration was given to having the 1960 running mates, Henry Cabot Lodge and Lyndon Johnson, appear together for ten minutes at the beginning of one program before yielding to the top-of-the-ticket nominees.

Even as the series of 1960 was under way, Kennedy's negotiators were lobbying to add a fifth debate to the schedule. Five had been JFK's ideal number all along. "Basically, Kennedy wanted as many debates as possible to gain the television exposure, and we wanted as few debates as possible, possibly only one," said Herb Klein, Nixon's press secretary.[70] Through the end of October 1960, the issue of a fifth debate remained alive, sparking a flurry of bargaining sessions and accusations in the press; when agreement could not be reached, the series ended at four.

Nixon's team had already made a costly blunder about the debate schedule, wrongly reasoning that the final match of the series would draw the largest audience. As it turned out, nothing could wipe away the impression left in the first encounter. "When the debates were held," Nixon wrote, "at least twenty million more people listened to and watched the first than any of the others, including the fourth and final appearance. I turned in my best performance before the smallest audience."[71]

In 1984 Mondale's negotiators initially proposed a whopping six presidential and two vice presidential debates. The outrageousness of the demand, particularly from an underdog campaign, illustrates how debate negotiations resemble haggling in a Middle Eastern carpet bazaar. According to Mondale's aide Richard Leone, six was never a realistic consideration; the Democratic side hoped for three and settled on two, plus one vice presidential debate.[72]

Beyond number, another recurring point of campaign disagreement has been program length. In 1960 each of the four debates ran only an hour, the shortest in history. They might have been even a few minutes shorter: NBC's Robert Sarnoff argued for "appropriate" commercial sponsorship of the debates, an idea quickly scuttled by cosponsor CBS.[73] Since Kennedy–Nixon, all but two of the programs have been ninety minutes long; the exceptions are the sixty-minute Reagan–Anderson debate in 1980 and the vice presidential debate in 1976, which at an hour and fifteen minutes represented a compromise between Dole, who wanted an hour, and Mondale, who wanted an hour and a half.

As President Reagan learned in his first match with Walter Mondale in 1984, one and a half hours is an extraordinarily long time for any individual to perform at capacity on live television. That event, which ran beyond its scheduled time slot, clocked in at one hundred minutes. Reagan's doddering performance—"the worst night of Ronnie's political career," in the words of Nancy Reagan[74]—brought into the open a previously unmentionable topic: the seventy-three-year-old president's ability to withstand the physical and mental rigors of the office.

According to Elizabeth Drew, "Getting the debates to last an hour and a half was one of the Mondale negotiators' major strategic achievements, even though they held few cards; they figured that Reagan would not have sufficient stamina to last that full time in good form."[75] The Republicans wanted the debates to last sixty minutes, but swapped the extra half hour for the supposed safety of a panel of questioners.

THE DEBATE OVER FORMAT

Given the importance of format in debates, it comes as no surprise that campaigns obsess over how the programs are designed. Functioning in their role as executive producers manqué, political strategists seek structures that are comfortable for the candidates first, and educational for the voters second. In practice, this meant that for three decades presidential debates remained locked in a single, candidate-friendly format: the joint news conference, with a panel of reporters posing a series of disconnected questions.

The press conference format endured because candidates took comfort in its strictures. By directing their answers to a panel, debaters could avoid confronting each another in ways that might prove unseemly in front of a viewing audience. Furthermore, with three or four reporters asking a succession of disparate questions, the discussion could not dwell on any single issue for very long, allowing candidates easy segues into their predigested messages. Douglass Cater, a questioner in the second Kennedy–Nixon debate, complained that the panel's mission "was hardly more than to designate categories—animal, vegetable, or mineral—on which the two might or might not discourse."[76]

Thanks in large measure to the intercession of Bill Clinton, the debates in 1992 inaugurated looser formats: the "town meeting" or "people's debate," in which an audience of voters questions the candidates, and the "single moderator," used twice in 1992 and in all presidential and vice presidential debates thereafter. The original proposal by the debates commission in 1992 also called for a single-moderator format throughout the series. George H. W. Bush resisted this idea, telling CNN's Bernard Shaw, "I thought when you and others asked tough questions at the 1988 debates, it livened things up. I saw nothing wrong with the former format."[77]

Clinton himself suggested the town hall meeting that would produce the year's most talked-about debate. According to Mickey Kantor, the candidate raised the issue in a phone call during a break in one of the negotiating sessions. "He thought you'd probably get more-substantive questions," Kantor said. "He thought he'd do quite well in it, and that it would show the difference in his ability to relate to people and President Bush's. To my surprise, the Bush people accepted immediately."

Recalled Clinton's aide Paul Begala, "When the word came back that the president's folks had agreed to it, we were hooting and hollering. We couldn't believe it."[78]

Why did Bush's negotiators go along with the Richmond town hall debate? According to Edward Fouhy, producer of the debate in 1992, "They thought that Richmond, a conservative city, could be relied on to produce uncommitted voters sufficiently in awe of the president to ask softball questions." James Baker said Bush agreed because he was "really good with small groups. When we started his presidential campaign, we had something called 'Ask George Bush' forums, and they were extremely successful."[79] In the end, Bush would have reason to rue the town hall debate.

The single-moderator format made its debut with the rollicking vice presidential debate in 1992. According to Fouhy, it was Dan Quayle who persuaded Bush's campaign to accept the idea. After suffering at the hands of a press panel in his debate with Lloyd Bentsen in 1988, Quayle had cause to favor a less rigid format. As Fouhy put it, "Quayle knew that his hopes for helping the ticket and building his own candidacy for the future were riding on his debate performance."[80] Indeed, Quayle improved considerably in the give-and-take of the single-moderator structure, though many critics condemned the program as a free-for-all.

The innovations of 1992 finally dragged presidential debates into the modern era. At the end of the series, political reporter Richard Berke of the *New York Times* analyzed how the three candidates had fared in the various formats: "Before the debates, President Bush's aides wanted a panel of journalists to pose questions; now they say that approach was least helpful to their man. Governor Bill Clinton's side wanted a single moderator to ask the questions but ended up preferring another format, too." Concluded Berke, "Presidential campaigns don't know what's good for them."[81]

In 2000 a new format variation joined the roster: the table debate, with candidates and moderator seated a few feet apart from one another behind a desk. This format was used for the second Bush–Gore match and the vice presidential debates of 2000 and 2004. It resurfaced in the final presidential debates of 2008 and 2012.

The discussion about whether debaters should stand or sit extends back to 1960, when Kennedy's handlers sought a stand-up format in order to exploit Nixon's knee injury. Said JFK's aide J. Leonard Reinsch, "If Nixon had to shift his weight every now and then, it would give the impression that he was uncomfortable and ill at ease."[82] Reinsch was surprised when the Republicans raised no objections; Nixon did visibly shift his stance on the air, adding to his impression of physical debility. In 1976 representatives for Jimmy Carter and Gerald Ford argued at length over whether the candidate not speaking ought to be seated, as was the policy in 1960. According to debate scholar Sidney Kraus, this discussion "probably consumed more time than any other single point in the substantive or technical negotiations and necessitated a series of telephone calls to each of the principals."[83]

After the successful introduction of sit-down formats in primary and state-level debates, the CPD in 1996 sought a table debate between Bill Clinton and Bob Dole. The effort failed when both campaigns objected. According to co-commissioner Frank Fahrenkopf, "Experts tell us that the nature and context of discussion changes when people are seated around a table. We threw it out—the candidates were not interested."[84]

Some candidates feel more at home in a table debate. Vice presidential contender Dick Cheney pressed for the sit-down format in both of his general election debates, in part because it followed the familiar contours of Sunday morning Washington talk shows like *Meet the Press* and *Face the Nation*. In 2004 Kerry–Edwards negotiator Vernon Jordan suggested that the vice presidential candidates hold a less traditional event, perhaps a town meeting with citizens asking questions. According to Jordan, "I told [James] Baker when we were negotiating that I wanted to have the vice presidential debate standing up. He said, 'Cheney can't stand up, he's had a heart attack,' and I said, 'That's why we want him to stand up!' "[85] In the end, according to Baker, "We were adamant that we were going to have that debate sitting down. The vice president's not going to stand up and walk around the room with a trial lawyer. We're going to have that debate seated or we might not even have it."[86]

Despite a successful table debate against Al Gore in 2000, negotiators for George W. Bush opted to avoid the format four years later, and except for the town meeting, Bush and Kerry remained perched behind lecterns throughout their appearances in 2004. According to Bush's deputy campaign manager, Mark Wallace, the candidate "thought his best version would be at a podium. There was a design to make it clear that the president was just that—the president."[87] Brett O'Donnell, the Liberty University debate coach who served as an adviser to Bush's campaign, was among those opposed to a table format. "It would put [Bush] in very close proximity to Kerry, which might have led to a breaking of the rules," O'Donnell said.[88]

In 2008 and 2012 the debate commission again sought to seat the candidates at a table for all their debates. In both cycles the campaigns insisted that the first event of the series be a lectern debate. "When you've got the non-incumbent candidate, you want the presidential appearance," said Ron Klain of Obama's team. "Nothing looks more presidential than a podium."[89] Janet Brown, executive director of the debate commission, said that campaigns resist table debates "based on a perfectly legitimate observation, which is that Americans see the president standing behind a podium for a lot of different events, ranging from the State of the Union to press conferences to joint press conferences with foreign leaders." On the other hand, she said, moderators "vastly prefer" the sit-down format, where close proximity and the ability to make eye contact allow for greater interaction and conversational control.[90]

Campaigns fixate on the sitting-versus-standing question because it is one of the few areas in which they still wield influence. Negotiators also flex their muscles in attempting to shape town hall formats. The unpredictability of citizen-questioners gives candidates and their advisers plenty to worry about. George W. Bush, for one, had little use for town hall debates. In 2000, recalling his father's experience against Bill Clinton, Bush told reporters, "Sometimes the formats lend themselves to who best can walk around the stage, act dramatically. I'd rather have a good discussion."[91]

In the end Bush reluctantly accepted a town hall debate against Al Gore, with mixed results. For the town meeting in 2004, Bush's negotiators changed the composition of the audience from undecided voters to "soft supporters" and, in the memorandum of understanding, drafted four pages of detailed guidelines governing how the town hall questioners would operate—again, with a less than stellar outcome for their candidate.

Limitations on the town hall continued apace in 2008 and 2012. No predebate audience warm-up. No follow-ups from questioners or the moderator. Microphones cut after a question is asked. Reaction shots of audience members prohibited. No rephrasing of questions by the moderator. And so on. To a great extent these prohibitions and protections have been illusory. After the town hall debate in 2012, Josh Voorhees of *Slate* compiled a list of sixteen rules from the memorandum of agreement that had been flouted; violators included the moderator, audience members, and the candidates themselves. In Voorhees's estimation, "The town hall debate became one giant string of rules violations."[92]

THE DEBATE OVER STAGING

No detail being too small for campaign negotiators, a number of other production points bear mention in our discussion of predebate haggling.

One of the most contested matters in televised presidential debates is height. Because history shows that the taller presidential candidate dominates at the ballot box, campaigns strive to mitigate a debater's relative shortness. The height issue first cropped up in the 1976 series between Gerald Ford and Jimmy Carter. Although Ford was only three and a half inches taller than Carter, negotiators for the Democratic challenger sought compensatory measures. The two sides reached what became known as the "belt buckle compromise": Ford's lectern was built to intersect his torso two and a half inches above the belt buckle, while Carter's podium intersected an inch and a half below his buckle point. In exchange for this concession, Carter's camp agreed to let Ford's people choose the color of the backdrop, something the Republicans wanted in order to mask the incumbent president's thinning hair. "We worried about the height, they worried about the hair," Carter's aide Gerald Rafshoon told *Newsweek*.[93]

George H. W. Bush's six-foot stature posed a height challenge to both of his first two debate opponents, Geraldine Ferraro and Michael Dukakis. In 1984 Ferraro's people demanded and got a riser on the stage that made her five-foot-four-inch frame appear less diminutive. The piece was designed as a gently sloping ramp, so that Ferraro would not have to take a noticeable step up to her podium; instead, the candidate had to concentrate on staying in place atop the riser, lest she appear to be listing.

Michael Dukakis, at a six-inch stature disadvantage, got a similar ramp four years later, though Baker and his team did not yield this concession until the final round of the debate talks. "What are you going to do when you have to negotiate with Gorbachev?" Baker taunted his opponents. "Call for a little platform?"[94] Not inaccurately, Bush's aides referred to the riser as a "pitcher's mound"; at the second debate, a Republican advance man sneaked a softball onto the set intending to leave it on Dukakis's lectern, but no opportunity arose to make the drop. In the end, stratagems to downplay the Democratic nominee's relative shortness were of mixed value. At the close of the debate, when Dukakis stepped down from his podium to shake Bush's hand, the height difference between the two men seemed all the more pronounced.

"All three of my candidates—Ford, Reagan, and Bush 41—were taller than their opponents, so we always held a bargaining chip on height," wrote James Baker in his autobiography. "Each time, we let the other side adjust the podium, add a riser, or do something else to compensate, but we always got something good in return."[95]

In 2000 negotiators for George W. Bush unsuccessfully sought a lower lectern for their candidate, in view of Al Gore's slightly superior height, but both pieces ended up measuring an identical forty-eight inches from top to bottom. A more pressing concern for the Bush campaign was keeping Gore tied to his home base. According to Bush's media adviser Stuart Stevens, "One of our major requests was for microphones attached to the podiums, rather than lapel mikes, so that each candidate would be more or less tethered to the podiums. We were trying to discourage Gore's ability to pull some stunt, like walking over to the governor with a pledge to end global warming by that weekend or some such nonsense."[96]

Debate negotiators approach the art of podium design with the utmost seriousness. The Republican team of 1976, mindful of Ford's reputation as a klutz, made sure to insist on a brace for securing the presidential water glass. Carter's people successfully demanded smaller-than-normal lecterns in order to more fully display their candidate's physical grace. "Jimmy uses his hands and body language beautifully," one of Carter's officials told *Time* magazine. "The president [Ford] has zero body language."[97]

Carter's negotiators also won the skirmish over whether Ford would be allowed to affix an official presidential seal to his lectern. Four years later, handlers for then-incumbent president Carter co-opted this tactic for themselves. According to a prenegotiation strategy memorandum of 1980, "The presidential seal should be on his [Carter's] podium. Obviously, we won't get this but it's something to trade away."[98] More recent debate agreements have specified that no decorations may appear on the lecterns.

Over the years, negotiators have also grappled with whether to allow debaters to bring notes or props onto the stage. John F. Kennedy used this trick in a West Virginia primary debate in 1960, producing a government-surplus food package to make a point about federal programs for the undernourished. Dan Quayle's aides sought approval to have props in the vice presidential debate in 1992; they planned for Quayle to read passages from *Earth in the Balance*, Al Gore's newly released book on the environment. Gore's negotiators agreed, on the condition that their man could bring a potato, the vegetable whose name Quayle had misspelled in a widely publicized incident earlier in the year. The matter was quickly dropped.

Negotiators in 2004 added another prohibition on the debaters: in addition to a ban on notes, props, and "other tangible things," the contract specified that "neither candidate may reference or cite any specific individual sitting in a debate audience at any time during a debate." According to the terms of the memorandum, if such a reference was made, or if notes or props were produced, the moderator had to interrupt the proceedings and explain to the audience that rules had been violated. The document of 2004 also required candidates not to issue any challenges for more debates, ask their opponents to take a pledge, or directly address each other.[99]

The most contentious staging issue faced by negotiators in 2004 was the use of timing lights. In hammering out an agreement with John Kerry, Bush's campaign insisted on a timing device that would be visible to the audience at home—a shift from the usual procedure, in which only the candidates could see the lights. "Their feeling is John Kerry talks too much," explained *Time* magazine's Karen Tumulty in an interview on CNN. "And they essentially want to make it obvious to the viewing audience when he has gone over his time."[100] Despite their initial objections, Kerry's debate advisers came to regard the device as an asset, because it pushed their candidate to compress his responses. In a

,essment of the series of 2004, *New York Times* columnist called the timing lights "a godsend for Mr. Kerry. They do what his advisers had been fruitlessly wishing he would do on the campaign trail: come to the point and stop talking."[101]

THE DEBATE OVER QUESTIONERS

The television networks that sponsored the debates in 1960 originally hoped to enlist a prominent jurist or university president as the program moderator. It was the campaigns' uneasiness with this idea that handed the job to journalists instead. Fearful that even a highly respected national leader could not suppress his bias, representatives for Kennedy and Nixon argued that members of the press would be less inclined to play favorites. The networks, recognizing an opportunity to promote their own personnel, gladly assented, inaugurating a long-standing tradition of journalistic participation in presidential debates.

In keeping with the general pugnacity of the deliberations in 1960, a new controversy soon erupted: the campaigns' demand that newspaper and magazine reporters be included in the debate panels along with television people. After initial resistance from the broadcasters, an accommodation was reached that gave the networks all four panelist slots in the first and fourth debates, and two slots to print reporters in the second and third. When neither the networks nor the handlers wanted the responsibility of picking the print panelists, names were drawn at random from a list of reporters traveling with the candidates.

Never again would campaigns take so lightly the task of selecting moderators and panelists. The resumption of presidential debates in 1976 brought a radical change in procedure: for the first time, the participants had an active hand in choosing their questioners. When network news officials learned that the League of Women Voters had invited Ford's and Carter's campaigns to submit suggestions for debate panelists, a brief public spat ensued. Again in 1980, media outlets objected to the league's collaboration with the campaigns in picking questioners, but as before, the journalists soon relented.

In 1984, when Reagan debated Mondale, panelist selection took center stage, erupting in the media as an ugly sideshow. On the eve of the opening debate, the League of Women Voters broke the long-standing code of silence between sponsors and negotiators and called a news conference to denounce the campaigns' high-handedness in rejecting eighty-three journalists for the first panel. Dorothy Ridings, the organization's president, publicly chastised both sides for having "totally abused" the process.[102]

The league had initially supplied the campaigns with a list of twelve possible panelists for each of the year's three debates. All but one of the thirty-six names were rejected. League officials submitted more names, and were met with more rejections. "It was one of those things that takes on a life of its own," recalled league debate producer Victoria Harian. "They weren't really legitimate concerns—it just became a game between the two campaigns." Ridings said journalists were stricken from the list for reasons "that had nothing to do with their professional capabilities."[103]

In protest, news organizations like the *New York Times, Washington Post*, and CBS announced that their employees would not serve as panelists. (CBS let correspondent Diane Sawyer appear in the first debate because she had signed on before the ban.) Press reaction to the panelist selection story was predictably harsh. A piece in the *Post* compared the exercise to both a college fraternity rush and Nixon's list of enemies.[104] Network newscasts the evening of the first debate in 1984 showed footage of the panelists' desk being reconfigured after one of four participants resigned in a last-minute boycott. The shrunken desk provided a visual metaphor for the predebate tussle between campaigns and reporters.

Like other political professionals, James Baker maintained that campaigns deserve veto power over moderators and panelists. "I've never been a believer that you turn all of this over to some allegedly nonpartisan, objective group. There's too much at stake," Baker said. "The campaigns have a legitimate right in making sure they're not going into a debate with moderators or questioners who are biased. And don't tell me that these people don't have biases, because they do."[105]

Following the controversy in 1984 over panelist selection, the campaigns tightened their grip, giving themselves a more active hand in the decision making. The debate agreement of 1988 devoted a full page to codifying the process for selecting questioners. In legalistic language the document laid out an intricate procedure in which each campaign prepared a list of names that the other side could then approve or delete, until a proper number was reached—a process akin to jury selection.

Recent changes in debate formats, particularly the phase-out of press panels, have given moderators a far more substantive role. In 1996 and 2000, absent any behind-the-scenes drama, PBS's Jim Lehrer was chosen as solo moderator of all but one of the presidential and vice presidential debates. (Bernard Shaw of CNN handled the Cheney–Lieberman debate in 2000.) In 2004 the CPD returned to a different moderator for each debate. Furthermore, to reduce campaign meddling in the process, the CPD announced its roster of moderators in mid-August, well before the two sides sat down to iron out a debate agreement. When it came time to negotiate, both Bush and Kerry accepted the proposed slate without objection. According to Janet Brown, executive director of the debate commission, "There was absolutely no problem with the individuals who were announced."[106]

In 2008 and 2012 the CPD followed the same pattern, announcing its slate of moderators in August, before the campaigns met to draft their memorandum. Although the campaigns raised no objections to the names on the list—initially, at least—the selection of presidential debate moderators has become an increasingly fraught business, not just from an ideological standpoint but from a diversity standpoint as well. Going forward it appears likely that campaigns will attempt to reassert their influence over who gets chosen.

Although predebate negotiations have become standard operating procedure in presidential campaigns, at the end of the day, nitpicking and dealmaking can provide only so much security. Democratic media consultant Robert Squier offered this advice to candidates headed into the debate arena: "The first thing to remember in a debate is that once you're on stage, everything that's been negotiated is out the window. There are no rules, except the rules of fair play."[107]

In other words, presidential debates are live television. And, inevitably, live television trumps written contracts.

2 / PREDEBATE STRATEGY

In the seconds leading up to the presidential debate of 1980, President Jimmy Carter and challenger Ronald Reagan strode onto the stage from opposite sides of the Cleveland Music Hall to assume their positions at the lecterns. Instead of stopping at his designated spot, Reagan bounded across the set directly to Carter and, unexpectedly, shook his hand. "Carter's look of surprise suggested that he thought he was about to be knifed," wrote communication scholar Kathleen Hall Jamieson.[1]

As with all political kabuki, such moments are part of a candidate's master strategy—in this case, to knock the president of the United States off his game just before a live debate. Again at the end of the program, in violation of the agreed-upon rules, Reagan marched over and shook hands with Carter, this time on camera, under the watchful eye of perhaps the largest television audience ever assembled for a presidential debate. The move served a dual purpose: making Reagan look amiable and flummoxing Carter.

The handshakes in 1980 epitomize a fundamental quest of debaters on live television: to seize control of the narrative. In an unscripted setting like a presidential debate, candidates attempt to impose their own story line through the use of calculated gestures, prepackaged sound bites, and audience-tested messages. What makes debates compelling in spite of their choreography is the skill with which the leading players apply these tools. Debaters operate simultaneously as competitors and collaborators, coauthors of a work in progress that each wishes to steer in a different direction. Any small narrative edge, such as Reagan's on-camera handshake at the end of the debate in Cleveland, can affect the audience's perception of which star deserves top billing in the drama.

But an obverse tendency tempers this principle: live television creates its own momentum, apart from the strategic desires of the candidates. Presidential debates have thus spawned a litany of errors both serious and silly:

- Richard Nixon declaring that "America can't stand pat," inadvertently making a double-entendre of his wife's name
- Gerald Ford's erroneous claim that Eastern Europe was not under Soviet domination
- Bob Dole blaming the country's war dead on the Democratic Party
- Jimmy Carter's discussion of nuclear weaponry with daughter Amy
- Ronald Reagan, meandering down the Pacific Coast Highway in a closing statement that had to be curtailed by the moderator
- Michael Dukakis reacting dispassionately to Bernard Shaw's question about the hypothetical rape and murder of Kitty Dukakis
- Dan Quayle venturing into the land of Camelot for a JFK analogy
- George Bush the father looking down at his watch during the town hall debate in 1992
- George Bush the son scowling and squirming his way through the first debate of 2004
- John Kerry gratuitously referencing Vice President Cheney's gay daughter
- John McCain condescending to Barack Obama

Though debaters strive to inoculate themselves against missteps of this sort, the high-combustion nature of live television renders such episodes impossible to prepare for. Candidates instead devote their predebate energy to planning *positive* tactical moments, snippets that will play favorably during the live telecast and in postdebate media coverage as well. According to Democratic debate coach Tom Donilon, "You hope in a debate there will be a moment . . . where your candidate can make an impact. You don't know when it's going to come."[2] The savvy debater does not wait for the high points to occur naturally; he manufactures them, polishes them, and finds a way to deploy them.

Let us trace the evolution of several classic moments from presidential and vice presidential debates, and then consider the overall strategic imperatives debaters face as they prepare to do battle.

CLASSIC DEBATE MOMENTS

Like Reagan's surprise handshakes, most classic debate moments share a common heritage as the products of careful plotting. At the end of that same debate with Carter in 1980, Reagan posed a question in his closing statement that struck its target with the accuracy of a heat-seeking missile: "Are you better off now than you were four years ago?" The line, scripted by speechwriter David Gergen, had the feel of folk wisdom, like the insightful query of a commonsense neighbor. In fact, the language stemmed directly from polling data: by a two-to-one margin, Americans considered themselves in worse shape than they had been at the beginning of Carter's presidency.

As this example from 1980 shows, opening and closing statements lend themselves particularly well to strategic planning. But Reagan's other, seemingly more spontaneous rejoinders were also devised ahead of time, albeit by the candidate himself. In the Reagan–Carter debate, Carter tartly reminded the audience that his opponent had begun his political career campaigning around the country against Medicare. "There you go again," Reagan replied, more in sorrow than in anger. This simple line accomplished two of Reagan's objectives: diminishing Carter by questioning his veracity, and bolstering Reagan's own standing vis-à-vis health care. According to Reagan's biographer, Lou Cannon, "The reply was the Great Deflector's high point of the debate and perhaps of the campaign itself. It seemed such a wonderful, natural summation of an opponent's excess that overnight it became part of the political language."

Cannon described the phrase as having "all the careful spontaneity of a minuet."[3] During debate rehearsals, Reagan had resisted advice that he bone up on issues, concentrating instead on one-liners, which he believed the viewing public would be more likely to remember. According to debate coach Myles Martel, Reagan was urged to use lines that could "dramatically differentiate" him from Carter, a tactic Carter had successfully employed against Ford in 1976. Martel noted, " 'There you go again,' crafted by Reagan himself and practiced on [mock debater David] Stockman two days earlier, successfully elevated Reagan without projecting him as unduly strident or defensive—indeed a formidable challenge when refuting an incumbent president."[4]

Of the presidential debate in 1980, Reagan wrote that the event "may have turned on only four words" that "popped out" of his mouth. "I think there was some pent-up anger in me over Carter's claims that I was a racist and warmonger," he said, adding that his response "just burst out of me spontaneously."[5]

Four years later, Reagan would make the same dubious claim of spontaneity for his response to a panelist's question about whether he was too old to handle the presidency. The line became another instant classic: "I want you to know that I will not make age an issue of this campaign. I am not going to exploit for political purposes my opponent's youth and inexperience." In his memoir, Reagan wrote that the words "just popped off the top of my head. I'd never anticipated it, nor had I thought in advance what my answer might be to such a question." Reagan continued, "Well, the crowd roared and the television cameras flashed a shot of Mondale laughing. I'm sure that if I had been as stuffed with as many facts and figures as I was before the first debate, I wouldn't have been able to come up with that line; your mind just isn't flexible enough if it's saturated with facts because you've been preparing for an examination."[6]

Reagan's aide Richard Wirthlin recalled the story somewhat differently: After a practice session, Wirthlin reminded the president he would surely be asked a question on age. "His eyes twinkled and he said, 'Don't worry, Dick. I've got a way to deal with that question, and I'm just waiting for it to come up.' Now he said that it just popped off his head—and it did. But when that thought came to him it was at least two days before the actual debate."[7] Whatever the timing, observers agreed that the riposte hit its target. Wrote David Broder, "It well may have been that the biggest barrier to Reagan's re-election was swept away in that moment."[8]

The unforgettable line of 1988—Lloyd Bentsen telling Dan Quayle "You're no Jack Kennedy"—also had a less than spontaneous provenance. In an August appearance at the Missouri State Fair, Quayle boasted to his audience, "I'm very close to the same age of Kennedy when he was elected, not vice president but president."[9] The remark, like others from Quayle's stump speeches, was duly recorded by Bentsen's campaign staff and passed along to headquarters. In debate rehearsals, when Quayle's surrogate Dennis Eckart drew a JFK comparison, Bentsen responded, "You're no more like Jack Kennedy than George Bush is like Ronald Reagan."[10] In the televised debate, Bentsen omitted the Bush–Reagan reference, and another catchphrase entered the political lexicon.

These and other debate triumphs stand out not just for the rewards they bestow upon a particular candidate but for the damage they inflict upon the opponent. As ABC's Sam Donaldson pointed out, "It's not just the clever line, it's the reaction. Had Jimmy Carter come back with a line that topped 'There you go again,' Carter would have had the headlines. Had Dan Quayle . . . been able to handle 'You're no Jack Kennedy,' that would have made it, too."[11]

In fact, Walter Mondale used just such a tactic in 1984, turning Reagan's "There you go again" around on its speaker. Attempting to invoke past glories, Reagan walked right into a Mondale trap by using the line again. "Remember the last time you said that?" Mondale asked, and Reagan nodded. The effect on camera was unsettling: suddenly the president seemed vulnerable. "You said it when President Carter said that you were going to cut Medicare. . . . And what did you do right after the election? You went out and tried to cut $20 billion out of Medicare." The bit that had worked so beautifully in 1980 now came flying back in Reagan's face.

UNIVERSAL DEBATE OBJECTIVES

As the previous examples suggest, debate strategy is greatly situational, tied to the moment and tailored to the personalities of the participants. But five decades of presidential debates have produced a set of objectives that apply to candidates across the board, which are outlined in the following sections.

Projecting Leadership

The most basic goal in a presidential debate is to command the stage. By virtue of their competitive structure, debates provide a natural forum for the expression of authority. This is why debaters struggle to control the narrative; when someone takes ownership of the event, audiences are witnessing executive ability in action. "What wins a political debate," said Democratic strategist Richard Leone, "is if one candidate seems in command—of himself, of the environment, of his opponent." Republican Roger Ailes expressed it another way: "People reduce it down to fairly simplistic language: I want a president who can hit a home run."[12]

Leadership in presidential debates is demonstrated in various ways, from seizing the spotlight to maintaining calm in the face of pressure. The track records of John F. Kennedy, Ronald Reagan, and Bill Clinton indicate that the public responds favorably to debaters who display a high degree of self-possession. As Michael Deaver, Reagan's longtime media adviser, observed, "What is important is how comfortable the person is with himself. If you can get that across in the debate, that's what people are hungry for."[13]

Any hint of nervousness or inauthenticity undermines a candidate's effort to project leadership. George W. Bush in 2004, for example, was so fidgety and ill at ease in his first two debates that he appeared less presidential than John Kerry, the nonpresident with whom he shared the stage. Al Gore's shifting personalities in the debates of 2000 similarly worked against his credibility as a leader. In 2008, calm, confident Barack Obama came across as more statesmanlike than John McCain, a man old enough to be his father.

"We had one objective in that debate," recalled Ron Klain of Obama's campaign: "to look presidential." In Klain's judgment, voters in 2008 were ready to reject Republican economics, particularly after the financial crash that dominated news coverage just before the first Obama–McCain debate: "The only question left on the table: was Barack Obama ready to be president? That's what we had to prove in that debate, that was the objective, that was the whole thing."[14]

Since debates serve as an audition for the presidency, voters naturally prefer to see performers who fill the role. While a debate may not parallel the job of being president, it is a place where candidates put their personal qualities on display for citizens to gauge. According to Bill Clinton, debates "give people a feel for what kind of leader the debater would be, how much the person knows, and how they approach the whole idea of being president."[15]

Being Likeable

In addition to projecting leadership, debaters must also connect with voters on a human level. In a column in the *Washington Post* in 1980, television consultant Jack Hilton offered a series of suggestions to that year's presidential contenders. High on the list was the imperative to "be liked." As Hilton saw it, "The emotional content of the debate will remain in the viewers' memories for longer than the ideas expressed. A candidate can fail in all of his objectives for the debate and still win if the viewers at home feel empathy or sympathy for him."[16]

The ethos of television demands that its star performers be audience friendly. For presidential debaters, likeability functions as a wild card, a commodity much prized yet impossible to generate on cue. Those who lack charisma—charisma through the lens of a camera—face an uphill battle.

Such was the case with the Democratic nominee in 1988, Michael Dukakis, whose strategic objective entailed, in effect, a personality overhaul. To the candidate's credit, but also to his misfortune, Dukakis did not attempt to remake himself into Mister Congeniality in order to please the audience and the press. According to biographers Christine Black and Thomas Oliphant, "Dukakis was more serious than Bush, more articulate, more overtly aggressive, scored many more debating points, and, ultimately, was less likable."[17]

This deficiency became a discussion topic during the debates themselves. "Wouldn't it be nice to be perfect?" George Bush asked viewers sarcastically. "Wouldn't it be nice to be the Ice Man so you never make a mistake?" Margaret Warner, a questioner in the second debate in 1988, put the issue directly to Dukakis: "Governor, you won the first debate on intellect and yet you lost it on heart. . . . The American people admired your performance but didn't seem to like you very much." By way of reply, Dukakis declared himself a "reasonably likeable guy." But when a candidate must publicly defend his appeal, the matter has already been decided.

Conversely, debaters who have the audience on their side enter the arena with a head start—again, the examples of Reagan and Clinton spring to mind. Yet debates cannot be reduced to mere popularity contests. A more suitable analogy is that presidential debates function as job interviews. As in all job interviews, it is normal for those sitting in judgment to prefer applicants with whom they click. "When we vote for a president, we are deciding not just whose finger will be on the nuclear button but whom we want televised into our homes for the next four years," David Broder of the *Washington Post* wrote in an advice-to-the-candidates essay in 2000. "It doesn't hurt to show you'd be good company."[18]

Dispelling Negative Perceptions

Presidential candidates must use debates not only to communicate positive traits but also to counteract perceived weaknesses. Because individuals at this level rarely step before the camera as unfamiliar entities, this goal can prove elusive. "By the time they engage in presidential debates," wrote political communication scholar Robert V. Friedenberg, "most presidential candidates are reasonably well known and already have firmly established images with the public. Consequently, presidential image goals often involve modifying existing images."[19] Friedenberg dates this trend back to 1960, when Nixon sought to soften his "political assassin" reputation in the debates while Kennedy tried to offset doubts about his lack of executive experience.

The Reagan–Carter match of 1980 offers a textbook instance of a debater making the most of his opportunity to upend public perceptions. In that encounter Ronald Reagan set out to allay voters' concerns that he was a warmonger who lacked the gravitas to be president. He surprised many in the audience by coming off as thoughtful and reasonable, more the wise grandfather than Dr. Strangelove. According to Michael Deaver, "He was always thought of as this dumb actor, so when he actually used his brains and was on his feet without notes, people were blown away, because they just assumed there was nothing there."[20]

In 2008 Sarah Palin used her vice presidential debate with Joe Biden to staunch the hemorrhaging of credibility that had beset her candidacy. Palin had barely survived a series of humiliating network news interviews, solidifying the impression that she was unready for the political big-time. The night before her debate with Biden, Jay Leno joked in his *Tonight Show* monologue that Palin had been busy prepping for the encounter: "I understand she now knows all three branches of government."[21] In the end, Sarah Palin rose to the occasion with enough skill to halt her downward trajectory.

The competitive structure of presidential debates means that each candidate can expect to have his deficiencies pointed out by his opponent. Debaters must therefore be prepared to play both defense and offense. In the first match of 2004, George W. Bush eagerly reminded viewers that John Kerry had flip-flopped on an $87 billion supplemental bill to fund the war in Iraq—a favorite Republican talking point of the campaign. Kerry had his response ready: "When I talked about the $87 billion, I made a mistake in how I talk about the war. But the president made a mistake in invading Iraq. Which is worse?" In this artfully constructed statement we see a first-rate example of a debater using his platform to spin a negative into a positive. As an added benefit, the pithy wording of the remark made it a much-played sound bite in media recaps.

Candidates triumph in debates when they manage to overcome a bad rap. Candidates lose when they fail to shake off unfavorable stereotypes: Bob Dole the hatchet man in 1976, unfeeling Dukakis in 1988, out-of-touch Bush 41 in 1992, exaggeration-prone Gore in 2000, intransigent Bush 43 in 2004, distant Obama in 2012. Each of those candidates misjudged how the audience read him—unlike Ronald Reagan, who accurately diagnosed his negative image and took proactive measures to remedy it, or John Kerry, who in acknowledging error turned the tables on George W. Bush.

John McCain fell into the negative perception trap by treating his opponent with testiness and condescension—exactly as Obama's team had hoped. Democratic debate coach Michael Sheehan told Obama that their mission was to make McCain come off like Mr. Wilson, the grouchy next-door neighbor on *Dennis the Menace*. Only in the last of their three debates together did McCain transcend this stereotype.

When a candidate appears in a presidential debate, he performs before some of the largest audiences he will ever face, minus the usual filters. This hands every participant a giant megaphone with which to address the viewing public on his own terms. Debaters succeed when they grab that opportunity to dispel negatives. They fail—often spectacularly— when they do not.

CHALLENGERS AND INCUMBENTS

The Reagan–Carter match illustrates the risks that incumbent presidents face in television debates. In seven election years, sitting presidents have appeared alongside their challengers. With the exception of Bill Clinton in 1996, the incumbent is generally thought to have faced the more difficult task. According to political scientist Austin Ranney, "Most pundits naturally believe that either the challenger or the underdog has an inherent advantage—the biggest advantage, of course, going to an underdog challenger. Challengers allegedly have that advantage because they get to stand next to a sitting president, increasing their credibility and their visibility."[22]

Carter's strategist Patrick Caddell defined debates as "the vehicle of challengers. . . . They are the best device for a challenger to reach and cross the Acceptability Threshold."[23] Until Bob Dole took on Bill Clinton, one could argue that just such a threshold was crossed by every upstart candidate. For these would-be chief executives, the strategic objective meant positioning oneself as equal in stature to the most powerful individual on the planet.

In 1976, when Jimmy Carter became the first challenger to debate a sitting president, Carter's team correctly identified its mission as separating Ford from the trappings of his office. Nonetheless, they feared a backlash if the upstart candidate appeared overly antagonistic toward so revered a figure as an American president. "I would say that it was one of the most difficult challenges that I had ever faced in my life," Carter said, "to be appearing before 70 to 100 million people on the same level with the president."[24]

For their part, Ford's handlers took pains to frame their candidate's participation in the debates in 1976 as an act of political noblesse oblige. Media consultant Doug Bailey wrote that the debates were "not between two candidates but between one candidate and the president. Everything said, done, and projected by the president should emphasize that fact. If the president is consistently, persistently presidential, Carter (no matter what he does) will not measure up."[25]

Four years later, incumbent president Carter staked out this same territory for himself against Reagan. In 1980, Caddell wrote in a memorandum, "The president's role is not to debate Ronald Reagan. We are letting the American people compare responses to similar questions. Reagan is the foil for the president."[26] As it happened, executive aloofness afforded no protection against Reagan's potent charm, and Carter's attempt to marginalize his opponent backfired.

Incumbency does offer advantages. Sitting presidents accrue a vast store of information, much of it unknowable to challengers. Furthermore, by virtue of their office, incumbents typically hold a strong hand in the negotiation process. But there are negatives. As Reagan's adviser Richard Wirthlin put it, "When a president sits in the Oval Office, in most cases, he lives in a White House cocoon. Everyone is deferential to him. Very seldom is he attacked one on one. And suddenly he is put in a position where not only his issues are being questioned, but his motives are being questioned as well." In the first debate of 1984, Wirthlin said, this sense of isolation bedeviled Ronald Reagan: "He wasn't used to someone talking to him as forcefully as Mondale did, and it took him off balance."[27]

Despite the windfall of Reagan's poor performance in the first debate of 1984, Mondale could not accomplish what every challenger must: persuading voters to trade in their old president for a new model. The next time an incumbent participated in a television debate, this mission proved less daunting. George H. W. Bush, rarely a lucky man in debates, found himself doubly threatened in 1992, having to defend against both Bill Clinton and Ross Perot. Bush's failure to understand what was required of him until too late in the process greatly benefited the opposition.

Like other presidents before and after, Bush allowed personal disdain for his competitors to blind him to the attraction Clinton and Perot held for much of the electorate. By underestimating the threat, Bush got left at the starting line, particularly in the town hall debate that so heavily abetted Clinton. Clinton, meanwhile, used the debates of 1992 to "close the deal" with voters. Said Clinton's campaign manager Mickey Kantor, "In a sense, we had a Ronald Reagan 1980 problem; the final sale had to be made that Bill Clinton was credible."[28]

Four years later, as a popular incumbent, Bill Clinton had no difficulty prevailing over Bob Dole in the debates of 1996. Ever the political analyst, Clinton defined a new objective for himself: "to keep the race focused on the future." No incumbent in a presidential debate, he felt, should dwell excessively on the past. "What's really relevant is evidence that you're moving in the right direction, that you're changing in the right way, that you're pointing toward the future," Clinton said.[29]

The most recent sitting presidents to debate their opponents, George W. Bush in 2004 and Barack Obama in 2012, vividly illustrate the hazards of incumbency. "Presidents think, well, I won last time; I must be a pretty good debater," said Republican debate coach Brett O'Donnell. "So it's harder to convince them that they need to work at it to take the rust off—to convince them this set of debates is entirely unique from the last set because they're facing a different candidate."[30]

Challengers almost always have recent experience in primary forums, leaving them better toned for general election debates than their out-of-practice competitors. This was certainly the case for John Kerry, who had appeared onstage with his Democratic rivals for nearly twenty formal debates, not to mention dozens of other, equally freewheeling campaign events around the country.

Bush, on the other hand, had not debated in four years. Compounding his creakiness, the incumbent president spent the entire campaign of 2004 in front of exclusively friendly crowds that had been scrubbed of potential dissenters. By the time he reached the debates, he was ill equipped to defend his controversial first term. "If you don't talk to the press and deal with audiences with some degree of skepticism, you can't build understanding so people have confidence in you in hard times," presidential scholar Wayne Fields told the *Washington Post*. "His handlers think they're doing him a favor, but they're not."[31] Only in the third match with Kerry did George W. Bush regain his equilibrium, and then just barely.

In 2012 President Obama faced different problems. His opponent, Mitt Romney, had survived a strenuous, often incendiary series of twenty primary debates, emerging battle tested and ready to rumble. Obama's peevishness toward debates in general—and toward Romney in particular—led to a halting, passive performance that drew uniformly negative reviews. The Barack Obama of 2012 stepped into a different, more aggressive debate environment than the one that had existed four years earlier—familiar turf to Romney but terra incognita to Obama. Out of practice, unhappy at having to defend himself, and oblivious to the shift in tone wrought by social media, Obama failed to adapt, permitting his better-prepared challenger to grab the win.

ATTITUDE TOWARD OPPONENT

Democratic media consultant Tony Schwartz has described the presidency as "the only job in the world for which all of the applicants show up at the interview and attack each other."[32] The nakedness of the clash is a distinguishing feature of television debates. Presenting one's own case will not suffice; one must also bash the opposition, and do so in a way that passes the smell test of tens of millions of viewers. Each debater straddles a line between disparaging the competition and showing proper respect. Balancing these contradictory imperatives calls for a good deal of strategic forethought.

"At all times be courteous, respectful, friendly in manner, even when vigorously disagreeing or criticizing, even when unfairly attacked," Theodore Sorensen counseled Jimmy Carter in 1976. Sorensen had been brought into the campaign as an adviser because of his experience with John F. Kennedy in the debates of 1960. "Do not call your opponent names or slur his character or criticize his wife. But beware of appearing too agreeable to the point of passivity; be vigorously assertive and positive; take the initiative, avoid being on the defensive."[33]

Before the Cleveland debate in 1980, Reagan's campaign brain trust advised their candidate to "show righteous indignation" in responding to suggestions that he was dangerous or that questioned his California credentials. "Looking directly at Carter in such instances can be very effective," Reagan's coaches told him. "Humor or a confident smile can also disarm Carter when he thinks he's got you where he wants you."[34]

Four years later, Walter Mondale made the decision to surprise Reagan by treating him with gracious deference. "I wanted to show that I was more alert than the president, without being negative," Mondale recalled in an interview with Jim Lehrer. "And I wanted the debate to build around that."[35] Strategists devised what they called the "gold watch" approach: the popular incumbent had done his job, but now it was time to move on—"sort of embracing a grandfather and gently pushing him aside," in the words of adviser Patrick Caddell.[36] Caddell suggested that Mondale begin the exchange with an informal greeting to Reagan, perhaps even present his opponent with a humorous gift. Mondale did not go that far, but in the opening debate, he conceded that the president had "done some things to raise the sense of spirit and morale—good feeling—in this country," and added, "I like President Reagan." According to Elizabeth Drew, although Mondale had not planned the latter remark, he ad-libbed the extra compliment when he realized his affability was rattling Reagan.[37]

In 1988, strategist Tom Donilon articulated a definition of victory for Michael Dukakis that would seem to apply to debaters across the board: whoever emerges the "appropriate aggressor" wins the match. Being an appropriate aggressor means going on the offense without being offensive; making moves that are bold but not reckless; appearing confident but not condescending. "If he could be nice, okay," Donilon said, but the top priority for Dukakis was to answer Bush's attacks on his character. "To the degree that we had to sacrifice likeability for that, we did."[38]

George H. W. Bush, by contrast, faced not a deficit, but a surfeit, of niceness. Fearing that their candidate's good manners would be misconstrued as passivity, Republican debate coaches in 1988 worked to uncork Bush's repressed competitive juices. According to adviser Lee Atwater, Bush needed to be a "counterpuncher." Said Atwater, "The nature of the man is such that he does not go out and start a fight, he doesn't start controversy or confrontation, but if he gets hit, he hits back."[39]

In the election of 1992, incumbent president Bush continued to resist an aggressive stance. His complacency in the first debate allowed Bill Clinton to pull off a maneuver that dominated postevent coverage. When Bush questioned Clinton's patriotism in the first debate—a ploy Bush had also executed against Dukakis—the Arkansas governor forcefully reminded his opponent that Senator Prescott Bush, the president's father, had led the fight against Joseph McCarthy during the Communist witch hunts of the 1950s. "Your father was right to stand up to Joe McCarthy," said Clinton. "You were wrong to attack my patriotism." For most of this exchange, Bush self-consciously scribbled notes, as Clinton stared him down. According to George Stephanopoulos, the confrontation played out "word for word, the way we wanted it."[40]

As though surrounded by a protective force field, Bill Clinton never got stung in any of his five general election presidential debates. In 1996, predebate hype called for Bob Dole to assail Clinton on the "character issue," but no such lambasting took place. "Dole could not attack his opponent's character at the eleventh hour without bringing his own character disastrously into question," concluded *U.S. News & World Report*.[41]

Twenty years after the fact, Bob Dole still bore the scars of his abrasive, misconceived performance in the vice presidential debate of 1976. A *New York Times* headline from October 1996 indicates the pressure Dole faced vis-à-vis his own reputation: "Searing Images from Debates Past Are Continuing to Haunt Dole." The story revisited not only the infamous match with Walter Mondale but also Dole's controversial senatorial debate in Kansas in 1974. In that encounter the candidate was booed by the audience for snarling at his opponent, a Topeka obstetrician, "I want to know how many abortions you've done."[42]

Although he exceeded expectations by not devolving into "the mean Bob Dole," the senator could make little headway against the gilded persona of President Clinton. If anything, media observers were disappointed that the irascible Dole of old had gone soft. Joe Klein described Dole as a "halfhearted gladiator" who was "too limited a political performer to provide a very compelling alternative to Bill Clinton."[43] Like every born entertainer, Clinton understood the first rule of stardom: grab the lead role for yourself, and by default the other fellow gets cast as second banana.

STRIKING THE RIGHT TONE

Few maneuvers are more difficult for debaters than balancing the contradictory goals of criticizing one's opponent and simultaneously showing respect. On the campaign trail, presidential candidates make great sport of demonizing their opponents. When they meet as rivals, face-to-face on a debate stage, the antipathy is not easy to turn off.

According to Jonathan Alter, Barack Obama in 2012 "didn't trust himself to tangle with Romney." Obama regarded his challenger as an opportunist and a liar, and he feared that a Romney win would undo the progress Democrats had made in his first term. "Obama had long worried that his attitude would spill out," Alter said. "Suppressing that was part of what threw him off his game" in the opening debate of 2012.[44]

Obama was hardly the first debater to grapple with such sentiments. In 2004 Republican strategist Karl Rove faced similar concerns about George W. Bush heading into his debates with John Kerry. "Bush thought Kerry was a pedantic and arrogant flip-flopper and didn't like the Massachusetts senator. I was worried those feelings would show through," Rove wrote in his political memoir.[45]

Handled improperly, disdain for one's opponent can lead debaters and their strategists down a dangerous path. During prep sessions in 2008, advisers to John McCain counseled the candidate to avoid eye contact with Barack Obama as a way of suppressing McCain's hostility toward his rival. McCain internalized this lesson too well: a key story line to emerge from the first Obama–McCain debate was the Republican candidate's unwillingness to look his opponent in the eye. "When McCain was talking, Obama looked at him, like he was a listener," observed John Dickerson in *Slate*. "McCain stared straight ahead as Obama was speaking, which at times made it appear as if Obama was scolding him for denting the car."[46]

Asked about this matter of optics two days later by ABC's George Stephanopoulos, McCain offered a less than convincing explanation: "I've been in many, many debates and a lot of time I don't look at my opponents because I'm focusing on the people. . . . That's what the debate's all about."[47]

Supplementing his nonverbal aloofness in the first debate, McCain repeatedly used condescending language toward Obama: "I don't think that Senator Obama understands . . ."; "I'm afraid Senator Obama doesn't understand . . ."; "What Senator Obama doesn't seem to understand . . ." As television critic Tom Shales noted, "Many of McCain's answers were preceded with belittling references to Obama as if he were talking to a college freshman way out of his depth."[48] Beyond the appearance of rudeness, McCain was also playing with fire: by harping on Obama's lack of experience, he ran the risk of highlighting his own running mate's even slimmer political biography.

Still another factor contributed to McCain's attitude of imperiousness toward Barack Obama. In 2008, for the first time in presidential debate history, the format allowed for direct exchange between candidates. Both Obama and McCain were nonetheless disinclined to avail themselves of this rule change, leaving moderator Jim Lehrer to jump-start the candidate interplay.

"Do you have something to say directly to Senator McCain, Senator Obama, about what he just said?" Lehrer asked early in the debate. When Obama began to answer generically, Lehrer twice urged, "Say it directly to him," at which point the candidate rephrased his comment: "John, ten days ago you said that the fundamentals of the economy are strong. And—"

Looking at Lehrer, with his thumb pointed at Obama, McCain interrupted: "Are you afraid I couldn't hear him?"

"I'm just determined to get you all to talk to each other," replied Lehrer. "I'm going to try."

Despite one more attempt, Lehrer never got McCain to address his opponent directly. Furthermore, while Obama frequently referred to McCain as "John"—twenty-five times, according to media scorekeepers— the Republican nominee stuck with "Senator Obama" as his preferred form of address. To debate viewers this all added up to a sense that Obama was being treated in a less than courteous manner. Lehrer recalled, "I had a feeling sitting there that night that McCain's refusal to address Obama directly, as well as McCain's tense body language, would affect the final outcome of the election."[49]

In the follow-up debate, a town meeting in Nashville, McCain compounded his previous errors by dismissively labeling Obama as "that one" during a discussion of the senator's vote on an energy bill. "You know who voted for it? You might never know. That one," McCain said, pointing an accusatory finger at his opponent. "You know who voted against it? Me." With the debate still under way, Obama's press secretary, Bill Burton, fired off an e-mail to reporters: "Did John McCain just refer to Obama as 'that one'?" In the postdebate spin room, Obama's chief campaign strategist, David Axelrod, pressed the issue, saying, "Senator Obama has a name. You'd expect your opponent to use that name."[50]

As Chris Cillizza wrote in his *Washington Post* blog, McCain's reference—off-the-cuff as it may have been—immediately dominated postdebate chatter. "In a debate almost entirely devoid of news or quotable one-liners, it stood out," Cillizza said. "And that is unlucky for McCain." To Ron Klain of Obama's team the gaffe reinforced the "Get off my lawn, you kids" narrative already forming around McCain. "If he hadn't done that, the debate probably would have been seen as a tie—not a changer either way," said Klain.[51]

In their third debate together McCain finally managed to tamp down the disdain, turning in his best performance of the series. Obama by then had figured out that looking directly at McCain was the most effective way to rattle him. "Obama went in there to psych out McCain and he never broke eye contact with him," recalled Bob Schieffer of CBS News, who as moderator sat in close proximity to the candidates. "Nobody's going to scare John McCain after what he's been through in his life, but I think it may have been a little bit unsettling to him."[52]

As political polarization deepens, presidential debaters face mounting pressure to find the sweet spot between civility and clash. Mitt Romney approached his debates against President Obama in 2012 with a clear, simple imperative: "to be aggressive," according to Romney's media adviser Stuart Stevens, "and to prosecute Obama and make him defend his record."[53] At their opening debate in Denver, this hard-charging attitude caught the president off-guard.

"In the past," wrote Jonathan Alter, "incumbents didn't take shots at their challengers; it was considered unpresidential. The pugilistic GOP primary debates had changed that, with the most combative candidate usually declared the winner." In the election of 2012, Alter concluded, "partisans on both sides were looking for their man to land blows."[54]

Obama's team quickly realized their error. "We underestimated how aggressive Romney would be," said Ron Klain. "And what we completely missed was the impact that social media would have on demanding a level of aggressiveness out of candidates that heretofore had never been seen." In Klain's opinion, 2012 was "one of the great change years" in presidential debate history. Until that point, he said, the arbiter of debates had been dial-groups, in which participants armed with measuring devices invariably rewarded a candidate's positive expressions and punished the negative. "The arbiter in 2012 was Twitter. Twitter loves a food fight, Twitter loves a punch-fest, Twitter loves the takedown. And that's why Obama got crushed."[55]

After the president's loss in Denver, his team retooled its approach and sharpened the candidate's fangs. "They realized that in this atmosphere, no one would be penalized for being too aggressive in the debates," Dan Balz wrote in his book about the campaign of 2012. "The country was so polarized, and the undecided voters so few, that nothing was more important than giving every potential Obama supporter a reason to get out and vote."[56]

The second Obama–Romney debate was a town hall, traditionally a venue in which debaters soften their attacks so as not to alienate the live audience. Prior to the encounter, Bill Clinton urged Obama to resist the temptation to throw punches at Romney—such was the conventional wisdom about town halls. In the end, Obama chose not to heed Clinton's counsel, opting instead for a relentless assault on his opponent. "From the moment he strode onstage," wrote Todd Purdum in a *Vanity Fair* blog post, "the president seemed coiled like a big cat, and he pounced on Mitt Romney from their very first exchange."[57]

For a town hall debate, the interaction was unusually sharp, unusually personal, and unusually physical. To MSNBC's Chris Matthews, the debate felt "like a scene from *West Side Story*." During postdebate coverage on ABC, George Will observed that both candidates "tip-toed right up to the point of rudeness, but stepped back." Noting that he had watched every presidential debate from Kennedy–Nixon forward, Will added, "This was immeasurably the best."[58]

Obama continued his aggressive posture in the final debate, whose foreign policy theme gave the incumbent a decided home-field advantage. The most memorable moment of the evening came when the president regaled his rival with a tutorial on modern warfare: "You mentioned the Navy, for example, and that we have fewer ships than we did in 1916. Well, Governor, we also have fewer horses and bayonets, because the nature of our military has changed. We have these things called aircraft carriers, where planes land on them. We have these ships that go underwater, nuclear submarines. And so the question is not a game of Battleship."

New York Times columnist Frank Bruni described the rebuke as "clever all right, and plenty fair in its way, but it had a schoolyard nastiness to it." Jonathan Alter saw "horses and bayonets" as emblematic of the shift in tone that now held sway in presidential debates: "A line dripped with sarcasm that would have backfired as recently as the Denver debate—and been viewed as far out of bounds in earlier elections—was now toasted as clever on Twitter."[59]

Is a stepped-up level of contentiousness the new normal for general election presidential debates? Although it is too early to render a verdict, the combination of social media, a divided electorate, and barroom-brawl primary debates points toward a less genteel future.

THE INAPPROPRIATE AGGRESSOR

In the town hall debate of 2000, against the advice of his campaign team, Al Gore executed a move that he had first tried out in rehearsal. About ten minutes into the program, as George W. Bush was answering a question about patients' rights, Gore got off his stool and slowly advanced on his opponent, "looking oddly like Gort—the robot in *The Day the Earth Stood Still*," according to analyst Jeff Greenfield. Bush shot a pointed glance at his would-be stalker, followed by a quick, dismissive nod of the head. "The audience laughed," Greenfield wrote, "and Al Gore was finished for the night."[60]

Gore's incursion into George Bush's territory backfired for a variety of reasons, all of which boil down to this: Al Gore was behaving as the "inappropriate aggressor." He had reasoned that a physically assertive gesture would unnerve the Texas governor; instead, the action looked petty and phony. For his part, Bush handled the episode perfectly, exposing Gore's action as hokey stagecraft worthy of audience ridicule. The exchange quickly became one of the most replayed moments of the debate, provoking a stream of commentary from pundits, comedians, and campaign surrogates—like former first lady Barbara Bush, who said she thought Gore "was going to hit George. It sort of scared me."[61]

Gore ought to have known better. One month earlier, in a much-discussed New York senatorial debate, Republican Rick Lazio marched over to the lectern of his opponent, Hillary Clinton, and demanded that she sign a pledge for campaign finance reform. To viewers watching the event on television, Lazio came off as a bully; his invasion of Clinton's space played not as commanding but as disrespectful. In Al Gore's case the maneuver had the added disadvantage of taking place in front of a live audience of town hall questioners, whose laughter instantly punctured the seriousness of his effort.

Any attempt to challenge an opponent in a presidential debate, either physical or verbal, must be handled with subtlety and deftness. Democratic coach Michael Sheehan has recommended that a debater use the first part of his answer to critique his rival's positions; then, in the final thirty seconds, the debater should make a "clubhouse turn" and wrap up with a positive statement touting his own vision.[62] A single response thus leaves a dual impression: negative about one's opponent, positive about oneself.

In order to avoid inappropriate aggression, candidates tend to moderate the language they use with their competitors. In the vice presidential debate of 2004, John Edwards kicked off his first response by telling Dick Cheney, "You are still not being straight with the American people." In rehearsal the line had been even stronger—"You're lying to the American people"—but Edwards decided against the less diplomatic wording.[63]

The principle of inappropriate aggression applies not only to individuals sharing the debate stage, but by extension to members of their families as well. In the final match of 2004, moderator Bob Schieffer asked the candidates whether they believed homosexuality was a choice. John Kerry's response included a mention of Vice President Cheney's lesbian daughter, Mary. Though Kerry and his campaign team later insisted that the reference had been unplanned, to many viewers it felt forced and out of bounds.

"I wish he hadn't done that," a Democratic voter from Iowa told the *New York Times* in a typical reaction. "I don't think he meant anything by it, I just think he could have done without it."[64] Though Kerry stood by his comment, it came at a cost; what initially appeared to be a third consecutive victory against Bush soon morphed into an extended dissection of the senator's motives in mentioning the vice president's gay daughter.

A more positive example of debaters citing family members came at the start of the first Obama–Romney face-off in 2012. In his opening response, President Obama noted that the debate was taking place on his wedding anniversary. Acknowledging the First Lady in the audience, he promised that "a year from now we will not be celebrating it in front of

40 million people." Mitt Romney followed up by congratulating the president on his anniversary. "I'm sure this was the most romantic place you could imagine, here—here with me," Romney added, getting a laugh from the audience. The self-deprecating nature of Romney's joke stood in contrast to Obama's more mordant tone, which betrayed the president's all-too-obvious lack of desire to be there.

Inappropriate aggression can also manifest itself against debate moderators. Several times during the town hall debate in 2012, Mitt Romney crossed swords with moderator Candy Crowley over supposed rules violations—arguing for more time, demanding the last word, insisting that it was his turn. Crowley at one point had to ask Romney to sit down. Romney's doggedness in squabbling over the rules did him no favors; instead, it served to reinforce the candidate's image as a greedy plutocrat, more concerned with grabbing his piece of the pie than with the needs of voters. In the town hall setting, this egocentric attitude came off as especially tone-deaf.

Because moderators serve as stand-ins for the public, candidates must be careful not to treat them in a manner that can be perceived as discourteous. In the vice presidential debate in 2008, Sarah Palin opted for a passive-aggressive attitude toward both moderator Gwen Ifill and opponent Joe Biden. "I may not answer the questions the way that either the moderator or you [Biden] want to hear," Palin said, after being challenged on her evasiveness, "but I'm going to talk straight to the American people and let them know my track record also." Asked about Palin's comment on *Meet the Press*, Ifill said, "She blew me off, is I think the technical term."[65]

No debater can afford to alienate the audience, which is why smart candidates avoid any maneuver that might smack of the unseemly. Presidential debate history is rife with gambits that were contemplated but not executed. After Walter Mondale's win against Ronald Reagan in the first debate of 1984, Democratic advisers briefly considered dropping a bombshell in the follow-up encounter. In the course of the debate, Mondale would produce a letter the president had written in 1960 to Richard Nixon, a letter that compared John Kennedy's ideas to those of Karl Marx and Adolf Hitler. Mondale himself dismissed the suggestion as undignified.[66]

The threat of another mystery document surfaced in 1992, when aides to Bill Clinton fretted that George Bush might flourish a letter in which the collegiate Clinton had weighed renouncing his American citizenship. "They're signaling like crazy that they have something dramatic," James Carville warned his candidate before one of the 1992 debates. "But I think it's a 75 percent chance they're just playing mind games with us."[67] Indeed, no such letter materialized.

Bush's team did discuss a different surprise involving Bill Clinton and a letter. In this scenario Bush was to send his opponent a debate-day demand that he honor an earlier promise to release his complete draft records. During the telecast Bush would then challenge Clinton to set the matter straight. "The handlers liked the idea," wrote *Newsweek*, "but Bush, worrying about op-ed types fussing over McCarthyism, decided the ploy would only worsen his press."[68]

In 1988 Bush's advisers feared that Michael Dukakis would break format at the beginning of one of the programs by challenging the vice president to dismiss the press panel and debate him one-on-one. When one of Bush's aides overheard a rumor to this effect from a member of the technical crew, the Republicans cobbled together a last-minute counterstrategy: if the governor abrogated the rules, Bush would step out from behind his lectern and ask Dukakis to come down from his podium. Viewers would then see that the shorter Dukakis had been perched atop a height-enhancing riser.

During the technical rehearsal preceding the second Bush–Dukakis debate, Bush's aides checked their man's microphone to see if it could be disengaged and swung around in case Bush needed to move out in front of his podium. This repositioning caught the attention of Democratic handlers in the hall. Assuming that *Bush* was planning to break format, they cautioned Dukakis to expect the worst, possibly even the presence in the debate audience of the victims of Willie Horton, the Massachusetts prisoner who committed crimes after being released on furlough during Dukakis's tenure. The governor's aides thought Bush might ask his opponent to justify himself to the victims in front of the nation.

"This is the level of obsession, I guess, that presidential campaigns go through in these things," Dukakis's coach Tom Donilon later said of the incident. Republican strategist Charles Black agreed: "Part of the problem is you get there the last afternoon and evening, and there's nothing to do, so you think up all these cute things."[69]

RHETORICAL STRATEGIES

In the first debate of 2008, Barack Obama strove to present himself as a politician eager to work across the aisle. Six times he called his opponent "absolutely right" about one thing or another. Twice more he said he agreed with McCain. Describing this approach as "sportsmanlike conduct run amok," critic Tom Shales wrote, "Obama supporters must have been displeased. . . . Doesn't Obama want to win?"[70]

McCain's campaign quickly produced a web ad that strung together Obama's expressions of comity. On CNN's media criticism program *Reliable Sources*, Chris Cillizza pointed out that Obama's team was "thrilled" with the web ad, because it played into their strategy. "I think Obama is making a calculated gamble," Cillizza said, "which is, people really do want a different kind of politics."[71]

But danger lurks for debaters who come off as excessively agreeable, just as it does for debaters who come off as excessively confrontational. Several days after the debate, linguist and political theorist George Lakoff posted a checklist of areas in which Obama needed improvement. "Instead of saying 'I agree with Senator McCain . . . ,' Obama should try 'Senator McCain agrees with me that . . . ,'" Lakoff wrote. "The former frames McCain as setting the standard. The latter frames Obama as setting the standard." If Obama's objective was to strike a bipartisan tone, Lakoff suggested the phrase, "Senator McCain and I agree . . ."[72]

These subtle differences underline the importance of word choice in debate strategy. Like soldiers armed with hand grenades, candidates march into televised debates bearing an arsenal of rhetorical ammunition. Whatever the topic being raised, debaters are instructed to deliver the desired, predetermined response. This goal of staying on message, borrowed from the worlds of marketing and advertising, ties debaters to a set of narrowly conceived themes, themes that have been audience tested and painstakingly rehearsed.

In 1976 Gerald Ford's "basic message" was divided into seven points. According to press secretary Ron Nessen, "No matter what specific question was asked, the president was to answer it briefly, then slip into one of the seven points." Each of the seven points came with its own one-liners: "A president cannot be all things to all people"; "There is no button in the Oval Office marked 'maybe'"; "Surely Mr. Carter understands why vetoes are necessary. As governor of Georgia, he vetoed his own legislature 138 times in four years"; and so forth.[73]

Jimmy Carter, meanwhile, chose a strategy of identification with "the people." Scholar Stephen Brydon noted that Carter used the word *people* more than seventy times over the three encounters, compared with Ford's thirty. "The challenger claimed that the people were the source of his own strength and knowledge," Brydon wrote. "Carter portrayed himself as one of the people, representing their needs, hopes, and aspirations."[74]

In 1980, running against Reagan, incumbent president Carter shifted to a top-down, leaderly approach. The Democratic candidate was coached to use definitive language as a means of enforcing his air of authority: "I strongly believe . . ."; "I have always stood for . . ."; "I have always had a firm commitment to . . ." Carter's strategists devised phrases that would paint Reagan as too much of a simpleton to serve as president: "You make it sound as easy as one, two, three"; "You make it sound as easy as apple pie"; "That sounds good but nostalgia won't solve our problems."[75]

For his part, Ronald Reagan used a verbal strategy in 1980 that called for the repeated use of a single reinforcing word: *peace*. In his first response of the debate in 1980, the Republican candidate got straight to the point: "I'm only here to tell you that I believe with all my heart that our first priority must be world peace," Reagan said, informing viewers, "I have seen four wars in my lifetime. I'm a father of sons. I have a grandson." Wrote Lou Cannon, "Reagan mentioned 'peace' so often it sounded like he had invented the word."[76]

Throughout his career, Reagan employed a rhetorical deftness that vexed his competitors. Before the debates in 1984, Mondale's campaign sought advice from former California governor Pat Brown, who had debated Reagan in the gubernatorial race in 1966. "Everybody who had experience with Reagan had essentially the same story, which was, there's only so much you can do," said Mondale's aide Richard Leone. "You can't draw him into an intellectual tennis match at the net, and his lobs are going to drive you nuts because you can't really pound them back." According to Leone, Brown's advice to Mondale's campaign was grim: "Don't think there's anything you can do that will get him off his script."[77]

As it turned out, Reagan's rustiness gave Mondale an unexpected edge in the first debate of 1984. Mondale spooked Reagan, causing him, in essence, to forget his lines. In the wake of this disaster, media coach Roger Ailes urged the president to get back to rhetorical basics: "You didn't get elected on details," Ailes reminded Reagan. "You got elected on themes. Every time a question is asked, relate it to one of your themes."[78] This advice apparently worked, for in the second debate, Reagan discarded the flawed facts-and-figures approach for what scholars Craig Allen Smith and Kathy B. Smith described as "his familiar cinematic language."[79]

Audience researcher Diana Carlin said voters strongly approve of debaters who, like Reagan, are able to translate abstract issues into the language of everyday lives: "They like the metaphors, they like the stories."[80] On this count, Bill Clinton fared particularly well in the audience participation debates of 1992 and 1996. Clinton's psychobiographer Stanley Renshon saw evidence in these town hall performances of the candidate's gift for "strategic empathy,"[81] a skill highly prized among audiences weaned on confessional talk shows and reality television.

At the opposite end of the strategic empathy spectrum is a debater like Michael Dukakis. Democratic adviser Frank Mankiewicz aptly defined the problem when he told *Newsweek*, "Dukakis has a tendency to say things like 'We must be concerned about health care for the elderly.' He needs to say, 'What about your 90-year-old mother?'"[82] In practice sessions before the debates of 1988, Mario Cuomo encouraged Dukakis to tell stories, while Bill Clinton exhorted him to get angry.

Not all political candidates possess the gift of connecting conversationally. Like Dukakis, John Kerry tended to orate rather than talk. In a predebate column in the *Boston Globe*, Democratic consultant Dan Payne advised Kerry to "avoid stuffiness: No sentence that begins 'Ladies and gentlemen' should leave your lips."[83] The advice went unheeded: during the town hall Kerry lapsed into the phrase fourteen times. However suitable "Ladies and gentlemen" may be for the floor of the Senate, in the less formal setting of a television debate it feels stilted and remote.

John McCain, another man of the Senate, likewise suffered from sounding too much like a career politician in debates. In the town meeting with Obama in 2008, McCain addressed the live audience nineteen times as "my friends"—not an egregious rhetorical offense, certainly, but language that lost its freshness during the presidency of Franklin Roosevelt. Too much of McCain's debate rhetoric seemed grounded in the past. After the first debate, James Fallows catalogued the infractions: "The forced and unsuccessful Bob Hope–style jokes, the repeated reference to the 'overhead projector,' the prevalent allusions to an era much of the electorate considers past. Tip O'Neill, the early Reagan, the Marine disaster in Lebanon—important all, but dated-sounding in 2008."[84] These examples seemed even more out of touch against the visual backdrop of a much younger opponent.

Too often debaters lapse into the language of statistics and bureaucracy, when they ought to be concerned with matters of immediate relevance to real-life voters. Democratic coach Sam Popkin has instructed candidates to bone up on the price of simple consumer goods, in case such a question arises. "The single defining moment of François Mitterrand's defeat of Valéry Giscard D'Estaing was when Mitterrand asked in a debate, 'Do you even know the price of a metro ticket?' and Giscard hadn't a clue," Popkin wrote in a memo for Clinton in 1996. "Knowing the prices people pay for products and services every day is important evidence for continued connectedness."[85]

Staying connected to the audience also means not insulting them. In the vice presidential match of 1976, Bob Dole's disdain for the entire debate process unwittingly extended to the body politic. Dole referred to the viewers as "those who may be still tuned in" and "those who may still be with us." As communication scholar Kevin Sauter wrote, "The implication that those watching the debate should probably have tuned out earlier may not have been a direct affront . . . but after an evening of Dole's sharp attacks on the Democrats, to make an unflattering remark about the audience was not an astute rhetorical move."[86]

Dole's bad-mouthing of the debate had started well in advance of the televised encounter. "I assume the audience will be smaller," Dole quipped to one reporter, "but I think we can put them to sleep quicker than the presidential candidates did." In another television interview, Dole could scarcely contain his peevishness: "It really bugs me to have to interrupt our campaign here for a week to prepare for this." And "I think we both have a mission in this debate. I haven't quite figured out what it is."[87] With such an openly hostile attitude, can we wonder that Dole lost his debate to Walter Mondale?

SELLING THE MESSAGE

James J. Pinkerton, who covered the town hall debate in 1996 for *New York Newsday*, wrote that he "groaned out loud when Bob Dole started to tell his little gag about the need for litigation reform." Reminding the audience of a recent episode in which he had tumbled from the stage at a political rally, Dole said, "Before I hit the ground, my cell phone rang and this trial lawyer says 'I think we got a case here.'" As Pinkerton noted, Dole had used the line hundreds of times on the campaign trail—"and yet the bit got a healthy laugh. Real people, who pay only intermittent attention to the campaign, hadn't yet heard it. The moral of this media story: repeat, repeat and repeat—and then repeat some more."[88]

"Debate messages don't necessarily have to be new to be effective with viewers," wrote political analyst Blake Zeff. "Indeed, it's in the candidates' interest to reiterate the biggest critiques or flaws of their opponents as much as possible during the debate, even if they *aren't* new. Because they *will* be to many of the people watching." Zeff likened presidential debates to Super Bowls, whose massive audience includes tens of millions of casual viewers with only a limited understanding of football—just as tens of millions of debate watchers have not obsessively been following the campaigns. From a strategic communication standpoint, repetition of the basics makes sense.[89]

But repetition has its dangers. In the vice presidential debate of 1996, Al Gore repeatedly referred to Bob Dole's tax plan as a "risky scheme"—"a zillion times," according to ABC's Sam Donaldson, who said the vice president seemed to be "reading a teleprompter in his mind." Lisa Myers on NBC described Gore as a "digitalized telephone operator,"[90] while other critics reached for unflattering metaphors of their own. In the first debate of 2000, Gore's robotic term of choice was *lockbox*, repeated so incessantly that it became the central gag in *Saturday Night Live*'s debate parody. Instead of reinforcing his points, Al Gore's transparently predigested rhetoric invited ridicule.

Catch-phrases and scripted lines have become inevitable components of presidential debates, focus-grouped and poll-tested and crafted for maximum political return long before the live event begins. But just because a slogan works as rhetoric does not mean it will play within the context of a television debate. The trick for debaters in delivering these lines is to strike the proper balance between following the script and seeming spontaneous—which is more of an acting challenge than a rhetorical challenge.

"I'm very anti-lines," said Romney's media guru Stuart Stevens. After working in the entertainment industry in Hollywood, Stevens came to the conclusion that even professional actors have difficulty bringing scripted words to life: "Most candidates are less qualified to deliver lines than actors. And I've found that if you give people lines they'll spend the whole debate saying, 'Is this the time for this line?'" In Stevens's view, candidates like having scripted moments at the ready "because they're safe places they can go. But I think the best lines are those the candidates come up with themselves, in the moment, that are driven by a strategic understanding of the debate."[91]

Bill Clinton, a master at political theater, made it a practice to arm himself with several scripted sound bites for each debate, but he would use them only if he found a natural opportunity to do so. Drawing on his experience as a musician, Clinton likened the process to jazz: "There's a melody that has to be played, and you have to play it in the right key, but there comes a time when you have to adlib. If you totally adlib and you play out of key and you forget what the song is, you're in trouble. But if you never vary from the melody line, you won't be very effective either."[92]

Problems arise when candidates try to shoehorn into a live debate what they have so painstakingly rehearsed in practice sessions. Most scripted lines sound like scripted lines, and it is not difficult for voters to see through the faux spontaneity. Linda Grabel, an audience member in the town hall debate of 2004, told the *National Journal* that as she watched Bush and Kerry in action, she found herself anticipating their stock phrases: "Yep, here he goes again. Yep, I can see this one coming." Grabel added: "I found it very irritating."[93]

A message that gets overexposed, or that in some way fails to hit its target, can be just as annoying as one that is overly obvious. Early in the final debate of 2008, John McCain cited an Ohio man named Samuel Joseph Wurzelbacher, who three days earlier had had a brief back-and-forth at a campaign stop with Barack Obama on the topic of taxes. "Joe the Plumber," as McCain dubbed Wurzelbacher, became a central theme in the debate, a metaphor for hard-working Americans worried about their finances. Both McCain and Obama mentioned Joe the Plumber numerous times—McCain called him "my old buddy"—and both candidates directed remarks to him into the lens of the camera. "At times," wrote Dan Balz in the *Washington Post*, "it seemed that the entire campaign came down to which candidate could win over Wurzelbacher's vote."[94]

Dial-groups being conducted during the debate by Obama's campaign showed that voters were less enthralled with Joe the Plumber. As the program wore on, the dials went down each time his name was mentioned. According to Obama's pollster Joel Benenson, "Then we did a focus group session afterwards with people, and they said to us, 'What does Joe the Plumber's life have to do with me?' It just wasn't connecting with them."[95]

For Wurzelbacher the attention was a mixed blessing. Although he became an instant media celebrity, particularly among right-wing news outlets, the spotlight also brought trouble: questions over his credentials as a plumber, charges of unpaid taxes, conspiracy theories about his motives in confronting Obama. Appearing on the *Late Show with David Letterman* a couple of days after the debate, McCain said, "Joe, if you're watching, I'm sorry."[96]

Selling the message in presidential debates also means having the right message to sell. Part of Barack Obama's difficulty in the debate with Mitt Romney in Denver sprang from the muddled strategy of Obama's advisers. Unwilling to jeopardize the president's likability, Obama's team settled on an approach that emphasized restraint. "I didn't want caustic exchanges, and so we kind of warned him off of those," said David Axelrod, "and in a sense he was left in a no-man's-land when he got out there."[97]

"Obama seemed caught between what he wanted to say on stage and what his agreed strategy was," wrote Richard Wolffe. "He couldn't attack in case it destroyed his own popularity. But he needed to attack to show some backbone. He looked indecisive and weak because his game plan was itself conflicted and weak."[98] Without a properly conceived message, the messenger found himself flailing.

As the campaign of 2012 demonstrated, social media have given debaters new mechanisms for getting their messages across—and new ways to be assailed when they don't. One of Twitter's most tangible effects on the debates in 2012 was to compress what used to be full sound bites into compact hash-tags: "Big Bird" and "binders full of women" (Romney), "horses and bayonets" (Obama), "malarkey" (Biden). Entire sound bites still matter, particularly for the purposes of television news and video file sharing. But catch-phrases, with their ability to drive traffic in social media, now matter too, giving candidates and campaigns one more strategic tool with which to promote a message.

WORKING THE CLOCK

Like musicians, actors, athletes, and others who perform live before the public, presidential debaters must develop a well-honed sense of timing. The first order of business—and the most difficult for many candidates— is fitting one's answers within the allotted time constraints. As Republican adviser Sig Rogich put it, "In the debate setting, your succinct 60- or 30-second response is the essence of success or failure."[99]

Except when they debate, presidential candidates are accustomed to speaking for as long as they want. Adjusting to a circumscribed debate format can therefore be challenging, especially for individuals like Barack Obama, who more comfortably traffic in nuance than in sound bites. "I came in, and still do, with a very conversational, professorial style," Obama told Richard Wolffe during the primaries in 2008. "I think of these things (debates) as conversations, and they're not."[100] Throughout his career a critical goal of Obama's debate preparation was compressing complex ideas into bullet-list talking points.

Facing a similar situation in 2004, John Kerry's handlers brought a prop to the practice sessions: the loudest, most obnoxious buzzer they

could get their hands on—"something between electroshock ther-
apy and the electric fence for dogs," in the words of coach Michael
Sheehan.[101]

That same year, when George W. Bush's aides practiced with their
candidate to condense his responses, the student took his lessons too
much to heart. As a result, in the actual debates some of Bush's answers
came up short. According to Bush's adviser Mark McKinnon, "If he didn't
have anything particular to add to what he'd said, he just repeated himself. It became awkward because there were questions where he had a
very succinct answer that he'd deliver in fifteen seconds, but then he
would need to fill two minutes." McKinnon attributed Bush's timing
problems to "overcoaching."[102]

Format rules are a major determinant of how loquacious a debater can
be. Negotiators for Sarah Palin won a significant victory in limiting response times in the vice presidential debate of 2008 to ninety seconds
per candidate, followed by two minutes of joint discussion. Under this
structure, topics clicked along as if to the beat of a metronome, allowing the underinformed governor of Alaska to emerge unscathed.

By contrast, the looser structures of the debates of 2012 permitted
longer disquisitions by candidates—hazardous for any participant already inclined toward monologue. The opening debate between Barack
Obama and Mitt Romney was divided into six segments, with fifteen
minutes per topic: two minutes per candidate for opening statements
and eleven minutes of open discussion. This format "played to the president's worst instincts," wrote Mark Halperin and John Heilemann,
"feeding his case that he had plenty of time to make multiple, complex
points."[103]

In their postmortem of the disaster in Denver, Obama's advisers noticed that although their candidate had spoken for several minutes longer than Romney in the debate, he had uttered several hundred fewer
words. To prepare Obama for the follow-up encounter, coaches ran drills
to quicken the president's rate of delivery. "By increasing the speed we
thought he would seem more energetic," said Ron Klain. "He would be
less contemplative about his answers, a little more instinctual. It sounds
so simplistic, but it made a big difference."[104]

For presidential debaters, understanding the clock also means pacing
one's output and husbanding one's energy over the duration of the pro-

gram. Michael Sheehan warns candidates to beware the "witching hour"—the sixty-minute mark in a ninety-minute event.[105] This is when many of the best-known debate moments have occurred, like Lloyd Bentsen's "You're no Jack Kennedy" and Gerald Ford's insistence that the Soviets did not dominate Eastern Europe. Live high-stakes debates are physically exhausting, and the two-thirds mark—the end of Act Two, in theatrical terms—is apt to be a point at which the debater's energy flags, before the final push into the home stretch.

"I don't think you're ever out of the woods on these things," said Stuart Stevens of Romney's campaign. "People usually make mistakes at the end of debates. You get unforced errors, you get tired, you get overly relaxed and you start to feel cocky and you can press things too far."[106]

Debate scholars generally concur that the first part of a debate has the strongest effect, both on viewers and on the media pundits scoring the event. "The first 30 minutes of the first debate are the most important," wrote Republican coach Brett O'Donnell in a preview piece the day of the opening Obama–Romney match. "That will set in motion the narrative, and help determine whom voters perceive to be winning the debate."[107]

In the age of social media, that imperative to succeed early assumes added urgency, for the wisdom of the crowd comes swiftly into focus. According to Democratic debate strategist Ron Klain, "Twitter exacerbates this even more because the Twitter analysis of the thing is set early and then develops, so it's hard to change that."[108] In modern presidential debates, there is no time to waste.

HUMOR IN PRESIDENTIAL DEBATES

Bob Dole's vice presidential debate of 1976 highlights the riskiness of wisecracks as a rhetorical device. In that program, Dole let loose with a steady flow of sharp-edged remarks. He accused Walter Mondale of enlisting union leader George Meany as his makeup man. Referring to Jimmy Carter's controversial *Playboy* magazine interview, Dole said, "We'll give him the bunny vote." And so on. The net effect of the sarcasm was to turn viewers off. According to James Hoge, who moderated the Dole–Mondale debate, "Humor is a very dangerous thing in politics, particularly if it's ironic or sarcastic. With that huge an audience, most good politicians tend to avoid it."[109]

Dole himself would come to agree with this assessment. Interviewed in 1999, he admitted that the debate in 1976 had taught him to resist the temptation to go for the easy laugh. "You've got to be very careful with humor and you've got to point it at yourself," he said. "It's got to be self-deprecating or it can be terminal, fatal, if you're out there just slashing away at someone else."[110]

Natural wit being a rare commodity among presidential contenders, debaters over the years have relied heavily on scripted zingers. This practice hit rock bottom in 1988, when George H. W. Bush dropped all pretense a few minutes into the first debate and asked, "Is this the time to unleash our one-liners?" Bush then proceeded to unleash: "That answer was about as clear as Boston Harbor." Michael Dukakis had prompted Bush's outburst with his own creaky one-liner: "If he keeps this up, he's going to be the Joe Isuzu of American politics," Dukakis said, invoking the prevaricating star of a series of popular television commercials. One could almost hear the grinding of the gag writers' gears.

For the debates in 1992, Bush was given a laundry list of suggested jokes, most of which, mercifully, he ignored: "That last answer was almost as inflated as prices would be in a Clinton presidency." "I'd find broccoli easier to swallow than that last answer." "Listening to Governor Clinton talk about integrity is like listening to Madonna talk about chastity."[111] Roger Ailes weighed in with his own suggestion: "You can't turn the White House into the Waffle House," which Bush did manage to work into the second debate, but not quite as Ailes had planned. Before delivering the gag, Bush was supposed to set it up with three prior uses of the word *waffle*; instead, he offered the punch line minus the setup.[112]

As it developed, the scripted bon mots of President Bush were no match for the organic, almost relentless wit of rival Ross Perot. Perot's skill with homespun one-liners reflected the candidate's true personality, not the labor of anonymous jokesmiths. Addressing his lack of government experience, Perot declared in the first debate, "I don't have any experience in running up a four trillion dollar debt," as the audience roared with laughter. A few minutes later, he shot back with what would become the signature sound bite of the night. Asked about his proposal to offset the deficit by raising gasoline taxes, the jug-eared Perot said, "If there's a fairer way, I'm all ears."

What was the effect of Perot's jocularity? As scholar Dan Hahn pointed out, the zingers drew audience applause and gained extensive replay as media sound bites: "Yet it is not clear whether these bites, successful in the short run, ultimately redounded to his benefit or came to be seen as just a little too simple for someone who would be president."[113] By the end of the series the jokes had worn thin. In a focus group discussion after the third debate, a woman in Boston remarked, "It's nice that someone has some humor and lightens things up, but now it seems like every opportunity he had to speak he had a quick one-liner."[114]

Like Perot, George W. Bush brought to his political career a natural sense of humor. This asset was of particular value in 2000, when the relatively unknown Bush went up against the considerably less lighthearted Al Gore. In a *Washington Post* column before that year's first debate, Michael Kelly suggested that the Republican nominee use his platform to "make 'em laugh." "Having established a measure of gravitas," Kelly said, "Bush can now afford to display his easy wit and genuine good humor. Nothing will more effectively highlight Gore's priggishness."[115]

But the high-stakes nature of the events kept Bush from giving his comedic side much of a workout. His debate jokes in 2000 leaned toward gently self-deprecating remarks about mangling the English language. In the subsequent series against John Kerry, George W. Bush found it necessary to enlist his sense of humor for damage control. After he had been roundly criticized for making angry faces in the first debate, Bush responded to a Kerry comment in the follow-up encounter with, "That answer almost made me want to scowl." Similarly, in the third debate, when asked what he had learned from the strong women in his life, he answered, "To stand up straight and not scowl." Whether these lines succeeded depended on how viewers felt about Bush—and in 2004 few Americans took a neutral position.

Like Al Gore, John Kerry did not exactly qualify as a sparkling wit. "Being lectured by the president on fiscal responsibility is a little bit like Tony Soprano talking to me about law and order in this country," Kerry proclaimed in the final debate, and though the joke felt forced, it did generate a good deal of replay in postevent press coverage. No matter how contrived the gag, candidates can count on the media to trumpet a one-liner.

An off-the-cuff attempt at humor proved more perilous for Senator Kerry. In the town hall debate in 2004, the Democratic candidate joked that of all the people in the room, only he, Bush, and moderator Charles Gibson would benefit from a Republican tax cut for the wealthy. In effect, Kerry was relegating the studio audience to the status of hired help. A comment intended to be witty instead confirmed John Kerry's social distance from average Americans.

VICE PRESIDENTIAL DEBATE STRATEGY

As the first of her gender to participate in an executive-level debate, Geraldine Ferraro stepped up to the lectern both blessed and cursed. On the plus side, as Ferraro told campaign journalists Jack Germond and Jules Witcover, she "could hit [George H. W. Bush] as hard as she liked, and he would not be able to return her fire in kind for fear of being cast as a bully."[116] At the same time, enormous pressures fell upon Ferraro, not only as a political standard-bearer but as a symbol of womanhood. According to Ferraro's debate coach, the candidate "could be ladylike, which would make her appear uninformed and too delicate to do the job; or she could be assertive, which would make her appear bitchy."[117] Ferraro saw herself as "standing in for millions of women in this country. If I messed up, I was messing it up for them."[118]

Opponent Bush had his own hobgoblins to tame. As communication scholar Judith Trent wrote, "He needed to find the acceptable 'twilight zone' between being perceived as an unacceptably aggressive attacker or an unacceptably passive lap dog." Moreover, Trent added, Bush's aides worried that Ferraro's assertive style might unhinge him, "and thus reveal the kind of high-strung and nervous manner that had hurt him in other debates."[119]

Vice President Bush was advised to win, but not to have Ferraro go down in defeat. Observed Bush, "I don't think they would have said that if I had been debating Tony Coelho."[120] In a day-of-debate story in the *Wall Street Journal*, future vice presidential debater Dick Cheney cautioned, "I think he's got a lot to lose . . . and I think she's got absolutely nothing to lose whatsoever."[121]

Beyond gender, the Bush–Ferraro debate embodied a second strategic consideration, one that applies to all encounters between vice presidential candidates: "junior" debaters have substantially more room to maneuver. As political scientist Michael J. Robinson wrote of the Dole–Mondale encounter, "Small stakes make for more fun and quicker moves."[122] This first vice presidential debate in 1976 proved far livelier than any of that year's Ford–Carter programs; subsequent vice presidential matches have also surpassed the bigger-name broadcasts for sheer entertainment. (The exception is Al Gore versus Jack Kemp in 1996, perhaps history's dullest general election debate.)

Part of what makes second-string debates more watchable is the latitude the running mates have to "go negative." Traditionally a vice presidential debater's role has been to lambaste the opposing presidential candidate. As Dan Quayle put it, "In a vice presidential debate, you really do ignore the person on the stage."[123] The object of the game: to strafe the top of the ticket.

This freedom to cut loose has generated sparks in vice presidential debates that could not have ignited in the more rarefied air of the top-of-the-ticket appearances. In 1992, for example, Quayle proved to be a formidable attack dog on the issue of Bill Clinton's character. Four years later Jack Kemp was criticized for failing to do the same. Debate researcher Diana Carlin explained that second bananas can be more aggressive "because they aren't expected to be presidential the way the presidential candidates are. And they can say things about their own candidate that the candidate cannot say about him- or herself."

As a baseline requirement, vice presidential debaters must also reassure voters about their suitability for stepping into office. "This is not just another presidential debate with surrogates," said Carlin. "There should be a question in every single vice presidential debate about why are you qualified to take over—the Dan Quayle question."[124] A running mate who can demonstrate his or her presidential timber passes the test.

In the debate with Joseph Lieberman in 2000, Dick Cheney not only met this mark, he managed to neuter his opponent in the process. Cheney employed a strategy unusual in general election debates. He kept his presentation deliberately low-key and reasonable, and he discarded the time-honored bag of debate tricks: the scripted zingers and sneak attacks and false intimacy. "Sitting around a table talking issues without rancor, he looked at ease and in command," said Kevin Merida in the *Washington Post.*[125]

Like Jack Kemp in 1996, Joe Lieberman opted to maintain a sunny outlook during the debate with Cheney. Though this approach drew favorable reaction from civic-minded pundits, as a political strategy it failed to accomplish the task at hand. "Lieberman seemed to be consciously offering a counterpoint to the growing bitterness of the presidential contest," wrote James Traub in the *New York Times,* "which was not necessarily what the party needed."[126]

Four years later, Cheney faced a very different opponent, North Carolina senator John Edwards, whose pugnacity revived the tradition of bare-fisted vice presidential debates. Cheney seemed genuinely rattled, and in his discomfort he made the ludicrous assertion that he had never met Edwards, despite photographic evidence to the contrary. "Edwards' assault took Cheney completely off his game," concluded William Saletan in *Slate.* Of Edwards, Saletan asked, "Now are you sorry you didn't nominate this guy for president?"[127]

History's most-watched vice presidential debate came in 2008 when media comet Sarah Palin took on Senate stalwart Joe Biden. The first dual-gender debate since Bush–Ferraro drew enormous interest from the public and the press, not just for the wild-card presence of Palin but also for the prospect of watching two strikingly different politicians in pursuit of two strikingly different goals.

For Palin the charge was clear: to avoid anything that might undermine her already tenuous viability as a candidate. This she accomplished. In saving her own skin, however, Palin did little to boost her running mate. Biden's objective was equally well defined. "We sent Biden in there with a simple imperative," said Ron Klain. "Make your points, make our case, don't give her any basis for aggrievement."[128]

Four years after deliberately staying out of Palin's way, Biden deliberately got in the face of Republican vice presidential candidate Paul Ryan. Trading kid gloves for boxing gloves, Biden in 2012 put on one of the most boisterous—or obnoxious, depending on your view—displays in presidential debate history. To John Dickerson, "Biden's performance was aimed at one thing: painting the Romney and Ryan agenda as a flim-flam operation. He did it with style as much as substance."[129] When it was all over, Biden–Ryan entered the annals as yet another raucously entertaining running mates' debate.

By definition, even victorious vice presidential debaters bump up against the political equivalent of a glass ceiling. "The truth of the matter is the vice presidential debates are really unimportant in the big picture," said James Baker. "It's great theater but it doesn't matter. People aren't making their voting determinations based on who's vice president."[130]

DEBATES AS DRAMA

A winning debate strategy hinges in large measure on how well a candidate apprehends the experience as televised drama. Smart debaters understand that part of their mission is to stage a performance for an audience—an audience that expects to be simultaneously enlightened and entertained. Debates demand theatricality, not to the exclusion of substance but in ways that hold viewers' attention. Presidential debates consist of equal parts bread and circus: bread representing content, and circus representing everything else. Politicians generally have the content down cold. It's the everything else that provokes angst.

Even candidates with impressive performing gifts must adapt their talents to the idiosyncratic specifications of debates. It is not enough to know how to put over a campaign speech, or navigate a live televised press conference, or deliver a rousing State of the Union address. Debaters must assimilate the particulars of live television debate, a strain of political communication that entails its own set of skills—skills not otherwise pressed into service.

"Political debate is not, of course, like other forms of debate," wrote James Fallows. "It is not primarily a dispassionate contest of logic, in which ideas are pitted against each other to see which is most compelling. It is debate as political combat, in which the contest of ideas is subordinate to the struggle for dominance between the debaters."[131] Translated into show business terms, debates are a battle to determine which performer on the stage deserves to have his name above the title.

Meeting the theatrical challenge of presidential debates requires candidates to master the relevant mechanics; hence the heavy emphasis on rehearsals and obsessive predebate efforts to replicate debate-night conditions. Participants must have a firm grasp of the nuances of each debate format and modulate their delivery accordingly. Lectern debates are more formal than sit-down debates. Sit-down debates call for a different dynamic than podium debates. The town hall, once the least confrontational format, is now a place to show aggression. Open discussion periods are opportunities to seize control of the narrative.

Mastering the mechanics also means technical proficiency. When should you look at your opponent? At the moderator? Into the lens? How much should you smile? What should you do when you're listening but not speaking?

"They say actors have a hard time knowing what to do with their hands," wrote Democratic strategist Paul Begala in a perceptive column in 2008 about how to win debates. "The best debaters—Reagan, Clinton—spent much of the time creating moments by either fixing their eyes on their opponent when launching a barb or looking directly into the camera." One of a debater's most important skills, Begala said, "is knowing what to do when the other candidate is attacking you." As a negative example, Begala cited Dan Quayle's deer-in-the-headlights moment during the "You're no Jack Kennedy" exchange. More positively, Begala pointed to Barack Obama in his opening debate with John McCain. "Every time McCain launched a broadside, Obama would shake his head slowly, paint a half-smile on his face, look down and jot a note. He did not glare angrily or stare blankly."[132]

Even an action as basic as note-taking has its camera etiquette. After the first debate in 2012, President Obama was reproached for scribbling too much at his lectern. "We kept telling him not to write a novel," said coach Michael Sheehan. "He wished the whole thing could be an essay exam and he could use two blue books if he needed to."[133]

Beyond a mastery of technique—stagecraft, camera angles, timing, format nuances—perhaps the single most crucial quality a candidate can bring to a presidential debate, theatrically speaking, is his or her desire to be there. Audiences take delight in performers who relish the performance. This is something that first-rate debaters like Ronald Reagan and Bill Clinton understood instinctively. "Reagan always enjoyed the contest," Michael Deaver recalled. "He always believed that if he had the opportunity he could win people over."[134] Debate viewers sensed Ronald Reagan's eagerness to connect with them, and reciprocated by according him their approbation.

In the view of playwright Arthur Miller, Bill Clinton "was relaxed on camera in a way any actor would envy. And relaxation is the soul of the art, for one thing because it arouses receptivity rather than defensiveness in an audience." Miller made this observation during a fascinating lecture, "On Politics and the Art of Acting," delivered in Washington several months after the election in 2000: "Like all great performers [Clinton] loves to act, he is most alive when he's on; his love of acting may be his most authentic emotion, the realest thing about him, and as with Reagan there is no dividing line between his performance and himself—he is his performance."

Miller went on to analyze the two men who had debated a few months earlier, Al Gore and George W. Bush: "There is no greater contrast than with Gore or Bush, both of whom projected a kind of embarrassment at having to perform, an underlying tension between themselves and the role, and tension, needless to say, shuts down love on the platform no less than it does in bed."[135]

Much of Barack Obama's troubles in the debate arena stemmed from just such a reluctance to put on a show. "These debate formats are not a natural form of communication for me," Obama lamented in 2008. "My natural instinct is not to try to beat the other person down, but rather to understand their point of view, and then see if we can find common ground. Well, that is completely contrary to what a debate is about."

Exactly. Television debates differ from other forms of political dialogue, because they are dialogues only in the strictest sense of the word. Candidates who take part must accept debates at face value, as theatrical exercises that turn more on personality than on policy. Arthur Miller correctly categorized presidential debates as a branch of show business. And a fundamental truth of show business is that audiences love performers who give it their all.[136]

3 / CANDIDATE PREPARATION

"If it takes a village to raise a child," wrote Joseph Lieberman in his campaign memoir, "it apparently takes an army to prepare a vice presidential debater, or so I learned in 2000."[1] Like many a candidate before him, Lieberman discovered that campaigns do not take lightly the task of readying a debater to meet his or her opponent on live television. In the innately unpredictable realm of presidential debates, candidate prep is one of the few aspects of the process over which political professionals exert total control—and rarely do they pass up the opportunity.

Since 1960 all but a handful of presidential debaters have set aside significant chunks of time to tone up for this most exacting of telecasts. In the days and weeks before a debate, presidential campaigns shift their focus to the mission at hand. Rehearsing for debates has evolved from briefing books and off-the-cuff Q&A sessions to full-scale dress rehearsals with lights, cameras, costumes, and role-playing. In the words of Republican adviser Sig Rogich, debate prep constitutes "a life unto itself."[2]

John F. Kennedy's predebate preps were limited to informal drills with aides reading questions off index cards. According to Kennedy's aide Ted Sorensen, "There was no rehearsal, no debate coach, no strategy discussions on being aggressive or warm."[3] By contrast, today's candidates go through detailed simulations that duplicate the format, timing, and production circumstances of the actual program. Stand-ins for moderators, panelists, and town hall questioners grill the debaters in sessions that are videotaped, then played back for critiquing, sometimes in front of focus groups. Each campaign amasses a team of experts to attend to its candidate's every need: political strategists and policy specialists, speech-writers and voice coaches, lighting technicians, and makeup artists.

The utility of debate prep is one of many legacies of the Kennedy–Nixon "Great Debates." Although both Republicans and Democrats in 1960 compiled massive briefing books—JFK's people called theirs the "Nixopedia"—only Kennedy bothered to practice for the debate with his advisers. According to Nixon's campaign manager Bob Finch, "We kept pushing for [Nixon] to have some give-and-take with either somebody from the staff . . . anything. He hadn't done anything except to tell me he knew how to debate. He totally refused to prepare."[4]

From Nixon in 1960 to Barack Obama in 2012, nominees have ignored at their peril the preliminary conditioning that presidential debates demand. With so much riding on performance, only the most cavalier of candidates—or, like Perot and Stockdale, the most unorthodox—fail to subject themselves to a strict predebate regimen. The goal of rehearsal is simple: to ready the debater for any contingency. As Bill Carruthers, television adviser to President Ford, put it, "When the president walks out onto that stage, nothing can be a surprise to him."[5]

DEBATE BOOT CAMP

The lessons of Kennedy–Nixon loomed large for the candidates and their staffs in 1976. Aides on both sides pored over the preparation materials of 1960, while the star performers, like football players studying classic game footage, watched at least part of the historic broadcasts.

In Plains, Georgia, Jimmy Carter held a Saturday night screening of the Kennedy–Nixon debates for a handful of relatives, aides, and friends. Included in the group was actor Robert Redford, who had recently starred in the classic political film *The Candidate*. "I was probably president because of Bob Redford," Carter told an audience at Redford's Sundance Institute in 2004. "You can imagine the feeling of a Georgia peanut farmer who is scheduled to have three televised debates with the incumbent president of the United States: I didn't know what in the world I was going to do.

"And here came Robert Redford to Georgia, and he had a 16-millimeter film of the Nixon–Kennedy debates, and he sat on our living room floor and we played the debate over and over, and he gave me advice."[6]

It is Gerald Ford, an individual not normally associated with theatrics, who became the first presidential contender to stage full-scale practice debates, complete with lecterns, stand-in questioners, cameras, lights, and makeup. Earlier in the year, Ford had used a similar video setup to rehearse his acceptance speech before the Republican convention, with positive results. Hoping to repeat this success, advisers scheduled a series of predebate run-throughs to be staged, recorded, and dissected in the White House family theater.

Videotape of these rehearsals shows a no-nonsense, highly professional operation at work. Ford's team took advantage of its practice sessions to deal with both content and stylistics. At the end of one gathering, Ford crumples a paper at his lectern and says, "Okay, let's see how the clothes look, and any other comments that you have." When not practicing with a live stand-in for Jimmy Carter, President Ford shares the stage with a television monitor set up to play sound bites from an appearance by Carter on *Meet the Press*. The mock panelists ask questions of the monitor; Carter's taped response plays back. As coached, Ford gazes forcefully at the television version of his opponent during these replays.

The president does not always seem to be enjoying himself in the rehearsals. At one point, he stops a session in progress, looks down at his watch, and announces, "I think this is enough," whereupon the proceeding immediately ends. But reflecting on the experience later, Ford credited the preparation process. "Over a four-day period, I spent nine hours under the lights, and the grueling interrogation boosted my confidence," Ford wrote in his autobiography.[7]

Because rehearsals of this magnitude were unheard of in 1976, the White House sought to downplay Ford's debate preps. Carter's forces, meanwhile, attempted to capitalize on what they viewed as efforts to program the Republican candidate. Of his own debate preparations, Carter pointedly assured a reporter, "I am not going to go off and practice against a dummy opponent or memorize any cute speeches or anything like that."[8]

True to his word, Carter at first would not even let his aides run questions by him, preferring instead to read his briefing books in private—Richard Nixon's approach. "He read every single page and corrected typographical errors and grammatical mistakes in what had to be, I would say, easily 200 pages of written material," recalled Carter's aide Stuart Eizenstadt.[9] After the opening debate in Philadelphia in 1976, in which Carter seemed cowed by Ford and reticent to attack, he did agree to parry questions with his senior staff. But for the duration of the series, Carter steadfastly refused to participate in a mock debate.

In 1980, against show business veteran Ronald Reagan, Jimmy Carter dropped his objections. The president's team scheduled a series of mock debates, first at Camp David and then at Carter's hotel in Cleveland just before the appearance with Reagan. For the ninety-minute, real-time session at Camp David, lights, cameras, and lecterns were installed at Hickory Lodge, and political science professor Sam Popkin arrived from California to portray the Republican nominee.

Popkin, an expert in the rhetoric of Ronald Reagan, had come to Carter's attention with a strategy memo called "Popping Balloons," the aim of which was to help the president navigate the rocky shoals of Reagan's deceptively benign communication style. Among other suggestions, Popkin advised, "You don't beat a story with a fact—you beat a story with another story." In their first practice session, when the "stunt Reagan" trounced the president of the United States, Carter realized the challenge he would face against so folksy a rival. At the end of the practice, Popkin recalled, "I thought they were going to have the Marines break my kneecaps."

Of no small help to Carter's prep squad was the utter predictability of their opponent's language. Reagan had spent many years on the hustings delivering essentially the same message, and for the debates the script did not change. According to Popkin, "With one exception, every single Reagan speech I gave in every single practice was actually used."[10]

In Carter's final run-through before the debate in Cleveland, the president told his aides about a conversation he had had with his daughter, Amy, on the subject of nuclear war; Carter wondered if this might be something to raise during the debate. "We had all argued against it," said chief of staff Hamilton Jordan, "perhaps not as bluntly as we should have." According to Sam Popkin, just as advisers were recommending against the Amy anecdote, an inopportune phone call distracted Carter, and the message never sank in. "That's why when you watch the tape, he clutches when he brings it up," Popkin said. "He knew he wasn't supposed to."[11]

To no one's surprise, Hollywood candidate Ronald Reagan perfected the art of full-scale debate rehearsals in 1980, mounting elaborate mock debates at an estate in the Virginia countryside that belonged to Senator John Warner and his wife, actress Elizabeth Taylor. Reagan's team converted the garage into a professional-quality television studio, and enlisted Michigan congressman David Stockman to play John Anderson, and later Jimmy Carter. Some twenty advisers attended these practice sessions, not counting stand-in questioners. (Among the advisers was columnist and ABC News commentator George Will, who went on camera after the Reagan–Carter debate and praised Ronald Reagan's "thoroughbred performance," neglecting to disclose his role in prepping the candidate.)[12]

Despite his years as a professional showman, Reagan was notoriously bad in rehearsal. After the first dry-run for the debate with Anderson, Stockman wrote, "You felt kind of sorry for the guy, but his lack of agility was disquieting." As an outsider in Reagan's campaign circle, Stockman was astonished to observe that none of the senior aides wanted to take charge of the critique: "The campaign staff treated him with kid gloves. . . . It was all on-the-one-hand . . . on-the-other-hand."[13]

Stockman's observation underscores one of the ongoing conundrums of debate preparations: who will tell the emperor he has no clothes? Advisers involved in practice sessions can find it difficult to balance candor with deference, criticism with praise. Their diffidence is understandable. In order to execute the stunt at hand, presidential debaters must draw from a deep well of self-confidence. Anything less than a wholehearted endorsement by one's own campaign staff might rattle the star at just the wrong moment.

Ronald Reagan was savvy enough in 1980 to understand that he needed to keep practicing. According to David Gergen, a member of the debate prep team, Reagan asked for an immediate rematch after his disastrous first rehearsal with David Stockman. "Round two was a draw," Gergen wrote. "Would Reagan now say he was ready? I wondered. Nope, he wanted round three. I still don't know what he did overnight, but this time he was in full command of his arguments and funny rejoinders. As strong as Stockman was, Reagan knocked him out of the ring."

Among Gergen's responsibilities in 1980 was preparing Reagan's debate briefing books. "The first book I gave to Reagan was quite thick," Gergen recalled. "He passed it off with a joke but I noticed Nancy looking daggers. I made sure the next book was drastically shorter."[14]

As Gergen's comment indicates, campaigns have a tendency to overprepare debaters by saddling them with too much information. This was the case in 1984, when Reagan's advisers so miscalculated their candidate's needs that they prepared him in exactly the wrong way before his disastrous first debate in Louisville. "Everybody forgot that he'd been president of the United States for four years, so we briefed him the same way we did in 1980," said Michael Deaver.[15] Instead of concentrating on broad themes, the debate advisers stuffed their candidate full of facts.

Reagan wrote in his memoir that he was "hurt" by the people trying to help him in 1984. "They fill your head with all sorts of details, technicalities, and statistics as if you were getting ready to take an exam on those topics," he said. "Finally, when you're in a debate, you realize you just can't command all that information and still do a good job as a debater."[16]

After the debacle in Louisville, Nancy Reagan angrily confronted Deaver back at the hotel. "What have you done to my husband?" she demanded. "Whatever it was, don't do it again." Reagan's long-time confidant Paul Laxalt, who drew the postdebate assignment of flying back to Washington with Mrs. Reagan, "heard for two or three hours how this debate had been screwed up."[17]

As the press delved into the particulars of Reagan's preparations, Republican advisers began a round of finger-pointing. Laxalt told the media the president had been "brutalized" and "smothered" by the briefing process.[18] Unnamed members of the debate prep team hinted that Reagan's own indolence was to blame.

To avert another disaster, campaign commanders imported a high-powered guru for Reagan: Roger Ailes, a New York communication consultant who had served as Richard Nixon's media adviser in the election of 1968 and who would go on to create and run the conservative Fox News Channel. In the view of Lou Cannon, "Ailes was to reassurance what Nixon was to foreign policy."[19] The coach began his workout by putting Reagan through a quick question-and-answer exercise called a "pepper drill." "Go back to your instincts," Ailes exhorted his student. "Just say what comes to you out of your experience." For an hour, the drill continued. "Every time he'd start to stumble," Ailes recalled, "I'd ask, 'What do your instincts tell you about this?' and he'd come right back on track. He was very good. Finally I said, 'Mr. President, if you can do that Sunday night, you're home free.' "[20]

Under Ailes's tutelage, Reagan regained his confidence and showed considerable improvement. To further boost the president's spirits, staffers staged a pep rally at his hotel in Kansas City immediately before the debate. Beneath a banner reading "Hail to the Kansas City Chief," Reagan greeted supporters with an anecdote about a young American soldier who had relayed a message to him from Germany: "We're proud to be here, and we ain't scared of nothin'." Reagan thanked the crowd, looked down at his watch, and, with a self-effacing grin, said, "I guess now I've got to go to work." Then, amid chants of "U-S-A, U-S-A!," the president departed for the auditorium.[21] According to Michael Deaver, "Reagan was always buoyed by something like that. He was, after all, an entertainer."[22]

DEBATE PREPS IN THE 1980S AND 1990S

Geraldine Ferraro's autobiography of 1985 offers an insightful firsthand account of debate preparations from the candidate's perspective. Like other debaters, Ferraro viewed her boot camp experience with ambivalence. "It seemed like such a waste of my time, and everybody else's as well," she observed. "I felt embarrassed sitting there, surrounded by three people the first afternoon and many more in subsequent sessions, giving thoughtful answers in such an artificial circumstance."[23]

Mondale's campaign managers assigned a cadre of advisers to Ferraro. Some, like future secretary of state Madeleine Albright, dealt with matters of substance, while others concentrated on style. Ferraro was urged to speak slowly and to enunciate; her rapid-fire delivery may have been acceptable to New Yorkers, but for the American masses it sounded too rat-a-tat. To reinforce this notion, Ferraro's debate coach ordered the candidate to watch a videotape of *Mr. Smith Goes to Washington*. "Jimmy Stewart was relaxed and easygoing to a fault," Ferraro said. "I fell asleep in front of the VCR and never got to see how it all came out."[24]

In spite of her misgivings, Ferraro came to appreciate the value of preparation, especially after the sessions moved into a Manhattan television studio configured to replicate the debate site in Philadelphia. "My answers got clearer and more detailed," Ferraro wrote. "People remember only those points made in the first two sentences, I had been told. By Wednesday morning everyone agreed that my replies were sharp and focused, with the key points in the first two sentences."[25]

Ferraro, like others who have run the debate prep gauntlet, saw both pluses and minuses in extensive rehearsal: "All this preparation was essential, but at the same time it magnified the significance of the debate. I'm not one for butterflies in the stomach, but I will not deny that I felt a lot of pressure."[26] As Ferraro indicates, the run-throughs designed to put a debater at ease may produce the opposite effect.

With so many experts offering advice, debate preparations can lead a candidate to doubt his own instincts. "Over days of cramming and rehearsal," Dan Quayle wrote of his experience in 1988, "there was only one general idea being pounded into me: don't plow any new ground. Don't make a mistake. If you feel unsure of an answer, just fall back on old rhetoric. In other words, don't trust yourself." In his autobiography, Quayle blamed Republican handlers for not preparing him before his debate with Bentsen, especially on content. "The real problem with the questions they anticipated was that they were too issue-oriented," Quayle complained. "The staff didn't seem able to imagine the more general, reflective questions that have become a part of these debates."[27]

Others pointed out that Quayle himself had approached his debate preps too casually. Maureen Dowd, in the *New York Times*, reported that the candidate gave up one study session on a flight back to Washington in favor of an impromptu photo opportunity. According to Dowd, Quayle invited members of the press into his cabin "to watch and photograph him posing with sleeves rolled up and a serious expression, as if he was making notes on his briefing papers. Then he used his study time to amiably chat with the journalists about his hopes for the debate."[28]

During his rehearsal sessions, Quayle received a spectacularly bad piece of advice from Bob Packwood, the senator who served as Lloyd

Bentsen's stand-in. After antagonizing Quayle in the run-through, Packwood assured him that the real debate would be less brutal. "I know Lloyd Bentsen," Packwood said. "He won't attack you the way I did today. He's a gentleman." Quayle also ignored the counsel of his aides, who warned him to forgo any references to John F. Kennedy. "I probably should have avoided it," the candidate later admitted, "but I only brought it up to make a single, valid comparison about our experience in the Congress."[29]

Like Quayle, Michael Dukakis paid a toll for not heeding his coaches' advice. Strategists had worked with Dukakis to devise a response to the charge that he was soft on law and order—what the staff called "the crime question." The answer, which Dukakis had gone through at least a dozen times in the prep sessions, involved a highly personal account of his own father and brother as victims of violent crime. When moderator Bernard Shaw asked the Massachusetts governor about his stand on the death penalty vis-à-vis the hypothetical rape and murder of his wife, Dukakis was supposed to plug in the rehearsed response.

"Every step of the way he fought me on this, and fought his campaign on this, because he didn't like dealing with the crime issue this way," recalled Susan Estrich, Dukakis's campaign manager, at a symposium in 1996. Aggravating his problems, Dukakis had fallen ill with the flu just before the Los Angeles appearance. "And so feeling lousy that night maybe," said Estrich, "or feeling a little resentful at the last hundred times your advisers had told you to look deeply into the camera when you talk about your brother, he just didn't do it."[30]

Four years later, the next Democratic presidential nominee had no such misgivings. Both in 1992 and as an incumbent in 1996, Bill Clinton set a new standard for diligence in debate rehearsal. Clinton's debate team, most of them veterans of previous Democratic campaigns, had never encountered so eager a pupil. Said Michael Sheehan, a media trainer, "For me, working with Clinton is like Kazan getting to work with Brando."[31]

According to Tom Donilon, Clinton's debate coach in 1992, Clinton spent an "enormous amount" of time preparing: "He knew how important it was, he understood that it was a special skill that had to be practiced, that it was a point in the campaign when you really did get a chance to explain yourself, and if you were going to do it within the confines of the debate structure, you really had to work at it."[32] With his elite group of debate strategists, Clinton ran drills on everything from physical posture to facial expressions.

For the first-of-its-kind town hall debate in Richmond, Hollywood producer and Clinton's confidant Harry Thomason laid out the rehearsal stage in a grid so the candidate could learn to manipulate the space to maximum advantage. Cameras were positioned just as they would be for the telecast, and doubles for Bush, Perot, and the audience took their places on the set. With the help of the grid, Clinton choreographed his moves so as to keep one or the other of his competitors in the camera shot at all times, a maneuver that circumvented the prohibition on cutaways of one candidate while another was speaking. According to journalist Roger Simon, Clinton's campaign hoped to catch Bush and Perot on camera with "bad facial expressions." When Bush was shown looking down at his watch, "the result exceeded their wildest expectations."[33]

President Bush, on the other hand, had not bothered to rehearse in the town hall format. Ross Perot did not prep at all for any of the debates in 1992, other than to read background papers. Said Perot's aide Clay Mulford, "I was delighted if I could spend 30 or 40 minutes with him the day before the debate to go over a couple of things. I thought that was an unusual concession on his part."[34]

In 1996, Clinton's debate-prep juggernaut was back in business, so methodical that rehearsal sessions for the debate in San Diego took place in New Mexico in order to get the presidential body clock ticking on Western time several days before the event. Clinton's well-oiled machine provided a sharp contrast to his competitor Bob Dole's laissez-faire approach. Dole submitted to only the most minimal predebate conditioning. A telling photo op showed Dole blithely tossing his briefing papers off the balcony of his Florida condominium. As Dole said to reporters, "You reach a point and you just stop. It's like filling up your tank with gas. It can only hold so much."[35]

However dismissive his remark was, Dole does raise a valid question about debate preparations: how much better can any performer get? In the quest to be thorough, campaigns too often drain the naturalness out of their debaters. Amid the strategizing and contrivance and plotting, what human qualities get lost?

On the eve of the town hall debate in San Diego in 1996 between Bob Dole and Bill Clinton, Dukakis's campaign manager Susan Estrich was asked what advice she would give Dole in using the debate to stage a comeback. Her answer is eminently reasonable, if just as far-fetched:

> I would tell him to get rid of all his debate advisers, to burn the briefing books, to kick out all the people who are scripting him. . . . What are the two things he cares most deeply about? Say them. And talk to people, not with a script and not with scripted attack points. If he's troubled by Clinton's character, say it. Say it the way you would say it to me if you were sitting here.
>
> But nobody will do that because he's off closeted with fifteen people who are now reviewing the tapes.[36]

DEBATE PREPS IN 2000 AND 2004

As a candidate with limited experience on the national stage, George W. Bush had to master both substance and style in his debate preps in 2000. Bush participated in an estimated fifteen to twenty practice debates between May and Labor Day, some staged in a rented theater at the Texas Bar Association headquarters in Austin and others at the governor's ranch in Crawford. One of the more intensive sessions at the ranch featured a format that Bush's campaign hoped, but ultimately failed, to secure for their man: a special edition of *Meet the Press* in which the debaters would sit at a table and answer questions from moderator Tim Russert. Duplicating a favorite Russert tactic, handlers set up a video playback unit and ran clips of "particularly embarrassing" sound bites by Bush for the candidate to respond to.

The weekend before the first match in 2000 in Boston, the campaign relocated its debate camp to a rural Methodist church a few miles from the governor's ranch. "Amazingly, we had never done a 90-minute debate straight through," wrote media consultant Stuart Stevens in his memoir about Bush's campaign. "Our custom had been either to concentrate on one subject for 20 to 30 minutes, touching on every possible angle of a question on Social Security or taxes or education, or to stage more realistic sessions with questions on various topics, but limited to 45 minutes or so, followed by a critique and then another session."[37]

Among the campaign advisers in attendance was future secretary of state Condoleezza Rice. An accomplished classical pianist, Rice likened mock debates to rehearsing for an arduous musical performance, telling colleagues, "You run the whole concert and if you make a mistake, you keep going, just like when you're onstage."[38] Although the practice debate lasted for the full ninety minutes, aides made little attempt to replicate the conditions that would face Governor Bush at the debate site a few days later. Lecterns were set up, but no lights, cameras, or other technical accoutrements. In the view of Stuart Stevens, "There was something about this approach that terrified me and something about it that was very endearing."[39]

Standing in for Al Gore in Bush's preps in 2000 was Ohio representative Rob Portman, who would go on to play everyone from Hillary Clinton to Barack Obama in practice sessions with Republican candidates. Portman pointedly violated the negotiated agreement by interrupting Bush's answers, approaching his podium, and demanding that he sign pledges on various issues. In the rehearsal before the town hall debate, Portman-as-Gore got up off his stool during one of Bush's responses, walked over to his opponent, and glared—much as the real Gore would do in the actual debate. The key difference: in the mock session, Bush threw his arms around Portman and kissed him on the head.[40]

By contrast with Bush's inconspicuous and informal rehearsals, Al Gore turned his debate preps into something of a media spectacle. When Gore headed to a debate retreat in Florida, he brought along a demographically diverse collection of "citizen-advisers," including three educators, a high school student, a construction worker, a firefighter, and a retiree. "Not coincidentally," noted the New York Times, "almost all of those Mr. Gore has invited come from important swing states where newspapers and television stations are likely to compile reports about the new Gore advisors."[41] In fact the campaign bought satellite time so Gore's crew of citizens could do interviews with hometown journalists. The group also appeared in a photo op the morning before the first debate, strolling with the vice president along the beach.

For his rehearsal before the town hall debate in St. Louis in 2000, Gore again enlisted the support of "real people": the original citizen-advisers plus another thirteen voters from Missouri. Reporters were invited to watch the first few minutes of the mock town meeting, a rare departure from the usual veil of secrecy that surrounds debate prep. According to press accounts, Gore found the rehearsal with average Americans so helpful that he brought them back for an unscheduled second round. Away from the cameras and minus the citizen-advisers, the candidate also practiced with his team of professional consultants. "Not all of us were enthused about the 'real people,' because we thought we were the real people," joked Gore's media strategist Robert Shrum at an election postmortem at Harvard. "But the truth is he actually did learn from them. They actually did have good suggestions and good ideas and good comments. It was a useful part of the preparation and he was very serious about it."[42]

Had Al Gore succeeded in the debates of 2000, subsequent candidates might have copied his creative approach to debate prep. Instead, Gore's preps became an example of what *not* to do before a presidential debate. According to Mary Beth Cahill, John Kerry's campaign manager in 2004, "Everybody wants to be involved in debate prep. . . . But we were very much informed by what happened with Gore, and what a sideshow that was. We were not going to let that happen."[43] In the words of Bob Shrum, a strategist for both Gore and Kerry, "Less is more in terms of a debate prep. I've done it two different ways, in 2000 and in 2004. And a tight team and tight discipline are the keys to effective preparation."[44]

Kerry rehearsed extensively in all three formats that were used in 2004, with Washington attorney Gregory Craig standing in for George W. Bush. "I was amazed at how close to the real thing our sessions turned out to be," Craig observed. "President Bush said nothing that came as any surprise to Senator Kerry, and that was my job: to make certain that nothing came out of Bush's mouth that Kerry had not already heard from me—ideally, more than once."[45] It bears mention that Kerry's debate preps did not anticipate moderator Bob Schieffer's question in the third debate about whether homosexuality was a choice—a question that caused trouble for Senator Kerry when he responded by invoking the name of vice presidential daughter Mary Cheney.

As an incumbent president, George Bush devoted less time to his debate preps in 2004 than Governor Bush had in 2000. Although he did take part in mock debates, by the time Bush stepped onto the stage with John Kerry, he was ill equipped to face his competition. After a widely panned performance in the opening round, Bush put renewed energy into his preps, beginning that night on Air Force One, when aides sat him down to watch a replay of the debate during the flight home.[46]

Bush's experience in 2004 is not unusual for incumbents who debate. "I've worked with a lot of incumbents, and incumbents never like to debate," said Mark McKinnon, the media adviser for Bush's campaign. "He didn't want to be there, he didn't want to be debating, and he didn't want to have to be defending himself, which is typical of any incumbent up for reelection." It took the first match with Kerry to snap Bush into shape. "He understood that he had to up his game," McKinnon said, "and he did that in round two and more so in round three."[47]

DEBATE PREPS IN 2008 AND 2012

In 2008, with no incumbent president in the race, both presidential candidates entered the fall election season fresh off an extensive series of primary debates—around twenty apiece for Barack Obama and John McCain. There any similarity ends.

In preparing for the general election, Obama took the mission far more seriously than his opponent, subjecting himself to a busy slate of practice drills, mock debates, and briefing books. "I get more work done with [Obama] in two hours than I would with others in eight," said performance coach Michael Sheehan. "Because he just has that ability to focus."[48] Obama's debate camps took place in three swing states: Florida, North Carolina, and Ohio, with exact replicas of the set constructed for each format.

When John McCain announced the suspension of his campaign two days before the first debate, preparation efforts by both candidates fell by the wayside. Obama curtailed his preps in Florida in order to join McCain, President Bush, and congressional leaders in Washington for a last-minute meeting on the financial crisis. Instead of a final round of full-scale rehearsals, Obama and his advisers had to settle on back-and-forths in Mississippi the day of the debate.

McCain, meanwhile, had done relatively little to get ready—not a single formal run-through, according to *Game Change* authors Halperin and Heilemann. McCain "detested debate prep, resisted it with every fiber of his being," they wrote. "He thought he didn't need it, thought he knew the issues, and hated being quizzed."[49] Only after losing the first match to Obama did McCain get serious about preps.

McCain's sparring partner in his mock debates was Republican standby Rob Portman, enlisted to play Obama. Before Portman assumed the role, McCain's campaign had offered the job to Michael Steele, former lieutenant governor of Maryland and future chair of the Republican National Committee. As an African American, Steele would have been of enormous value in helping McCain navigate the subtleties of history's first biracial presidential debate. But after spending the summer studying Obama, Steele was unceremoniously dropped in favor of Portman. According to Halperin and Heilemann, McCain "worried that the press would find out that he had picked a black Obama placeholder and accuse him of tokenism."[50]

If McCain's preps were desultory and disorganized, those for running mate Sarah Palin smacked of desperation. Palin's inexperience on the national stage was compounded by her profound lack of knowledge, particularly on the international front. Under the gun and overwhelmed by tutorials from well-intentioned handlers, the Alaska governor essentially lapsed into a state of hibernation. The HBO movie *Game Change* vividly depicts the situation, with Julianne Moore as a mute, inert Sarah Palin, oblivious to the debate advisers buzzing fruitlessly around her.

Uncertain how to proceed, the Palin team summoned former vice presidential candidate Joe Lieberman to Philadelphia, where debate preps were being held in a downtown hotel. Under the circumstances, about the best Lieberman could offer Palin was a religion-infused pep talk. Only after the prep operation was moved to John McCain's home in Sedona, Arizona, did the candidate improve. Reunited with her family in a tranquil setting and given a simplified list of talking points to assimilate, Palin got her confidence back.

One of Palin's recurring mistakes in debate prep was to call Joe Biden "Senator Obiden." This prompted a suggestion by staffers that during the debate she refer to her opponent as "Joe." When the candidates met onstage in St. Louis, Palin's first words of the night—"Nice to meet you. Hey, can I call you Joe?"—led analysts to speculate that she was playing head games with her opponent. In reality she was just trying to get his name right; during the actual debate, Palin did at one point call him "Obiden."

Not surprisingly, Biden's own debate preps placed heavy emphasis on gender dynamics. Drawing on his extensive political contacts, Biden sought input from colleagues like Hillary Clinton, Barbara Boxer, and Geraldine Ferraro, the first woman to participate in a vice presidential debate. "It seems like the only people in the room that think that debating a woman is going to be fundamentally different are people who don't hang around smart women," Biden told reporters on his campaign plane.[51]

Instructed by campaign strategists to ignore Palin, Biden devoted much of his practice time learning to steer clear of his opponent's orbit. Michigan governor Jennifer Granholm, brought in to play Palin, subjected Biden to a three-day workout, challenging and baiting him mercilessly. "The whole goal was to try to get under Joe Biden's skin," Granholm said. "Try to throw as much his way that could possibly come up during a real debate and see how he handled it." Though she accurately forecast most of Palin's mannerisms in rehearsal, Granholm failed to anticipate one detail: "I missed the wink."[52]

Four years later Biden would undertake a completely different sort of prep for a completely different sort of candidate, Wisconsin congressman Paul Ryan. Untethered from gender constraints and hungry for a victory after Obama's opening loss, Biden armed himself for all-out verbal and nonverbal combat. For mock debates, he brought in Ryan's Democratic counterpart on the House Budget Committee, Chris Van Hollen.

Ryan, who as a young staffer in 1996 had helped prep Jack Kemp for his debate with Al Gore, enlisted former solicitor general Ted Olsen to play Biden. According to Dan Balz, Olsen portrayed the vice president as "a boorish and somewhat obnoxious character."[53] As part of his prep, Ryan reviewed the Biden–Palin debate of 2008. Asked on CNN if he had called Sarah Palin for advice, Ryan replied, "You know, I haven't. I don't really know her."[54]

At the top of the ticket in 2012, debate preps took on extra urgency after Barack Obama's defeat in Denver. Where did the president go wrong? Obama had kicked off his predebate strategizing in May, with a briefing from his advisers about the difficulty incumbents face in first encounters. Mock debates began in mid-August, with John Kerry playing Mitt Romney. "There was probably more formal prep in 2012 than there was in 2008," according to Obama's strategist Anita Dunn. Said debate coach Ron Klain, "I would bet he practiced more for this first debate than almost any sitting president."[55]

Yet the lessons did not sink in—or perhaps the wrong lessons sank in. Just before the opening debate in Denver, Obama spent several days outside Las Vegas in debate camp. Behind the scenes, he was struggling, constrained by a strategy that required him to suppress his instinct to confront Romney. Advisers instead sought to preserve Obama's likability by holding him at a distance, above the fray. When the president called on local campaign volunteers during a break from the prep sessions, he told one that prep was "a drag. They're making me do my homework."

After the debate in Denver, Obama would have a new homework assignment: a retooled strategy that demanded tighter responses, quicker delivery, and—most of all—a stepped-up level of aggression. The town hall format meant a more physical encounter than the previous lectern debate, giving athletic Obama an edge over awkward Romney. "We did a lot of practicing around where Obama wanted to be on the stage when he made certain points, when he wanted to face the audience, when he wanted to take it to Romney," said Klain. "We spent a good amount of time practicing the physicality of the performance."[56]

The theatrical denouement of the town hall debate involved a charge by Romney that Obama had failed to label the death of the American ambassador in Benghazi, Libya, a terrorist act. Citing evidence to the contrary, Obama expressed anger at Romney for politicizing the incident; the debate moderator then backed up Obama's version of events. On camera this exchange played out as high drama, with the candidates maneuvering their way upstage and down as they jockeyed for control. "Please proceed, Governor," Obama said at one point from the safety of his stool, happy to give Romney all the rope he needed to hang himself. Solid on the facts and physically in command, the president left his opponent looking flummoxed.

As it happened, several hours prior to the debate, Obama had had occasion to revisit his original Benghazi remarks. Before leaving for the debate site, Ben Rhodes, deputy communications director for national security, went over the transcript with Obama one last time, fixing in the president's mind the wording of his initial statement. In this as in so many other instances, debate preparation reaped dividends.

Mitt Romney in 2012 devoted more time to formal debate preps than any other candidate in history. By season's end, Romney's team had staged sixteen mock debates, an apparent record. The candidate dubbed this effort "the Manhattan Project," and charged campaign manager Beth Myers with bringing the plan to fruition. While media attention was focused on the Democratic national convention, Romney retreated to the Vermont home of his former lieutenant governor for three days of intensive prep, including five mock debates. "Then, for fun at night, we'd do white-board sessions," said Myers.[57] Other full-scale mock debates were held at locations around the country.

To prep for the town hall, Romney's advisers considered inviting citizens to ask questions. "We actually had some real people lined up to do this," said media strategist Stuart Stevens, "but there were a lot of concerns"—concerns about the participants posting on social media or talking with reporters, for instance. In the end the plan fell through.

Just before the town hall debate, CNN's Dana Bash reported another element of Romney's debate prep: how to perch on a barstool. "Mitt Romney is a Mormon," said Bash, "so he doesn't spend a lot of time on barstools, according to his aides, because he doesn't drink." In getting ready for a presidential debate, no detail goes unrehearsed.

A strategy memo written to George H. W. Bush before a primary forum in 1988 summarizes the case for thorough preparation by all debaters, whatever the year and whoever the players: "A relaxed, confident and knowledgeable demeanor flows directly from the sense that you have prepared fully. Irrespective of whether you actually use more than just a small percentage of what you prepare for the debate, the process of mastering the substance and sharpening your thinking and rhetoric causes you to be visibly more confident and relaxed."[58] Though these words were aimed at a specific individual on a specific occasion, its anonymous author has astutely assessed the broader value of debate preps: the greater a debater's command of the situation, the more likely he or she is to loosen up and deliver the goods.

Of course, debate prep involves more than a mastery of content. Candidates must also be physically and psychologically poised for battle. "Too much debate preparation is cognitive, fact-filled, rational and focused on verbal game playing," wrote Republican presidential candidate Newt Gingrich in a tips-for-Mitt-Romney column in 2012. "The most important aspect of a debate is how you feel."[59] In his autobiography, Dick Cheney offered this advice to future presidential and vice presidential debaters: "Get some rest. Once you've gone over the issues and know what message you want to convey to the voters, you can do yourself a real favor just by taking a nap. You've got to be relaxed—or at least look like you are—when the moment comes. I think voters figure out pretty quickly that if you can't handle the stress of a political debate, you're not going to be much good in an actual crisis."[60]

DIRTY TRICKS IN DEBATE PREPARATION

Two incidents twenty years apart illustrate the seriousness campaigns attach to their debate preparation, and the cloak-and-dagger secrecy that shrouds the effort.

In 1980 the campaign of Ronald Reagan came into possession of several hundred pages of debate briefing materials that had been prepared for President Jimmy Carter. The provenance of the materials was never determined, despite investigations by Congress and the Justice Department in the mid-1980s. In the confusing thicket of claims and counterclaims surrounding the incident, two indisputable facts can be established: first, Reagan's debate team used the information to prepare Carter's stand-in David Stockman for his practice sessions with Reagan, and second, news of the maneuver did not leak out for nearly three years.

Had the national media been paying attention, the so-called Debategate saga might have come to light much earlier, perhaps even before the election. On the day of the Carter–Reagan debate in 1980, Stockman, a Michigan congressman, boasted at a luncheon at the local Optimist Club that he had used a "pilfered copy" of Carter's briefing book in prepping Reagan. Stockman's claim appeared halfway through a description of the luncheon that ran on page 15 of the Elkhart, Indiana, newspaper, where it was promptly ignored.[61]

The tale of the mystery briefing book did not gain traction until 1983, when it surfaced in a book by Laurence Barrett, a White House correspondent for *Time* magazine. "Apparently a Reagan mole in the Carter camp had filched papers containing the main points the President planned to make when he met Reagan for the debate," Barrett wrote, adding that David Stockman "was delighted to find most of his homework done for him as he outlined his own script for the dry run."[62] It would soon emerge that Stockman had been Barrett's source for the information.

Once the *New York Times* and *Washington Post* picked up the story, news coverage mushroomed, generating a round of negative press for Reagan that culminated in an uncomfortable presidential press conference in June 1983. The intensity of journalistic interest in the stolen briefing book appeared to catch Reagan off-guard. "It seems strange to me that since I was the debater, no one on our side ever mentioned to me anything of this kind, or that they had anything, or told me any of the things that supposedly were in there," he said.[63]

How did the briefing materials find their way from Carter to the Republicans? James Baker, senior adviser to the Reagan campaign, said he received a black binder containing the pages from William Casey, Reagan's campaign manager and future CIA director. "Casey did not tell me how he came into possession of the book and I did not ask," Baker wrote in his autobiography.[64] For the rest of his life, Casey would steadfastly deny any knowledge of the briefing book.

In Baker's opinion, the material had several possible sources: "Someone in the Carter campaign could have provided it. Someone from our campaign could have stolen it. Or someone outside either campaign, but sympathetic to Reagan, could have found it and passed it on to Casey, perhaps after it was misplaced by a Carter staffer." Baker considered the first possibility the most likely, explaining, "It was no secret that many people in the Carter administration were dissatisfied with the president."[65]

Two Debategate investigations failed to produce evidence of any criminal wrongdoing, and eventually the story receded into memory. Within political circles, however, the episode stands as a reminder of the high-stakes nature of presidential debates. Years later, Baker admitted that he had mishandled the situation. "Should I have asked Casey where he got the book?" Baker asked. "Should I have refused to pass the material on to those preparing Reagan? These are legitimate questions. In hindsight, my answer to both questions is yes."[66]

A similar incident in 2000, also involving purloined debate materials, indicates that the lessons of Debategate have not gone unheeded. In early September former congressman Thomas Downey, who was scheduled to play George W. Bush in mock debates with Al Gore, received in the mail a mysterious package postmarked Austin, Texas, headquarters of Bush's campaign. Inside was a videotape of Bush in a practice debate, along with a stack of confidential debate-related documents. Recognizing the significance of the materials, Downey turned the package over to the FBI and withdrew from participating in Gore's debate preps.

As the FBI opened its inquiry, charges and countercharges flew back and forth between the campaigns. Bush's people claimed that Democrats had planted a mole in their operation. Gore's staffers suggested that the mailing of the package had been an inside job, designed to set them up as dirty tricksters. "The mystery has set off high-stakes maneuvering that is consuming countless hours and brain cells at the top levels of both campaigns," wrote the *Washington Post*, "at a time when those aides normally would be focusing on the real debates."[67]

The investigation quickly coalesced around Yvette Lozano, an employee of Maverick Media, the Austin-based firm that handled campaign advertising for Bush. A post office surveillance camera had recorded Lozano mailing a package around the same time the materials were sent to Downey. She told investigators she had been returning a pair of mail-order trousers for her boss, Bush's advertising guru Mark McKinnon, who initially backed up her story. Upon further scrutiny, Lozano's claim fell apart.

Several months later, Lozano was indicted on charges of mail fraud, perjury before a grand jury, and false statements to the FBI. In June 2001 she pleaded guilty to the first two charges; prosecutors dropped the remaining charge. She received a one-year prison sentence and a $3,000 fine.

Particularly devastated by the turn of events was Mark McKinnon, who as Lozano's boss and friend had been one of her staunchest defenders. "There was obviously a lot about her I didn't know that I learned through the course of that investigation," McKinnon recalled. "She was a pretty troubled person as it turned out." Throughout the ordeal, McKinnon said, George W. Bush kept an admirably level head. "He said, 'Listen, McKinnon, don't worry about this, stay focused on your work. I'm not worried about it. There are no state secrets in there.'"[68]

Given the level of obsession opposing presidential campaigns have with each other, Bush's assessment of the situation was probably accurate. All debate prep teams follow essentially the same model in compiling briefing materials, whoever the candidate may be. Having access to an opponent's study guide may seem like the political equivalent of gaining an answer key in advance of a big exam, but in reality each side can pretty well predict what the other has up its sleeve with no assistance from purloined documents.

4 / PREDEBATE NEWS COVERAGE

On the morning of the first Kennedy–Nixon debate in 1960, the *Washington Post* devoted not a single news story to the broadcast that would become a seminal event in American politics. The main debate article in the same day's *New York Times* ran four short paragraphs on page 22, while the predebate edition of *Time* magazine failed to note the candidates' meeting altogether. Even the host medium of television paid scant attention; with only hours to go before opening statements, the three network newscasts mentioned the debate just briefly, and not as a lead.

By contemporary standards of coverage, the first meeting between John F. Kennedy and Richard Nixon caught the press napping. As if to compensate, journalists in subsequent years have pursued these events with messianic fervor, casting off the shackles of subtlety that restrained the reporting of 1960. This heightened interest has accompanied a seismic shift in debate journalism, as the locus of coverage has moved, with profound consequences, from print to television to multiscreen platforms.

To be sure, a few journalistic outlets grasped the importance of the first debate in 1960. The *Los Angeles Times* and *Boston Globe*, each with a hometown contestant in the race, ran front-page debate-day stories. So did papers in Chicago, where the event took place. In general, however, little of the momentousness that routinely attends modern presidential debates preceded this landmark telecast.

Several factors explain why the press underplayed the story. First, as with all events lacking a precedent, the novelty of joint appearances by presidential candidates presented journalists with an institutional challenge: how to report an event that had not yet occurred. Reporters in

1960 took refuge in history; a favorite predebate news angle was comparing the Kennedy–Nixon broadcasts to the senatorial debates in 1858 between Abraham Lincoln and Stephen Douglas. On the eve of the televised debate, the *Chicago Tribune* ran two such stories in its Sunday edition. "It is fitting that the Kennedy–Nixon duel should kick off Monday in Chicago, the heart of Lincoln–Douglas land," one article noted. "The series of clashes between the giants of a century ago started at Ottawa, Illinois, scarcely 80 miles from today's TV studio in Chicago."[1] With no other signpost to guide them, writers sought comfort in the familiarity of a 102-year-old analogy.

Other observers cast their gaze not backward but forward into the immediate future. The *Boston Globe*'s political editor John Harris accurately forecast the gravitas of the event: "Both Nixon and Kennedy, and their staffs, busy with final preparations, are keenly aware of the high stakes. . . . They well know, skilled as each is in handling impromptu questions, that they risk losing the White House prize on the drop of an ill-chosen phrase."[2]

CBS's president Frank Stanton, who for years had lobbied to bring presidential debates to television, told the *New York Times* the discussion would create "a whole new sense of values" for the American electorate. Each candidate "will be peeled right down to the man himself," Stanton predicted, adding that televised debates would forever alter the practice of presidential campaigning.[3] What must have seemed like hubris at the time turns out to have been trenchant analysis.

For each of the debates in 1960, the networks took out advertisements in major newspapers around the country. Here, as in journalistic accounts, the tone is muted: "The Television and Radio Networks and their affiliated stations throughout the United States urge you to be present during the first in a series of historic face-to-face discussions between Senator John F. Kennedy and Vice President Richard M. Nixon. Tonight from 9:30 to 10:30."[4] The word *debate* never appears. According to Don Hewitt, producer-director of the first Kennedy–Nixon program, the networks consciously avoided the term so as not to promote a win–loss expectation among viewers.[5]

The cautious mood of advance coverage in 1960 reflects a code that no longer obtains between campaigns and the media. Audiences today expect candidates and the press to act as eager partners in setting the predebate table; in 1960, no such arrangement existed. One of the rare instances in which a principal player even mentioned the debates came not in a news setting, but during an interview on the *Tonight Show* between Jack Paar and Richard Nixon a month before the first event. Paar asked the candidate if he looked forward to the so-called Great Debates. Presciently Nixon answered that the broadcast would be a "very rugged experience—it will be for Senator Kennedy, it will be for me." Beyond that, he was unwilling to speculate.[6]

Other factors contributed to the subdued coverage of the first debate in 1960. In the hierarchy of news stories, the telecast took a back seat to another groundbreaking event that was concurrently under way at the United Nations: the gathering, at the height of the Cold War, of fifteen Communist bloc leaders, including Fidel Castro and Nikita Khrushchev. On the afternoon of the initial debate, as Kennedy and Nixon went through their preshow paces in Chicago, Castro was wrapping up a four-and-a-half-hour anti-American peroration to the U.N. General Assembly that would run alongside the next morning's debate stories. Castro's speech included an unsolicited assessment of the contenders for the White House: both Kennedy and Nixon, he said, "lack political brains."[7]

Probably the best explanation for the sedateness of advance debate coverage in 1960 is the higher standard of objectivity to which journalists of that era held themselves. Political communication scholar Thomas Patterson, in a study of the front page of the *New York Times* between 1960 and 1992, found a tenfold increase in the proportion of interpretive election stories, and a concomitant reduction of descriptive stories. In the race between JFK and Nixon, only 8 percent of front-page election stories in the *Times* could be called interpretive; in 1992 the level jumped to 80 percent.[8] By definition, most predebate reporting tends to involve speculation; the main event has not yet transpired, and observers have few concrete facts with which to work. In the absence of reportable data, the press corps of 1960 largely resisted the temptation to engage in the speculative analysis that is now de rigueur.

Television news, then in its infancy, had its own problems with advance debate coverage. Network newscasts, which at the time ran only fifteen minutes, were geared less to "futures" stories than to events that had already happened, events that could therefore be illustrated. The combination of television's visual demands and the reluctance of reporters to postulate made presidential debates an unlikely subject for advance television coverage in 1960.

The story got a somewhat higher profile on radio, where the personalized nature of the storytelling more readily lent itself to commentary. Lowell Thomas on CBS Radio noted in the hours before the first debate, "The series that begins tonight, I suppose, could also determine the next president of the United States." Fulton Lewis on MBS Radio offered a skeptical preview: "Whether or not the occasion has been so hamstrung by artificialities and rules and red tape as to take the life out of it remains to be seen."[9]

One of the most incisive pieces of predebate journalism came from a newspaper reporter who would serve as a panelist in the third Kennedy–Nixon debate, syndicated columnist Roscoe Drummond. Drummond stressed the responsibility of the *audience* in the debate-viewing transaction: "If the candidates are prepared to encounter each other face-to-face and to let the public hear both sides simultaneously at no small risk to themselves—then we ought to be prepared to weigh, examine, compare, and ponder their arguments as free from partisan prejudice and pre-judging as we possibly can."[10] Heading into the debates in 1960, it was still possible for Americans to do this, thanks to the low-key media atmosphere that prevailed. After the fact, as journalists realized the degree to which they had underreported the story, the nation's press would quickly shift course.

The *Washington Post*, whose front page had contained only a two-sentence programming advisory the day of the first debate, came back for the second Kennedy–Nixon encounter with a full-length, morning-of story on page 1. The tone of this article by Robert J. Donovan demonstrates the rapid metamorphosis in predebate reporting: "The drama of the Nixon–Kennedy debates will go into its second act tonight when the candidates square off," the story began. Donovan wrote of the "enormous tension" building up over the confrontation and noted that Nixon "is under particularly heavy pressure to make up for a shaky start in the first debate . . . due in considerable measure to ill-advised lighting or makeup or both, which distorted his image on television screens."[11]

To a remarkable degree, this report in the *Post* presages the sensibility that would come to typify most predebate news coverage. Brashly predictive, the writing tackles issues of performance and strategy and cosmetics that other press accounts in 1960 either downplayed or avoided. A benchmark had been set for advance coverage of presidential debates: in the absence of any actual substance, journalists would find alternate ways to stoke the story. In print, on television, and online, predebate news began to center on expectations-setting, tactics, and endless speculation about what each candidate needed to accomplish. Never again would the press deprive itself of a seat at the table.

FINDING THE ANGLE

Just as Kennedy and Nixon drew comparisons to Lincoln and Douglas, so did the debaters in 1976 enter the arena under the shadow of their television predecessors. The news media now had a precedent to follow, a navigational chart with which to plot coverage of the first debate series in sixteen years. The iconographic images of JFK and Nixon would hover over Gerald Ford and Jimmy Carter like gods gazing down from the video pantheon.

A month before the first debate in 1976, Joseph Lelyveld of the *New York Times* screened the first two Kennedy–Nixon broadcasts in search of clues to the upcoming Ford–Carter debates. "In one way," Lelyveld wrote, "the experience was similar to that of sitting through an old movie that was considered bold and exciting in its day but now seems mannered and coy." Lelyveld, like others before him, concluded that "the interplay of personalities, not ideas" was what had figured most strongly in the debates of 1960.[12]

Conventional wisdom from the Kennedy–Nixon series informed much of the predebate coverage in 1976. Jules Witcover in the *Washington Post* noted that for Ford and Carter, substance would most likely matter less than "how each candidate looks, sounds, and handles himself vis-a-vis his opponent. That is the one clear lesson that came through in the only previous televised presidential campaign debates."[13] On NBC, Douglas Kiker revisited the Kennedy–Nixon matches with a series of clips that contrasted the Democrat's grace under pressure with the Republican's unfortunate reaction shots. Interestingly, among the excerpts was a debate sound bite from 1960 in which JFK offered a rhetorical litany of typical American voters, a list that included "a peanut farmer in Georgia."[14]

In the *New Yorker*, Elizabeth Drew sought to deflate the buildup of the debates of 1976, attributing the anticipation to a "retrospectively distorted view" of the series of 1960. "A number of people now see those debates as events in which a good guy in a white hat met and bested a bad guy in a black hat," Drew wrote. "I wonder how much enthusiasm there would be for debates this year if Kennedy were deemed to have 'lost' in 1960."[15]

All these stories use 1960 as a touchstone, just as future reports would feed off the series of 1976 and its successors. With each new round of candidates, the body of debate history expands, making presidential debates an ever-more-self-referential genre. Television, always keen to relive its classic moments, has been an especially effective medium for sustaining the highlights of debates past, a collection that functions as a sort of "greatest hits" reel to be trotted out with each new run for the White House.

In 1976, when the predebate story migrated from newspapers to television, a reliable pattern of coverage took hold: the narrative line would begin at the negotiations, move to an intense period of expectations-setting both by campaigns and journalists, touch briefly upon candidate preparations, and conclude with a flurry of last-minute handicapping and spin. Every four years, from the Ford–Carter debates to the present, this process has repeated itself like clockwork. The occasional wrinkle may vary the plot from race to race, but essentially the press strays little from its familiar script.

To each series, reporters assign a story line that establishes the agenda for that year's predebate coverage; thus, the emphasis in 1976 was on the restoration of debates after a sixteen-year hiatus. Once a series is in motion, events in one program dictate the narrative through the remaining installments. The first Ford–Carter debate set the tone for its successor when, just as the candidates were wrapping up their final answers of the night, the sound got knocked off the air for an excruciating twenty-seven minutes.

Going into the follow-up match two weeks later, the press exhibited a sudden interest in the previously eye-glazing particulars of television audio production. Jack Kelly, CBS's pool producer for debate number two, recalled being "driven crazy" by media inquiries about audio arrangements. "That's the only thing people cared about," Kelly said. "I'd get calls in the middle of the night from radio stations. And it was always the same question."[16] All three networks aired footage of Jimmy Carter personally inspecting the sound board in San Francisco's Palace of Fine Arts during his tech check the afternoon of the debate, with NBC reporting that "Carter gave close attention to the maze of audio equipment and its backup system."[17]

That same day, Carter furnished ABC's Sam Donaldson a sound bite that would prove prophetic in defining the next chapter of the debate saga. "If one of us makes a mistake," the Democratic challenger said, "that will be damaging."[18] Hours later, Ford committed his verbal blunder about Soviet influence in Eastern Europe, giving the press an angle not just for the final Ford–Carter encounter but for the ages: the imperative not to err. Into the stone tablets of debate lore, journalists would carve this new message, just below the lesson about Richard Nixon's makeup.

On the morning of the last debate of 1976, David Broder wrote in the *Washington Post*, "Both Gerald Ford and Jimmy Carter have been told by their top advisers that they can win the presidential election if they avoid a serious misstep in tonight's final television debate." ABC's Barbara Walters said, "Both sides agree that the most important element in winning is to make sure that a major mistake is not made either in fact or style." Bob Jamieson on NBC reported that another error "could be fatal" to Ford's campaign.[19]

This journalistic obsession with mistakes has colored all predebate coverage since Ford–Carter. The issue returned with a vengeance in 1984, when Ronald Reagan's disjointed performance in the first encounter handed the press one of the most dramatic plot twists in debate history. Advance coverage of the second and final Reagan–Mondale debate two weeks later converged on a single point: would the seventy-three-year-old Republican nominee survive the evening with his dignity intact?

Reagan's preparations for the debate in Kansas City sparked fervent media interest, as did the altered stakes for both candidates. On ABC, White House correspondent Sam Donaldson raised what he called "the senility factor." Said Donaldson, "People will be watching tonight because of Louisville, to see whether the president stands up, makes sentences that make sense from the standpoint of not stammering and stuttering, and doesn't drool." (Before the earlier debate, in a *Los Angeles Times* interview, Donaldson had erroneously predicted a victory for Reagan. "He'll get his facts wrong and his figures wrong. But so what?")[20]

Perversely, Reagan's poor showing in the first debate complicated the mission of Walter Mondale heading into the second. As *Newsweek* observed, "His [Mondale's] problem is that in Louisville his success was surprising; in Kansas City it will be expected. In Louisville, his style of respectful dissent seemed to take Reagan aback; in Kansas City, Reagan will be ready."[21] Clearly the debate with the strongest fascination for the press was not the president against Mondale, but the president against himself.

EXPECTATIONS-SETTING BY THE CAMPAIGNS

In 1976 Carter's pollster Patrick Caddell boasted to the *New York Times* of his candidate's television prowess. Carter "is very good with the camera," Caddell said. "He treats it like a person—one person. It's his strength."[22] This quote is remarkable in its braggadocio. Today's campaigns work diligently to lower the standing of their own candidate while raising the bar for the adversary.

Several weeks before the first debate, Jimmy Carter downplayed his skills in a luncheon interview with a trio of prominent political writers. Over milk and bologna sandwiches at his home in Plains, Georgia, Carter offered this partisan preview: "I think President Ford is expected to know a great deal more about domestic programs and foreign programs than I do. He's been in Washington 27 years. And to the extent that I come out equal to him in my apparent knowledge of issues, I think that would be equivalent to a victory for me."[23]

By the second debate, Ford's aide Michael Duval was arguing the opposite case, telling a reporter from ABC it was the *president* who would be operating at a disadvantage, because "when he speaks, it's the policy of the United States of America, and that is a major constraint."[24] With a single sound bite, Duval sent a double-edged message: lowering the standards for Ford while reasserting Ford's status as chief executive.

In Duval's and Carter's quotes we discern competing press strategies at work, as each side jockeys for position in the media. Beginning in 1976 and continuing through the present, journalists have been co-conspirators in this game of brinksmanship, serving as a kind of political message board that keeps the story alive and kicking until airtime. This practice marks a radical shift from the cautiousness of Kennedy–Nixon coverage, when neither the campaigns nor the reporters had much to say in advance of the first presidential matchups.

Today, in the weeks before a debate, politicos and journalists link hands in a feverish dance of expectations-setting. Each side has something the other wants: campaigns have information; the press has an audience. Individually these commodities are of limited value; together they form a symbiotic juggernaut with the power to predispose public perceptions. For both parties, the trick is finding an acceptable level of reciprocity in the merger.

In 1980 the campaigns' desire to position themselves favorably against the opposition assumed particular urgency, thanks to the presence of Hollywood veteran Ronald Reagan. For Reagan's two opponents, the strategic objective could not have been clearer. In the face of the Republican nominee's overwhelmingly superior media skills, the only logical choice was to prepare the audience for the worst.

"I, of course, was not the emcee for the twenty-mule team Borax," John Anderson reminded a reporter, "and I was not the host on the *General Electric Theater*."[25] President Carter told the *Washington Post*, "I'm a careful enough observer to know that Governor Reagan is a professional in dealing with the media. He's articulate and I don't underestimate him."[26] In an interview on ABC, Carter ventured hopefully that the audience would not be watching to decide "who is the most professional debater or the best orator or the most professional television performer," but rather "who will be the best president for the country during the next four years."[27]

In recent debate cycles the ritual of expectations-setting by the campaigns has grown ever more entrenched. In 1988 handlers for George H. W. Bush took pains to portray their candidate as an ineffectual performer, especially compared with Michael Dukakis, who had moderated a public affairs series on Boston's prestigious WGBH-TV. "We capitalized on that, frankly," Bush's campaign manager James Baker later admitted, "and the vice president was perfectly willing for us to do that. It wasn't an insult to his manhood for us to go out and say, 'Hey, wait a minute. Our guy's not that good a debater.' He basically let us go out and trash his debating ability, but it paid off."[28]

So contrived had the machinations become that Bush himself found it impossible to sustain the charade. At a predebate news conference, Bush went through the motions of playing up Dukakis's debating prowess, then pointed out that he was "lowering expectations. My wife, Barbara, when I practice debating, she falls asleep and I have to do something about that."[29] As Dukakis's press secretary Dayton Duncan commented, "When your candidate comes out and says it, there's not even any pretense to it."[30]

In 1992 Al Gore complained to a rally of supporters that he was at a "terrible disadvantage" in his upcoming vice presidential debate. "Dan Quayle's expectations have been pushed down to such an unreasonably low level that the news media has declared him the winner in advance," Gore grumbled.[31] Quayle sought to protect his underdog status by drawing a tongue-in-cheek class contrast with Gore. "He has a big advantage over me," Quayle told reporters. "He grew up in Washington, D.C., and I'm a product of the public schools." As the *New York Times* pointed out, "Mr. Quayle himself had a privileged upbringing as the scion of a wealthy newspaper family."[32]

In 1996, expectations-setting reached new levels of inanity, with debate maestro Bill Clinton portrayed by the opposition as superhuman and by his own side as woefully out of practice. Bob Dole's people had the easier task, and in raising the stakes for Clinton, they spared no rhetorical excess. Reagan's former press secretary Marlin Fitzwater called Clinton "the greatest television performer in American presidential history." Dole's spokesman Scott Reed described Clinton as "a great debater. He's capable of charming the birds out of the trees every day." Dole himself said, "He is so good, if I show up, I think I will win."[33]

During breaks in his debate rehearsals, Clinton tried valiantly to lower his standing. "I'm badly out of shape on this," the president told reporters in Chautauqua, New York. Hillary Clinton did her part in an appearance on the television talk show *Live with Regis and Kathie Lee*, saying that "for more than 35 or so years [Dole] was in the Congress and was a very good debater, so I expect it will be a very tough debate for my husband." Press secretary Mike McCurry reported that Clinton "feels like he has not had the time he had allotted" for debate preparation.[34] All of these lines were delivered—and reported in the press—with a straight face.

In 2000 George W. Bush's team went to greater-than-usual lengths to lowball their candidate and heap praise upon the opposition. Karl Rove called Al Gore "the world's best" debater. Karen Hughes described Gore as "the most experienced debater in American politics today. We expect that he'll have some of the best lines that Hollywood can write at his disposal."[35] In return Gore offered the not entirely credible assertion, "I don't have an overconfident bone in my body."[36]

The strategy bore fruit: stepping onto the debate stage in 2000, Bush wore the coveted crown of the underdog. "To listen to many strategists and pundits," wrote Richard Berke in the *New York Times*, "Mr. Bush might as well put away his briefing books and sit out the debates. The common wisdom is that Mr. Gore . . . is such a vaunted debater and Mr. Bush is such a novice, sometimes even a stumblebum, that it would be like watching a karaoke competition between Barbra Streisand and a barroom crooner."[37]

In 2004 John Kerry's campaign took measures to avoid being tarred with the same brush. "We looked very closely at what had been done in 2000," said Stephanie Cutter, communications director for Kerry–Edwards. "They set their expectations game very low and we weren't going to allow them to do that this time." According to Cutter, efforts to equalize the playing field began six weeks before the first debate: "We weren't ever going to be able to say Kerry was a bad debater, but we could ensure that the expectations were at least kept even."[38]

As they had done with Gore, Bush's operatives labored to tout Kerry's oratorical skills. In the words of campaign strategist Matthew Dowd, "John Kerry, as everybody knows, has debated and debated and debated. He's the best debater since Cicero."[39] But this time the Democrats gave as good as they got. "The president has won every debate he's ever had," declared John Kerry in an appearance on *The Daily Show*. "He beat Ann Richards. He beat Al Gore. So he's a good debater."[40] Democratic National Committee chair Terry McAuliffe kicked the talking point further down the road: "Let's face it, George Bush is a great debater. He wins them on style not substance, and he wins them because he isn't always honest."[41]

In 2008 the game again played out along predictable lines. "Have no doubt about the capabilities of Senator Obama to debate," John McCain assured voters at an event in Ohio. "He's very, very good." Meanwhile, Obama's strategist Robert Gibbs argued the opposite case: "These debates are not by any stretch of the imagination [Obama's] strong suit."[42] That neither debater held an obvious advantage in 2008 somewhat reined in the expectations-setting—but only somewhat.

More complicated was the predebate positioning of vice presidential candidates Joe Biden and Sarah Palin. Ancient Rome got pressed back into metaphorical service, this time by Biden's press secretary David Wade, who dubbed the Alaska governor "Cicero of the Snow"—and, for good measure, "a leviathan of forensics." These descriptions rang especially hollow in the wake of Palin's recently aired television interviews, which had been roundly panned. For her part, Palin said on *Fox News* that Biden came to the debate with a "tremendous amount of experience. I think he was first elected when I was like in second grade."[43]

In 2012, in a rare departure from the script, New Jersey governor Chris Christie pointedly *raised* expectations for Mitt Romney. Making the rounds of the Sunday morning talk shows, Christie predicted that on the morning after the first Obama–Romney debate, "this whole race is going to be turned upside down."[44] That Christie's prognostication came true got lost in the shuffle; what mattered was that he had ventured where few campaign surrogates dare to go.

For its part, Obama's expectations-setting effort trumpeted several themes: Romney had dominated the Republican primary debates. His prep was the most extensive in campaign history. The president was rusty and too preoccupied with affairs of state to properly rehearse. Asked by reporters to envision the debate's worst outcome, Obama's press secretary Jen Psaki replied, "Well, he could fall off the stage."[45]

In the weeks before the first debate of 2012, the two campaigns released dueling strategy memoranda, chock full of praise for the opponent. "He's quick, polished, and ready with a punchy attack against the president," wrote Obama's campaign manager Jim Messina in the opening volley. Romney's folks countered with their own memo, praising

Obama as "a uniquely gifted speaker" and "one of the most talented political communicators in modern history." Obama's team fired back a day later, reminding journalists that debates favor challengers. And so on.[46] Hungry for predebate conflict, the political press breathlessly relayed each new attempt at one-upmanship.

To the delight of reporters, campaigns regularly use predebate media coverage to taunt their opponents. Democrats in 1984 portrayed Geraldine Ferraro as itching for a fight with George Bush, a theme journalists seized upon. In campaign appearances around the country, Ferraro repeatedly brought up the impending match. Before an Italian American audience, she needled Bush in Italian, asking, "George, are you ready to start the debate?" At another event, claiming to have gotten hold of Bush's briefing book, the congresswoman previewed what she said were her opponent's preppy-flavored attack lines: "Gosh," "Gee whiz," "Zippity-doodah," and "Let's win, win, win!"[47]

Ferraro's antics apparently succeeded in unsettling Bush's campaign, as demonstrated by a pair of incidents that occurred shortly before the vice presidential debate in 1984. In a conversation with two reporters aboard Air Force Two, Barbara Bush referred to her husband's opponent as "that four-million-dollar—I can't say it, but it rhymes with rich." She later said she believed the comment to have been off the record, and that the word she had been thinking of was "witch."[48] The future first lady telephoned Ferraro to apologize, interrupting a debate rehearsal. "I was dumbfounded," Ferraro wrote in her memoir. "The issue of rudeness aside, it was an astonishing thing to say to the press. And, of course, they jumped on it."[49]

Just as the controversy began to subside, Bush's press secretary Peter Teeley took aim at Ferraro in a story in the *Wall Street Journal* that ran the morning of the Bush–Ferraro debate. Said Teeley, "She's too bitchy. She's very arrogant. Humility isn't one of her strong points, and I think that comes through." Compounding the insult, Teeley offered a "clarification" in the *Washington Post* the next day: "What I meant by that is that . . . essentially she has to come across as not being screechy or scratchy. If you have to use the word 'bitchy,' that's adequate."[50] The press, always a sucker for conflict, had found an irresistible predebate sidebar.

EXPECTATIONS-SETTING BY THE PRESS

In the period before a presidential debate, journalists happily take on the role of political strategists. Since 1976, debate analysis has developed into a cottage industry in the press, accounting for an ever-increasing share of preevent coverage. With input from their campaign sources, reporters craft a conventional wisdom that departs from the traditional journalistic mission of factual storytelling; in turn, this predebate "morning line" becomes the yardstick by which postdebate judgments are rendered.

Handicapping the horse race has long been a fixture of campaign journalism, but where live debates are concerned, the impulse to speculate is particularly enticing. Political journalists approach the debate story the way sports reporters approach a major athletic event. "This reminds me a lot of the Super Bowl," said columnist George Will on ABC the morning of the first debate in 1992. "Each year the hyperbole and rubbish and pageantry and marching bands surrounding the little kernel of football in the middle gets larger and larger."[51]

The accelerated pace of predebate coverage mirrors institutional changes in the American news media. Pressure to generate stories is enormous, particularly for television, where the dependence on visuals further complicates advance coverage of an event like a presidential debate. Because most predebate events are pictorially lacking, television instinctively fills the gap with pundits. These talking heads cram the airwaves, spouting predictions, analyzing strategy, and revisiting debates past.

In the view of Thomas Patterson, as television news extended its influence, print journalism began taking more of its cues from television, with substantive reporting yielding to interpretive stories. "The television model gradually affected the print media, to the point where the difference in the styles of television and newspaper reporting is now relatively small," Patterson wrote after the election in 1992.[52] In practice this has meant more predebate stories about tactics and performance, and fewer reports that link debates with candidates' stands on the issues.

As Patterson's study shows, the shift toward interpretive analysis has been incremental. When presidential debates resumed in 1976, coverage was considerably more speculative than it had been for Kennedy–Nixon, but considerably less speculative than it has become today. With every election, the border between fact and opinion, description and interpretation, gets spongier—now more than ever, thanks to digital media.

In 1980, when a truncated debate season heightened the stakes, journalists handicapped the candidates' odds as enthusiastically as professional bookies. Coverage of the single Carter–Reagan debate focused on the "high noon" riskiness of the event. The *Christian Science Monitor* called it a "one-to-one shootout . . . which could decide the outcome." "A single roll of the dice with the White House at stake," said the *Washington Post*. "It is not inconceivable that the election could turn on what happens in the next 90 minutes," CBS's anchorman Walter Cronkite said in comments just before the debate began.[53] "Less than a month before the election," Jimmy Carter complained in his memoirs, "the press continued to ignore the substantive issues in the campaign and to concentrate almost exclusively on who might debate whom, Reagan's 'blunders,' and my 'meanness' to my opponent."[54]

The game-playing between campaigns and the press got even meaner in 1984. In a memorandum to colleagues, Mondale's adviser Patrick Caddell proposed engaging journalists in a "pantomime of deception." Caddell wrote, "If expectations are to be overturned, then they must be built up to a maximum degree. The strategy must be protected by a 'Bodyguard of Lies.'"[55] Caddell's antagonistic language mirrors the intrinsic testiness of the campaign–journalist interaction. To political handlers, the press is putty that needs molding. Meanwhile, journalists regard *themselves* as the rightful sculptors of predebate expectations; campaigns merely supply the raw materials.

If hostility toward the media increased in 1984, so did reporters' willingness to shed their reliance on campaign sources in predebate coverage. In a piece on NBC two days before the first Reagan–Mondale match, Roger Mudd delivered a classic example of insider analysis, presenting what he described as "the book" on each of the presidential debaters. The story abandons the traditional use of interviewees, consisting instead entirely of the journalist's opinions.

According to Mudd, Reagan was expected to be camera savvy, cavalier with numbers, a whiz with one-liners—and "from time to time he will not make sense." Mondale would have a "sharp edge" from his appearances in primary debates, and would be combative and specific. "So the contrast will be sharp," Mudd offered in his closing comment, "Mondale trying to nail Reagan with a mistake that accentuates his age and isolation, Reagan trying to make Mondale look shrill and frantic by exuding his 'aw, shucks' optimism."[56] That Mudd was largely correct in his assessment does not lessen the radical nature of the story: predebate reporting had leapfrogged over the long-standing journalistic insistence on external sourcing.

For better or worse, Mudd's style of interpretive journalism has become the norm in contemporary predebate reporting. The press does its own expectations-setting, separate from, yet influenced by, the spin of the campaigns. If political handlers fail to plant a story line of interest to the media, reporters create their own.

In 1988 the journalistic weakness for predebate speculative analysis manifested itself in the weightless matter of Michael Dukakis's likability. The story surfaced before the first Bush–Dukakis encounter, but gained strength going into the second, after news analysis and polling determined that Dukakis had won the first debate on substance but lost it on heart.

The debate-day edition of the *New York Times* addressed the subject in two articles. The first cited a poll in which voters named Bush the more likeable candidate by a margin of 47 to 37 percent—close enough, and irrelevant enough, that one might have expected the *Times* to ignore the finding altogether. The second story, by Bernard Weinraub, dealt exclusively with Dukakis's public image as a cold fish. "There is no master plan to warm up the Massachusetts governor, whose performance in the first debate was considered skilled but rather chilly by many reviewers," Weinraub wrote.[57] Television journalists made similar points, sounding more like meteorologists than reporters with their descriptions of Dukakis's "icy" personality and need to project "warmth."

In the end, when the candidate fulfilled expectations by giving a technocratic response to the question about his wife's hypothetical rape and murder, journalists may have felt vindicated. But the test the press had applied to Michael Dukakis was a false one. How could a fifty-four-year-old man—how could *anyone*—suddenly make himself more likable on national television? And what did such a transformation have to do with one's fitness for the presidency in the first place?

Al Gore, another politician with few natural allies in the press, faced a different problem. Several months before his televised encounters with Bush in 2000, conventional wisdom coalesced around an influential *Atlantic Monthly* cover story by former presidential speechwriter James Fallows. In an exhaustive examination of Gore's history as a debater, Fallows described the vice president as "America's most lethally effective practitioner of high-stakes political debate." The article defined debates as "the medium in which Al Gore has displayed the least attractive aspects of his campaigning style: aggressiveness turning into brutality, a willingness to bend the rules and stretch the truth if necessary."[58]

This diagnosis set the terms for predebate speculation in the news media, with an eager assist from Bush's campaign. According to Mark McKinnon, media adviser to George W. Bush, "We were passing out to the press articles we'd found that were very positive about Gore. We planted a million of [the Fallows piece]. We airdropped it over the national press corps."[59]

Journalists and commentators internalized the message en masse. "In more than three dozen national debates over the past thirteen years, Gore has developed a practiced, methodical debating technique that has earned him a reputation as one of the most formidable practitioners of rhetorical warfare in American politics today," wrote Ceci Connolly in the *Washington Post*, adding that "Gore's success is built on a ruthless go-for-the-jugular style." Political scientist Larry Sabato, in an interview on CNN, said, "When Gore is given a choice between a subtle attack and an attack with a two-by-four, he almost always grabs for the two-by-four."[60]

When Gore fulfilled expectations with an aggressive performance against Bush that also included a couple of minor factual misstatements, reporters jumped on the twin story lines. "We clearly lost the expectations game," admitted Carter Eskew, senior strategist in charge of the Gore–Lieberman message team, "and I'm not sure that we could have won it. The bar was set very low for Bush. Let's face it. He jumped over it, and he deserves credit for that."[61]

For the debate series of 2004, James Fallows returned with another cover story for the *Atlantic Monthly*, but this time George W. Bush took center stage as the focus of heightened expectations. "Bush has been far more skillful in his debating career than is generally appreciated," Fallows wrote, "and his successes in that realm put his widely noted lack of eloquence in a different light."[62] As if to redress the imbalances of 2000, Al Gore echoed this praise in an op-ed article for the *New York Times* that ran the morning before the first Bush–Kerry match. Gore's advice to John Kerry: "Be prepared for the toughest debates of your career."[63]

Neither the press nor the public fully swallowed the formulation of George W. Bush as a dragon-slayer, not as they had for Gore. Any such suggestion instantly evaporated in the first encounter with Kerry, when Bush delivered the most embarrassing performance of his career. Almost before the debate had ended, journalists began devising a new narrative: could Bush heal his self-inflicted wounds? A few hours before the second Bush–Kerry match, John King of CNN declared, "The president simply cannot have a poor performance tonight." On NBC Norah O'Donnell said, "The goal for the Bush–Cheney campaign is to regain some of the momentum and avoid a repeat of last week's debate."[64] As these comments attest, the preshow story line is a malleable thing. If one set of assumptions does not pan out, reporters are only too happy to push a new angle.

In 2008 predebate expectations got sidelined by John McCain's surprise campaign suspension, redirecting the conversation at a crucial moment from what-must-the-candidates-do to will-they-or-won't-they. Once in debate mode, however, the press resumed its familiar script: Obama needed to legitimize himself as presidential, while McCain had to decouple himself from the unpopular George W. Bush. Obama, wrote Katharine Q. Seelye in the *New York Times*, "will try to overcome the impression . . . that he is hesitant and overly nuanced." McCain, she added, would probably "dial back" his pugilistic tendencies.[65]

After the first debate, media attention turned to the town hall—McCain's supposed forte. "The spontaneous, unpredictable conversational style of the events and the informal interaction with voters seem to bring out the best in Sen. McCain," wrote Amy Chozick in the *Wall Street Journal*. Nedra Pickler of the Associated Press described the town hall as "McCain's signature" and a chance for the candidate to "come across to voters as feisty, warm, engaging and quick-witted."[66] In the final analysis, a format that allegedly favored McCain had no such effect.

After McCain lost two debates in a row, with Obama solidly leading in the polls, press speculation before the final debate centered on whether the senator from Arizona would go negative—and, if so, how negative? On ABC George Stephanopoulos asserted that McCain would "have to draw some blood" on his opponent. Mark Halperin of *Time* listed several ways McCain could produce a "major memorable moment" at Obama's expense—"by forcing an error, exposing a flaw or unattractive trait, or revealing an inconsistency or weakness."[67] None of which came to pass.

Four years later Obama entered the debates amid high expectations, never a good place to start. According to the polls, voters overwhelmingly expected the president to prevail over Mitt Romney. On NBC Chuck Todd predicted a pumped-up, proactive Obama. "He's going to be a little more aggressive tonight than maybe people realize," Todd said, a couple of hours before the candidate turned in one of the least energetic performances of his career.[68]

After Romney's conclusive victory in the first debate, press coverage coalesced around a new narrative: could Obama get his mojo back? "Obama's ability to show some fight . . . will be the dominant story line Tuesday night," said the *Washington Post*'s Chris Cillizza.[69] As things turned out, Obama gave the press what it wanted: a "comeback kid" plot twist. Just as Romney's triumph in the opening debate had upended the original narrative, reporters and pundits now had new trails to blaze.

NOVELTY AND PERSONALITY IN PREDEBATE COVERAGE

The debate in 2008 between Joe Biden and Sarah Palin ignited an explosion of media interest inordinate to a vice presidential match. To journalists and pundits, this spectacle offered a tantalizing bounty of story lines: male-versus-female, insider-versus-outsider, colorful character–versus–colorful character. In the words of Associated Press reporter Beth Fouhy, it was a match between "often ill-informed newcomer" Palin and "often gaffe-prone veteran" Biden.[70]

Biden's image as a generator of foot-in-mouth moments enchanted journalists. The candidate "is known for his windiness, zingers and gaffes," wrote Martha Moore in a debate-day preview in *USA Today*. "The unknown for tonight: Whether the Delaware senator will say something condescending, controversial, or clumsy." In a witty advice-to-Biden column, *Slate's* Dahlia Lithwick recommended, "No compliments. Don't say you like her shoes." And: "Even if she pulls out her breast pump during commercials, keep your eyes glazed over on the middle distance."[71]

Flamboyant as Biden may have been, the real star of the show was Sarah Palin, particularly at that moment when stumbling interview performances had put her under intense national scrutiny. "Sorry, Joe, most of America is tuning in to see only one of the two candidates on stage," wrote Rick Klein in ABC News's "The Note." In *Politico* Jonathan Martin and Ben Smith said the predebate buildup felt "more like a NASCAR race than a serious political forum: the audience may be tuning in as much in anticipation of cringe-inducing pile-ups as they are to watch the typical parry-and-thrust of debate."[72]

The attention heaped on Biden–Palin conjured memories of the precedent-setting match in 1984 between Geraldine Ferraro and George Bush. The prospect of history's first male–female debate had left the press salivating, with gender the key talking point. Hours before the encounter, ABC's Carole Simpson summed up the conventional wisdom for Bush: "He's really got to be careful not to attack her too much for fear of being accused of beating up on her, and yet he can't be too polite to her for fear of being called patronizing." Lynn Sherr identified Ferraro's hurdle as "proving she is qualified to be president."[73]

Beginning with Bob Dole in 1976, vice presidential debaters have often made juicier copy than their top-of-the-ticket counterparts. Joseph Lieberman was a media favorite in 2000, anointed by the press as the year's most colorful candidate and a likely victor in his debate with Dick Cheney—though the prediction got turned on its head. Reporters in 2004 reveled in the pairing of staid Cheney with youthful John Edwards. "It is a compelling matchup," wrote the *New York Times*. "Vice President Dick Cheney, the somber voice of experience, versus Senator John Edwards, the newcomer with the dazzling smile. The former chief executive of Halliburton versus the populist trial lawyer. No hair versus good hair."[74]

Debate journalists strongly prefer vivid characters, individuals whose personalities can be sketched in the broadest of strokes. Perhaps no vice presidential debater has been more sharply defined by reporters than Dan Quayle, the unexpected running mate of George H. W. Bush in 1988. In advance of Quayle's joint appearance with Lloyd Bentsen, journalistic speculation built to a crescendo. "For all practical purposes, the debate now features Dan Quayle versus Dan Quayle. Will he be as 'bad' as expected?" asked *Newsweek* magazine, the quotation marks around "bad" supposedly softening the question.[75] A story in the *New York Times* by Gerald Boyd reprised Quayle's remark that he "did not live in this century," and quoted an unnamed "top official" in the Bush campaign as saying the Indiana senator was no "rocket scientist."[76] And these stories ran *before* Quayle had been eviscerated by Lloyd Bentsen.

The vice presidential debate of 1992 whisked Dan Quayle back to the epicenter of media attention. "Expectations for his performance tonight are so low that the vice president is almost bound to do better than expected," said Mary Tillotson on CNN. In an op-ed piece in the *Washington Post*, Tad Devine, campaign manager for Lloyd Bentsen in 1988, described Quayle as "the only candidate who can't lose, and thus will most likely emerge as a real winner when all the spin has been spun."[77]

Beyond the return of Dan Quayle, the groundbreaking debate series of 1992 offered other narrative riches: three candidates for each event, the debut of the town hall and single-moderator formats, and a schedule of four debates compressed into nine days. From the standpoint of news coverage, this last circumstance loomed particularly large. In previous years debates had existed as isolated events, demarcated by distinct periods of buildup and wind-down. The abbreviated run of the programs of 1992 threw this familiar rhythm out of whack, obliging reporters to rethink their approaches both before and after the individual broadcasts.

A story in the *Washington Post* headlined "Punditocracy Faces Dizzying Spin Cycle" captured the journalistic mood heading into the series. "For the men and women who fill America's airwaves with spin and opinion, this could be Gallipoli," wrote David Von Drehle.[78] In deference to the timetable, advance coverage of the first match of 1992 dealt not just with that encounter but with the collective effect of them all. "The stakes are very, very high because we have this truncated debates period," said Ken Bode on CNN immediately before the first meeting of Bush, Clinton, and Perot. "This is the beginning of a dialogue that will dominate the news cycles over that period of time."[79] As indeed it did.

Reporters being suckers for larger-than-life personalities, the immediate beneficiary of predebate coverage in 1992 was Ross Perot. Through his previous television appearances, most notably on CNN's *Larry King Live*, Perot had become a familiar presence—if not exactly endearing, then compulsively watchable. His effect on the debates caused much rumination among journalists, who almost uniformly described him as a *wild card*. "With Perot the wild card in the deck," said Brit Hume on ABC, "some kind of peculiar new chemistry could emerge here."[80] Although Perot was judged the winner of the first debate, his whimsicality soon lost luster. "While he scored well with viewers during the first outing," said CNN's Tony Clark, "by the second, his stories and one-liners seemed to wear thin."[81] Perot had committed a mortal sin of journalism: he allowed his act to get stale.

In the vice presidential debate in 1992, Admiral James Stockdale briefly inherited the "wild card" label from running mate Perot. CNN referred to Stockdale as "the stealth candidate." On ABC, reporter Mike Vom Fremd, noting the admiral's credentials as a scholar of Greek philosophy, mused that Stockdale "could make it more of a highbrow affair."[82] The paucity of footage of this little-known candidate left television producers scrambling, especially when Stockdale himself went into what was described as "virtual seclusion" in the days prior to the debate. No candidate had ever stepped onto the debate stage with so cryptic a media image, or left so pummeled.

Over the years the press's interest in predefining the story has led journalists down the occasional blind alley. CBS had egg on its face after a story that aired the day of the first Ford–Carter match in 1976. During an interview with Ed Bradley, Carter's press secretary Jody Powell slyly alluded to a potential twist in the evening's plot. "In order to go beyond what's assumed and make this a dramatic point in the campaign," Powell said, "something has to happen—and perhaps some sort of an off-the-wall announcement or whatever would be a way to do it."[83] No such "off-the-wall announcement" took place, but this would not be the last time campaign staffers sought to unsettle the opposition by planting red herrings with journalists eager for a scoop.

In 1992, predebate buzz began building over Bill Clinton's alleged inability to keep cool under fire. "There had been this idea developing in the press, about ten days before the debate, that Clinton couldn't control his temper," Clinton's aide George Stephanopoulos recounted at a campaign postmortem.[84] In part the charge stemmed from an appearance Clinton made on the *Phil Donahue Show* on television a few days before the first debate, described by both the *Washington Post* and the *Los Angeles Times* as a "testy exchange."[85]

As the "temper" story gained momentum, Clinton's handlers prepared for the possibility that President Bush would deliberately try to rattle the Arkansas governor, perhaps even provoke a fight on camera. In print and on television, media analysts recounted past instances in which Clinton had publicly vented his spleen. But in the actual debate, such journalistic speculation proved to be wholly unfounded, a triumph of wishful thinking over reality.

Similarly, coverage of the Clinton–Dole appearances in 1996 hinged on the possibility that Dole would launch a character attack on his opponent. When such a stratagem did not materialize in the first debate, reporters reassigned the prediction to running mate Kemp, who was supposed to pursue the matter in the vice presidential match. But Kemp did not attack either, shifting the onus back to Dole in the third and final debate of the series—which once again failed to include the long-promised character attack.

COVERING NEGOTIATIONS AND REHEARSALS

Buried in the avalanche of predebate media hype are two topics that typically receive short shrift from the press: negotiations and candidates' preparations. Because these activities take place behind closed doors, journalists must depend on morsels of information from inside sources, sources who are predisposed to spin favorably for their candidate. Television, with its addiction to pictures, has particular difficulty addressing these nonvisual portions of the tale. Cameras do not record the negotiations for later excerpting. On those rare occasions when campaigns do share video or stills from debate rehearsals, the images exude all the spontaneity of a military parade.

In 2008, for example, McCain's campaign released an unusual photograph of Sarah Palin during her debate prep at John McCain's retreat in Sedona, Arizona. The shot showed a pair of wooden lecterns incongruously positioned on a grassy, tree-shaded lawn alongside a creek. Behind them stood Palin, wearing a baseball cap, and sparring partner Randy Scheunemann.

Even stranger than the outdoor setting was the campaign's decision to share the photo. "We were curious about why images from Arizona were being supplied to the media," recalled Jennifer Granholm, who at the time was playing Palin in Joe Biden's mock debates. "We thought, 'Wow, isn't that interesting,' because our debate prep was quite different."[86] Only later did it emerge that Palin's preparations had come close to melting down—the photo, presumably, was intended to signal otherwise.

It is interesting to note that in the campaign of 1976, journalists criticized Gerald Ford for staging mock debates before his televised meeting with Carter. ABC's Tom Jarriel disparaged the "top-secret coaching" the incumbent president had received: "They've told him what to wear, where to look, and have carefully edited his answers to fit into the three-minute debate format."[87] Ford's press secretary Ron Nessen wrote in his memoirs, "I could never figure out why reporters made such a fuss about the president rehearsing. Television correspondents and anchormen rehearsed to polish their performance for a big program. Why shouldn't the president rehearse before the debates? The stakes on a good showing were enormous."[88]

After 1976 the press no longer bothered to register its astonishment at the preparation process. Today candidate warm-ups are another routine stop on the predebate trail, accepted unquestioningly by a campaign press corps excluded from covering them. In 2012, when Mitt Romney did more debate prep than any previous candidate in history, the media barely bothered to mention it.

Somewhat more attention is accorded to predebate negotiations. Although reporters lack direct access to the bargaining table, they rely on leaks from the principal players to round out the picture. "Every side wants to get out that they were less worried than the other side, so they'll leak out details," said Richard Berke, a journalist for the *New York Times* who broke a number of negotiation stories. "And you just sort of work them against each other."[89]

In certain years—1980, most notably—negotiations constitute a driving force of the predebate narrative. In that race, campaign officials argued for weeks about the conditions under which debates would take place or if they would take place at all. Carter's refusal to participate in any forum that included independent candidate John Anderson generated extensive media coverage, but after a short-term burst of negative publicity for the president, the fallout dissipated. In the *Washington Post*, Robert Kaiser described press reaction to Carter's decision as "the furor that wasn't." For three days, Kaiser wrote, debate developments dominated the headlines. "Once the news was conveyed and initially analyzed, it seemed there was nothing more to say."[90]

When Carter and Reagan opened negotiations for a two-way match, media interest reignited. Reporters camped outside the closed doors of the meeting room, hungry for a breakthrough. No scrap of information was too inconsequential to be passed along. "Roast beef and turkey sandwiches were brought in as the talks dragged on through the afternoon," wrote the *New York Times*'s reporter Terence Smith of one session. Smith and other journalists at one point overheard—and reported— Democratic negotiator Robert Strauss through the conference room door exasperatedly telling his opponents, "I don't think you've heard anything I've said since we came in here."[91]

The press did gain access to the sanctum sanctorum for a brief photo opportunity. According to an account by ABC's Susan King, "Verbal gamesmanship dominated the picture-taking ceremony, and it was clear not just the date but the debate idea itself was up for grabs. Both sides agreed on one thing: to answer no questions."[92] Negotiators in later years stopped providing even this much of a stage-managed photo op, or letting reporters anywhere near.

In 2004, with Washington heavy-hitters James Baker and Vernon Jordan leading the talks, debate negotiations evolved minus the usual media theatrics—and with an unexpected outcome. Once the campaigns struck an agreement, for the first time in history they publicly released their negotiating document, a thirty-two-page "memorandum of understanding" jointly posted on the websites for Bush's and Kerry's campaigns. In previous election cycles, well-connected reporters had had to dig up isolated nuggets of what the agreement contained. In 2004 any voter with access to the Internet could peruse the entire litany of mind-numbing details.

According to Vernon Jordan, the original plan had called for him and Baker to announce their debate deal in a joint press conference, an idea they both scuttled: "Had we had a press conference, then Baker would have had to do his posturing for the benefit of his side, and I would have had to do posturing for my side. And we didn't need that." As Jordan saw it, "the debate was not between me and Baker, the debate was between Bush and Kerry. So we said no press conference. This thing is *res ipsa loquitur*—it speaks for itself."[93]

By posting the memorandum for all to see, the campaigns subjected themselves to several days of tut-tutting in the press. But according to Bush's negotiator Mark Wallace, "We made the decision that selective leaking prolongs the story ad nauseam."[94] The release of the agreement did produce a burst of unflattering media stories, the common theme of which was the campaigns' obsessiveness in trying to stage-manage the debates.

"The document is crammed with sections and subsections spelling out almost every imaginable rule of engagement and detail about how the debates will look. Or will be prohibited from looking," wrote Paul Farhi and Mike Allen in a typical account in the *Washington Post*. "In its precision and seeming fussiness, in its attempt at control, it often reads like an agreement between a concert promoter and a particularly demanding pop diva."[95] Just as the campaigns hoped, once the novelty of the memorandum wore off, political reporters moved on to greener predebate pastures.

LAST-MINUTE COVERAGE

Weeks of predebate coverage culminate in a home-stretch sprint that has generated its own customs and folkways: debate-day photo opportunities, afternoon technical checks in the debate hall, down-to-the-wire saber-rattling by the campaigns, and a final frenzy of handicapping in the media. With the countdown clock ticking, story lines are whipped to a climax: Will Ford make another mistake? Will Dukakis become likeable? Will Reagan make sense? Will Quayle humiliate himself? Will Gore tell a tall tale? Will Biden insert foot into mouth? Will Palin betray geopolitical ignorance? Or will something else spin the tale in an unforeseen direction?

History's first debate-day photo op was an impromptu exchange between Kennedy and Nixon, who awkwardly shook hands for photographers in the WBBM studio shortly before the first broadcast. In their enthusiasm to document this historic occasion, cameramen managed to knock over several studio lights. The raucous spontaneity of that scene led subsequent political handlers to exert greater control over how candidates are packaged in the run-up to a debate.

In 1976 Gerald Ford and Jimmy Carter appeared in a variety of stage-managed predebate contexts: poring over briefing books for photographers, arriving at the auditorium for tech checks, greeting crowds on the way back to the hotel. It was vice presidential candidate Walter Mondale who introduced the tradition of the athletic debate-day photo op. Newscasts the day of the Dole–Mondale match in Houston in 1976 showed the Democratic nominee playing a round of tennis, pointedly unconcerned about the event at hand.

Bob Dole's predebate coverage in 1976 took a different tack, prominently featuring the senator's bride of less than a year, future presidential candidate Elizabeth Hanford Dole. She accompanied her husband to his technical check, posing with him at the lectern for photographers. When Dole's handlers recommended a change of necktie for the television appearance, video crews trailed the newlyweds to a Houston department store, where they shopped for a substitute.

From wives to parents to children, candidates' family members have regularly turned up as characters in predebate coverage. In 1976 First Lady Betty Ford made her only debate appearance of the year at the third and final event in Williamsburg, Virginia. Described in a debate-day ABC story as "the campaign's secret weapon," she joined her husband at his afternoon tech check on the campus of the College of William and Mary. There, as the president posed at his lectern, she stepped over to Carter's podium and scrawled a note: "Dear Mr. Carter, May I wish you the best tonight. I am sure the best man will win. I happen to have a favorite candidate, my husband. Best of luck, Betty Ford." President Ford's press secretary displayed the note to reporters and promised to deliver it to Carter later. "The pre-debate psychological warfare is under way," reported Tom Jarriel on ABC, perhaps too cynically.[96]

Former Hollywood actress Nancy Reagan served as a reliable costar in her husband's predebate photo ops. For the Reagan–Anderson debate in 1980, the couple made a dramatic arrival at the airport in Baltimore in a helicopter, deemed by the campaign to be a "more presidential" mode of transportation.[97] Jimmy Carter, meanwhile, turned up on the evening newscasts in an especially unflattering predebate photo op. Cameras captured Carter out for a waterlogged run in the cold rain; the pictures called into question the president's common sense. Sam Donaldson made the point on ABC that "some people may not think it's very smart to go jogging in the driving rain on the morning of a day when your presidency could be at stake." NBC's Judy Woodruff linked the soggy run to Carter's recent bout with laryngitis.[98] The footage diminished the candidate, making him look silly just hours before tens of millions of voters would evaluate his suitability for reelection.

A story that aired the evening of the Carter–Reagan debate illuminates the ambivalence journalists feel toward covering this most contrived of political events. Dan Rather's no-nonsense debate preview on the *CBS Evening News* opened on a note of barely concealed hostility: "There are the makings of high drama here. There also are aspects of what some see as a parody of true debate." Rather then proceeded to scold the campaigns for micromanaging the event, noting that "the candidates were even instrumental in choosing the panel of reporters who are here tonight supposedly to ask them tough questions."[99] However contemptuous the tone, Rather deserves credit for pointing out more frankly than most the reality of campaign string-pulling.

Dan Rather returned to his role as debate skeptic four years later. Just before the first debate in 1984, he offered viewers this tart advisory: "Inside the hall everything from the stage setting to the rules under which the candidates are appearing makes it clear that this will not be an actual debate." Before the second debate, Rather reiterated his hard-line stance: "It will not be an actual debate, not with the rules set by the candidates themselves and with the candidates having a hand in selecting their own questioners. What it will be is a candidates' forum—a kind of expanded joint news conference."[100]

Rather's comments betray an antagonism toward presidential debates that other journalists suppress. Reporters assigned to cover these events find themselves trapped in a paradox: scoffing at the manipulations of the campaigns on the one hand, while promoting their agenda on the other. As much as journalists resent being treated as puppets, they see little choice but to embrace rules of engagement that are devised by the candidates. Occasionally, perhaps inevitably, the coverage turns nasty.

For a performer about to embark upon a live television debate, the least welcome media send-off is a last-minute round of negative press. Such was the fate of the hapless Dan Quayle heading into his appearance with Lloyd Bentsen. Two stories that aired on the evening of the vice presidential match in 1988 threw a harsh glare onto Quayle's image problems, just as the public was preparing to tune in.

The first, on ABC's *World News Tonight*, featured uncharacteristically candid footage of the candidate inside Omaha's Civic Auditorium during his predebate technical check. As Quayle was shown at the podium practicing his lines in a low voice, his obviously memorized words appeared in the form of subtitles on the screen. Reporter Jackie Judd narrated the scene: "On the most important day of his political career, Quayle turned often to his media handler, Roger Ailes." "Hey Roger," Quayle said to his adviser. "On this, if I decide I want to gesture over there—that's all right? You don't mind that?"[101] Quayle came off in this video clip as a human marionette, nervous and profoundly insecure, in need of guidance for even the simplest thought or physical movement.

The second, more devastating television story ran on PBS's *McNeil–Lehrer NewsHour*. In a report billed as a "Peer Review" of the two vice presidential candidates, correspondent Roger Mudd interviewed half a dozen senators from both sides of the aisle. The bulk of the thirteen-minute piece was devoted to Quayle, who drew sharply incriminating comments from Democrat Alan Cranston. "I don't think he has been taken seriously by his colleagues," Cranston said. "Most senators have been laughing about the nomination, Republicans with tears in their eyes, and they tell a lot of jokes about him. Their private remarks are quite different than their public remarks." Without prompting, Cranston offered an example: "What were the three toughest years in Dan Quayle's life? The second grade."

Cranston continued, recalling a Republican senator's description of Quayle as "two pounds lighter than a straw hat." When Mudd asked why Cranston had chosen to break the rules of senatorial courtesy by publicly excoriating a fellow member, the senator from California cited the significance of the vice presidency. Anyone with knowledge of "the capacities or incapacities" of a vice presidential nominee "has some responsibility to level with the American people," he said. Mudd, in his closing standup, sustained the negative tone: "Privately the senior senators from both parties would not be too upset if young Dan Quayle falters tonight. It is, they say, dignity and maturity and seniority and reliability and comity which are to be admired."[102] Implicit in this statement is Quayle's perceived lack of all these attributes.

Lloyd Bentsen, by contrast, attracted considerably friendlier press from Mudd and other network reporters. Where the dominant visual of Quayle's prebroadcast tech check showed the candidate consulting his television coach, Bentsen was photographed on the debate stage playfully picking up his wife, demonstrating, in the words of a story by ABC, "that at age 67 he has the stamina of a man Quayle's age, 41."[103] With messages like these filling the airwaves in the hours before broadcast, one could argue that Quayle had already lost the debate on the basis of unfavorable pretrial publicity.

Bentsen's "he-man" photo op underscores the importance campaigns attach to preevent visuals. For the second Bush–Dukakis debate several days later, Democratic handlers concocted a less successful picture. Hoping to melt Dukakis's frosty image, the campaign arranged for photographers to take pictures of the governor tossing around a ball by the pool of his hotel in Los Angeles, wearing a UCLA sweatshirt and striving mightily to look like a regular guy. But as Lesley Stahl pointed out on CBS, the visual setup left it unclear whom Dukakis was playing catch with, reinforcing a sense of isolation and loneliness.[104] Vice President Bush also selected a baseball backdrop for his preproduction photo session, attending game seven of the Dodgers–Mets playoffs on debate eve. In this venue, however, the candidate was surrounded by crowds, an undisputed man of the people.

The athletic settings in turn provided a handy theme for predebate commentary, inspiring journalists to formulate playing-field analogies of their own. On CBS, Bob Schieffer compared the Los Angeles debate to a "ball game where [Bush] is ahead. These are the late innings, he's got to hold his lead." ABC's Sam Donaldson began his report on Dukakis's technical rehearsal with a different comparison: "Day of game. And the Democratic quarterback is on his way to check out the field." And, from Dan Rather on the *CBS Evening News*, still another sport: "Jump ball tonight here at Pauley Pavilion," Rather began, referring to the UCLA basketball Bruins who normally inhabited the debate site.[105] If athletic metaphors were good enough for the candidates, they were good enough for the press.

Candidate photo ops in 1992 presented a three-way contrast in image management. On opening day of the series, George Bush made a campaign stop, Ross Perot got a haircut, and Bill Clinton went to church. In each instance, the candidate was using the press to send a not-so-subtle message: Bush has the common touch, Perot is unflappable, Clinton is a God-fearing Christian.

Four years later, Clinton was photographed arriving in San Diego for the final debate of his career. As reported on ABC, Hillary Clinton was "conspicuously at his side, as she has been in the past when anyone attacked her husband's character. They were very much the devoted couple at the airport here."[106] The video showed the Clintons standing hand-in-hand on the tarmac, talking intimately and stealing a kiss, obviously aware of the camera's gaze.

In 2000 Al Gore's predebate photo op of choice involved a stroll on a Florida beach with the crew of "citizen-advisers" who had taken part in his rehearsals. As Jonathan Karl reported on CNN, "Even a walk on the beach can get rough. As Gore took a stroll with his special advisers, attention temporarily turned to a battle between a seagull and a crab. Perhaps a metaphor for the debate?"[107]

Though George W. Bush kept a low profile before his debates in 2000, in 2004 the candidate made a show of visiting hurricane victims in central Florida the day of his first televised encounter with John Kerry. That evening the Republican-friendly Fox News Channel reported that Senator Kerry, by contrast, had opted for a manicure at his Miami hotel. Fox correspondent Carl Cameron first shared the item with anchor Brit Hume around 6:00 P.M., three hours before the start of the television debate. Although no other network mentioned the manicure, Fox News gave the tidbit several airings. Shortly after Cameron's initial reference,

Hume and his panel of pundits chewed over the significance of Kerry's grooming regimen. Concluded Fred Barnes, "This is a man who needs to stop windsurfing, stop getting a manicure, and desperately needs to go bowling."[108]

Just before the debate, Fox News host Bill O'Reilly asked former House Speaker Newt Gingrich what advice he would offer Kerry. "Well, the first thing I would tell him to do is don't get a manicure," Gingrich responded. "I can't imagine a dumber thing going into the debate . . . because it makes him look silly. And it guarantees that everyone in the country's going to look at his fingers early in the debate."[109] At least everyone watching on the Fox News Channel.

The next day, reporter Carl Cameron's fixation on Kerry's cuticles took a new twist. Cameron posted a bogus story on the Fox News website consisting of made-up quotes from Kerry, including the comment "Women should like me! I do manicures." After the falsification came to light, the network pulled the report and issued a statement of "regret," claiming that the error occurred "because of fatigue and bad judgment, not malice."[110] Yet as blogger Joshua Marshall asked in *Talking Points Memo*, "Why did comments very similar to Cameron's fabrications come up again and again from Fox commentators on debate night?"[111] Carl Cameron received an unspecified reprimand from his network, and for the remainder of the campaign he continued to cover John Kerry as chief political correspondent for Fox News.

Recent presidential campaigns have taken a low-visibility approach to debate day, with photo ops generally limited to candidate departures and arrivals. Thanks to social media, that may be changing. In 2012 Romney's campaign was particularly active in using Twitter to disseminate debate-day visuals of the candidate. For each of the events, Mitt Romney's personal aide tweeted a series of photos of Romney: attending afternoon tech checks, playing Jenga with his family, eating dinner at the hotel, waiting in the wings as he was about to step onstage. These images present a fascinating portrait of a candidate in the nerve-racking moments before a debate—and they do so in a way that circumvents journalistic interpretation altogether.

PART II / EXECUTION

5 / THE DEBATERS

Walter Mondale called it "the longest walk I've ever taken": the approach to the stage in the fateful moments before a presidential debate.[1] For the layperson, it is difficult to imagine the stress that accompanies candidates as they venture onto this battlefield. A host of factors converge to intimidate: enormous stakes, vast audiences, historical implications—all under the magnifying glass of live television. For debaters, the risks could scarcely be higher.

As unscripted performances, presidential debates transcend the months of negotiation, preparation, and speculation leading up to the featured event. Once a debate begins, all previous maneuvering yields to a superior force: the on-camera prowess of the candidates. As shown by the diverse experiences of the twenty-seven men and two women who have competed at this level, no strategy memo, no negotiated agreement, no amount of rehearsal can thoroughly condition a debater for the exigencies of a live television performance.

"It's like a championship fight," said presidential historian Doris Kearns Goodwin. "You feel a sense that you're watching these candidates under pressure. And what matters even more than what they say is how they respond to that pressure."[2] Each debater appears before the nation as a solo act, succeeding or failing in an utterly personal way. For ninety minutes the support systems and defensive armor of a presidential campaign are stripped away, leaving only the mystical bond between audience and star.

The rules of debate performance defy easy explanation, and, in the last analysis, it may be impossible to articulate why viewers respond favorably to some on-screen personalities and unfavorably to others. At bottom, debates are exercises in alchemy, subject to the hazy laws of political celebrity. With this limitation in mind, let us evaluate the individuals who have taken the "longest walk" in a presidential or vice presidential debate. What advantages and disadvantages did they bring to their matches? What response did they draw? And what is the legacy that each of the members of this elite club has left to the debate institution?

JOHN F. KENNEDY (1960)

A single hour of live television was all it took to canonize John F. Kennedy as the patron saint of presidential debates. Though Kennedy would make three more appearances with Richard Nixon, it is their first meeting in Chicago that conferred upon JFK the iconic status that he holds among campaign debaters even today. Subsequent candidates might outshine him in technique, but none has better understood debates as the ultimate star turn.

Like Nixon, Kennedy had proven himself in the broadcast arena well before the "Great Debates." In 1952 the young JFK successfully grappled with senatorial opponent Henry Cabot Lodge in a joint appearance that aired live around Massachusetts. Eight years later, in the West Virginia presidential primary, Kennedy met Hubert Humphrey for a televised matchup that served as a dress rehearsal for the general election debates against Nixon. Media historian Erik Barnouw wrote that Kennedy "impressed viewers with the brevity and conciseness of his replies, an engaging wit, and apparent grasp of local issues."[3] Kennedy also briefly debated his rival for the Democratic nomination in 1960, Lyndon B. Johnson, in an informal exchange that was broadcast during the party convention.

In view of his less than dazzling delivery on the stump, the senator's skill as a television communicator might not have been expected. Political scientist Harvey Wheeler wrote that the same characteristics that worked against Kennedy in person benefited him in the television debates: "His unadorned style of delivery fitted well into the viewer's living-room. And although his rapid rate of speech prevented much of his content from being assimilated, what did come through was the picture of a bright, knowledgeable young man of great earnestness, energy, and integrity."[4]

As the famous White House press conferences would later attest, Kennedy's verbal dexterity and natural wit played particularly well on live television. In an effort to seem more mature, JFK deliberately restrained his sense of humor in the 1960 debates, though occasional flashes of cleverness nonetheless peeked through. In the third debate, a panelist asked Kennedy if he owed Nixon an apology for a remark Harry Truman made suggesting where the vice president could go. Answered Kennedy, "I really don't think there's anything that I could say to President Truman that's going to cause him, at the age of 76, to change his particular speaking manner. Perhaps Mrs. Truman can, but I don't think I can."

The most valid criticism of Kennedy's debate performances is that they lack the common touch. Not surprisingly, some viewers interpreted Kennedy's air of detached confidence as patrician arrogance. Adviser Clark Clifford, in a memo after the first debate, suggested that "attention must be given to adding greater warmth to your image. If you can retain the technical brilliance and obvious ability, but also project the element of warm, human understanding, you will possess an unbeatable combination."[5]

Offsetting JFK's deficiency in chumminess was an abundance of attitude. Kennedy ran for president not just as a politician, but as a leading man. In the debates as in the overall campaign, this positioning paid off. Presumed stardom led to genuine stardom.

Compounding his other advantages, Kennedy was blessed with fortuitous timing. The Kennedy–Nixon debates took place against a backdrop of media calm, in an era when audiences had not yet grown cynical about the merger between television and politics. Like no subsequent debater, JFK was given an unfiltered opportunity to connect with voters on his own terms, and he was smart enough to seize it. Reviewing a tape of his broadcast appearances after the election, Kennedy said, "We wouldn't have had a prayer without that gadget."[6]

RICHARD M. NIXON (1960)

Thirteen years before Richard Nixon met John F. Kennedy in Chicago for the first televised presidential debate, the two then-freshman congressmen held their first in-person debate in a hotel ballroom in McKeesport, Pennsylvania. Before a boisterous crowd, Nixon and Kennedy, both members of a subcommittee that had drafted the Taft–Hartley employment bill, argued the fine points of labor-management relations. That night, on the train ride home to Washington, the lawmakers shared a sleeper compartment, drawing straws to see who got the bottom berth. Nixon won.

By the time of the campaign in 1960, the career of Richard Nixon had eclipsed that of his rival, due at least in part to Nixon's relationship with television. A riveting nationwide broadcast—the "Checkers" speech in 1952—had helped the candidate retain his slot as Dwight Eisenhower's running mate. In 1959 Nixon strengthened his anti-Communist credentials in the equally famous "kitchen debate" with Nikita Khrushchev in Moscow, shown to approving audiences in the United States. As vice president, Nixon commanded the media spotlight for eight years, his tenure in office neatly coinciding with the exponential growth of American television.

Given this head start, how did Nixon go astray in the debates in 1960? As we have seen, the Republican nominee arrived in Chicago physically ill, overfatigued, and otherwise unprepared to meet his rival. But beyond poor health, Nixon had fundamentally misconceived the event, viewing it as a rhetorical exercise, while Kennedy approached it as a television show. "His varsity instincts at the ready," wrote communication expert Kathleen Hall Jamieson, "the vice president marshaled his facts against Kennedy's, contested points, and defended his ground. He instead should have showcased himself against the backdrop Kennedy provided."[7]

Harvey Wheeler speculated that the "Checkers" experience had deceived Nixon into adopting a similar style for the debates. "But the 'Checkers' speech was over a moral issue, not policy questions," Wheeler wrote. "And in that speech he was by himself on television—unchallenged by opponent or reporters."[8] Indeed, a major explanation for Nixon's failure in the debates in 1960 is the relative lack of charisma he exudes alongside his costar. Eugene Patterson, in a column in the *Atlanta Constitution* after the second debate, stated the matter bluntly: "The medium is good to Kennedy and most unkind to Nixon. It makes Kennedy look forceful. It makes Nixon look guilty." In Patterson's opinion, Nixon's demeanor on the small screen was that of a "salesman of cemetery lots."[9]

Visual factors conspired against Nixon in another way. Six years after the Kennedy–Nixon debates, network news producer Wallace Westfeldt had occasion to observe the former vice president as he was being interviewed on a Miami talk show. From the vantage point of a television control room, Westfeldt watched Nixon on a pair of side-by-side monitors, one color, the other black and white. The difference was "stunning," Westfeldt recalled. "Nixon looked good in color. He looked like hell in black and white."[10] In 1960 black-and-white television was the only option.

In both appearance and performance, Richard Nixon got considerably better over the remaining three debates of 1960. To combat his skeletal visage in the first encounter, he embarked on a "milkshake diet," and recovered his normal weight and collar size. He agreed to wear makeup, and a certified Republican cosmetic artist joined the campaign entourage. Still, improvement in the later debates could not counteract the profoundly negative impression left in the first.

Although Nixon's refusal to debate in 1968 and 1972 may be understandable, the lack of these events is history's loss. Imagine Nixon in a three-way match against Hubert Humphrey and George Wallace, or one-on-one with George McGovern. As it happened, 1960 represented both the beginning and the end of Richard Nixon as presidential debater. Eventually Nixon would find bitter humor in the experience, describing himself as "a dropout from the Electoral College—because I flunked debating."[11]

GERALD FORD (1976)

As the first incumbent to meet his challenger on the playing fields of television, Gerald Ford made a significant contribution to the institutionalization of presidential debates. But even if Ford had not shot himself in the foot with his claim that Eastern Europe was not under Soviet domination, the matches in 1976 would have offered this accidental president little gain against Jimmy Carter. Ford did not exactly hurt himself by debating, but neither did his lackluster performance rouse much enthusiasm.

Two factors operated against Gerald Ford the debater: a loud, monotonous voice and a narrow range of facial expressions. Together, this combination rendered Ford spectacularly unscintillating on television; by comparison, the low-key Carter leapt off the screen. Ford's relentless delivery had a narcotic effect, like the drone of a didactic speaker at a chamber of commerce luncheon. "He is forceful in his way of speaking, but he doesn't say very much," observed Elizabeth Drew, one of the panelists in the first debate in 1976. The president's debate coach warned Ford that "many viewers perceive you to be shouting." Communication scholars clocked Ford's speech rate as so slow that he needed almost thirty extra minutes to match the total number of words spoken by Jimmy Carter.[12]

President Ford's three debates with Carter cast him in the role of solid, upstanding burgher. Every inch the midwestern Republican, Ford even wore a vest beneath his suit coat in the first debate, as though to underscore his conservatism. In a more animated individual, Ford's lack of theatrical pretense might have seemed disarming; instead, he came off more as a local businessman than the leader of the free world. Compared with later such performer-presidents as Ronald Reagan and Bill Clinton, Gerald Ford looks and sounds like a relic from some preelectronic age.

Ford did bring one visual asset to the debate: like Reagan, he possessed a commanding physique that contrasted favorably with the slighter build of Jimmy Carter. James Gannon of the *Wall Street Journal*, a panelist in the first debate in 1976, described Ford as "an imposing presence" who looked as though "he could lift (the podium) over his head and throw it at me." Jules Witcover wrote that Ford gripped his lectern "like some big, menacing bear straining to leap at his adversary."[13]

Ford's track record as a klutz, reinforced in the public consciousness by Chevy Chase on *Saturday Night Live*, may have handed the incumbent president an inadvertent advantage. According to press secretary Ron Nessen, Ford "had the image of being a plodding speaker, slow-witted and clumsy. Thus, when he did not trip or bump his head, when he spoke with style and clarity, he appeared to be doing even better than he really was."[14] All the same, aides took no chances. A strategy memo drafted before the first debate addressed the specifics of Ford's stage exit at the end of the event. The memo stressed that the president would be attached to a microphone cable connected to the base of his podium, information that the memo's recipient had hand-bracketed for emphasis.[15]

Videotape of one of Ford's practice sessions shows the debater in a rare candid moment, smoking his pipe just before a run-through begins. In this footage he appears to be the very picture of relaxation and fatherly wisdom. Unfortunately for Ford, once he looked into the lens and began to speak, this easy grace devolved into dullness—and dullness is the enemy of television.

JIMMY CARTER (1976, 1980)

After the media-wise presidencies of Ronald Reagan and Bill Clinton, it is easy to forget that in 1976 Jimmy Carter was regarded as an accomplished television communicator. But strategists for Gerald Ford found cause for concern in their opponent's performance during the primaries. A predebate memorandum described Carter as "controlled," "confident," and "resolute." A television adviser to Ford warned, "He does not offend anyone, either through his answers or visually. He is an appealing figure who comes across as smooth and calm."[16]

Like JFK before him, Carter entered the debates in 1976 as the lesser-known commodity. Unlike Kennedy, Carter seemed subdued, even intimidated during his first encounter with Ford. "I didn't know exactly how to deal with the fact that Mr. Ford was president," Carter confessed afterward.[17] For the second debate, Carter adopted a more confrontational stance, intensified his preparations, and, with unexpected assistance from Ford's gaffe about Eastern Europe, emerged the clear victor. "Self-confident and acerbic, he fired aggressive and sometimes pointed charges at Gerald Ford," wrote Richard Steele in *Newsweek*.[18] Carter drew even better reviews in the third and final debate of the series. "If you were scoring by rounds," said the *Washington Post*'s William Greider, "Carter seemed to be the clear winner. His presence, which was steady and confident, was less abrasive than at the second debate, more self-assured than in the first."[19]

Against the lackluster Ford, Carter had little trouble prevailing as the star debater in 1976. Four years later, with Ronald Reagan as his opponent, the tables were turned. The Reagan–Carter match provided viewers with one of the sharpest polarities in debate history. An editorial in the *New York Times* saw it as a case of Carter winning on words, Reagan winning on music—and in presidential debates, music matters more. "Carter comes across like a teacher we don't really want to listen to," wrote Elizabeth Drew. "He's not interesting to listen to, it's not fun to listen to him, he doesn't engage us."[20] Ironically, Carter's strength—his command of facts and issues—became his undoing, making him seem didactic instead of commanding, humorless instead of reassuring.

Physically, too, Carter suffered by comparison with Reagan. David Broder in the *Washington Post* noted that while individual close-ups showed both men looking equally composed, Reagan "was the dominant figure with his greater height and bulk in the longer-range shots." According to NBC's Tom Brokaw, "When Carter bumped up against Reagan, he seemed small, and kind of wonkish."[21]

In the evening's most ridiculed moment, Carter made an ill-advised reference to his thirteen-year-old daughter. "I had a discussion with Amy the other day before I came here," Carter told the audience, "to ask her what the most important issue was. She said she thought nuclear weaponry and the control of nuclear arms." In the crowd at the Cleveland Music Hall, scattered snickers could be heard. Far more damning was the postdebate commentary, not just by journalists but by comedians and even Reagan himself, who told a rally in Milwaukee, "I remember when Patty and Ron were little tiny kids, we used to talk about nuclear power."[22]

In the end, the so-called Amy gaffe was merely a symptom of Carter's larger problem in debating Reagan. "The optimism in Carter's camp was always misplaced," said Broder. "People were ready to elect a new president, and all they needed was some assurance that Reagan was not going be some sort of crazy person."[23]

Like other debate victims before him, Jimmy Carter believed that he lost the match in 1980 not on content but on theatrics. The night after the event, he dictated some thoughts about the debate in Cleveland for his diary. Said Carter of Reagan, "He has his memorized lines, and he pushes a button and they come out." Carter then added what might be read as an epitaph for the debate of 1980: "Apparently made a better impression on the TV audience than I did."[24]

WALTER MONDALE (1976, 1984)

Walter Mondale's career as a debater brought him up against both ends of the personality spectrum: Bob Dole's prince of darkness in 1976 and Ronald Reagan's sunny optimist eight years later. Largely on the basis of not being Dole, Mondale won history's first vice presidential debate. Against Reagan, Mondale had a mixed record: a remarkable, well-conceived victory in the first debate of 1984, and a second debate that rendered him not so much a loser as a footnote.

Compared with both his opponents, Mondale lacked a clearly defined on-camera presence. Earnest but unexciting, Mondale had a way of seeming graceful at the lectern without leaving much of a mark. In 1976 Dole gave perhaps too colorful a performance, which worked to Mondale's advantage. The series with Reagan in 1984 cast Mondale in the role of underdog, hopelessly inferior to his opponent both in popular appeal and on matters of style.

"The public would especially expect Reagan to be glib and adroit," wrote William Henry of the first debate, "while Mondale had built up a reputation for being dull; measured against those expectations, Mondale had every chance to offer a pleasant surprise to the electorate."[25] And surprise the people he did. Mondale's performance in the Louisville debate presented a political variation of the tortoise-and-hare parable. This time, strategic preparation overtook presumptive ability.

Early in the program Mondale established a tone that shrewdly combined aggression with respect. "His principal purpose was not to explain himself," said Hugh Sidey in *Time*, "but to confuse, anger, and outscore his opponent." John Corry in the *New York Times* noted that for the first time since taking office, Reagan was being openly patronized: "His strength has been in the strength of his convictions, but Mr. Mondale was suggesting that the convictions didn't amount to much."[26]

The debate in Louisville, which marked Reagan's worst public performance, briefly lifted Democratic spirits. "Walter Mondale flew into New York today," reported ABC's Brit Hume the next evening, "but the way he was feeling after last night's debate, he probably didn't need the plane."[27] Needless to say, such euphoria could not last. Heading into the second and last debate of 1984, Mondale found himself trapped in a no-win situation: The bar for Reagan had been set extraordinarily low.

"I believe if it hadn't been for the first debate," Mondale told journalists Jack Germond and Jules Witcover, "the reports on my performance in the second debate would have been far better. But I think the contrast between the two—all he had to do was stay on his feet the second time around."[28] Edwin Newman, who moderated the second debate, described Mondale as so nervous that "when he came on stage, he did not even say hello to me and the questioners."[29] Postdebate commentary suggested that the two candidates had reversed roles, Mondale seeming old and tired while Reagan crackled with vitality.

In a news conference the day after his defeat at the ballot box, Mondale lamented the inordinate power of television in presidential campaigns. "I've never really warmed up to television," the candidate told reporters. "And in fairness to television, it's never warmed up to me."[30]

BOB DOLE (1976, 1996)

A candidate as naturally witty as Bob Dole faces a dilemma in the risk-averse setting of a presidential debate: whether to curb his humor or direct it at the opposition like artillery. In 1976 Dole's refusal to sugarcoat his acerbic personality led him into a series of verbal miscalculations; twenty years later, against the masterful Bill Clinton, the longtime Kansas senator reined himself in to the point of blandness.

The earlier Dole, appearing with Walter Mondale in history's first vice presidential debate, approached the event with unconcealed disdain. No other performer in the annals of debating has been so openly contemptuous of the exercise or so loath to prepare for it. According to Dole's biographer Richard Ben Cramer, the candidate delayed rehearsals for

Mondale's debate until the day of the broadcast, "but by then he was so offhand (or trying to look offhand), he'd just toss off wisecracks."[31]

During the debate, Dole's proclivity for one-liners manifested itself in remarks that seemed ill-considered at best, and mean-spirited at worst. Announcing at the outset that "tonight may be sort of a fun evening," the Republican candidate went on to needle his opponent: "We've been friends . . . and we'll be friends when this election is over—and he'll still be in the Senate." Dole dismissed the vice presidency as a job that is "mostly indoors and there's no heavy lifting." He insulted his hosts, the scrupulously fair-minded League of Women Voters, as being "a little bit liberal."

Most damaging, however, was Dole's offensive reference to the 1.6 million Americans killed in "Democrat wars." This charge led the laid-back Mondale to rebuke his opponent in uncharacteristically sharp language: "I think Senator Dole has richly earned his reputation as a hatchet man tonight." Wrote William Greider in the *Washington Post*, "Dole was relentlessly loose, a man whose wit is irresistible in one moment and outrageous in the next."[32]

Two decades later, when Dole made an improbable comeback as his party's nominee for the White House, the nimbus of the debate in 1976 hovered over him still. In a pair of joint appearances with Bill Clinton, Dole seemed to be battling his own reputation as much as his opponent. Postdebate analysis of the first match of 1996 stressed Dole's personality overhaul. Tom Shales in the *Post* called the Dole strategy an "attempt to dispel his image as Snidely McNasty, the meanest man in American politics." Sam Donaldson, on ABC, allowed that the candidate had not come off as a "dour troglodyte."[33] Others mentioned Dole's failure to take advantage of the opening that moderator Jim Lehrer had provided for a critique of Clinton's character.

Ten days later, in the second and final presidential debate, predictions that Dole would hammer the "character issue" again failed to pan out. In the setting of a town hall forum, before more than one hundred un-committed voters in San Diego, Dole had an even narrower window of opportunity to question his opponent's moral rectitude. "There weren't the kind of fireworks that Bob Dole promised," said NBC's Jim Miklaszew-ski the next morning, "because every time he lit the fuse, President Clinton managed to snuff it out."[34] Although Dole did sneak in a few references to Clintonian ethics, he got no assistance from the audience members, whose own questions pointedly excluded matters of personal conduct.

By all rights, a candidate with Bob Dole's verbal agility and straight-shooting appeal ought to have been a natural in the arena of a live presidential debate. Instead, the necessity for debaters to confine themselves within a tightly delineated safety zone defanged this most watchable of politicians. Regrettably for Bob Dole, caution proved to be just as misguided a strategy as insouciance.

RONALD REAGAN (1980, 1984)

Could any presidential debater have been better prepared for the task than Ronald Reagan? The cumulative experience of five decades as a radio announcer, film actor, television host, corporate spokesman, and political celebrity gave Reagan an edge in debates that other candidates could only dream of. He started his broadcasting career at an Iowa radio station in the 1930s, vividly describing baseball games he had not actually seen. In 1955, after a long stint in movies, Reagan served as co-host of one of early television's riskiest live telecasts, the grand opening of Disneyland; in the face of one embarrassing technical disaster after another, the future governor of California maintained an admirably cool head. Reagan more than held his own in a televised debate with Robert Kennedy in 1967, defending an unpopular stance on the Vietnam War before a hostile group of international students. Leaving the set at the end of the program, RFK warned an aide, "Don't ever put me on with that sonofabitch again."[35]

By the time Reagan entered the presidential primaries in 1980, he was completely at home in the pressure-cooker of unscripted television. That year, at a forum in Nashua, New Hampshire, Reagan demonstrated how formidable a live performer he could be. The event, sponsored by the *Nashua Telegraph* but underwritten by Reagan's campaign, had originally been scheduled as a two-man confrontation with fellow front-runner George Bush. At the eleventh hour, the Reagan organization saw political advantage in extending invitations to the other Republican primary contenders, four of whom appeared at the hall at the appointed hour, ready for a showdown.

The debate began with an announcement from the publisher of the *Telegraph*: the last-minute arrivals, now standing onstage, would be allowed only to give closing statements. When Reagan protested, the moderator ordered the candidate's microphone turned off. "I am *paying* for this microphone," Reagan retorted, lifting a line from Frank Capra's political comedy *State of the Union* and drawing cheers from the crowd. Although the other candidates did not ultimately join the debate, Reagan's act of bravado instantly became the stuff of campaign legend. David Broder of the *Washington Post*, who was seated in the hall, called it "one of the most electrifying moments I've ever known in covering politics."[36]

In his two general election debates in 1980, first with John Anderson, then with incumbent president Carter, Reagan deftly accomplished a critical objective: to dispel his image as a right-wing warmonger by seeming trustworthy, avuncular, and optimistic. His closing statement in the debate with Anderson, in which Reagan described America as "a nation which is for all mankind a shining city on the hill," ranks among the Great Communicator's finest rhetoric.

The higher-stakes debate with Carter proved even more beneficial. Reagan's naturally cheerful disposition contrasted sharply with Carter's pinched demeanor; the difference seemed most pronounced when Reagan chided his opponent with the rueful line, "There you go again." According to historian Gil Troy, Carter unwittingly found himself cast as Richard Nixon to Reagan's John F. Kennedy. "The Carter-Reagan debate marked a clash between two styles," Troy wrote, "between a linear, formalistic print culture and McLuhan's blurry visual culture, between a politics of issues and a politics of images."[37]

As in the Anderson debate, Reagan delivered a powerful closing statement, asking Americans, "Are you better off than you were four years ago?" Broder wrote in the *Post*, "Reagan used all the skills acquired in 40 years before the cameras—shrugs and smiles and easily inflected small jokes—to tell the viewers that the portrait of him Carter was drawing . . . was a political caricature." Daniel Yankelovich, pollster for *Time*, saw a radical shift in public opinion after the telecast. "The dissatisfaction with Carter was there all along," he said, "but people couldn't bring themselves to vote for Reagan. The debate changed all that."[38]

Four years later, in the first of two joint appearances with Democrat Walter Mondale, Reagan would suffer his greatest humiliation as a public figure. The seventy-three-year-old president gave a performance so disconnected it caught his competitor off guard. "This guy is gone," Mondale commented to an aide immediately afterward. "It's scary. He's not really up to it." Reagan's defeat inspired a tidal wave of negative press. "The old actor, a ghost of his 1980 self, missed cues, flubbed lines, lost his place," wrote columnist Mary McGrory in a typical account. "He seemed lonely and afraid, just another politician clinging to his job."[39]

Reagan came into the second debate of 1984 keenly aware of his mission. This time his aides agreed to "let Reagan be Reagan," a decision that accrued to the president's advantage when one of the panelists brought up the inevitable age issue. With a perfectly detonated joke—"I refuse to make my opponent's youth and inexperience an issue in this campaign"—Reagan succeeded, perhaps too easily, in silencing his critics. Even a semicoherent closing statement, halted in progress by the moderator for running too long, did not hurt Reagan. The old magic had cast its spell.

As critic William Henry observed, "In politics, there is one gift that outshines all others, and that is the gift of luck."[40] Among presidential debaters, no one exemplifies this maxim better than Ronald Reagan.

JOHN ANDERSON (1980)

The debate in 1980 between John Anderson and Ronald Reagan illuminates the problem that such events pose for independent and third-party candidates. Like Ross Perot twelve years later, Anderson upset the political applecart by threatening the traditional one-on-one structure of debates; unlike Perot, Anderson failed to win a seat at the grown-ups' table. Jimmy Carter refused to share the stage with both Anderson and Reagan, creating a lopsided, lackluster exchange between a pair of unevenly matched challengers. As Hedrick Smith put it in the *New York Times*, "The Reagan–Anderson confrontation had all the trappings of a full-fledged presidential debate except for the president."[41]

Badly trailing both his opponents, Anderson entered the event under intense pressure. "For John Anderson," reported CBS's Bob Faw, "the debate is a make or break proposition. He must not only do well, but well enough to show he's a genuine contender and that a vote for him is not wasted." Anderson, who had debated Reagan in the primaries, fell far short of his opponent in the charisma department. As Faw pointed out, "The trouble is that the public John Anderson tends to sound preachy and self-righteous."[42]

Anderson's performance in Baltimore did little to dispel his advance billing as a scold. The candidate's closing statement makes the point:

> Do you really think that our economy is healthy? Do you really think that eight million Americans being out of work and the fifty percent unemployment among the youth of our country are acceptable? Do you really think that our armed forces are acceptably strong in those areas of conventional capability where they should be? Do you think that our political institutions are working the way they should when literally only half our citizens vote? I don't think you do think that.

Compare this with Reagan's closing statement in the same debate, in which he painted a word picture of America as a "shining city on a hill."

The appearance with Reagan represented both the zenith of Anderson's campaign and its swan song. Within days, poll numbers for the former congressman from Illinois began a slide from which they would not recover. By the time the Carter–Reagan debate rolled around a month later, Anderson's candidacy had flatlined into irrelevance. CNN, then a struggling news operation seen in only a fraction of the nation's homes, electronically inserted Anderson into a three-way version of the debate, but by this point the third man in the race had become an also-ran.

In the end, Anderson could not capitalize on the sixty-minute window of opportunity his single debate afforded. "Anderson failed in part because he did not understand debates," wrote Democratic strategist Patrick Caddell. "He was more interested in promoting his own ideas in a vacuum than in challenging Reagan. In retrospect only a total destruction of Reagan offered Anderson any hope—looking all right was fatal."[43]

GEORGE H. W. BUSH (1984, 1988, 1992)

No other presidential candidate of the twentieth century debated more, or enjoyed it less, than George H. W. Bush. "I'm trying to forget the whole damn experience of those debates," Bush told interviewer Jim Lehrer in 1999. " 'Cause I think it's too much show business, and too much prompting, too much artificiality, and not really debates."[44] After a high-strung, eccentric debut in the vice presidential match in 1984 against Geraldine Ferraro, Bush went on to five top-of-the-ticket debates, two with Michael Dukakis in 1988 and three against Bill Clinton and Ross Perot in 1992. His erratic track record in these encounters spanned a dizzying spectrum, from flashes of effectiveness to moments of near-incoherence.

Failing to comprehend that American voters *like* evaluating their potential leaders side by side, candidate Bush never learned to mask his fundamental testiness toward debates. He viewed debates as irritants, roadblocks to be gotten around as quickly as possible. According to Republican adviser Mary Matalin, Bush was "generally cranky about the whole process."[45]And his crankiness showed.

In the chaotic debate negotiations of 1980, Bush managed to escape a face-to-face meeting with his opponents. Four years later he became an unwitting guinea pig in a new political tableau: the first male-versus-female debate. This juxtaposition disconcerted Bush, and against Ferraro he gave an almost comically hyperactive performance. "In a reversal of stereotypes," wrote columnist Ellen Goodman, "Ferraro was subdued, lawyerlike, and cool . . . while Bush was shrill, strident, and, gasp, hysterical."[46]

The debate with Ferraro may have been the "nadir" of Bush's career, said David Hoffman in the *Washington Post*, "in part because it spawned the notion that he was a whiny and awkward communicator in comparison with [Reagan]."[47] Emerging from Reagan's shadow in the first debate of 1988, the incumbent vice president got off to a shaky start, mangling an abortion question, demonizing Dukakis, and regularly lapsing into semi-intelligible "Bush-speak." Wrote *Post* columnist George Will, "Tracing a Bush thought back from its manifestation in speech to its origin in his thinking is like seeking the source of the Blue Nile."[48]

In the second debate in 1988, Bush got an unexpected boost from the unfeeling response Dukakis gave to Bernard Shaw's question about the theoretical rape and murder of Kitty Dukakis. "Bush's performance was hardly hall of fame material," observed *Newsweek*, "but he was steady, commanding and, measured against the governor, an appealingly mortal man."[49]

This "mortal man" may have been mortally wounded in his final round of debates, the series in 1992 with Clinton and Perot. Just as Bush's advisers had feared, the three-way structure set up a two-against-one dynamic. After the first encounter, Michael Kelly wrote in the *New York Times* that Bush had spent much of the debate "playing variations on the theme that things were not as bad as they seemed. He drew mostly modest applause, and on several occasions actually finished speaking to a dead silence, a surprising thing given that a quarter of the people in the hall were friends, family, and selected Republican guests."[50]

The second debate in 1992, the town hall in Richmond, was even more disastrous. Bush joked to an unappreciative audience that his wife would probably make a better president than he would. Then, in the night's signature moment, he got caught on live television stealing a glance at his watch. When a young African American woman asked how the national debt had affected Bush personally, his response was, "I'm not sure I get it." Clinton strategist James Carville, watching backstage at the debate hall, was heard to say, "Bush just lost the election."[51]

Recovering in time for the last installment of the series in 1992, Bush turned in the best debate performance of his career. Still, a late, isolated victory could not stop the momentum that had been gathering for Bill Clinton. "This won't be enough to give Bush the win," Richard Nixon told a colleague, "but at least he will have gone down fighting."[52]

Although Bush's inconsistent, inelegant delivery ranks him in the lower tier of presidential debaters, an endearing genuineness redeems all his performances. "Bush was not a good debater in the natural sense," said veteran Washington journalist Brit Hume, "but there was a slightly goofy good will that came through. You could tell he was a real person."[53] For George Bush, authenticity may have been an asset, but it was insufficient to win debates.

GERALDINE FERRARO (1984)

As the first woman on a major-party presidential ticket, Geraldine Ferraro entered the vice presidential debate in 1984 under microscopic scrutiny. Could she hold her own against George Bush? Would she rattle him? Would she overcome doubts about her suitability for office? "I was doing two things," Ferraro said of the match. "I had to not only debate George Bush on substance, but I had to let the public know that a woman—this woman—was able to take over the job of president."[54]

The congresswoman from Queens, selected by Mondale at least in part for her television skills, had been dubbed by the media as "scrappy" and "feisty" and "acerbic." Hoping to soften that image, Ferraro's handlers sanded away at the sharper edges of her personality. But in their attempts to craft a stateswoman, they may have imposed too many checks. "Ferraro was in a bit of a box," wrote Elizabeth Drew, "and her discomfort there showed."[55]

In the debate's flashiest moment, Ferraro's fighting spirit surfaced when Bush offered to help her understand the subtleties of international diplomacy. Looking directly at her opponent, Ferraro let him have it: "I almost resent, Vice President Bush, your patronizing attitude that you have to teach me about foreign policy." Was the moment planned? "Absolutely not," Ferraro said in an interview on CNN twelve years later. "He kept talking down to me."[56] Particularly irritating, said the candidate, was Bush's habit of calling her "Mrs. Ferraro," despite an earlier agreement that she be addressed as "Congresswoman Ferraro."

Boston Globe reporter Robert Healy, who had covered the debates in 1960, praised Ferraro, likening her to John F. Kennedy. "Ferraro has the unusual faculty of being able to talk to the television audience as if she were sitting in their living room having a cup of coffee," Healy wrote.[57] Indeed, the candidate seemed remarkably at ease before the vast viewership, especially in contrast to her opponent's nervous zippiness.

But the general response to Ferraro was less enthusiastic, most notably on matters of style. Perhaps the salient image from the Bush–Ferraro debate was of the Democratic candidate looking not at the camera but down at her lectern, either jotting or referring to notes on a legal pad. "She had fallen back on the body language appropriate to a court of law," said campaign authors Peter Goldman and Tony Fuller. According to

William Doerner in *Time*, "The down-and-low delivery was such a departure from her brassy style on the stump . . . that some observers thought she came across as cowed."[58]

As is so often the case in presidential debates, Geraldine Ferraro's performance could not live up to its advance hype. Although she acquitted herself admirably on content, in the end she was punished for not having mastered the stylistic niceties of television debating. "But in terms of the substance and my handling of the issues," Ferraro wrote in her memoir, "I think I did extremely well."[59]

MICHAEL DUKAKIS (1988)

If television is a cool medium, then Michael Dukakis ought to have been the most blessed of presidential debaters. Instead, in his two matches in 1988 with George Bush, Dukakis's natural reserve functioned as an audience turnoff. Dukakis was widely thought to have won his first debate and lost his second, but in the end the distinction mattered little: win or lose, neither viewers nor the press could warm up to the unemotive governor of Massachusetts.

The first encounter gave Dukakis a much-needed opportunity to counter Bush's relentless campaign of ad hominem attacks, attacks that extended into the debate itself. Early in the program, within a single sixty-second rebuttal, Bush called his opponent a "liberal," a "card-carrying member of the ACLU," and "out of the mainstream," disingenuously adding in a follow-up, "I'm not questioning his patriotism." In what would become the evening's defining sound bite, Dukakis fired back: "Of course the vice president is questioning my patriotism. I don't think there's any question about that. And I resent it."

This newly aggressive tone helped propel Dukakis to a 45 to 36 percent victory over Bush in ABC's postdebate poll. But the win was hollow, observed *Newsweek*, the triumph of the smartest kid in the class: "He had got A's for his answers . . . and D's in popularity." As Dukakis's biographers Christine Black and Thomas Oliphant saw it, "Dukakis made substantive points while Bush scored with emotional and folksy ones."[60]

Any afterglow got swept away in the opening question of the follow-up debate: Bernard Shaw's hypothetical query about the rape and murder of Kitty Dukakis. The question harpooned the Democratic candidate, and for the rest of the debate he suffered a slow, agonizing, on-camera demise. In the view of columnist David Nyhan of the *Boston Globe*, Dukakis "went into the hole on the very first question and never climbed out. As the night progressed, Bush got better, and the Duke got worse."[61] In her memoir, Kitty Dukakis would describe Shaw's query as "the nail in the coffin" of the campaign. She wrote, "Michael made a mistake; he answered a question he should have hurled right back into the face of his questioner."[62]

Dukakis's observers were surprised that this veteran politician failed to seize the opening Shaw had presented, especially since a response had been rehearsed. "I think I went through 50-odd debates with Michael Dukakis," said campaign manager Susan Estrich. "And he was very good in most of them; he wasn't good in every single one of them. Unfortunately, this was the most important one of the season, and it was a disappointment."[63]

Ten years after the fact, Dukakis looked back on this, his best-remembered and most damaging debate moment. "It was not an unfair question," he said, "but I answered as if I'd heard it for the thousandth time. There is the danger that having done this over and over and over again, you forget that for most of the audience this may be the very first time they've watched you." He added, "I've listened to the response since—and it doesn't sound so bad."[64]

LLOYD BENTSEN (1988)

As David Broder of the *Washington Post* saw it, Lloyd Bentsen looked like "the reliable, white-haired corner pharmacist, with a store of experience as deep as his baritone voice."[65] In his vice presidential debate against Dan Quayle in 1988, this kindly druggist administered the verbal equivalent of a lethal injection.

Before the debate, Bentsen had been thought of as mild-mannered, even reserved. "Senator Bentsen is not a spellbinder and is unlikely to become one," wrote Warren Weaver in the *New York Times* the morning of the event. "He projects sincerity, experience and a command of complicated factual material, but he rarely has emotional impact on an audience." *Newsweek* predicted that "he may well prove boring and pedantic," while Texas Democrat Ann Richards said, "He's not going to be a standup comedian."[66]

Indeed, apart from the "You're no Jack Kennedy" line, little stands out from Bentsen's performance in Omaha. But that one exchange was all it took to stamp the debate with its signature moment. "Bentsen looked like the sorrowful uncle talking to the wayward nephew," observed NBC's John Chancellor,[67] and many viewers agreed.

Polls taken immediately after the program named Bentsen the overwhelming victor, and the candidate wasted no time savoring his moment of glory. Bentsen told postdebate audiences that Quayle "left Omaha with no forwarding address" and promised to "open the Quayle season a little early this year."[68] Dukakis's campaign advertisements, which had barely acknowledged Bentsen before the debate, now prominently featured the senator's name. Political pundits wondered aloud if the Dukakis–Bentsen ticket might be more electable with the order reversed.

Though Bentsen's performance in Omaha would give Democrats a badly needed shot of adrenaline, the effect was short-lived. The principal beneficiary turned out to be not Michael Dukakis, but Lloyd Bentsen. According to Elizabeth Drew,

> The emergence of this improbable star said some telling things about this election, and about how we choose candidates. Bentsen's new glory came not because he had got off his now-famous line about Kennedy; it came about because he was the most—in fact, the only—authentic figure in the race. What people were responding to was that for the first time this fall they had seen a genuine, whole person, someone at ease with himself and his knowledge.[69]

In the strange and bitter presidential race of 1988, these qualities placed Lloyd Bentsen in a class by himself.

DAN QUAYLE (1988, 1992)

Fairly or not, Dan Quayle will be forever remembered as the butt of Lloyd Bentsen's putdown in the vice presidential debate in 1988: "Senator, I served with Jack Kennedy. Jack Kennedy was a friend of mine. Senator, you're no Jack Kennedy." With these words, the young man from Indiana, who had been cautioned not to compare himself with the thirty-fifth president, went down in stunning defeat.

Descriptions of Quayle's performance in 1988 fell along two metaphorical lines: animal and schoolboy. Meg Greenfield saw "a deer caught in the headlights"; Tom Shales, "Bambi on ice"; Michael Dukakis, a "cornered chipmunk."[70] David Broder compared Quayle to the "senior class president of his high school or college," while Elizabeth Drew likened him to "a young man hesitantly reciting his lessons and knowing little else."[71] Even friendly analysts like George Will could muster no enthusiasm. "Quayle was so overprogrammed it seemed someone backstage was operating a compact disc—a very small compact disc—in Quayle's skull," Will wrote.[72] So deeply did the words sting that Quayle called Will from the road to complain.

What stands out about these assessments is their uniformity. Dan Quayle's performance in 1988 is one of the few in debate history to provoke an almost totally negative reaction. Quayle would attribute his problems to a bad night's sleep and having spent the whole of debate day "just endlessly replaying those rote answers in my mind." In his autobiography, Quayle recalled a conversation with Lesley Stahl of CBS about the peculiar effect the television camera has on certain people's eyes: "In my case, she says, it captures some look of uncertainty, even though my demeanor in person reflects otherwise."[73]

Quayle's opportunity for vindication came four years later in the three-way vice presidential debate with Al Gore and James Stockdale. "I threw away that campaign book," Quayle said, "and I focused on themes. And I was more relaxed and far more in control. I learned a lot from the 1988 debate, believe me."[74] Quayle's rock-bottom expectations also handed him a considerable edge. As Tad Devine, campaign manager for Lloyd Bentsen, put it, "Such low pre-debate standing is the political equivalent of an express elevator to the penthouse of debate victory."[75]

Indeed, the reviews in 1992 read like citations for "most improved" debater. "Quayle may be no Jack Kennedy, but he was no stumblebum either," wrote R. W. Apple Jr. in the New York Times.[76] Quayle was credited with hitting hard on the question of Bill Clinton's fitness for office, a charge Gore let slide. Gore may have been expecting another deer in the headlights, observed William Safire, but what he got was a "grizzly bear climbing up over the hood. Quayle was an imperfect but effective debater in command of his basic message: Even if you're unhappy with Bush, you can't trust Clinton."[77]

Dan Quayle was hardly an exemplary performer in 1992. He had not learned to calm himself down, and occasionally his voice dropped into a self-consciously melodramatic stage whisper. "He did maintain good eye contact with the camera," wrote Tom Shales, "but he still seemed essentially the same as when Bush chose him for the vice presidency four long years ago: unstable as all get-out."[78] Others found Quayle's debate turn in 1992 admirable, among them a fellow victim of the debate gods' disfavor, Richard Nixon. "They should bring him out more," Nixon said of the young vice president. "People will come out to see him in droves. For better or for worse, he's interesting."[79]

BILL CLINTON (1992, 1996)

Bill Clinton's lasting contribution to presidential debates may well be the citizen participation format, a structure he pioneered in 1992 and successfully revisited in 1996. What Clinton dubbed the "people's debate" offered an ideal showcase for the Arkansas governor's vaunted television skills, uniting electoral politics and show biz in a way that perfectly suited this schmoozy Southerner's empathetic style. Working the crowd like a televangelist, Clinton redefined the relationship between debaters and debate watchers, and raised the standard for future nominees.

The effectiveness of Clinton's delivery in the town hall debate stood in counterpoint to the less fluid performances of his older co-stars, George Bush and Ross Perot in 1992, and Bob Dole four years later. Clinton, a child of television, projected total ease in the audience participation setting. That Clinton had studiously rehearsed his apparently effortless on-camera maneuvers seemed not to matter. The proof was in the performance.

After the election of 1992, Clinton told journalists Germond and Witcover that he had given a great deal of thought to the town hall forum. He explained, "It's a lot easier to be a good talker than a good listener. But in that format, with all that pressure, with one hundred million people watching, it's probably even harder to be a good listener. And one thing I thought about going into that debate was that these are real people. . . . I saw the American people sort of screaming for me to pay attention to them and listen to them."[80]

Clinton's debut as a presidential debater had been preceded by a rigorous roster of primary debates—three within a single thirty-hour period—and these encounters taught the candidate the value of a well-executed moment. But Clinton entered the compressed round of general election debates in 1992 with mixed expectations. An early appearance in October on Phil Donahue's talk show provoked Clinton's short temper, making him look peevish. His voice had grown raspy and hoarse, and aides publicly fretted about the governor's well-known prolixity. "His defect is that he falls in love with his own rhetoric," adviser Dick Morris told the *New York Times*.[81]

Clinton soon put these concerns to rest. Strong performances in all three of the matches in 1992 showed the candidate to be fully at home as a debater. By 1996 Clinton's reputation as a television prodigy had assumed heroic proportions. The morning after the first Clinton–Dole debate, Lisa Myers on the *Today* show allowed that "the president could talk a dog off a meat wagon."[82]

Fittingly the last debate of his career was another town hall forum, the debate in San Diego in 1996 with Dole; again, Clinton triumphed. As the *Boston Globe*'s Thomas Oliphant said, "Clinton never strayed from his task during this game of twenty questions—a little of his record, a little diagnosis of remaining problems, and a script for the future."[83] Though Bob Dole tried valiantly to keep pace, the night belonged to the president.

An impromptu scene immediately after this debate ended may have better summarized Bill Clinton than any of his studied words and gestures. Viewers watching on C-SPAN saw Clinton talking with individual members of the studio audience who had remained in the hall. Jeffrey Rosen described the interaction in the *New Republic*: "His eyes fixed single-mindedly on his target, he continued to argue animatedly for four minutes. All told, Clinton lingered for forty minutes, debating undecided citizens, one by one. If there's a better way for the president of the United States to conduct his final campaign, I can't imagine it."[84]

AL GORE (1992, 1996, 2000)

Al Gore's unexpected flame-out in the presidential debates of 2000 serves as a cautionary tale for any candidate about to confront a political adversary on live television. The story offers two key lessons: first, general election debates are no place to tinker with one's persona. And second, being overestimated as a debater is a dubious honor.

On the latter point, Gore could exert little control, especially when juxtaposed against an inexperienced opponent like George W. Bush. By 2000 Al Gore was on his fourth national campaign, as battle-tested as any executive-level debater in history. After earning his stripes in the crowded primary forums of 1988, Gore graduated to the freewheeling, three-way vice presidential match with Dan Quayle and Admiral James Stockdale in 1992. In his opening statement he came out swinging, promising Quayle, "If you don't try to compare George Bush to Harry Truman, I won't compare you to Jack Kennedy." Gore then turned to Stockdale and said, "Those of us who served in Vietnam look at you as a national hero," not so subtly reminding viewers that Quayle was the only one on the stage who lacked Vietnam credentials. Wrote Elizabeth Kolbert in the *New York Times*, "For the innocent tone and brutal implications of his opening statement, Mr. Gore probably deserves the evening's Eve Harrington Award for adroitly undermining a rival."[85]

Four years later, against Jack Kemp, Gore again won the match while drawing unenthusiastic reviews. In postdebate analysis on ABC, George Will described the Democratic candidate as "relentlessly, robotically, Muzak-ly on message." David Broder of the *Washington Post* watched the debate of 1996 with a group of undecided voters in Ankeny, Iowa. "Many of them didn't like Gore at all," Broder recalled, "because they thought he was talking down to them. One woman said, 'He speaks to us like he thinks English is our second language.'"[86]

Gore's finest debate performance came not during an election campaign but in a televised forum in 1993 with Ross Perot over the North American Free Trade Agreement on CNN's *Larry King Live*, the program that had launched Perot as a political phenomenon the previous year. In the intimate setting of a broadcast studio, absent a live audience and minus a rigid format, Gore decisively got the better of his opponent.

Gore also prevailed in a series of nine primary debates against Democratic challenger Bill Bradley in late 1999 and early 2000.

As Gore entered the general election debates in 2000, his reputation as a fierce competitor had swollen to epic proportions, thanks in large measure to an influential cover story by James Fallows in the *Atlantic Monthly* magazine. "Al Gore is the most lethal debater in politics," the article's lead-in promised, "a ruthless combatant who will say whatever it takes to win, and who leaves opponents not just beaten but brutalized."[87] This conclusion became conventional wisdom in the press, paving the way for George W. Bush to exceed expectations.

If Gore could not tamp down his reputation, he at least ought to have been able to restrain his personality. In debates few qualities count for more than authenticity, yet almost nothing about Al Gore's approach to debating in 2000 rang true, from the "citizen-advisers" who attended his preparation sessions to the mannered performances he delivered on camera. The first Gore–Bush match became known as the "sighing debate" for Gore's strange and annoying habit of exhaling loudly when his Republican counterpart said something disagreeable. "Every time Bush spoke, it seemed, Gore would haul up another great gust of oh-really-now from his lungs and blow it all over the stage," observed Michael Kelly in the *Washington Post*.[88]

In the second debate, Gore let the pendulum swing too far in the other direction. He apologized for getting some of his facts wrong in the previous encounter, an attempt at contrition that came off as obsequious rather than genuine. "The humble act was self-defeating," wrote Maureen Dowd in the *New York Times*. "Gore was reacting to Gore, like the sheriff in *Blazing Saddles* who holds a gun to his own head and takes himself hostage." Jake Tapper in *Salon* magazine likened Gore to "a henpecked husband whose wife had insisted, before the party, that he remain civil."[89]

Not until the third match of 2000—the town hall forum—did Vice President Gore find something approaching a natural voice, though this improvement was undermined by gratuitous physical aggression toward George W. Bush. In an interview shortly after the third debate ended, Gore drew an analogy between his performances and the Goldilocks story: "The first was too hot, the second was too cool. The third one was just right."[90] Perhaps so. But when a presidential contender takes to comparing himself to a fairy tale heroine, the news cannot be good.

Several years after the election of 2000, Al Gore told a colleague that campaigning for the presidency had made him feel "as if he were that character in *Being John Malkovich*. There were all of these voices in his head telling him what to do."[91] Gore's problem as a debater was his willingness to listen.

ROSS PEROT (1992)

After the first debate of 1992, Richard Nixon offered a particularly astute assessment of Ross Perot. "The guy is just interesting," Nixon told an aide. "And I've always said that the only thing worse than being wrong in politics is being dull. If Perot weren't there, it would have been dullsville." Nixon then added the inevitable postscript: "It won't affect a damn thing, though."[92]

Ross Perot's eminently watchable trio of performances in 1992 points up a curious dynamic in presidential debates: unpredictability will almost always outmatch choreography, but unpredictability has its limits, too. Perot's irrepressible sense of humor, along with his laudable refusal to be professionally packaged, breathed new life into the ritualistic debate genre. Before the novelty paled, Perot had shown the political pros that there is value in breaking the mold.

Reentering the race less than two weeks before the first debate in St. Louis, Perot gained instant credibility from his appearance with rivals George Bush and Bill Clinton. "Let's call a spade a spade here—Ross Perot won this debate," pronounced Cokie Roberts during ABC's postevent analysis. "He made the other two sound alike." Wrote Michael Kelly in the *New York Times*, "Mr. Perot, with his hands clasped behind his back and his chest puffed out like a pouter pigeon's, played a role that was a sort of Will Rogers–Mr. Deeds hybrid. At his best lines, and there were many, the audience laughed out loud, and even cheered a bit."[93]

But in the next debate, when Perot repeated the "I'm all ears" wisecrack that had been such a crowd-pleaser in round one, the joke fell flat—an indication of the larger problem that plagued this unorthodox candidate. In the view of NBC's Tom Brokaw, "Perot didn't have a second act." Tom Shales of the *Washington Post*, describing the Texan as a "crabby Munchkin," similarly held that "his act seemed to be growing increasingly stale."[94]

If Perot could never quite replicate his initial success, he did leave an intriguing legacy for other presidential debaters to ponder. Journalist John Mashek, a questioner in the first Clinton–Bush–Perot match and a panelist in 1984 and 1988, called Perot "the most relaxed of all the people I've watched debate." According to Perot's campaign adviser Clay Mulford, "He wasn't unnerved by the debates or felt that he was doing anything different than whatever else he'd do on a given day."[95] Perot's straightforward self-possession should serve as a model for other candidates, who too often approach debates like actors at a casting call, willing to twist themselves into pretzels in order to land the part.

Ross Perot proved that in a star-driven vehicle like a presidential debate, an engaging personality goes a long way. Many observers directly attributed the high viewership for the debates in 1992 to Perot's presence as an offbeat character in the political drama. "He made everybody watch the debates," said Tom Brokaw, "because they didn't know when he was going to blow a gasket or say something really funny. He was great for the process because it really did bring people to the debates."[96]

JAMES STOCKDALE (1992)

"Who am I? Why am I here?" With these all-too-prophetic questions, Admiral James Bond Stockdale set sail upon the oddest, most improbable odyssey ever undertaken in a presidential debate. *Newsweek* compared Stockdale to "a kindly old owl that had somehow blundered into a video arcade." "Flustered and unprepared," said Tom Shales. "The clear loser of the evening," in the view of Germond and Witcover.[97]

Stockdale's excruciating performance offered viewers a fascinating bounty of the unexpected. The candidate cut short an answer to a health care question by saying, "I'm out of ammunition." Stockdale missed another question because he had turned off his hearing aid. Moderator Hal Bruno had to encourage him to join the discussion. Standing mute as Al Gore and Dan Quayle jousted, Stockdale commented, "I feel like I'm a spectator at a ping-pong game."

With his shock of white hair and black, professorial glasses, this unlikely debater looked nothing like his telegenic competitors. At sixty-eight, Stockdale was a generation older and an atomic lifetime away from their experience in the national spotlight. On one level, Stockdale's babe-in-the-woods status enhanced his standing. As Gore and Quayle attacked each other's economic philosophies, Stockdale said, "I think America is seeing right now the reason this nation is in gridlock." According to Elizabeth Kolbert in the *New York Times*, Stockdale "seemed to be speaking for the frustrated viewer sitting powerlessly in front of the set, unable to intervene in an escalating squabble."[98]

Amazingly, Stockdale's debate appearance marked his debut on national television. The candidate had not even known he would be debating until a week in advance, when running mate Ross Perot casually informed him that the invitation had been accepted, "and I forgot to tell you."[99] Stockdale practiced for the debate not in a television studio but on a home video camera set up by his son. Stockdale's son, an elementary school principal in Pennsylvania, wrote an op-ed piece for the *Times* a few days after the ordeal that attempted to salvage the family honor. The younger Stockdale chided Gore and Quayle—and, by extension, the system that produced them:

Two children of privilege have been handed title and authority because they play by rules of insensitivity and blind ambition. Snarling like savage poodles on choke chains one minute, and smiling with smarmy rehearsed sincerity the next, they remind us always to doubt the motives of the man who is too well-groomed. Mr. Quayle and Mr. Gore epitomized modern anger, with its hair combed.

And then there is my father. A man of compassion, truthfulness, and sincerity. He is not interested in power. He is interested in goodness, honesty, and responsibility. His experience in a Vietnam prison brought out his wisdom, a quality our modern world spurns.[100]

After the debate, Admiral Stockdale attributed his poor showing to being less packaged than the other candidates. "What I saw last night was an art form," the admiral told supporters at a rally, "an art form I've never been near before."[101] Hoping to contain the damage, Perot's campaign sent Stockdale around the country to meet with newspaper editorial boards, a setting in which this thoughtful man felt more at home. The debate, however, left an indelible mark; never had the audience seen anything like it.

The great lesson of James Stockdale for future debaters is clear: experience has no substitute. As the *Washington Post*'s columnist Mary McGrory put it, "Politics may seem incoherent, but it has its rules, too."[102]

JACK KEMP (1996)

Like a new cast member added to a long-running series, Jack Kemp debuted in the vice presidential debate in 1996 as the year's only nonveteran. The media widely touted Kemp's appearance with Al Gore as a dress rehearsal for the presidential race of 2000, a sneak preview of coming attractions for political connoisseurs to sit back and savor. As it happened, the Gore–Kemp meeting in St. Petersburg, Florida, received some of the lowest ratings and least enthusiastic reviews of any general election debate.

As an unsuccessful presidential candidate in 1988, Kemp had taken part in his share of primary debates. But in the telecast in 1996, this former football star left an overriding impression of nervousness, hardly a reassuring trait for a would-be national leader. "Kemp was winging it," said David Broder. "I think he had not really sat down and said, okay, what are my strategic goals, what are the three points I want to make no matter what they ask me."[103]

Moderator Jim Lehrer's opening question handed Kemp an easy opportunity to attack Bill Clinton's character: "Some supporters of Senator Dole have expressed disappointment over his unwillingness [in the first debate] to draw personal and ethical differences between him and President Clinton. How do you feel about it?" Kemp responded that attacks on the president were beneath Bob Dole, effectively prohibiting Dole from pursuing a character strategy in the days to come.

Conservatives disdained Kemp's kid-glove handling of Clinton and conciliatory attitude toward Gore. Bill Kristol, editor of the *Weekly Standard*, complained that "if you came down from Mars and saw this debate, you might think that Al Gore was the moderate Republican and Jack Kemp was the Democrat." Even Bob Dole, cracking wise on *Nightline*, said, "It looked like a fraternity picnic there for a while."[104]

Several days after the debate, Sam Donaldson put the charge directly to Kemp on the Sunday morning program *This Week*. Donaldson: "A lot of Republicans are saying they wanted a lean, mean fighting machine to show up, and they're saying that what showed up was a garrulous, unprepared wimp—you." After a few minutes of obligatory face-saving, Kemp gave in, confessing, "I'm just not an attack dog."[105]

Not all observers disapproved of Kemp's restraint. To Martin Nolan of the *Boston Globe*, this was "the best vice presidential debate ever, 90 minutes of serious issues rarely discussed." But those expecting sparks to fly reacted with disappointment. "The debate left little material for video editors to regale us with in 2000, should these two men meet again as presidential candidates," wrote Christopher Buckley in the *New York Times*. George Will made the point more bluntly in his postdebate analysis on ABC: "It seems to me that what happened tonight was the campaign of 1996 came closer to being closed, and the campaign for the Republican nomination in the year 2000 opened wider."[106]

GEORGE W. BUSH (2000, 2004)

As a debater, George W. Bush brought to the table a singular talent for staying on point. From his first gubernatorial debate in Texas in 1994 through his series ten years later against John Kerry, Bush demonstrated a consistent grasp of his objectives and the discipline not to venture beyond them.

Attorney Gregory Craig, who played Bush in Kerry's practice debates, closely studied his counterpart's rhetorical style, and concluded that Bush "never varied the message from what he had said in the past, no matter what the issue. He never ever left his home base." Bush's message, Craig discovered, "was simple, smart, well targeted, and easily understood. President Bush never made it up as he went along."[107]

Yet this same clarity of purpose locked Bush into something of a straitjacket. In the inherently spontaneous arena of political debates, George W. Bush too often seemed like a musician sticking to the written score while the rest of the band jammed. The perils of Bush's rigid approach to debates surfaced vividly in the primary campaign of 2000, in performances notable for their extreme caution. "He was trying harder not to get anything wrong than he was to get anything especially right," observed Frank Bruni of the Texas governor's first primary debate in 1999. "His diaphanous answers sometimes ended many seconds before they had to, creating moments of silence and awkward pauses before the moderators realized that he was done and they should move on." At every opportunity, Bruni said, "he pivoted into a regurgitation of lines from his stump speeches—a tactic that all of the candidates used, but that few did as transparently and consistently as Bush."[108]

Bush got lucky in the general election debates of 2000 when his opponent's inconsistent performances left him victorious by default. "On paper," wrote James Fallows, "George W. Bush lost the battle of logic to Al Gore. But he won the more important '*Saturday Night Live* primary,' when Gore was ridiculed for the three different personas he had presented in three debates."[109] In the view of Bush's media adviser Stuart Stevens, "Short of Gore declaring that he was an agent of Satan, it was hard to imagine how the debates could have turned out better."[110]

The Republican nominee did face demons of his own in the debates of 2000. Although the second encounter is generally considered Bush's best, the candidate disconcerted many viewers by appearing to boast about his state's eagerness to apply the death penalty. This issue cropped up a few days later in the town hall debate, when a questioner asked Bush if he was proud of Texas's track record in leading the nation in criminal executions. The governor conceded that, no, he did not take pride in that distinction. At times Bush did not entirely make sense, as when he described the word *insurance* as a "Washington term." But he offset his rhetorical missteps with flashes of humor: when a town hall audience member had difficulty reading her question from a card, Bush whipped out a pair of eyeglasses and jokingly offered them to her.

If George Bush had the benefit in 2000 of being an unknown and underestimated commodity, that advantage disappeared four years later in the debates with John Kerry. By that point the man who had run for office as a "uniter not a divider" had alienated huge swaths of the electorate. Almost no one who tuned in for the debates in 2004 did so without a strongly held opinion of Bush, pro or con.

It is no exaggeration to say that Bush's first debate in 2004 represents the sorriest performance ever given by a presidential candidate in a general election debate. His facial tics, scowls, slumping posture, and petulant attitude strongly signaled that he did not want to be there. The second debate, a town hall forum, proved only marginally less disastrous than the first. Bush was strident and whiny. His attempts at humor—usually a Bush strong suit—fell flat, and at times he seemed to be shrieking at the assembled voters. The low point came when a woman in the audience asked the president to name three "wrong decisions" he had made, and what he had done to correct them. Although Bush had been asked a nearly identical question at a press conference several months earlier, he could not muster a single concrete example.

Bush showed improvement in the third and final debate, and reaped a windfall from John Kerry's ill-advised reference to Mary Cheney, but by that point the damage had been done. "Where it has mattered most—the three debates—Bush has been wooden, ill at ease and downright spooky," wrote columnist Richard Cohen in the *Washington Post*. Comparing the candidate's demeanor to that of a "cinematic serial killer," Cohen opined that "he could take over the Bates Motel in an instant."[111]

If there is a lesson to be drawn from George W. Bush's performance, it is that repetition and a clear message do not in themselves win debates. Candidates must also demonstrate a genuine desire to step into the spotlight, to seize the opportunity and make a personal connection with voters. Much like his father, Bush could not grasp a simple truth about debates: they are occasions to be relished, not obstacles to be overcome.

DICK CHENEY (2000, 2004)

Dick Cheney's performance in the vice presidential debate of 2000 is worthy of study by any candidate undertaking a political debate. Consider his accomplishments:

- He defied predebate expectations by outperforming his opponent, Joe Lieberman.

- He suckered Lieberman into staying positive without ceding his own willingness to criticize.
- He critiqued Lieberman in a way that the audience found palatable—ruefully rather than scornfully.
- He dispelled the extremist caricature that had accompanied him into the debate.
- Last but not least, he made voters question the order of the ticket.

To the surprise of nearly everyone, the low-voltage man from Wyoming turned out to be the best debater of the season of 2000. True, the field was weak, but until that point Cheney had been considered the least capable campaigner of the bunch.

Dick Cheney's no-frills delivery had the effect of sounding both wise and reassuring. He gave a thoughtful answer to a query about racial profiling from moderator Bernard Shaw in which Shaw asked each candidate to "imagine yourself an African American." Cheney even came off as funnier than Lieberman.

Cheney's finest moment came in response to a question about whether gay citizens should enjoy the same constitutional privileges as heterosexuals: "The fact of the matter is we live in a free society, and freedom means freedom for everybody," he replied. "We shouldn't be able to choose and say you get to live free and you don't. That means people should be free to enter into any kind of relationship they want to enter into. It's no one's business in terms of regulating behavior in that regard."

Beyond his unanticipated expressions of tolerance and humor, Cheney showed a refreshing self-awareness of his limitations as a public figure. Unlike other candidates for high office, he refused to repackage himself in order to score popularity points on television. Encouraged by his handlers to integrate personal anecdotes into his presentation, Cheney resisted. Joe Lieberman in his closing statement talked about how he wished his late father could have watched the debate. Cheney's closer offered an impersonal litany of policy positions.

"That was my close," Cheney told a reporter for the *Washington Post* who asked why he hadn't used the debate to make a "human connection" with voters. "I come back to the proposition that I'm not ordinarily someone who talks about myself that much, or my feelings. I'm proud of my family and my family's background. They worked hard for everything that they had, but I don't go around and talk about it."[112]

By contrast with the humble, reasonable, and canny Dick Cheney of 2000, the man who showed up to debate John Edwards in 2004 had morphed into an altogether different guise: the mumbling, sinister Marlon Brando in *The Godfather*.

On the surface the two debates offered similarities: as in 2000, the format called for both candidates to be seated with the moderator at a table. The Republicans' insistence on a sit-down debate had both practical and cosmetic motivations. Cheney's history of heart problems made the prospect of ninety minutes on his feet inadvisable. And there were visual reasons for wanting the candidates seated at a table. As live pre-debate coverage on C-SPAN showed in 2000, when Cheney came out onstage to take his seat just before the program began, he looked old, overweight, and stooped. These disadvantages vanished the moment he sat down. According to Jonathan Sallet, who led debate prep for Joe Lieberman, "It was clear to us from the very outset that in a table format, Cheney was going to be very effective, that he had this kind of bulldog quality that worked in the sit-down setting."[113]

In 2004, however, the arrangement proved a mixed blessing for Cheney by situating the vice president in the direct line of fire of an opponent who eagerly pounced. Particularly in the first half of the debate, Cheney seemed like an old lion being challenged for supremacy by a younger, stronger, and hungrier rival. One reporter in the hall who had covered Cheney for years said it was the first time she had ever seen him nervous.[114]

"As the evening wore on," a next-day editorial in the *Los Angeles Times* declared, "Cheney's chin sank down his chest, his gravelly voice turned into an inarticulate rumble and he even started passing up opportunities to talk at all. Handed opportunities on a platter . . . Cheney waved them aside."[115]

Although he picked up steam and got in his licks as the debate proceeded, Cheney could never quite hide his contempt for John Edwards, or his contempt for the debate itself. Cheney played the hand he was dealt as best he could, but his opponent held higher cards. In debates as in gambling, high cards will always beat a poker face.

JOSEPH LIEBERMAN (2000)

"My 85-year-old mom gave me some good advice about the debate earlier today," Joseph Lieberman announced at the outset of the 2000 vice presidential match. "She said, 'Sweetheart'—as she's prone to call me—'remember, be positive and know that I will love you no matter what your opponent says about you.' Well, Mom, as always, that was both reassuring and wise. I am going to be positive tonight. I'm not going to indulge in negative personal attacks."

With that preface, Lieberman set about following his mother's advice to the letter—and in the process forfeited his debate to the less positively disposed Dick Cheney.

Lieberman entered the arena with a jovial image and reams of good press. According to predebate handicapping, he was expected to easily demolish his decidedly less happy-go-lucky opponent. "Where Mr. Cheney comes across as reserved on the stump, even dour," wrote the *New York Times*'s reporter Richard Perez-Peña in advance of the debate, "the main impression Mr. Lieberman leaves is that he is enjoying himself. Even on the offensive, his relaxed tone never varies, his voice never rises, no hint of distaste crosses his face."[116]

That sunny demeanor may have served Joe Lieberman well on the campaign trail, but in a face-to-face confrontation with his vice presidential rival, good will curdled into conciliation. When Cheney criticized Lieberman for a joke about George Bush's religion made at a Democratic fund-raiser, the Connecticut senator smarmily apologized. When Cheney absurdly claimed that government patronage had not contributed to his personal wealth, Lieberman opted to wisecrack instead of rebut. Even more surprisingly, Lieberman went out of his way to avoid criticizing Cheney's archconservative voting history as a Wyoming congressman, despite the rich targets it presented. "There was a lot of very strong counsel that I should be affirmative," he later explained, "that I should draw distinctions but I should not attack Cheney's record."[117]

In his memoir of the campaign of 2000, Lieberman wrote that "Cheney and I disagreed on most issues, but we managed to disagree without being disagreeable," and he described himself as "tremendously proud" of the debate: "We proved that political debates don't have to be all attacks or all sound bites; we treated the voters with respect by respecting the importance of the issues."[118]

Although commentators lauded the high-mindedness of the exchange, it also seemed that some necessary ingredient of political clash had been missing. "This debate was so polite it was almost antiseptic," said Judy Woodruff of CNN, a couple of minutes after the program ended.[119] In the weeks that followed, it became increasingly apparent that Lieberman had been skunked.

Joseph Lieberman offers evidence that as a strategy in presidential debates, civility may be a worthy goal. It may be good for your personal reputation and it may make your mother happy. But being agreeable does not win debates.

JOHN KERRY (2004)

John Kerry stepped onto the presidential debate stage in 2004 amid great expectations. Despite a reputation for plodding, long-winded oratory, in the parry-and-thrust of televised debates, Kerry had been an adept player. His track record included a highly regarded series of eight Massachusetts senatorial debates in 1996 in which he came across as authoritative and assertive. Opponent William Weld likened Kerry the debater to "an acrobat": "He is well informed, and he's not easily stampeded. And he is very, very quick."[120]

During the long primary season of 2004, Kerry participated in nearly twenty televised appearances alongside a slew of fellow Democratic candidates. Kerry acquitted himself favorably, even managing to lighten his humorless reputation. At a forum in South Carolina, moderator George Stephanopoulos challenged Kerry about his chilly image—that he was "just too aloof," that he lacked "the common touch it takes to win." Kerry did not miss a beat before responding, "Well, probably I ought to just disappear and contemplate that by myself."[121]

Less positively, the primary debates showed that Kerry's rhetorical repertoire did not include an ability to package political abstractions into anecdotes that resonated with voters. He had difficulty mining the emotional content of public policy issues, and he could never quite persuade the electorate of his passion for the presidency. Kerry's caution may nevertheless have helped him survive the primary season intact; after nearly a full year of cattle call events with the other candidates, John Kerry was the last man standing.

One of those competitors, Al Sharpton, described Kerry the debater as a prizefighter who scored consistently well on points without ever landing a knockout punch.[122] As it happened, this would also prove to be an accurate analysis of Kerry's three general election debates with Bush. Kerry inflicted plenty of flesh wounds, but never the coup de grâce that would dispatch his opponent.

On the plus side, Kerry easily passed the test that faces all challengers in general election debates: seeming presidential. A number of critics made the point that Kerry came off as a more plausible chief executive than Bush. Throughout the debates, Kerry remained in command of his facts, his positions, and his nerves—exactly the opposite of his rival. Even physically, Kerry's ramrod-straight military posture and immobile visage contrasted positively with Bush's twitchy slump and weird facial contortions.

Kerry took a prosecutorial approach to Bush that kept the incumbent president on the defensive. Especially in the second debate—the town hall—Kerry drew sharp and personal distinctions between himself and George W. Bush. Over and over Kerry would stand at a perpendicular angle to his co-debater, directing his message right at Bush, who looked extremely uncomfortable.

In spite of his technical fluency in the debates in 2004, Kerry could not overcome a fundamental, probably intractable, problem: his inherent lack of star quality. John Kerry did not naturally leap off the screen; he did not know how to make himself an interesting character to the audience. The physiognomy of Kerry's face, especially his massive brow and hooded eyes, made him difficult to light and less than fully expressive. Even his superior height did not count as much of an advantage, because he did not seem fully at ease with it.

Although he did succeed in curbing his prolixity, there would come a moment in Kerry's debate answers when viewers could see the circuitry kick in, and he would shift from talking to speechifying. Too often he gave the air of having been teleported back to the floor of the U.S. Senate, instead of shaping his presentation to fit the dramatic contours of high-stakes live television. As in the primary debates, Kerry's language leaned heavily on references to legislation and process—too many statistics and not enough stories.

Kerry used lots of hand gestures, but they were the studied motions of a classically trained debater. "At times," wrote Alessandra Stanley in the *New York Times*, "Mr. Kerry looked a little like a flight attendant demonstrating how emergency exits and oxygen masks work: when addressing a broader security issue, Mr. Kerry referenced identity-verification technology, pointing to his eyes when he said 'iris' scans, and gesturing broadly with his thumbs when mentioning 'thumbprint analysis.'"[123]

Whatever Kerry's shortcomings as a performer, critical consensus held that he prevailed in all three of his debates against George W. Bush—at minimum he won the first two and tied for the third. Yet in the end he failed to seduce the audience, even though much of that audience was eager to be seduced. John Kerry's three performances in 2004 show the limitation of technique in presidential debates. Winning a debate on points is one thing; giving the voters some music to dance to is another.

JOHN EDWARDS (2004)

The advantages that John Edwards brought to his vice presidential debate with Dick Cheney in 2004—youthful vitality, down-home eloquence, television anchorman looks—could also be viewed as potential liabilities. Was he too inexperienced for the job? Too glib? Too much of a Ken doll?

Alongside the grandfatherly Cheney, these qualities stood out in sharp relief. No Hollywood casting agent would dare to pit two such disparate personalities against each other as costars, yet there they sat, just feet apart and ready to tangle. For viewers the contrast was nothing short of fascinating: a political face-off that lived up to the hype of "must-see" television.

In the days before the debate, Republican spinners worked overtime to remind the media of Edwards's superior performing talents. Bush's strategist Matthew Dowd described Edwards as a "cross between Atticus Finch and William Jennings Bryan." Cheney's adviser Mary Matalin called Edwards the "man with the golden tongue . . . put on the ticket exclusively for this moment."[124]

In fact John Edwards had drawn mixed reviews in the primary debates in 2004. Though he made no obvious blunders, there were few high points. As it happened, two of his least impressive primary debates used the sit-down format that Cheney's negotiators had succeeded in getting for the vice presidential match. At least part of Edwards's mediocrity in the primary debates could be attributed to structural limitations: in a field of multiple candidates, it is difficult to distinguish yourself from the competition. One on one against Cheney, the challenge for Edwards was to summon the skills that had made him a formidable trial lawyer.

This courtroom persona of John Edwards emerged in the very first exchange of the debate when he fixed his gaze on Cheney and said, "Mister Vice President, you're not being straight with the American people." In addition to putting his opponent on the defensive, Edwards honored a key principle of show business: give the crowd a boffo opening.

Throughout the evening, Edwards displayed an impressive command of rhetoric. He tempered his criticism with Southern politeness. He spoke directly to the audience ("Listen very carefully to what the vice president is saying . . ."). He used anecdotes to convey his points: describing being in Jerusalem right before a suicide bomber attacked, recalling a severely injured child he represented in a lawsuit against a swimming pool manufacturer, weaving his own biography into the broader tapestry of the debate. And he fulfilled his obligation as a running mate, making the case for John Kerry far more convincingly than Cheney made the case for George Bush.

Edwards also effectively employed nonverbal communication cues. His facial expressions were animated, he gestured frequently with his hands, and he leaned his upper body forward in order to stress particular points. He seemed not the least bit intimidated by the redoubtable Cheney.

Some observers found Edwards's intensity off-putting. The *Washington Post*'s critic Tom Shales felt "there was no passion in his umbrage." A journalist in Cleveland, where the debate took place, wrote that "Edwards taxed his own talent at times, putting on an over-the-top tone of uplift that made him sound in his closing speech as if he felt a song coming on." The day after the debate, comedian David Letterman joked about the candidate's image as a lightweight: "Good news for John Edwards. If he doesn't win in November, he has a firm offer to be the new host of the *Family Feud*."[125]

Most analysts at the time declared the debate a draw, perhaps because reporters were reluctant to pile on the Republicans just days after George W. Bush had performed so disastrously in the first debate. In retrospect, however, Edwards's performance seems underappreciated. In the immediate aftermath of the encounter, Tom Brokaw on NBC said that "the vice presidential candidates demonstrated tonight that you could have hand-to-hand combat while seated."[126] When both men got up from the table, Edwards had fewer wounds.

BARACK OBAMA (2008, 2012)

Debates demand from their participants a certain buy-in. Axiomatic as this may seem, some candidates find it impossible to overcome their disdain for the ritual. Barack Obama, whose oratorical skills functioned most effectively as a one-man show, never acceded to the basic premise of debates; instead, he approached them with the wariness of a traveler entering hostile territory. Yet when he set aside his misgivings long enough to pull off a necessary win, Obama showed himself more than capable of playing the game.

As an office-seeker in Illinois, Obama participated in a handful of multicandidate scrums. According to biographer David Remnick, "he was in the habit of crossing his legs and holding his chin up at an imperious angle while an opponent spoke, as if his mind were elsewhere or the proceedings were beneath consideration." Reviewing a debate among Democratic candidates for the U.S. Senate nomination in 2004, a perceptive local blogger accurately pinpointed a fundamental Obama debate weakness: despite an "informed and articulate" presentation, Obama's message "was not as focused as [the message of] some of the other candidates and lacked clarity."[127]

Throughout his political career Obama was lucky in the opponents he drew. His first big-ticket debates came against perennial Republican candidate Alan Keyes, an unconventional adversary whose political extremism and moralistic hauteur played poorly with voters in Illinois. Obama took part in three debates with Keyes, one on radio and two on television. Largely by staying out of his opponent's way, Obama chalked up unflashy victories, but in his book *The Audacity of Hope*, Obama gave himself low marks as a debater: "I was frequently tongue-tied, irritable, and uncharacteristically tense." What particularly rankled Obama was Keyes's habit of impugning his opponent's bona fides as a Christian.[128]

Early in the presidential primary season in 2008, candidate Obama found himself part of an ensemble that included such skilled and experienced rivals as Hillary Clinton, John Edwards, Joe Biden, and Bill Richardson—and he suffered by comparison. "He was a tentative, awkward presence in the endless Democratic debates through the spring and summer of 2007," concluded *Newsweek*. "He didn't seem to have his heart in it."[129]

In an audiotaped conversation with advisers during a primary debate prep session, Obama candidly analyzed his own ambivalence. "I don't consider this to be a good format for me, which makes me more cautious. . . . I often found myself trapped by the questions and thinking to myself, 'You know, this is a stupid question, but let me . . . answer it.'"[130]

By the end of the primaries in 2008, the cast of characters had boiled down to Obama, Clinton, and Edwards, who met twice as a trio, then Obama and Clinton, who appeared four additional times in one-on-one debates. These encounters unfolded with varying degrees of candidate-to-candidate engagement. In Las Vegas, Obama and Clinton downplayed their differences; in South Carolina, they squabbled bitterly. In Hollywood, before a star-studded audience that included everyone from Leonardo di Caprio to Steven Spielberg, they made nice—"like co-anchors who despise each other but rally to look convivial during sweeps week," according to Alessandra Stanley in the *New York Times*. In Texas, they butted heads again. In Cleveland, Obama declined to take his opponent's bait, and in Philadelphia, the focus fell less on the debaters than on the overbearing ABC News moderators, Charles Gibson and George Stephanopoulos—who, in the view of Tom Shales, "turned in shoddy, despicable performances."[131]

Sparring partners like Hillary Clinton and John Edwards gave Obama an invaluable workout for his three-debate series with John McCain. Pursuing a strategy of deliberate steadiness, even blandness, Obama used the general election debates in 2008 to display presidential temperament, at a point in American history when a calm hand was required. "We've been watching Barack Obama for two years now, and in all that time there hasn't been a moment in which he has publicly lost his self-control," observed conservative columnist David Brooks. "There hasn't been a moment when he has displayed rage, resentment, fear, anxiety, bitterness, tears, ecstasy, self-pity or impulsiveness."[132]

Despite their twenty-five-year age difference, Obama assumed the adult role against McCain, who never managed to conceal his irritation at appearing alongside his wet-behind-the-ears challenger. As a debater, Obama proved far from perfect—he was too conciliatory, too unwilling to seize his opportunities, too professorial in tone. "He willfully refuses to accept what debates are about," complained Maureen Dowd. "It's not a lecture hall, it's a joust."[133]

These deficiencies amplified in the first presidential debate of 2012, Barack Obama's single worst turn as a public performer. Insulated for four years in the White House bubble and unprepared for the open, free-wheeling format of the confrontation in Denver, Obama got rolled by the hungrier, more aggressive Mitt Romney. "What was being presented wasn't leadership," Obama later complained at a campaign rally. "That's salesmanship."[134]

Precisely the point. Debates are opportunities for candidates to sell themselves and their visions to tens of millions of voters at once. "He came to Denver with no larger theme he wanted urgently to get across, no apparent passion for the chance to make himself understood and make his opponent look silly," wrote Matt Bai. "He was there to defend his policies, but he wasn't going to get all needy about it, and no one was going to make him have an ounce of fun." The postdebate cover of the *New Yorker* summarized the situation visually, with an empty chair behind a vacant lectern substituting for the missing-in-action president.[135]

In the two follow-up appearances with Romney, Obama dramatically upped his game. The town hall meeting saw him undo much of the previous damage with a vigorous performance that rendered Romney sputtering and out of touch. At the foreign policy debate, Obama continued to pound away at his less experienced opponent, whose strategy of floating regally above the fray could not withstand Obama's relentless jabs.

With his back against the wall, Barack Obama was able to vanquish his aversion to the street fighting that campaign debates necessitate. Still, the candidate might have saved himself—and his supporters—a good deal of anguish had he simply been willing to accept debates for what they are: superficial political theater, yes, but also priceless platforms for connecting with voters.

JOHN McCAIN (2008)

As an authentic American hero with a reputation for straight talk, John McCain brought to his political persona an uncommon degree of integrity. On the campaign trail and in media interviews, McCain deployed a naturalistic style that charmed audiences and set him apart from his more heavily programmed Washington peers. Upon the debate stage, however, McCain's gifts as a communicator lost something in translation. Over the course of several dozen presidential-level debates, he only occasionally managed to turn the exercise to his advantage. The enduring image of McCain the debater is not that of a straight talker, but that of a man aggrieved.

In the Republican primary debates of 2000, McCain seethed with anger at his principal antagonist, George W. Bush. At a South Carolina forum, after Bush had questioned McCain's commitment to veterans, McCain snapped, "You should be ashamed, you should be ashamed." Eight years later, McCain aimed his disdain first at Mitt Romney, then at Barack Obama. McCain seemed particularly riled by debate opponents for whom he lacked respect, a list that included virtually all of his serious competitors.

In 2000, in a Republican field that included Rudolph Giuliani, Mike Huckabee, Mitt Romney, Ron Paul, and Fred Thompson, McCain often came across as the most measured and thoughtful candidate of the bunch. He also showed a flair for the crowd-pleasing wisecrack. At a debate in Orlando, McCain noted Hillary Clinton's support for a museum commemorating the Woodstock festival of 1969. "Now, my friends, I wasn't there," he said. "I am sure it was a cultural and pharmaceutical event. I was tied up at the time." The line—both a joke and a reminder of McCain's prisoner-of-war status—drew the crowd to its feet.

Moments of this sort became hallmarks of McCain's town meetings with voters on the campaign trail, though sometimes the candidate's responses came tinged with acid. At a forum in New Hampshire in 2007, a high school student asked McCain, who had celebrated his seventy-first birthday the previous week, if he worried about dying in office or becoming debilitated by Alzheimer's. After delivering a boilerplate answer about his physical fitness for the job, McCain turned back to the student. "Thanks for the question, you little jerk," he said. "You're drafted."

Though generally unmemorable in the Republican primary debates of 2008, in late summer McCain outperformed Barack Obama at two events in which the two presidential contenders appeared serially: the interviews with Rick Warren at Saddleback Church and the ServiceNation forum at Columbia University. Heading into the general election debates, McCain was by no means the underdog. In the view of Katharine Q. Seelye in the New York Times, "he is an aggressive competitor who scolds his opponents, grins when he scores, and is handy with the rhetorical shiv."[136]

John McCain's threat to skip the first debate placed the candidate on unsure footing when it came time to actually take part. For many viewers the main takeaway was McCain's unwillingness to make eye contact with his opponent. Coupled with a tendency to lecture his upstart challenger, McCain projected a peevishness that left Obama looking statesmanlike by comparison.

In their next debate, a town hall format that was supposed to be the Arizona senator's métier, McCain again hurt himself by dismissing his opponent as "that one." Tom Shales, critic for the Washington Post, thought the reference "contributed to McCain's image as a kind of mean old Scrooge, not so much a battle-scarred warrior as an embittered one."[137]

The third and final debate of the series in 2008—the debate that added Joe the Plumber to American political lore—turned out to be

McCain's best, yet reviews were mixed. McCain "drew sharp contrasts with his opponent," according to the *Economist*, and "managed to land some good jabs on his rival." *New York* magazine's John Heilemann was less enthusiastic: "McCain twitched, smirked, glowered, smoldered, rolled his eyes. And when he opened his mouth, what came out was too often a tonal match for his facial expressions."[138] Although Barack Obama had delivered only adequate performances, McCain was roundly adjudged the loser of the debates of 2008.

As a presidential debater, John McCain struggled to capitalize on his political assets—candor, humor, and the ability to make human connections. Instead, the quality that emerged was testiness. And testiness in debates inevitably backfires, because it has more to do with the candidate than it has to do with voters.

JOSEPH BIDEN (2008, 2012)

Lest there be any doubt that campaign debates rank among the performing arts, consider the example of Joseph Biden. In two vice presidential debates four years apart, Biden presented the American public with two distinct versions of himself. Against Sarah Palin, he was the restrained elder statesman, careful not to inflame his opponent's self-victimization or his own reputation for verbal faux pas. Against Paul Ryan, he was the very opposite of restrained—unleashed if you were a supporter, unhinged if you weren't.

That a single candidate can pull off such contrasting characterizations tells us something about Biden and something about debates. About debates we can infer that these are situational events, tailored to fit not just specific electoral circumstances but also the specific personalities of their leading players. About Biden the shape-shifting betokens a knack for political theater and the savvy to modulate his delivery as needed—important advantages for any debater.

Little in Biden's early career would have pointed toward this mastery of the milieu. In his first run for president in 1988, it was a closing statement at an Iowa debate that eventually forced Biden out of the race. Declaiming in lofty language about his humble origins, Biden lifted words from a speech by British Labour Party leader Neil Kinnock. And not just words, but key biographical details that did not even apply to Biden, such as being the first in his family to attend college. Exposure of Biden's plagiarism quickly spawned other, similar charges stretching as far back as law school, and one month after the debate in Iowa, Biden aborted his candidacy. He would wait twenty years before making another presidential run.

In 2008 Biden's Democratic rivals included Barack Obama, Hillary Clinton, and John Edwards. Despite his back-of-the-pack status, Biden managed to make his presence felt in the crowded primary debates, as in this much-replayed exchange at a forum in South Carolina in April 2007:

> *Brian Williams* (moderator): An editorial in the *Los Angeles Times* said, "In addition to his uncontrolled verbosity, Biden is a gaffe machine." Can you reassure your voters in this country that you would have the discipline you would need on the world stage, Senator?
>
> *Biden*: Yes. (followed by silence)

At a debate in Philadelphia six months later, Biden launched an attention-getting broadside against a Republican presidential rival, former New York City mayor Rudolph Giuliani. The delivery was classic Biden: "Rudy Giuliani . . . I mean, think about it! Rudy Giuliani. There's only three things he mentions in a sentence—a noun, a verb, and 9/11. There's nothing else! There's nothing else! And I mean this sincerely. He's genuinely not qualified to be president."

But such sound-bite moments were isolated. More typically, Biden found himself ignored in the primary debates in 2008, overshadowed by the juggernaut of Obama, Clinton, and Edwards. At a CNN forum in Las Vegas, when he was finally called upon after waiting silently for fifteen minutes, Biden exclaimed in mock horror to moderator Wolf Blitzer, "Oh, no, don't make me speak!" Although Biden's candidacy ended a few weeks later, the senator's solid performances in the primary debates helped him clinch the slot as Obama's running mate.

Heading into the vice presidential debate in 2008, the media focused on two points: Palin's low expectations and Biden's potential for sticking his foot in his mouth. As Mark Leibovich said in the *New York Times*, "He is a distinctive blend of pit bull and odd duck whose weak filters make him capable of blurting out pretty much anything." A few hours before the debate, McCain's campaign released a web ad that posed the question, "What might Joe Biden say at tonight's debate? Anything's possible." The ad replayed some of the senator's memorable gaffes, including a town hall event in which Biden told an audience member, "I think I probably have a much higher IQ than you."[139]

No such gems were in the cards for the Biden–Palin debate. Although most of the spotlight fell on Governor Palin, Biden drew the better reviews, particularly for his deft handling of a tricky opponent. "I was trying to be a good boy," Biden told an audience a few days later.[140]

Four years later the good boy vanished. The Joe Biden who showed up to debate Paul Ryan had no intention of being taken down by the young gun seated across the table, and throughout the match he kept Ryan in a defensive crouch. Like a master thespian on opening night, Biden conspicuously deployed his entire bag of performing tricks: dramatic line-readings, asides to the audience, toothpaste smiles, exaggerated laughter. "I wasn't laughing at him," Biden would later insist. "I was laughing at some of the answers coming forward."[141]

The debate's most striking characteristic was the twenty-seven-year age gap between candidates. In the optics of televised debates, a generational difference can cut either way: the older candidate might look out of date and past his prime, or wise and experienced. The younger candidate might look fresh and energetic, or not ready for the big leagues. In this case, Biden's age worked in his favor; Ryan's youth worked against him. Biden won the debate not just by demoting Ryan from costar to supporting player, but by arguing the case that Barack Obama had failed to argue a week earlier. In focusing the debate on Mitt Romney, Biden helped reset the terms of engagement for the principals' subsequent town hall.

Throughout his ninety minutes upon the stage, the vice president reminded America that he is a larger-than-life character, a throwback to a time when, for better or for worse, picturesque politicians roamed our electoral landscape. Among campaign debaters, Biden-style theatricality is a rare commodity. Even rarer is the discipline to approach each debate with a distinct objective—and then carry out the plan.

SARAH PALIN (2008)

For one brief moment, before her public image hardened into self-parody, Sarah Palin stood poised to infuse something fresh into American presidential politics: a down-to-earth, next-door-neighbor sensibility that prized common sense over calculation, the wisdom of the people over the wisdom of the elites. Unfortunately for Palin, that moment lasted about as long as the forty-five minutes it took to deliver her star-is-born speech at the Republican National Convention. One month later, as she made her debut on the vice presidential debate stage, Sarah Palin had degenerated into a national punchline. Even a face-saving performance against Joe Biden could not wipe away the negative perceptions that clung to her like barnacles.

Televised debates had been a generally felicitous milieu for Palin during her Alaska gubernatorial campaign in 2006, first in the primary and then in the general election. As a former television sports reporter, the candidate approached debates with considerable technical skill, bolstered by unusually camera-friendly looks and a homespun style that lifted her apart from the standard bureaucratic politician. What Palin lacked in policy credentials she made up for in folksy charm. "Her métier was projecting winsomeness," wrote Joel Millman in the *Wall Street Journal*, "making a virtue of not knowing as much about the minutiae of state government because, for most of her adulthood, she was immersed in small-town life and raising a family."[142]

Yet behind the Everywoman façade lurked warning signs of the trouble ahead. Staffers tasked with preparing Palin for the debates in Alaska found her unfocused and incapable of absorbing information. During the events themselves, Palin relied heavily on handwritten, color-coded note cards, cribbing on the sly while her opponents delivered their responses. Asked during one forum to name a legislative bill with which she either agreed or disagreed, she came up blank. Although Palin got off some good lines, she also emanated a sense of being less than fully committed to the task at hand.

In 2008 this same disengagement resulted in a disastrous rollout for Palin's vice presidential campaign. Two national television interviews, first with Charles Gibson of ABC and then, more memorably, with Katie Couric of CBS, exposed in stark terms Palin's lack of preparedness. Even more devastating was comedian Tina Fey's spot-on *Saturday Night Live* imitation, which cemented the perception of Palin as a woman whose brain was as scrambled as her syntax. The weekend before Palin debated Biden, the Couric interview received a full *SNL* parody. Fey needed little help spinning Palin's words into comedy gold; the sketch-writers simply appropriated the actual transcript.

As though these public embarrassments were not enough, Palin's behind-the-scenes debate preps had deteriorated into chaos, playing out amid a backdrop of mistrust between candidate and handlers, internal power struggles, and a ticking clock that gave Palin limited opportunity to study. Palin's interview missteps heightened media chatter about her debate prospects, producing an atmosphere that mixed the soft bigotry of low expectations with breathless anticipation of an on-camera crack-up. "Not since Dan Quayle took the stage in 1988 have debate expectations for a major party candidate been as low as they will be on Thursday for Gov. Sarah Palin of Alaska," wrote Katharine Q. Seelye in the *New York Times*. In predebate coverage on NBC, Chuck Todd put it more bluntly: "The goal, really, is for Sarah Palin to survive."[143]

Survive she did, with an ease that belied her previous tribulations. Palin's performance against Biden brought back echoes of the perky hockey mom who enthralled the Republican convention. Winking, grinning, dropping her *g*'s, and pointedly ignoring the moderator, Palin projected what former Miss America Kate Shindle described to the *Washington Post* as the "cheerful aggressiveness" of a beauty pageant contestant: "part cheerleader, part news anchor, and part drill sergeant."[144]

Outgunned on substance, Palin took advantage of the format's ninety-second response times to unfurl talking points that required little talking. Even with this safety net, she occasionally diverged off-course, as when moderator Gwen Ifill asked whether any trigger might justify the use of nuclear weapons. "Nuclear weaponry, of course, would be the be-all, end-all of just too many people in too many parts of our planet," Palin replied. ("Mostly the end-all," wrote Maureen Dowd.)[145] Palin demonstrated no coherent political philosophy in the debate, nor anything approaching a mastery of policy details, but neither did she humiliate herself, as she had done in the encounters with Gibson and Couric.

On some level Palin's vice presidential debate performance seems almost miraculous. That she was able to pull it off is undoubtedly a credit to some innate competitive quality within Sarah Palin. But Palin's experience also affirms how superficial debates can be, especially when structured to elicit deliberately short responses that require memorization but no real thought.

MITT ROMNEY (2012)

As a debater Mitt Romney can be likened to a German luxury sedan: efficient but bloodless, sleek but unexciting—a product of engineering more than political passion. Romney hit his high-water mark with a well-conceived, well-executed victory over incumbent president Barack Obama in the first of their three clashes in 2012, and on balance the dozens of debates over Romney's career helped him more than hurt. His successful track record nonetheless contained significant trouble spots, weaknesses in delivery that the candidate never brought under control.

In his first high-profile debate in 1994, as Republican challenger to Senate fixture Ted Kennedy, Romney functioned essentially as a sacrificial lamb. That event brought to the fore several Achilles heels that would dog Romney throughout his debate career: sanctimoniousness, a sense of entitlement, and a tin ear. Asked to identify his greatest personal failing, Romney launched into a self-congratulatory peroration about the weekly visits he made to patients in Massachusetts hospitals. After the moderator interrupted to remind him that it was a question about a personal failing, Romney finally named "my inability to fulfill what I think is a God-given obligation to do more." In the same debate, Romney expressed outrage at distortions of his record in Kennedy's political ads, asking, "When will this end?" More than once, Kennedy reminded his opponent that perhaps the debate ought to focus on issues affecting the voters, not the candidates.

Over the next two decades of campaigns, narcissism became something of a trademark for Romney in debates. Shannon O'Brien, Romney's opponent in the Massachusetts gubernatorial race of 2002, detected in him a "lack of empathy."[146] Romney regularly provoked spats with moderators and opponents over such matters as whose turn it was to speak, how much time remained for answers, and whether debate rules had been violated—which is to say, violated at Romney's expense.

One of many examples: at a Republican primary forum in Las Vegas in 2011, Mitt Romney lost his cool and petulantly insisted that moderator Anderson Cooper make Rick Perry stop talking. The problem for Romney was that these outbursts animated him in a way that policy issues did not, creating the impression that what really mattered to Mitt Romney was Mitt Romney.

This tendency to place himself on a pedestal drove Romney's opponents crazy. In 2007, Republican primary candidate Rudolph Giuliani derided Romney's attitude about hiring undocumented immigrants as "holier than thou." Four years later, Newt Gingrich expressed frustration at Romney's attempts to depict himself as a political outsider, despite having served four years as governor, waged two campaigns for president, and one more for senator. "Can we drop the pious baloney?" Gingrich demanded. "Just level with the American people. You've been running since the 1990s."

Outsider or not, Romney did sometimes project an aura of not quite breathing the same air as his rivals on the debate stage. There was the famous moment in Iowa in which Romney challenged Rick Perry to a $10,000 bet over an arcane point of fact. As debate analyst James Fallows noted, "If Romney had said 'a million bucks,' it would obviously have been hyperbolic; if he had said 'a hundred bucks,' it would have been a serious sum but comprehensible. Romney had instinctively found exactly the wrong number."[147]

Perry, a particular thorn in Romney's side, inspired another verbal slip when the Texas governor accused his opponent of prevaricating about firing the undocumented workers who mowed his lawn. Romney, repeating what he had told the lawn service company, said, "I'm running for office, for Pete's sake, I can't have illegals." This unscripted remark provided ammunition to his critics and reinforced Romney's reputation for political expediency.

Awkward moments notwithstanding, Romney usually rose to the occasion in his primary debates in 2012, most notably when his survival was at stake. Heading into the Florida primary, with the quixotic candidacy of Newt Gingrich posing a late-breaking threat, Romney used debates in Tampa and Jacksonville to dispatch his rival. "When he needed a command performance," wrote Maggie Haberman in *Politico*, "he delivered."[148] Relentlessly attacking the Gingrich record, Romney not only caught his opponent off-guard, he halted Gingrich's momentum.

Mitt Romney brought this same battle-readiness to his opening face-off with Obama in Denver. In the opinion of journalist Jon Meacham, Romney gave "the strongest Republican debate performance in the history of televised debates," excluding the sainted Ronald Reagan.[149] Operating in an untested format, with two-minute opening statements followed by open-ended discussion, the candidates needed to move fast and think on their feet. Romney came across as the far more nimble performer, alert to his surroundings—and to the format—in ways that Obama was not. Romney eagerly exploited the presidential debate platform to unveil a new, improved version of himself, delivering a ninety-minute infomercial on Mitt Romney to 70 million viewers. Such an achievement could not have happened, of course, without the enabling passivity of Barack Obama.

Obama would not make the same mistake twice. In the town hall debate that followed two weeks later, the newly energized incumbent made it his mission to relegate Romney to playing defense. In the citizen-questioner format, Romney's physical stiffness and inability to connect with the live audience were glaringly apparent, especially in contrast with the looser Obama. Whenever Romney began a response with "I appreciate that" or "That's an important question," the words signaled his discomfort with the topics being raised: equal pay for women, a ban on assault weapons, immigration.

In the third debate, devoted to international matters, Romney faced the daunting challenge of seeming equal to the sitting president on affairs of state. Rather than trying to outfox Obama, Romney adopted a strategy of magisterial detachment, smiling tightly through the volley of criticism being fired by his rival. "Attacking me is not an agenda," Romney said, reworking a line that Bill Clinton first used in a debate with Bob Dole in 1996, but that was about the extent of his counterpunching. Romney drew positive notices from some for taking the high road, especially in contrast with the more belligerent Obama. Majority opinion, however, put Romney's losses at two in a row.

All debaters need a basic level of competence, and Mitt Romney exceeded that requirement handily. But when it came to recognizing his weaknesses and conquering them, Romney lacked the self-awareness to improve his performance to the necessary degree. Debates must be about the needs and concerns of the electorate; Romney's number one priority always seemed to be Romney.

PAUL RYAN (2012)

A potential outcome of any two-person debate is that one candidate forcefully claims the starring role for himself while reducing his opponent to sidekick status. Such was the predicament of Paul Ryan in his vice presidential match with Joe Biden in 2012. "We think he's going to come at me like a cannonball," Ryan told a radio host in the days before the debate,[150] yet Biden's opera bouffe performance appeared to catch Ryan by surprise; the young congressman was like a cartoon coyote unaware of the anvil looming overhead. By avoiding mistakes and keeping his cool, Ryan lived to tell the tale, but by the time closing statements rolled around, he had not cleared a path for himself through the tangle of Biden's exuberance.

In his congressional races in Wisconsin, Ryan had debated a string of opponents, none of whom gave him much fight. As Mitt Romney's surprise pick for running mate, the forty-two-year-old Ryan brought to the Republican ticket a fresh, youthful face and an inside-the-Beltway reputation as a policy wonk. *Washington Post* blogger Ezra Klein described the candidate as smart, well versed on issues, and eager to engage. "While he's a highly ideological thinker," Klein said, "he doesn't come off as particularly ideological. He comes off as an affable, decent, conservative guy who holds strong views, but recognizes that he doesn't have all the answers."[151]

Despite his popularity in Washington, at the national level Ryan remained a little-known commodity. Predebate, his aides sought to lower expectations by reinforcing Ryan's relative inexperience against Vice President Biden. As one spokesman reminded a reporter, Joe Biden was "the front-runner for the Democratic nomination when Paul Ryan was in high school."[152]

Coming into the debate, the congressman faced pressures that transcended the inevitable butterflies attending one's first time at the rodeo.

First, Mitt Romney's strong performance in the opening round against President Obama had sparked momentum for the Republican ticket, and it was now up to Ryan to perpetuate that forward motion. Joe Biden, naturally, had the opposite objective, thus setting the table for a potentially consequential vice presidential confrontation.

Second, on the day of the debate, *Time* magazine released from its vault a series of photos that featured Congressman Ryan working out at a gymnasium. Wearing shorts, T-shirt, earphones, and a backward ball cap, Ryan showed off his biceps, mugged for the camera, and in general made a fool of himself. His campaign admitted as much; an anonymous aide complained to CNN that *Time* had exercised "poor judgment" in publishing the photos just hours before Ryan's moment in the spotlight.[153] As a visual appetizer served just before the debate entrée, the widely viewed images reinforced Ryan's immaturity—exactly the wrong message to convey as he stepped before the largest audience of his career.

From the second he bounded onto the set, Paul Ryan's nervousness was apparent. In a fascinating postdebate interview on CNN, social psychologist and body language expert Amy Cuddy commented on what would become one of the event's signature visuals: the candidate's prodigious intake of water during the hour-and-a-half broadcast. Cuddy attributed this thirst to a case of anxiety-induced cotton-mouth. "[Taking a drink] is actually the first thing he did when he sat down," she noted. "So he was backstage, you know, 90 seconds earlier, yet still he had to come out and take a sip of water as soon as he sat down."[154] When *Saturday Night Live* aired its parody of the vice presidential debate, Ryan's water-gulping became a running gag.

In unintended ways Ryan's debate presentation exacerbated his youth. His wide eyes and prominent widow's peak gave him the countenance of a Japanese anime character, and in the relentless split-screens with Biden Ryan often resembled a puppy being scolded for leaving a mess on the floor. At times he would squirm in his chair or jerk his neck like a bobble-head doll, and his high-pitched, nasal voice lacked authority. In the view of *Politico*'s Roger Simon, as the debate progressed, "Ryan began looking younger and younger—and not in a good way."[155]

Furthermore, Ryan showed evidence of being a poor listener, which for debaters is a major no-no. At the end of the program, moderator Martha Raddatz cited a conversation she had had with an American soldier dismayed by the negativity of the presidential campaign of 2012. What would you say to him? Raddatz asked the debaters. And are you ever embarrassed by the tone?

Biden answered first, not very memorably. When Ryan's turn came, after the obligatory "Thank you for your service" and "We won't impose military cuts," the candidate reached his main point: "And then I would say, you have a president who ran for president four years ago promising hope and change, who has now turned his campaign into attack, blame and defame." For another 400 words, Ryan's anti-Obama rant persisted. The sheer cluelessness of this was stunning. Had Ryan even heard the soldier's question?

These missteps notwithstanding, the debate did not dent Paul Ryan's future prospects as a national politician. Vice presidential debates in particular have a way of either hurting or helping those who take part. In this instance, although Biden won the match by sheer force of personality, Ryan notched a valuable credential on his résumé.

6 / THE (

To complement the stars, presidential debates feature cast members who function in key supporting roles: the moderators, panelists, and citizen-questioners who have been an on-camera presence in every general election debate since 1960. In some cases, these scene-stealers may have affected outcomes. We can only wonder how the debate series of 1988 would have differed without anchorman Bernard Shaw's hypothetical question about the rape and murder of Kitty Dukakis. Or how Dan Quayle might have fared absent the sharp questioning of journalist-panelists who pressed him on his credentials. Or how George H. W. Bush would have come across had he better connected with the woman in the town hall audience who asked about his personal experience with the national debt.

In the tightly controlled world of presidential debates, the question-ers and their questions function as rare, much-needed wild cards. Although campaigns have influenced—sometimes controlled—the selection of moderators and panelists, interrogators have had free rein to pose whatever questions they choose. This freedom generates much of the tension that attends live debates, interjecting the element of surprise into a heavily stage-managed exercise. Campaign staffs labor mightily to anticipate questions, but in the end, the power of the query rests less with the debaters' preparedness than the interlocutors' spontaneity.

Format innovations in the past few rounds of presidential debates have dramatically altered the nature of how candidates are questioned. Gone are the press panels that once dominated the programs. Since 1996, debaters have answered questions posed either by a solo modera-tor or by members of a town hall audience. Although these new formats are not without their flaws, few observers lament the disappearance of the press conference debates of old—even the journalists who took part in them.

PRESS PANELS AND THE QUESTIONS THEY ASK

"Reporters should ask questions at news conferences and interviews—but not in debates," wrote David Broder. Like other traditionalists in the news media, Broder believed that journalists who appear on debate panels violate the separation of church and state by involving themselves as players: "Whether the question impales a candidate or offers him escape from the tight corner of the previous change, we are affecting history, not just writing its first draft."[1]

Expressions of ambivalence are not uncommon among reporters selected for debate panels. Jon Margolis of the *Chicago Tribune*, a questioner in the Bentsen–Quayle debate, said he had "mixed feelings" about being picked: "I knew you had to be approved by both campaigns, and that meant either they thought I was a harmless wimp or they thought I was fair and objective. I hope it was the latter."[2] Peter Jennings recalled feeling "very honored" to be chosen for the first Bush–Dukakis debate. "It's a dubious compliment," he said, "but it meant we were acceptable to both the Republicans and Democrats, reaffirming our own belief that we were fair people."[3]

Others view the matter in a more positive light. Jim Lehrer has made the point that just as lawyers and doctors are called upon to contribute to the public good, so do qualified journalists have a civic duty to serve in debates. "If we see ourselves as professionals," Lehrer said, "then we can't say no to this kind of invitation unless there's something that's improper about it."[4]

Some panelists have jumped at the chance to participate. Norma Quarles, a questioner in the vice presidential debate in 1984, received her summons shortly after being admitted to the hospital for surgery. Instead of proceeding with the operation, Quarles left her hospital bed in New Jersey to make the trip to Philadelphia. "I thought about saying no," she recalled, "but I considered this an opportunity of a lifetime."[5]

Jack White, a correspondent for *Time*, also selected for the Bush–Ferraro panel in 1984, felt pressure to accept on two fronts: as a magazine reporter and as an African American. White saw himself as representing *Time* but also standing in for black journalists, who had rarely been chosen for debate panels. "There were many things going on beyond 'Let me get up here and ask a dynamite question,'" he said. "There was also 'How are you coming across representing these other groups that don't get much chance to appear in these contexts?'"[6]

With the panel format out of fashion, the issue of journalistic participation has subsided, at least for the time being. But in the shift toward other structures, has the press ceded too much ground? In 1988, the last year in which media panels appeared in all three debates, political analyst Jeff Greenfield wrote an op-ed column in the *New York Times* defending journalists as questioners. "The much-maligned format," Greenfield said, "produced the most significant glimpses we have had into the thinking and character of the candidates since the general election campaign began on Labor Day."[7]

As one example, Greenfield cited a question from Annie Groer in the first Bush–Dukakis debate that forced Bush to address his murky stance on a woman's right to an abortion. Groer pointed out that Bush had taken several positions on the issue over the years, including support for a constitutional amendment that would outlaw most abortions. If abortions were to become illegal, Groer asked, should women who have them and doctors who perform them go to jail?

Bush's muddled response suggested that criminal sanctions indeed might be appropriate, sparking a quick postdebate clarification to the contrary by campaign manager James Baker. As Greenfield commented, "The exchange told us that in fact Mr. Bush hadn't pursued the subtleties of the abortion issue. It was exactly the kind of tough but fair prodding that debates are supposed to produce."[8]

Complaints against debate panelists' questions fall along several lines: the reporters play "Gotcha"; the questions are convoluted and tendentious; the topics focus too narrowly on the day's headlines. The loudest objections have come from fellow members of the press, as in a scathing column in 1992 by the *Washington Post*'s Mary McGrory. "Somehow the encounter is not so much to elicit information from the questioned," she wrote, "but to display the erudition of the questioner."[9]

Over the years, panel members have exposed themselves to carping on several fronts. Charles Warren, a panelist in 1960, received telephone calls from irate viewers after asking JFK why farms could not be operated like other businesses. One caller said, "I'm a farmer and you're a sonofabitch for asking Senator Kennedy a loaded question like that," while another warned, "You'd better watch out."[10]

Panelists draw even more notice *before* the debates, when they are inundated with suggestions for questions. A telegram delivered to the theater just before the first debate in 1976 urged a questioner to ask, "How soon do you think it will take for a complete Soviet take-over of the U.S.?" Annie Groer was offered $100 to pose a "nasty question about the personal life of one of the candidates." Andrea Mitchell's stint as a debate panelist in 1988 coincided with the dawn of fax machines, making for a sleepless predebate night at her hotel in Los Angeles. "Special interest groups were faxing suggested questions and ideas and background papers all night," Mitchell recalled, "and the hotel kept stuffing this rolled-up fax paper under the door and waking me up. It was like having hamsters in your room."[11]

Moderators and panelists routinely discard most over-the-transom suggestions. Occasionally, however, one finds its way into the broadcast. John Mashek, a panelist in the first debate of 1992 in St. Louis, used a question he had read in an article in the *St. Louis Post-Dispatch* in which citizens revealed what they would ask if they were on the panel.[12]

In deference to the gravity of the occasion, most journalistic participants have worked hard to polish their questions. Elizabeth Drew of the *New Yorker*, the first woman to serve on a debate panel, prepared for the first Ford–Carter appearance in 1976 much as the candidates themselves did. With help from a research assistant, Drew put together a notebook of information about various subjects that might come up. "And then I worked on and refined and refined the questions," she said.[13] Many other panelists report a similar process: organizing background materials by topic area, then honing specific questions.

"We all overprepared," said Peter Jennings. "We prepared to death. I remember an inordinate amount of constructing and deconstructing sentences, which I knew before and know subsequently is never the way to interview anybody." According to Andrea Mitchell, "The preparations are tough because what you're trying to do is come up with something that will elicit a revealing answer that hasn't been asked before and that they're not prepared for. And there's so much at stake."[14]

Sometimes a question is asked simply because it cannot be avoided. In the second debate of 1984, after Ronald Reagan had come under intense scrutiny in the wake of his faltering debate performance in Louisville, it fell to Henry Trewhitt of the *Baltimore Sun* to raise the issue of presidential competence. Because the stated theme of the debate was foreign policy, Trewhitt deliberately couched his query within that framework:

> You are already the oldest president in history, and some of your staff say you were tired after your most recent encounter with Mr. Mondale. I recall, yet, that President Kennedy . . . had to go for days on end with very little sleep during the Cuban missile crisis. Is there any doubt in your mind that you would be able to function in such circumstances?

Reagan, as we have seen, rejoined with what is regarded as a classic debate sound bite, leaving Trewhitt to deliver a less celebrated but no less amusing riposte: "Mr. President, I'd like to head for the fence and try to catch that one, but I'll go on to another question." In retrospect, Trewhitt wondered if he ought to have pursued his original line of inquiry. "I just let him go when I really should have said, 'Okay, fine, that's a wonderful line, Mr. President, but I really think you should try to address the question,'" Trewhitt noted. "I didn't do that because I thought it was such a good line."[15]

Beginning with the first question ever posed in a presidential debate, the tone of journalists' queries has often been aggressive. Bob Fleming of ABC News opened the debate in Chicago in 1960 by asking JFK for a response to Nixon's characterization of him as "naive and at times immature." Minutes later, Sander Vanocur questioned Nixon about a remark President Eisenhower had made at a news conference a month earlier; when pressed to name an idea Nixon had contributed to his administration, Eisenhower told reporters, "If you give me a week I might think of one."

In *Six Crises*, Nixon was still smarting from Vanocur's query, which he dismissed as being "of no substantive importance" and something that would "plague me the rest of the campaign." Nixon wrote that Eisenhower had phoned him to apologize for what had been intended as a "facetious" remark. "I am sure that to millions of unsophisticated televiewers, this question had been most effective in raising a doubt in their minds with regard to one of my strongest campaign themes and assets—my experience as vice president," Nixon said.[16]

Questions of a personal nature have propelled some of the sharpest exchanges in presidential debates. In 1984 Fred Barnes asked President Reagan (and Walter Mondale as well) for a description of his religious beliefs. After Reagan delivered a homily that invoked Mother, God, and Abraham Lincoln, Barnes moved in for the kill: "Given those beliefs, Mr. President, why don't you attend services regularly, either by going to church or by inviting a minister to the White House, as President Nixon used to do, or someone to Camp David, as President Carter used to do?" Reagan never did answer the question.

The vice presidential debate of 1988, in addition to probing Dan Quayle's fitness for office, offered other examples of pointed, personal interrogatories. Brit Hume asked the candidates to identify a work of literature, art, or film that had had a strong effect on them. Both debaters gave what seemed like well-coached responses that quickly segued into attacks on the opposition. But as CNN's media analyst Frederick Allen later pointed out, "When a debate panelist says to a candidate, 'Read any good books lately?' it's not a friendly question. It's asked with a certain degree of malice. It's asked in the secret hope that the answer will be 'I can't remember ever opening a book.'" Hume defended the query as one he had hoped would be "revealing of character." "I spent a lot of time trying to think of questions that might take them off the script, to illuminate something beyond the rap they have predigested and prememorized," he said.[17]

Tom Brokaw's first question to Quayle dealt with the plight of American families living in poverty: "I'd like for you to describe to the audience the last time that you may have visited with one of those families personally and how you explain to that family your votes against the school breakfast program, the school lunch program, and the expansion of the child immunization program." Unconvincingly, Quayle cited a stop at a food bank in Indiana, during which no one had asked him about those votes. Brokaw later explained, "I came to that question because one of the things I'm struck by is that so many politicians are isolated from real-life experience. I thought, looking at Quayle's experience and how he lived his life, it's worth finding out. I did think it was a legitimate question."[18]

In the first Bush–Dukakis debate of 1988, Peter Jennings took a similarly prosecutorial approach to Bush, reminding the vice president that he had said he was "haunted" by the lives of inner-city children. "If it haunts you so," Jennings asked, "why over the eight years of the Reagan–Bush administration have so many programs designed to help the inner cities been eliminated or cut?" Bush's fuzzy reply fell far short of the question. Soon after the debate, Jennings said, "George Bush took a disliking to me."[19]

Not all panelists have defined their role adversarially. Max Frankel, the *New York Times* reporter whose question to Gerald Ford led to the gaffe about Eastern Europe, saw his task in a different light. "I wasn't so much trained to fish for news on television, or to play any kind of game of 'Gotcha,'" he said. "My thought always was that the purpose of these things is to elucidate views."[20] In the debate in San Francisco, after Ford prematurely liberated Eastern Europe, Frankel gave the president an opportunity to dig himself out, an opportunity Ford did not take.

Another reporter from the old school was Harris Ellis of the *Christian Science Monitor*, a panelist in the lone Carter–Reagan debate of 1980. Ellis said he purposely shaped his debate questions to emphasize his own neutrality. "In those days, when TV on that scale was still relatively new, that is the way more journalists would have acted," he said. "Today I have the real feeling that many journalists distort their role before the television camera in challenging a president or candidate."[21]

PANELISTS' STRATEGIES

In their predebate meetings, panelists have sometimes previewed each other's questions in order to avoid duplication. But not always. Sander Vanocur, a questioner in the initial Kennedy–Nixon debate, recalled fearing that someone else would preempt his question about President Eisenhower's putdown of Vice President Nixon.[22] The four newsmen in that debate had no idea what topics the others would raise, which has also been true in subsequent programs. Essentially the matter of sharing questions is something each panel decides on its own.

Panelists in the vice presidential debate in 1976 not only read their questions to one another ahead of time but helped edit each other's copy. "We are to my knowledge the only panel that conspired to write the questions and to establish an order we wanted to ask them in," said Hal Bruno, a participant in that debate.[23] Bruno and his colleagues agreed to limit their questions to thirty seconds and pledged to avoid unnecessary follow-ups that might bog down the discussion.

Just before the telecast, the panel's prearranged sequence of questions bumped up against a last-minute obstacle. According to panelist Walter Mears of the Associated Press, two of the questioners decided to trade seats in order to maintain the order of topics they had agreed upon beforehand. "But when Dole's people heard about the switch, they objected, saying they had been preparing on the basis of the original order of questioning. I never did figure out how Dole could prepare for questions I might put as opposed to those Marilyn [Berger, another panelist] might ask."[24]

The three panelists in 1976's final debate carried the concept of collaboration one step further. In a meeting before the debate, they agreed that when the broadcast reached the sixty-minute mark, whoever had the floor would yield and ask the candidates to break format and directly question each other. Five minutes before air, Jack Nelson of the *Los Angeles Times* informed moderator Barbara Walters of the plan. "We had not told her in advance because we didn't want her to maybe scotch the idea or tell any of the producers of the program," Nelson said. "Of course, she didn't try to scotch it, but what happened was we didn't get the time cue." Thus was avoided what might have been one of the most spontaneous episodes in presidential debates. According to Nelson, "We intended to do that because we thought it would be better to have an actual exchange between the two candidates rather than what amounted to three separate press conferences."[25]

Perhaps the most unified group of questioners in debate history was the panel in 1988's Bentsen–Quayle match. The journalistic quartet of Judy Woodruff (PBS), Tom Brokaw (NBC), Brit Hume (ABC), and Jon Margolis (*Chicago Tribune*) functioned in a way debate panels almost never do, as a synchronized interrogation machine that hammered away at Dan Quayle's qualifications for the vice presidency. In their predebate gathering, the panelists discussed the value of follow-up questions and decided to join forces to hold the candidates' feet to the fire.

Hume said that by following up each other's questions, the panel hoped to circumvent the deliberately restrictive structure the campaigns had imposed. "I was last in the rotation, and it was agreed that I would keep my eye on questions that had been asked by my colleagues that might have gone unanswered," he explained.[26] In this capacity, Hume returned to Woodruff's opening question to Quayle about his qualifications for the job, and later Hume followed up his own follow-up. Each time, Quayle offered a response unsatisfactory to the panel.

Finally the rotation came back to Brokaw. "I had real mental anguish," Brokaw recalled. "I don't think Quayle's people will ever appreciate that, but I remember as it came around to me, I thought, 'Oh, God, do I want to ask this again?' But he was so inadequate in the first two answers, I thought in a way he deserved the third crack at it. Also I thought the country deserved to hear one more time what he would do as president. That's why we were there."[27] Brokaw's rephrasing led Quayle to liken himself to JFK. Which led to Bentsen's "You're no Jack Kennedy" line.

At the end of the day, how much difference have panelists' questions made in presidential debates? As Walter Mears pointed out, "For all the self-importance a lot of us like to put in our questions, debates have been more driven by things that were beside the point."[28] Mears cited Ford's gaffe about Eastern Europe and Dole's "Democrat wars" statement as examples of debate moments that sprang only indirectly from a panelist's question.

Furthermore, no matter what the question, clever candidates will always shape answers that match their political objectives. Robert Boyd of Knight Ridder Newspapers, a questioner in the Bush–Ferraro vice presidential debate, called the candidates' responses in that event a "classic dodge and feint." "They're pros at this," Boyd said. "There was no question they hadn't answered probably scores of times already before and there was no real way, and no desire, to trip them up."[29]

MODERATORS OF PRESS PANEL DEBATES

Under the old press panel format, some of television journalism's most venerated names stepped up to the microphone to moderate presidential and vice presidential debates. Barbara Walters, Bill Moyers, Judy Woodruff, Bernard Shaw, Howard K. Smith, Sander Vanocur, and Pauline Frederick are a few of the individuals who presided over press conference–style debates. Given the strictures of the format, their talents went largely underutilized. With a few notable exceptions, moderators of press panel debates have made only a limited contribution to the content of the discussion, serving less as interrogators than traffic cops and timekeepers.

In 1988, for the first time, debate moderators were given the opportunity to kick off the telecast with a question to each candidate. This change in rules made possible what is one of the most notorious exchanges between a debate moderator and a presidential candidate, Bernard Shaw's opening query to Michael Dukakis in the debate in debate Los Angeles: "Governor, if Kitty Dukakis were raped and murdered, would you favor an irrevocable death penalty for the killer?" Equally shocking to the audience as Shaw's question was Dukakis's dispassionate reply.

In the predebate meeting with fellow panelists Andrea Mitchell of NBC, Ann Compton of ABC, and Margaret Warner of *Newsweek*, Shaw had been reluctant to share his question, "petrified" that it would become known to Dukakis in advance. When the panelists pressed him, Shaw relented and read it to them precisely as he would read it on the air. Taken aback, Mitchell asked him to consider substituting the words "your wife" instead of citing Kitty Dukakis by name. The other panelists supported Mitchell—"delicately," according to one—but Shaw held fast. "We thought it was a little unseemly, a little undignified," Mitchell said. "And you have to think back to the context. This was before shock radio, tabloid television, the blurring of lines within the multiplicity of media, so we were a little uptight and stuffy."[30]

Shaw hoped that his question would be a "stethoscope" to probe Dukakis's attitude toward capital punishment: "Bush had been beating Dukakis severely about the head and shoulders, charging he was soft on crime. Many voters perceive seeing and hearing Dukakis but not feeling him. I asked that question to see if there was feeling." The idea had come to Shaw at two o'clock in the morning on the day of the debate. His initial worry was that Dukakis would "hit it out of the park," making Shaw seem too easy on the candidate: "I didn't know how he was going to answer. What surprised me was that he didn't stop to reflect at all before answering. It was as if he didn't hear the question."

At the end of the debate, Shaw recalled, "an eerie thing" happened: as he made his way from the stage to the CNN anchor booth, the audience silently parted to let him walk past. "Nobody said 'thanks' or 'good debate' or anything like that," Shaw said. "And then I realized I had walked through the Dukakis side of the hall, through his supporters. And that's when it struck me what impact my question must have had."[31]

Reaction to the question ran heavily against Shaw. Kitty Dukakis herself called it "inappropriate" and "outrageous." In *Time* magazine, Walter Shapiro wrote, "The question was in ghoulish taste, but it proved revealing." ABC's Hal Bruno, who had been at the debate, found himself seated next to Shaw the next day on the plane back to Washington. "He's a good friend; we were police reporters together in Chicago," Bruno said. "Bernie started talking about why he asked the question. And after my second scotch I said, 'Bernie—it was a shitty question.'"[32]

Though it is the Kitty Dukakis question that most viewers remember, Shaw had a similarly gruesome opener for George Bush. Quoting the Twentieth Amendment to the Constitution on the issue of presidential succession, Shaw asked Bush to comment on the possibility of Dan Quayle becoming president in the event of Bush's death. Midway through the question, after the words "if you are elected and die before inauguration day," Bush interrupted and exclaimed in mock horror, "Bernie!" The difference between this and the mechanical Dukakis response accentuated Bush's relative humanity.

Less notorious than Shaw's question to Dukakis was moderator Judy Woodruff's opening volley to Dan Quayle in the vice presidential debate in Omaha in 1988. Woodruff got the program off to a memorable start:

Senator, you have been criticized, as we all know, for your decision to stay out of the Vietnam War, for your poor academic record. But more troubling to some are some of the comments that have been made by people in your own party. Just last week former Secretary of State Haig said that your pick was the dumbest call George Bush could have made. Your leader in the Senate, Bob Dole, said that a better qualified person could have been chosen. Other Republicans have been far more critical in private. Why do you think that you have not made a more substantial impression on some of these people who have been able to observe you up close?

Quayle's programmatic, unsatisfying response started him down a perilous path. According to Woodruff, the decision to query Quayle about his qualifications was obvious. "I came to Omaha pretty much persuaded that I wanted to go to that first," she later said. "It was particularly relevant in Quayle's case because there were outstanding questions about his background and his selection."[33] Woodruff's sharply worded opener paved the way for her fellow panelists to pursue the issue.

It is interesting to note that all presidential debate moderators but one have come from the world of television. The exception is James Hoge, who as editor of the *Chicago Sun-Times* pulled duty at the vice presidential debate in 1976 between Walter Mondale and Bob Dole. Hoge is also unique in representing a news organization based neither in Washington nor in New York.

As moderator, Hoge found himself making a decision that would affect the substance of the event. The debate sponsors, Hoge said, had encouraged him to mediate if one of the candidates attempted to "demagogue" a response. "And when Dole gave his answer, the gist of which was that Democrats were responsible for all wars, his face screwed up and nasty, I was seconds away from saying, 'Excuse me, Senator Dole, but you really didn't answer the question. Would you take another stab at it?'" In his peripheral vision, Hoge could see Mondale signaling with a vigorous shake of the head that he did not want Dole interrupted. "I made a split-second decision," said Hoge. "It's their debate, they're the ones who are going to get elected, so I didn't intervene that way."[34]

Barbara Walters, moderating the first debate in 1984 between Ronald Reagan and Walter Mondale, began her opening remarks with a crisp rebuke of both camps' imperious tactics in selecting press representatives for the panel. Tersely explaining to the viewing audience the difficulties encountered in the process, Walters said: "As moderator and on behalf of my fellow journalists I very much regret, as does the League of Women Voters, that this situation has occurred."

"On reflection, I might have asked her not to do that," said Dorothy Ridings, president of the league at the time. Herself a newspaperwoman, Ridings sympathized with Walters's desire to stand up for journalists: "But for the historical record it probably would have been better if she didn't."[35] Ridings changed her opinion after screening the debate some ten years later with people who did not understand the context, and who found Walters's reference confusing. For their part, the campaigns scorned the moderator's impromptu editorial. "That was pretty badly received," recalled James Baker. "Everybody was a little pissed off," agreed one of Mondale's aides.[36]

The tartness of Walters's opening statement was consistent with her overall moderating style, an attitude that brooked no nonsense. When Mondale made reference to Lebanon, Walters sternly reminded him, "Foreign policy will be the subject of the next debate. Stop dragging it by its ear into this one." At another point, Walters congratulated the candidates for heeding her admonitions, saying, "You're both very obedient. I have to give you credit for that." In the view of the *Washington Post*'s television critic Tom Shales, Walters outdistanced both Reagan and Mondale in demonstrating leadership qualities. "She's a toughie," wrote Shales. "She laid it on the line."[37]

In some instances, the influence of the moderator is not evident to debate viewers because it manifests itself behind the scenes. According to panelists in the first match in 1988 between Bush and Dukakis, that program might have taken a dramatically different turn without the predebate intervention of moderator Jim Lehrer. Stories had appeared in the press speculating that the panelists might break format as a protest against the campaigns' high-handed tactics in choosing panelists. The *Washington Post* went so far as to suggest that the journalists "stand up at the outset, take off their microphones and tell Lehrer to launch a one-on-one exchange between the candidates—the one thing both campaigns have been trying to avoid."[38]

Joining Lehrer as panelists for that debate were Peter Jennings of ABC, John Mashek of the *Atlanta Constitution*, and Annie Groer of the *Orlando Sentinel*. In the group's preproduction meeting, Jennings argued for brushing aside the rules and forcing the candidates into direct engagement. According to those present, Lehrer steered the conversation back to an acceptance of the original terms. In the end, Jennings resigned himself to the inevitable. "You got hired by the rules and you played by the rules," he said.[39]

As in previous years, the panelists' frustration stemmed from restrictive format conditions imposed by the two campaigns. "We had some difficult moments because of the agreement," Lehrer said. "There was some discussion there about 'To hell with the rules; we can do any damn thing we want to,' and I kept saying we had made an agreement to come and do something. I felt it just as a matter of function, a matter of giving your word."[40]

The event came off as planned, and the panel stuck to its designated role. The discussions that took place among the journalists behind the scenes, however, would inspire Lehrer to write a novel in 1995 (later turned into a television movie) called *The Last Debate*, in which a quartet of reporter-questioners deliberately undertakes to sabotage a presidential candidate during a live televised debate. The idea for the book came to Lehrer as he left the hotel en route to the debate site at Wake Forest University. He was carrying a folder that contained his opening questions; as he walked past campaign officials from both sides, Lehrer commented to his wife, "'Boy, they would give anything to know what I've got in this folder.' That's when I started thinking . . . what if you were the candidate and you knew what the questions were going to be?"[41]

JIM LEHRER: "AMERICA'S MODERATOR"

"A moderator is like a body at an Irish wake," observed Bill Moyers, who performed the function in the debate in 1980 between Ronald Reagan and John Anderson. "You need it to have the party, but it doesn't say much."[42]

With the demise of the panel format, Moyers's description no longer fits; the corpse has risen from the dead. Though single moderators now operate with reasonable latitude, their task remains tricky: they must run a program negotiated by the participants, while simultaneously, and overarchingly, addressing the needs of the public. A moderator must be acceptable to each of the candidates and the debate sponsor, but also to constituent groups who lack direct veto power, namely, voters and the press. Moderators must be judicious and informed, telegenic and in control.

According to Janet Brown, executive director of the Commission on Presidential Debates, moderators need three sets of skills: "Great currency in the issues and the candidates. Extensive experience with live television, so that you can deal with the varied demands that it imposes. And perhaps most important, the moderator will remember that his or her job is not to compete with the candidates."[43]

History's most experienced moderator of general election presidential debates is Jim Lehrer, longtime anchor of *The NewsHour* on PBS. Between 1988 and 2012 Lehrer led the questioning in eleven presidential debates; he also moderated the vice presidential match in 1996. Over the course of Lehrer's twenty-four-year-run as moderator, debates evolved in subtle but important ways, granting moderators more power in the equation while simultaneously positioning them as targets for attack.

Jim Lehrer's first debate as moderator, the series opener in 1988 between Bush and Dukakis at Wake Forest University in Winston-Salem, followed a traditional press panel format; four years later, at the initial Bush–Clinton–Perot encounter in St. Louis, he would repeat this format. Lehrer's maiden voyage as a solo moderator came in the final debate in East Lansing, Michigan, in 1992. A clumsy compromise between Bush's and Clinton's campaigns gave Lehrer a solo shot at the candidates for the first half of the debate; halfway through the program, the format switched, and a panel of journalists joined him onstage for the remaining forty-five minutes.

The relaxed rules governing the first half of the debate in East Lansing in 1992 allowed Lehrer to operate free from the tyranny of the clock. "I was depending on my instincts and my experience to make sure it was fair, rather than time cues," Lehrer said. What Lehrer called "the hardest moment I've ever had in a debate" occurred during this telecast, when Ross Perot interrupted the dialogue to complain about the distribution of time. "Is there an equal time rule tonight?" a testy Perot asked. "Or do you just keep lunging in at will? I thought we were going to have equal time, but maybe I just have to interrupt the other two. Is that the way it works?" As Lehrer remembered the episode,

"I looked at him and I said with my eyes, 'Don't you dare accuse me of being unfair,' and he backed off."[44]

With three participants in the debates in 1992, another of Lehrer's challenges was devising questions of equal weight for each of the candidates. He explained, "I had to ask an apple, an apple, and an apple, always. If there was an edge to one, there had to be an edge to all of them. If there were lobs, they had to be lobs for all three." Lehrer was, he said, "free to choose every subject. There was no restriction on how much time was devoted to anything." This freedom both simplified and complicated his job.

Lehrer suffered a few anxious moments shortly before the debate in East Lansing, when he read his opening questions over the telephone to his wife and sounding board, novelist Kate Lehrer. Because she was in the middle of a book tour, Mrs. Lehrer had remained at the couple's home in Washington. "I told her the three questions and there was silence," Lehrer recalled. "I said, 'What's the problem?' and she said, 'You've got two apples and an orange.' She was very reluctant to say anything because she knew this was the worst time in the world." Realizing she was right, but fearing he would not have time to rewrite his questions, Lehrer set out for the debate hall. Although the Secret Service had planned the route in advance, they did not account for Lehrer's limo being delayed at a railroad crossing, which unexpectedly gave the moderator the time he needed to fashion a last-minute substitution.

In 1996, with only two debaters per program, and the precedent of the single-moderator format under his belt, Lehrer faced new challenges at the first Clinton–Dole debate in Hartford. To begin with, the candidates had tightened the rules, giving the moderator less elbow room than he had had in 1992. Furthermore, Bob Dole's twenty-point lag in the polls had led to press speculation about a debate "surprise," a dramatic gesture that Dole might make in order to turn the race around.

With this possibility in mind, Lehrer devised a contingency plan. "If either candidate violated the rules—their rules, not my rules—I was not going to step on the event," he said. "Once they broke their own rules, I was going to let it play to its natural conclusion, then say, 'Gentlemen, you have violated the rules. We can negotiate some new ones right here in front of everybody or we can continue this thing wide open—your decision.' I was all prepared to do that. And of course, nothing like that happened."

In the Gore–Bush debates of 2000, all three of which Lehrer moderated, the PBS newsman did find himself cast as a referee. "We had one candidate [Bush] who really wanted those rules enforced," Lehrer said. "We had another candidate [Gore] who had agreed to the rules, who wanted to push them a little bit." This tendency became most obvious when Al Gore intruded into his opponent's space in the town hall debate. "I was stunned when that happened," Lehrer recalled. As moderator, his first thought was how he would proceed if the maneuver escalated into a confrontation. "I'm sitting there thinking what in the world am I going to do?"[45] As it turned out, Bush managed to dispatch Gore singlehandedly.

It bears mention that although moderators have a ringside seat for presidential debates, they often perceive the experience differently from how it plays on television. In the first debate in 2000, Lehrer failed to notice the sighing and eye-rolling that generated so much negative commentary for Al Gore. Immediately after the debate, when Lehrer's daughter remarked on Gore's theatrics, Lehrer had to ask what she was talking about. Because he had decided early in the telecast to direct his gaze only at the person who was speaking, the moderator—the person in closest proximity to the candidates—had missed Gore's reactions.

The divisive election cycle of 2000 placed Jim Lehrer in a difficult spot as moderator. In previous rounds, his performance had drawn almost uniformly positive reviews. After the debates in 1996, for example, the *New York Times*'s television critic Walter Goodman praised the subtlety of Lehrer's approach. "This man of modest mien keeps the spotlight on the person being questioned," Goodman wrote. "His somewhat halting conversational manner invites rather than commands. And his professional principles dispel any fears that he is out to get not just his guests' point of view but also the guests themselves."[46]

But a story that ran in the *Times* the morning of the final debate in 2000 raised the charge that Lehrer "did not sufficiently probe the candidates in the first two debates and was not particularly aggressive in following up his questions." The article, by reporter Richard Berke, quoted Senator Bob Kerrey of Nebraska as saying, "You could have picked ten people off the street who didn't know Jerusalem from Georgia and they would have had better questions." Although most of the criticism came from Democrats, some Republicans also complained that Lehrer had not done enough to rein in Al Gore. In his defense, Lehrer told Berke, "If somebody wants to be entertained, they ought to go to the circus. They ought to go to the movies. Or they ought to go to the ball- game. I didn't sign on to entertain people for 90 minutes three times. These have been tremendous exercises for democracy."[47]

Other critics complained that Lehrer was too much of a Washington insider to effectively hold the debaters accountable. Jack Shafer of *Slate* said, "He's so plugged into a civil, placid, friendly, unaggressive Wash- ington that it speaks poorly of the political process and the press in general that this is the guy who gets picked to moderate the debates. Fairness is overrated if fairness means challenging nobody."[48] In Leh- rer's view, however, being an insider conferred advantages. "I'm not dealing with a bunch of strangers," he said, "and they're not dealing with a stranger, which gives me a tremendous leg up. They've agreed to let me do this, so they have some level of trust in me that gives me a lot more latitude and a lot more confidence to do what I want to do."[49]

Lehrer's mixed reviews in 2000 may have stemmed in part from his role as moderator of all three of that year's presidential debates, a con- centration of responsibility that debate sponsors have since avoided. In 2004 and 2008, when Lehrer moderated only the first debate of the series, the complaints largely vanished, though Lehrer's attempt to provoke Barack Obama and John McCain into direct engagement did generate a degree of media tut-tutting. "He sounded like a marriage counselor," said Jessica Yellin on CNN. "Turn to your partner and share with them how you feel."[50]

As it happened, Lehrer's final debate as moderator, the opening match in 2012 between Obama and Mitt Romney, also precipitated the stron- gest backlash. Operating under a new, looser format that emphasized candidate interaction over moderator-driven Q-and-A, Lehrer was viewed by critics as being insufficiently in control. The lopsidedness of Obama's loss in that debate intensified the spotlight on Lehrer, sparking a na- tional discussion about the purpose of debate interlocutors. Should moderators introduce topics, keep time, and otherwise stay out of the way? Or is their job to challenge evasions, probe with follow-ups, and actively set the conversational agenda?

Reaction fell largely but not wholly along partisan lines, with those on the left tending to criticize Lehrer and those on the right supporting him. Richard Kim in the *Nation* wrote, "The Lehrer/PBS school of moderation is fundamentally unequipped to deal with the era of post-truth, asymmetric polarization politics—and it should be retired." Peggy Noonan in the *Wall Street Journal* applauded Lehrer as "old-school and a pro. He didn't think it was about him. How quaint."[51]

"The thing that surprised me," said Lehrer, "was the ferocity of the comments and hostility level. I think in retrospect we didn't do enough to tell people what was going to happen, and so they were expecting another routine kind of debate." From Lehrer's perspective, the debate unfolded the way it was supposed to. "I am confident this is the way to go," he told *Politico* at the height of the controversy. "It's more revealing than any other format I've seen."[52]

After two days of pummeling, the Commission on Presidential Debates issued an unprecedented statement of support for Lehrer, asserting that the format had called for "minimal interference by the moderator" and that Lehrer had "implemented the format exactly as it was designed." According to debate commissioner Michael McCurry, "Given his record as a moderator, he deserved something better than the blasting he was taking."[53]

The legacy of the open format of 2012 remains to be seen. The legacy of Jim Lehrer, however, seems secure, resting as it does on his two key contributions to the institution of presidential debates: first and most obviously, the programs he moderated, and second, less visibly, his work as a proponent and scholar of presidential debates. In Lehrer's writing about the topic and most particularly in his detailed video interviews with nearly all of America's presidential and vice presidential debaters, he has added greatly to our understanding of the process.

OTHER DEBATE MODERATORS, 1992–2000

The first single moderator of a general election debate was not Jim Lehrer. That distinction belongs to Hal Bruno, who as political director of

ABC News moderated the boisterous vice presidential match in 1992 between Al Gore, Dan Quayle, and Admiral James Stockdale. Though deemed a "slugfest" and a "free-for-all" in the press, this debate also broke ground as the first to dispense with a panel of questioners. Minus any journalistic sidekicks, Bruno had his hands full with this raucous conversation, which is best remembered for two things: the aggressive posture of Quayle and Gore toward each other and, more famously, the excruciating disconnectedness of Stockdale.

"About three or four minutes into it, I realized, oh my God, this is trouble," Bruno recalled. Stockdale's rhetorical opening questions, "Who am I? What am I doing here?" had caught the moderator, as well as the audience, off guard. "That's when I realized how much out of his element he was," Bruno said. "Somehow I established kind of a mystic eye contact, and I could tell when he wanted in or out. About halfway through, I really did feel that this poor guy had no business being there."[54]

As for Gore and Quayle, "They really were absolutely wild with each other," Bruno said. "Gore was going after Quayle, Quayle was going after Clinton." When Stockdale announced that he had missed a question because his hearing aid was off, Bruno stopped himself from blurting out, "You may be the luckiest man in America."

Bruno's performance as moderator drew a mixed reaction. Some observers thought he ought to have been more forceful, while others believed he was correct to let Gore and Quayle go at it. "It's hard to judge when you're sitting there," Bruno said. "I took the attitude that as moderator I was to be like a potted palm, just simply steer the discussion, see that they got their time."

Like other moderators before and since, Bruno considered himself hamstrung by the "rigid structure" drawn up in advance by campaign negotiators. Both of the major party candidates, he said, "were programmed to say certain things no matter what, so you let them do that and try to snap them back to the question. But in that format there wasn't time to get them back." Bruno also felt constrained by the set, which placed the three debaters at individual lecterns, physically segregated from the moderator and from one another. Bruno would have preferred gathering everyone around a table, an arrangement whose logic was too radical for the negotiators who drafted the memorandum of understanding.

These challenges notwithstanding, Bruno found the experience exciting. "I'm not blasé about it at all," he said. As a young reporter, Bruno had been present in the studio at WBBM in Chicago for the first Kennedy–Nixon debate. Thirty-two years later, he made debate history on his own.

Carole Simpson, Bruno's colleague at the ABC News Washington Bureau, also entered the history books when she moderated the first-ever town hall debate in Richmond with George Bush, Bill Clinton, and Ross Perot in 1992. Simpson got the job, she said, because of a "flukey thing" that occurred that year. The three broadcast networks had proposed a series of three debates, each to be hosted by a major network anchorman. When that plan fell through, NBC and CBS barred its employees from participating as moderators or panelists, leaving ABC the only over-the-air network still in the mix. As a result, ABC News was represented in three of the four debates in 1992. "Things happen for a funny reason," Simpson said. "I'm sure had they come to ABC and said, 'Give us one of your anchors to moderate this debate,' I would not have been at the top of the list."[55]

Simpson's experience was in some ways more taxing than that of either Lehrer or Bruno, since she was inaugurating a riskier, untested format. Recalled Simpson, "I had been watching presidential debates all my career, and of course they had always been panels of journalists questioning the candidates, so this was totally different. There wasn't anything to go back and look at to see how to do this." Simpson said she was surprised to discover how much leeway the written debate agreement gave her. "The only things it said I had to do were to make sure they each had a closing statement of two minutes, that no one would dominate, that we would cover both domestic and foreign issues, and that I could follow up and press a question," she said. "I had all kinds of latitude to do things that I thought were necessary to get the people to question the candidates."

Though praised by many, Simpson did not emerge from the experience unscathed. In the days that followed, some Republican campaign officials openly charged that she had skewed the debate by the tone she set in her predebate audience warm-up, and by her choice of on-air questioners. Simpson spent about half an hour with the town hall audience before the telecast began. "I said, 'I want an idea of the kinds of questions you want to ask,' and they wanted to stand up and read me their questions," Simpson recalled. "And I'm going, 'No, no, no, I don't want to know your questions; I just want to get a sense of the issues you're concerned about because my job is to see that you get answers from these candidates to the questions that concern you the most.'" The issues the audience raised, Simpson said, were considerably more substantive than those reporters and the campaigns had been focusing on.

Early in the debate, when President Bush attempted to bring up Bill Clinton's draft status, Simpson invited the audience to share with the candidates what they had told her in the warm-up. "I thought given the guidelines that I had a perfect right to bring up my discussion with the audience in which they indicated that they did not want to hear about things like that. And I said, 'Would some of you like to express to the candidates what you told me?' and that's when the man with the pony tail got up and said, 'We want an end to the mudslinging, we're tired of the negative campaigns.'"

Simpson's critics charged that she had preselected the audience members whose questions ultimately made it on the air. In fact, that task fell to producer Ed Fouhy, who communicated his instructions to Simpson through her earpiece. As Simpson described it, "He was just trying to balance the audience, so that we got men, we got women, we got minorities. . . . We'd go from one side to another side. I had no control over that. I was being told who to go to, and purely based on where they were located, not because we knew what their questions were or anything like that." Fouhy confirmed this. "I was in her ear throughout, and I was telling her who to go to next," he said. "To suggest that somehow those questions were screened . . . it's simply not true."[56]

Simpson said that the accusations of question planting hounded her after the debate. "It was widely talked about on the Rush Limbaugh show," she said, "and I even got death threats. The Republicans had put out this line that I was pro-Clinton and that I had tried to make George Bush look bad." Bush himself sent Simpson a thank-you note, commenting that she had done a fair, professional job. "I have it framed," she said, "because people were so accusatory that I had made George Bush blow it. I didn't make George Bush blow it."

In a campaign postmortem at Harvard's Kennedy School of Government, Bush's aide Fred Steeper denounced the "iron hand" that Simpson exercised as moderator. His reasoning offers insight into campaign thinking on whom debates should rightfully serve. "Her interest seemed to be more to get as many questions as possible out of the audience, rather than having the candidates speak," Steeper said. "Somehow the audience's interest was more important than the interests of the three campaigns."[57] According to this view, even the "people's debate" belonged to the candidates.

In 1996 and 2000 all but one of the general election debates were moderated by Jim Lehrer. For the vice presidential match in 2000, Bernard Shaw of CNN returned for his first debate since the notorious Bush–Dukakis encounter in Los Angeles in 1988, when he opened by asking how Michael Dukakis would feel about capital punishment if his wife were raped and murdered. In view of that earlier episode, Shaw's selection came as somewhat of a surprise. "The question will follow me to my grave," Shaw told a reporter in advance of the Cheney–Lieberman debate in 2000. "My only defense is, since when did a question hurt a politician? It's not the question, it's the answer that counts."[58]

The Kitty Dukakis question hovered over debate preps for both Dick Cheney and Joe Lieberman. Cheney's mock debate team practiced what one insider called "Shaw-style questions"—highly personal queries designed to provoke an emotional response. Lieberman watched a tape of the Bush–Dukakis debate "in pained silence," adding, "God only knew what [Shaw] was cooking up for us."[59] Neither candidate, as it turned out, had reason to worry. In the vice presidential debate of 2000, Bernard Shaw proved to be a low-key, thoughtful moderator.

DEBATE MODERATORS: 2004, 2008, AND 2012

In 2004, for the first time in twelve years, each of the general election debates featured a different moderator: Jim Lehrer for the opener, Charles Gibson of ABC News for the town hall, Bob Schieffer of CBS News for the final debate, and Gwen Ifill of PBS for the vice presidential joint appearance. This mixture of personalities lent each event a slightly different flavor, adding variety and interest.

In preparation for her debate with Dick Cheney and John Edwards, Gwen Ifill enlisted research assistance from the staff of PBS's *NewsHour*, for which she served as a correspondent. She also sought counsel from her colleague Jim Lehrer, who advised her "that I shouldn't even tell my closest personal friend what I was thinking of asking. Because if anything was clear, it was that in the same way that the candidates were going to try to control the rules of the debate, they were going to spend a lot of effort and time trying to figure out what kinds of questions I would ask."[60] Ifill cast her net wide, compiling background on a "zillion things" and turning her dining room table into "debate central," where she organized material into about fifty subject areas. From this she devised about forty questions, twice as many as she ended up using.

"Preparing for that debate was probably the hardest thing I've ever done," Ifill said, "because I had to find a way to distill to their essence the most important issues that these men needed to be heard on, and also because I couldn't consult with anyone. And then on top of it all, try to find a way to boil it down to a question that might elicit an answer instead of a speech."

Once she arrived in Cleveland for the debate, Ifill was chagrined to discover that she had been assigned to the same hotel as John Edwards, whose quarters were just down the hall. "Every time I walked into and out of my room I would cover my face and sneak in," she said. "There were usually staffers in the hallway who knew me, and I would just wave and duck back into the room, because the last thing I wanted to do was have even a casual conversation with a campaign worker prior to the debate." This self-imposed isolation extended to the debate set itself, where in the moments before the program began, the candidates and the moderator all sat in awkward silence, barely acknowledging one another's presence. "I'm sitting there mostly looking down at my papers, because I don't want to be drawn into any kind of friendly eye contact or chitchat with them in advance," she remembered. "I think it's really important not to give a vibe to either candidate that I am more friendly or less friendly to one or the other."

Gwen Ifill returned to the debate stage four years later as moderator of the Biden–Palin event, history's most-watched vice presidential debate. This time Ifill's preparation resulted in literal injury when three days before the debate she tripped on a stack of research materials at her home and broke her ankle. At Washington University in St. Louis, where the debate took place, Ifill was assigned two solidly constructed student athletes to help her maneuver onto the set—"crutch patrol," in the words of Janet Brown of the debate commission.[61]

Beyond a broken ankle, Ifill faced another challenge in 2008. Heading into the debate, right-wing commentators raised objections to a book Ifill was writing about African American politicians, denouncing it as pro-Obama agitprop, even though the work had not yet been completed. This supposed bias quickly established itself as an article of faith among conservatives. "Frankly," said John McCain on Fox News, "I wish they had picked a moderator that isn't writing a book favorable to Barack Obama—let's face it."[62]

Ifill weathered this trumped-up tempest-in-a-teapot and emerged with her reputation intact. "The broken ankle, strange as it may seem, actually helped me get through that book storm," she said. "Between dealing with that and preparing for the debate itself I had no time or energy to deal with what I considered to be an unfair attack on my integrity."[63]

Predebate attacks on moderators have become increasingly common in recent campaign cycles, particularly from the right. In 2012 vice presidential moderator Martha Raddatz briefly came under fire when it was revealed that more than two decades earlier Barack Obama had attended her wedding to second husband Julius Genachowski. At the time, Obama and Genachowski were colleagues at Harvard Law School; the marriage later ended in divorce. A statement from Raddatz's employer, ABC News, dismissed the complaints as "absurd."[64]

Like Raddatz, Candy Crowley of CNN found herself at the center of a predebate dust-up in 2012, but this time the grumbling came from both sides—and it did not stop when the debate ended. Crowley's announcement as moderator of the Obama–Romney town meeting had begun on a high note: Crowley would be the first female moderator of a presidential debate since Carole Simpson twenty years earlier (Gwen Ifill's two debates were both vice-presidentials).

The issue of woman moderators had come to the fore thanks in large measure to three female high school students from New Jersey. What began as a classroom project morphed into a national crusade to ensure gender balance among the slate of moderators in 2012. Their petitions calling for female representation in the presidential debates drew tens of thousands of signatures, attracting high-profile endorsements and extensive media coverage. Crowley's choice as moderator constituted a victory for the students, even as other groups charged that the all-Caucasian roster failed to reflect the diversity of modern America.

For the past several election cycles, the debate commission has released the names of moderators several weeks prior to the debates. This has been a largely positive development, bringing an end to the campaigns' behind-the-scenes dominance of the selection process. But it also creates opportunity for backlash, inviting a level of predebate scrutiny that intensifies with each cycle. Advance announcement poses a further practical challenge: how should the journalists chosen as moderators comport themselves professionally in the weeks before the debate? As Jeremy Peters wrote in the *New York Times*, "A role that once stood as a crowning and coveted journalistic achievement is now subject—before a question has been asked—to partisan rancor in this hyper-politicized climate."[65]

Jim Lehrer, Bob Schieffer, and Martha Raddatz essentially withdrew from the media spotlight prior to their debates in 2012. Candy Crowley, by contrast, talked eagerly with journalists, not just about her selection as town hall moderator but about how she intended to approach the job. Crowley mused that she would step in as necessary to seek clarifications and ask follow-ups—both prohibited, according to the negotiated rules. As she told *Politico*, "I'm not a fly on the wall."[66]

In a highly unusual display of comity, Obama's and Romney's campaigns voiced their concerns about Crowley in a joint letter to the debate commission, which in turn relayed those concerns to Crowley. But neither Crowley nor the commission had signed the campaigns' memorandum of understanding, essentially allowing the moderator complete editorial control. During the debate, when Crowley backed up Obama's version of the White House's response to the attack on the U.S. consulate in Benghazi, Republicans saw their worst fears come true. "We were furious," said Romney's adviser Stuart Stevens. More than a year after the debate, Mitt Romney was still fuming, telling a radio interviewer, "She obviously thought it was her job to play a more active role in the debate than was agreed upon by the two candidates."[67]

Something similar had occurred in the town hall debate in 2008 in Nashville when moderator Tom Brokaw ignored the format negotiated by the campaigns and asked his own questions—to the exclusion of the voters who had been assembled as interlocutors. "Tom just decided he was going to do it the way he wanted to do it, and he did," said debate commissioner Frank Fahrenkopf.[68] After only a single question from the audience, Brokaw jumped in with a query of his own for John McCain: whom would he select as his treasury secretary? "Not you, Tom," McCain shot back.

The Obama–McCain town hall, one of the least satisfying presidential debates on record, underscores the downside of using big-name television personalities as moderators: too often they make the event about themselves. "I wonder about having network anchors in the moderating job," said John Reade, who served as CBS's pool producer for Brokaw's debate. "There's another game being played at the same time: that particular anchor's reputation. It can become intrusive."[69]

In fairness to Crowley and Brokaw, the mission of town hall moderators is difficult to get a fix on. Press critic Jay Rosen defined the job as "a kind of ventriloquism" in which the authority of the moderator gets mixed up with the authority of the citizen-questioners. With no one in full command, Rosen wrote, "the situation is in charge."[70] For risk-averse campaigns, this lack of clarity is particularly unsettling. In the view of Obama's adviser Anita Dunn, who portrayed Candy Crowley in mock debates, "When you have to spend as much time preparing for a moderator as you do for your opponent, there's something wrong with the system."[71]

The last controversy-free audience participation debate was the 2004 town hall between George W. Bush and John Kerry, moderated by Charles Gibson of ABC News. In choosing the questions that would be asked, Gibson felt he had considerable latitude in shaping the debate's content. "The fact that they allowed me to make up the rules and then to pick out the questions was really very empowering," he said. "I thought that in the end the public was pretty well served by the evening."[72] Indeed, the program stands as a positive example of town hall moderation, with Gibson keeping the focus on the audience and its questions.

Another positive role model is Bob Schieffer of CBS, who as moderator of the closing debates in 2004, 2008, and 2012 delivered consistently admirable performances. The table format of the Obama–McCain and Obama–Romney debates proved particularly well suited to Schieffer's relaxed, conversational style.

This close proximity also gave the moderator a unique view of the candidates under pressure. "When Obama was speaking, McCain was furiously taking notes, squirming around in his seat," Schieffer recalled. "But when McCain was speaking, Obama never took a note. The only thing he ever did with his pen and pad—I looked over at one point and he was just drawing straight lines across the pad. And I wondered, is this some kind of Zen exercise?"[73]

Like other moderators, Schieffer devoted extensive preparation to the debates he moderated. For each event, the veteran CBS newsman reached out to a wide network of sources, conducting informational interviews with politicians, policy experts, and academics. The final question of the debate in 2004 was inspired by Schieffer's twenty-two-year-old assistant, Kelly Rockwell, who urged her boss to invite the candidates to talk about their wives. Just before closing statements, Schieffer noted that he, Bush, and Kerry were all married to "strong women" and the fathers of two daughters. "What is the most important thing that you have learned from these strong women?" he asked. Both debaters responded with heartfelt personal remarks about their wives and daughters.

According to Schieffer, this came to be the question that "generated the most comment and the most pickup." The query also provoked some carping, which Schieffer addressed in a postdebate appearance on his Sunday morning talk show, *Face the Nation*: "These critics said I wasted valuable time just to get a Hallmark card moment. Well, they caught me, and I plead guilty. As our campaigns have become nastier and nastier, I think we all deserve a Hallmark moment from time to time. I hope the candidates give us a few more down the line. We know for sure there'll be no shortage of that other stuff."[74]

Schieffer had carefully plotted another question in that debate, one that led to John Kerry's ill-considered reference to Vice President Cheney's lesbian daughter. Schieffer asked the candidates, simply, "Do you believe homosexuality is a choice?" Bush answered that he didn't know, and proceeded to restate his opposition to gay marriage. Kerry said he did not see homosexuality as optional, and cited Mary Cheney as an example. Schieffer had been concerned that the question might seem homophobic, so he first ran it by a number of gay friends and acquaintances who assured him it was not. "It seemed to me that was the key question," Schieffer said. "John Kerry, I thought, gave quite a good answer, had he not mentioned the vice president's daughter."

A couple of nights before the debate, Schieffer had a dream in which he ran out of questions while moderating the program. "I literally woke up in a cold sweat and was determined that that wouldn't happen," he said. "As it turned out, I had tons of questions, more questions than they ever got to."

Although Bob Schieffer had been a fixture on television news since the 1960s, moderating his first presidential debate gave him pause, especially in the minutes before the telecast began. "As I was backstage, for the first time in I'll bet about thirty years, I got butterflies," he said. "I'm thinking to myself, the presidency could actually turn on what happens tonight, and I really was a little nervous about it." He calmed down when he thought about how unnerved the debaters themselves must feel. Months later, when Schieffer ran into George Bush, he asked him if he had been nervous that night. "Hell, yes, I was nervous," Bush responded. "How would you feel?"

After three debates as moderator, Schieffer has said that he plans to "quit while I'm ahead." His advice for future moderators? "The American people are not electing a moderator. They're electing a president of the United States, and this is not a place where you come to demonstrate how smart you are. You have one job, and that is to give the American people a better understanding of the people who are running for president."

BUILDING A TOWN HALL AUDIENCE

In every election since 1992, ordinary citizens have stepped up to the microphone and participated as presidential debate questioners. To the delight of some observers and the chagrin of others, these average

Americans have queried the candidates on a vast range of subject matter, with frequently illuminating results.

Because the town meeting has historically been a tricky format, campaign negotiators impose numerous restrictions on citizen-questioners and how they function. The first town hall debate in 1992 encouraged a relatively free-flowing dialogue between audience members and candidates, and gave the moderator complete discretion in choosing topics and questioners. Four years later, the campaigns abolished follow-up questions and reined in the moderator.

The rules tightened further after the town hall in 1996, when two audience members asked nearly identical questions about gay rights. In order to guarantee a broad distribution of topics, town hall participants since 2000 have been required to submit their questions in writing to the moderator, who then selects which ones will be used. Audience members do not know in advance whether they will be called upon.

The memorandum of understanding negotiated by the Bush and Kerry campaigns in 2004 added new restrictions: the questioner's microphone had to be cut after the question was asked, and moderators had to silence anyone who departed from the question as originally worded. Additionally, the rules required moderators to "ensure" an equal number of questions about foreign and domestic issues during the debate, no matter what the people in the hall wanted to discuss.

In their quest to reduce unpredictability, campaign officials also strive to shape the composition of the town hall audience. In the first few presidential town hall debates, this meant audiences of undecided voters; more recently campaigns have preferred "uncommitted" voters—those who express a preference for one candidate over the other, but who might still be persuaded to change their minds.

Town meeting participants are screened and selected by the Gallup organization, which starts with a random sample of voters in the host city. Researchers then conduct telephone interviews to determine whether potential questioners support a particular candidate, and how strongly; interviewees are not told they are being considered for inclusion in the town hall debate. Although the campaigns approve Gallup's screening questionnaire, they play no direct role in the interview process or in deciding who gets to be in the audience. (In 1996 the Secret Service removed fourteen individuals from the list of possible questioners when background checks revealed they were convicted felons.)[75]

Negotiators for George W. Bush instigated the switch from undecideds to uncommitteds in recognition of how few voters remained undecided in the election of 2004. Polling data also indicated that those who had not made up their minds tended to be anti-incumbent. "We didn't think you could really know anything about undecideds," said Bush's lead negotiator, James Baker. "You have no idea where they're coming from. And so it would almost be better to have soft supporters on each side and have an equitable way to call on them."[76]

Limiting the town hall audience to undecided voters had long been controversial. According to Monica Crowley, an aide to Richard Nixon, the former president was "horrified" by the first town meeting debate in 1992. "Wasn't that format miserable?" Nixon asked Crowley. "It made them all look bad. They claimed that it was an 'audience of undecideds.' Undecideds? Selected by whom? Come on. Undecideds don't know very much because they don't care!"[77]

Nixon's point is well taken. By limiting questioners to those who have not made up their minds, organizers of town hall debates run the risk of dumbing down the intellectual content. In every town meeting debate since the format's introduction in 1992, the principal criterion for participation was not having settled upon a candidate. But are these the most appropriate individuals to elicit information from would-be presidents? Might it be more enlightening to hear from politically engaged citizens?

A second problem occurs with audiences made up exclusively of uncommitted voters: they tend not to reflect the national populace, or even the populace of the city in which the debate takes place. Carole Simpson recalled being surprised to spot only five African Americans among the Richmond questioners in 1992; given the town's racial composition, she had expected a more diverse crowd. "How Gallup had chosen them was to go with people who were undecided. Most African Americans had decided they were going to vote for Clinton, so that's why they weren't part of the audience," she said.[78]

As the national electorate polarizes into distinct camps, it becomes increasingly difficult to identify neutral voters for town hall audiences. For the debate in Nashville in 2008, the number of questioners onstage had to be reduced, with unfilled chairs struck from the set the day before the broadcast. Further complicating this situation are the geographical locations of the town halls: neither red-state Tennessee in 2008 nor blue-state New York in 2012 was likely to offer vast numbers of uncommitted voters. As John Judis observed in a blog post in the *New Republic*, "The debate format reflects, above all, the tyranny of the opinion polls, which have become not merely an entertaining mirror on the electorate during election, but part of the elections themselves."[79]

QUESTIONERS IN TOWN HALL DEBATES

Efforts to curb spontaneity notwithstanding, town hall debates have produced insightful, sometimes uncomfortable, exchanges between candidates and voters. From their inception, town meetings have thrust individual citizens and their concerns into the national spotlight. The very first "people's debate" in Richmond cast Bill Clinton, George Bush, and Ross Perot as headliners, but it also made mini-celebrities of several lesser-known participants:

- Marisa Hall, the twenty-five-year-old who asked George Bush how the national debt had personally affected his life. Although Hall's question was confusingly worded, Bush's "I don't get it" response contributed to the public perception of a White House out of touch and gave Bill Clinton ammunition that would last throughout the campaign.
- Kimberly Usry, a young single mother who early in the debate wanted to know why the candidates spent such a "depressingly large" amount of time "trashing their opponents' character."
- Denton Walthall, a ponytailed father of two, who followed up Usry's question by asking the candidates to cross their hearts and pledge to "focus on the issues and not the personalities and the mud."

In postdebate analysis on ABC, Jeff Greenfield credited the questioners with knocking the candidates off their sound bites and keeping attacks to a minimum. NBC's John Chancellor was even more exultant, calling the debate "a shining example of how well things can work in presidential politics." An editorial in the *Christian Science Monitor* described what happened in Richmond as a "citizens' arrest": "The candidates had little choice but to be civil and engaging—not only because of the cautionary early questions, but also because they were compelled to look honest-to-goodness voting citizens in the eye and respond to their heartfelt concerns."[80]

In Richmond the town hall participants successfully steered the conversation toward substantive issues of general importance. Four years later the San Diego audience came closer to fulfilling the warning of government professor Michael Robinson that "there is nothing more self-centered than an audience of untrained voters who ask the same question: me, me, me."[81] A military man asked Dole about the gap between military and civilian pay scales. A landlady wanted to know about capital gains cuts. A minister spoke about returning the country to Christian values. Two of the twenty questions focused on gay rights. Moderator Lehrer had to actively solicit foreign affairs questions; only two were posed during the ninety-minute debate.

The questioning improved in 2000 and 2004, when both town meetings took place in St. Louis. The 2000 town hall included a fascinating moment when an audience member called on George W. Bush to explain the apparent glee with which he had discussed capital punishment in a previous debate. Jake Tapper of *Salon* magazine described it as "a question that many of us in the Fourth Estate haven't had either the opportunity or the guts to ask him about: that creepy smile that falls upon his lips whenever he discusses the death penalty."[82] However gamely Bush attempted to respond, the question spoke more forcefully than the answer.

Perhaps the sharpest of all town hall debates was the Bush–Kerry match in 2004. "Each man got his share of softballs," wrote James Bennet in the *New York Times*. "But for 90 minutes in a dressed-up basketball arena at Washington University, the two candidates were also forced to address the kind of questions they get rarely if ever on the campaign trail: from voters who doubted them and maybe did not even like them very much."[83]

A woman in the audience asked John Kerry to square his "concern for the rising cost of health care" with his choice as running mate of someone "who has made millions of dollars successfully suing medical professionals." Kerry's feeble response included a mention of his "tort reform plan" on the Kerry–Edwards campaign website.

The most pointed questioning was reserved for the incumbent president. An audience member asked George W. Bush how he would rate himself as an environmentalist, a question whose straightforward wording left Bush floundering for a response. Another man, referring to the Patriot Act, wanted to know, "Why are my rights being watered down?" The best Bush could come up with was, "I hope you don't think that." Noting America's low standing in the court of international opinion, another woman asked, "What is your plan to repair relations with other countries given the current situation?" While Bush lapsed into evasive non sequiturs—"We've got a great country. I love our values."—viewers on C-SPAN saw the original question superimposed on the screen, a visual reminder that the candidate was skirting the issue even as he blathered.

"Hats off to these questioners," analyst Tim Russert said on NBC immediately after the debate. "They framed this election and this debate better than I've ever seen before."[84] As Russert and other commentators observed, 140 citizens of St. Louis managed to draw out the presidential nominees in ways that had eluded campaign journalists.

The next two town halls, in 2008 and 2012, fell considerably short of that mark. The dull-as-dishwater debate in Nashville between Obama and McCain suffered at the heavy hand of moderator Tom Brokaw, whose dominance reduced the audience questioners to the status of extras. In 2012 the questioners took a back seat to the onstage struggle between Obama and Romney, and to Candy Crowley's proactive moderating.

The town hall in 2008 introduced one modest innovation, the inclusion of several questions submitted online. Four years later a brief flurry of attention fell on a question that did not get asked: whether the debaters preferred their pizza with sausage or pepperoni. In a press release one week before the town hall debate in 2012, the Pizza Hut restaurant chain announced that it would award free pizza for life to anyone in the live audience who posed that query during the telecast. After negative reaction on social media and in the press, the offer was quickly rescinded.

Given the mixed success of recent town hall debates, the future of this format may be in doubt. Yet the concept of citizens questioning the candidates remains attractive. Carole Simpson, among others, defends the idea. "I've had arguments with my colleagues who thought the public's questions were innocuous and inane, and I have just to yell back at them that this election is about the people and their questions. They're not the questions that we might ask, but this is what they want to know, and I don't think we should have any criticism of that."[85]

In the view of Jim Lehrer, town meetings serve a separate purpose from other debates: letting voters see how the candidates respond to ordinary citizens. "You get questions that might not be asked by professionals," Lehrer said. "Sometimes they're a little off the wall, but so what—it's a different function."[86]

The volatility of town hall audiences is one of their most intriguing qualities, not to mention one of the greatest challenges for producers. Officials from the debate commission tell the story of a member of the town hall audience in Richmond who never made it on television with his question. Shortly before airtime, the Secret Service informed Commissioner Frank Fahrenkopf that the man had been behaving erratically. "What happened," Fahrenkopf recollected, "is he'd brought a flask in. They'd been there since three in the afternoon, so he was drunk and we had to remove him." We can only wonder how the candidates might have handled an average American citizen under the influence.[87]

7 / THE PRODUCTIONS

With less than ten minutes remaining in the nation's first presidential debate in sixteen years, Jimmy Carter was wrapping up his final answer of the evening, talking about a breakdown in the trust between government and the people. Mid-sentence, in tens of millions of homes across America, a static buzz suddenly knocked Carter's voice off the air. Unaware of the disruption, the candidate continued to speak. Seconds later, anchormen on all three networks materialized onscreen to announce the unthinkable: Audio from the program had been lost. On ABC, the network charged with pool-producing the debate, Harry Reasoner reassured viewers, "It is not a conspiracy against Governor Carter or President Ford, and they will fix it as soon as possible."[1] "As soon as possible" turned out to be twenty-seven minutes, an eternity for live television.

"I don't think I've ever been in a situation more tricky than that," moderator Edwin Newman recalled. "I immediately thought to myself, what in God's name am I going to talk about? I can't talk about what they've said, or review it, or evaluate it, since I'm the moderator and I'm supposed to be impartial." Exacerbating the awkwardness of the situation was the all-too-apparent discomfort of the debaters themselves. Neither man wanted to make the first move, so, for the duration of the gap, both stood frozen in place like statues. "When I suggested that they sit down because there were chairs on stage, not only did they not sit down, they did not acknowledge that I had suggested it," Newman said.[2]

Carter and Ford would reminisce about this most stilted of public moments in a joint interview with Jim Lehrer for the Commission on Presidential Debates's Oral History Project:

Carter: I watched that tape afterwards, and it was embarrassing to me that both President Ford and I stood there almost like robots. We didn't move around. We didn't walk over and shake hands with each other. We just stood there.

Ford: I suspect both of us would have liked to sit down and relax while the technicians were fixing the system. But I also think both of us were hesitant to make any gesture that might look like we weren't physically or mentally able to handle a problem like that.

Carter: But the fact is we didn't know at what instant all of the power was going to come back on and the transmission would be resumed. So it was a matter of nervousness. I guess President Ford felt the same way.

Ford: Because that was 28 [*sic*] excruciating minutes. You're on TV nationally, and yet you're not doing anything.[3]

To media theorist Marshall McLuhan the sound failure represented "the rebellion of the medium against the bloody message." Joseph Lelyveld in the *New York Times* called it a "great equalizer": "Presidents and presidential candidates normally ride with sirens and motorcycle escorts to insure that they don't have to wait for anything. But there they were, for all the nation to see, alone with their thoughts like ordinary citizens caught in a traffic jam."[4] The episode also demonstrated to a nationwide audience that neither Ford nor Carter had a knack for improvisation.

The breakdown would be traced to a tiny piece of electronic hardware valued at less than a dollar. David Brinkley began the next evening's NBC newscast by holding up an example of the errant part whose malfunctioning had been responsible for "plunging President Ford and Jimmy Carter into unaccustomed silence" and "irritating maybe 90 million people."[5] A new chapter had entered debate lore, one that even today serves as an object lesson for the men and women who stage presidential debates.

The audio breakdown of 1976 underscores the fragile nature of live television. Although debates require choreography, they also operate according to the iron rule of spontaneity, meaning that even the most carefully laid plans will sometimes be subverted. Debate technicians strive for a program whose execution calls no attention to itself; when the production becomes the story, unhappy television functionaries result. Elliot Bernstein, the ABC pool producer in charge of the Ford–Carter debate, described himself as "very depressed" after the incident. "For a couple of weeks after that I felt really awful," he said. The morning after the broadcast, President Ford invited Bernstein and a production colleague for a conciliatory cup of coffee. "The meeting with the president was like taking two aspirin," Bernstein said. "I felt better for about two hours."[6]

On the heels of the audio problem in Philadelphia, technicians outfitted the subsequent debate site in San Francisco with a triply redundant sound system. "We had to add backups to backups," recalled CBS pool producer Jack Kelly,[7] and in every presidential debate since, caution has been the watchword. Debate producers make elaborate preparations for worst-case contingencies: extra cameras at the ready; candidates and questioners on multiple microphones; thicker-than-normal carpeting and drapes to muffle ambient sound. For the final debate of 1976, on the campus of the College of William and Mary, student volunteers oiled all 650 seats in Phi Beta Kappa Hall to prevent squeaking during the telecast.

Producers of presidential debates do whatever it takes to ensure a smooth-running production. In the middle of a rehearsal for the vice presidential match in 1988, Omaha Civic Auditorium lost electrical power when a bird flew into an auxiliary power supply. Determined to avoid a repeat of this during the live broadcast, executive producer Ed Fouhy placed a strongly worded phone call to an official at the local power company. The official's perfunctory reassurances did not satisfy Fouhy, who countered with a threat to distribute the man's home phone number to all 1,500 journalists covering the event should anything go wrong. The next day crews arrived to double-wire the facility, which, according to Fouhy, "cost them so much power that people who live in that part of Omaha weren't seeing a full picture on their television sets. They were getting about a two-inch picture on their eighteen-inch monitors."[8]

Not every potential disaster is technical in nature. Annie Groer, a questioner in the first Bush–Dukakis debate, spent the ninety-minute broadcast terrified that she and her fellow panelists would fall off the set. "Our chairs were all on casters which were literally about eight inches from the apron of the stage," Groer said. "So one false move and we all would have been pitching backwards."[9] Four years later, producer

Fouhy had similar worries during the split-format debate in East Lansing, in which the panelists were required to walk onto the set halfway through the telecast. "My greatest fear," Fouhy wrote, "was that one of the three—all debate rookies—would walk onto the stage . . . and literally fall flat on their faces, coming from the backstage darkness and having to negotiate two steps to get to their table in the blazing onstage lights."[10]

During the vice presidential debate in 1992, Admiral James Stockdale gave producers a scare when he began wandering away from his podium. Richard Berke of the *New York Times* monitored this drama-behind-the-drama from an on-site production truck, where he was able to observe the full range of cameras simultaneously. Berke described the scene:

> As the 90-minute event wore on, Stockdale ventured farther and farther away from his spot on the podium, as if he had had enough give-and-take and was ready for his daily constitutional.
>
> "He's going for a walk!" came the voice of a nervous network producer in New York over a squawk box in the control room here. "I don't know if anyone can suggest something be done—he's got bad legs from the war, and he's going to fall down!"
>
> Nothing could be done, but luckily for the anxiety-ridden producer, as well as for Stockdale, he never fell.[11]

DEBATE VENUES

Although presidential debates were hatched in the sterile environment of a television studio, 1960 was the first and last year the programs took place in this setting. Since 1976 all general election debates have been produced in front of live audiences at auditoriums and arenas throughout the United States, mostly on university campuses.

Venues for presidential debates must be booked well ahead of schedule, which is to say months before the candidates have committed themselves to participate. The down-to-the-wire timing of debate negotiations sometimes means a subversion of the sponsors' carefully laid plans. Political wrangling has forced last-minute cancellations and facilities substitutions, leaving beleaguered sponsors to mop up the mess.

On paper, the process for site selection seems fairly straightforward. The debate commission invites cities to submit bids based on a set of logistical criteria. Obviously a suitable hall is needed, but so are the accoutrements that come with the traveling circus of a presidential debate, including transportation, hotel space, and work facilities for several thousand journalists and technicians. To offset production expenses, host institutions must also make a financial contribution, $1.65 million in 2012. And they must invest in infrastructure to make the campus debate-ready—another $3.5 million, for example, spent by the University of Mississippi for the first debate of 2008.

Debates take place in two types of on-location facilities: theaters and field houses, each with its benefits and drawbacks. "A modern and well-equipped theater means almost a turnkey operation," said Janet Brown, executive director of the debate commission. "You can move in and a great deal of the equipment is there. By the same token, our crew brings in a great deal of the equipment from scratch. I think in many cases it surprises them that we bring in as much equipment as we do."[12] Even state-of-the-art facilities undergo adjustments. Beyond the needs of debate producers, network news operations require major remodeling efforts to accommodate their on-site anchor booths for pre- and post-debate analysis.

In contrast to a production-ready theater, the field house setting means building a stage from the ground up; the advantage for producers is that they can create whatever space suits their needs. For the town hall debate in Richmond, for instance, crews constructed a facility-within-a-facility in the middle of a 15,000-seat basketball arena, exactly to the desired specifications. But field houses also present a liability: an atmosphere that encourages the live audience to approach the debate as an athletic competition. According to producer Fouhy, "You put people in a sports arena and they behave like they're at a sporting event."[13]

No better illustration of this exists than the Bentsen–Quayle match in 1988, whose spirited in-house spectators constituted the rowdiest debate audience in history. Democratic campaign officials later confessed that they had imported 300 partisan supporters to make noise and generate pro-Bentsen energy inside Omaha Civic Auditorium. For each row, a designated leader cued applause and led cheers for the senator from Texas.

"That was an attempt to take advantage of television," strategist Tom Donilon acknowledged at a symposium two years after the fact. "Because if you look at that tape, you can give people the sense that all of America is supporting your man's position when you have a kind of roar behind him."[14] For the next round of debates, campaign negotiators put an end to such shenanigans by stipulating that "the supporters of each candidate be interspersed among supporters of other candidates."[15]

According to Brown, a live audience of several hundred is ideal for a presidential debate; "over a thousand is where you get into a problem." UCLA's Pauley Pavilion, site of the final Bush–Dukakis debate and home court of Bruins basketball, regularly seats 14,000. Reconfigured for the debate, the space held only 1,500. Still, Brown said, "people realize they're in a cavernous space and it does change the feel of the event."[16]

As part of the audience warm-up in Los Angeles, debate co-commissioners Frank Fahrenkopf and Paul Kirk went through their regular preshow paces of exhorting those in attendance to comport themselves civilly. According to Fahrenkopf, a particularly defiant guest at Pauley Pavilion was the actress and Dukakis supporter Sally Field. "She just turned around and stared at me, giving me the finger with her look," Fahrenkopf said. "I'll never forget that as long as I live."[17] For the town hall debate in San Diego in 1996, moderator Jim Lehrer enlisted the support of audience VIP Gerald Ford in enforcing decorum. In his predebate warm-up, Lehrer informed the crowd he was appointing Ford "hall monitor," and told Ford, "You can discipline anybody who gets out of line."[18]

Except for the town hall forums, tickets for debates are split three ways among the sponsor and the campaigns, which then parcel them out to supporters. Often the candidates invite high-profile guests from the worlds of politics and entertainment. In the final debate in 1976, singer Pearl Bailey sat with First Lady Betty Ford. Running mate Joe Lieberman turned up for Al Gore's last match with George W. Bush in 2000, actor Michael J. Fox sat next to Teresa Heinz Kerry in the final debate in 2004, and Al and Tipper Gore attended the 2008 Obama–McCain town hall in Nashville. With tickets in high demand, average citizens have almost no opportunity to be part of a presidential debate audience. When the first Bush–Dukakis meeting in 1988 took place on the campus of Wake Forest University in Winston-Salem, North Carolina, only thirteen seats were earmarked for a student body of 5,000. (The students did receive a consolation: Because the school cafeteria was commandeered for use as a media center, dorm residents received breakfast in bed.)

However exclusive the ticket, a spot inside the auditorium does not offer the best vantage point for debate watching; after all, the production is designed as a television show and not a theatrical event. Acoustics and sight lines can be poor, and temperatures in the brightly lit hall are often uncomfortable. Describing the second meeting in 1976 between Ford and Carter, James Wooten in the *New York Times* referred to San Francisco's Palace of Fine Arts as "the largest sauna in the country." Unseasonably hot weather had turned the hall into an oven; spectators fanned themselves with their programs "like ladies at a country church in the deep of summer."[19]

The two candidates had no such worries. Production crews had gone to great lengths to keep Ford and Carter comfortable, installing an ad hoc air conditioning system in the otherwise uncooled theater. According to debate scholars Herbert Seltz and Richard Yoakam, "large flexible ducts, looking like elephant trunks, wound their way onto the stage and the debate set, where they were suspended from the light grid and aimed at the lecterns."[20] Taking no chances, technicians diffused the air blowing out of these hoses so as not to tousle the debaters' hair.

This image—Gerald Ford and Jimmy Carter standing onstage beneath separate but equal air ducts—offers a useful visual metaphor for presidential debates. In the never-never land of television debates, where reality intersects with contrivance, it is fitting that each candidate existed in what amounted to his own microclimate. Temperature-controlled and wind-free, these artificial zones of perfection underline what an exacting pursuit debate production can be.

ON-SITE NEGOTIATIONS

Once at the debate site, the campaigns intensify their efforts to anticipate the unexpected. This task begins about a week before the debate, and involves anywhere from a dozen to twenty people per campaign, headed by one or two lead representatives on each side. Also on hand are the nonpolitical personnel who will execute most of the production specifics: the debate sponsors and their team, plus a crew from the pool network charged with getting the program on air. From 1960 on, the major networks have shared responsibility for televising presidential debates, taking turns at staging the various events. The network in charge supplies a director, a technical crew, and, in the end, a fully produced feed of the program that is sent out for use by all members of the pool and by other media entities that pay to receive it.

The stakeholders at the debate site do not share power equally. To a great extent, campaigns maintain the upper hand in on-location dealings, leaving sponsors and television networks in a reactive posture. With the negotiated memorandum of understanding as their charter, the handlers set about converting the dry prose of the contract into a live television show. Up to this point, the debate has been all theory and bluster; now it becomes tangible.

The differing requirements of each physical setting make it impossible for drafters of the debate agreement to foresee every contingency. For this reason, campaign representatives continue to hammer out production details even as the hall is being set up. The goal on each side is simple: to protect one's candidate. "The stakes are such that you do literally everything you can think of to maximize the advantage, even if it's point-zero-zero-one percent," said Brady Williamson, an on-site negotiator for Democratic candidates. "Sometimes in hindsight, the trivial turned out to be sublime, and the sublime turned out to be trivial."[21]

At the debate venue, negotiators must settle a variety of issues, both procedural and production related. Coin tosses determine many of the procedural questions—things like which candidate speaks first, the sequence of the candidates' arrival at the hall, the order in which the spouses take their seats, and so on. More complicated staging points may call for a session at the bargaining table—or, when practical, on the set itself.

As production arrangements evolve, on-site handlers maintain close contact with their counterparts involved in candidate preps. The objective is to communicate details about the location that can be incorporated into mock debates. Bill Clinton's advance teams in 1992 and 1996 were particularly effective in conveying production minutiae that were then applied in the practice sessions. For the logistically complicated town hall sessions, the Clinton prep operation received precise measurements of the debate stage that were used to lay out an accurate replica for rehearsals.

Depending on the situation, and the dynamic between opposing handlers, negotiations on-site may or may not be thorny. Generally the campaign reps on both sides are experienced hands at presidential debates, and many of the key figures have worked with each other in the past. "I think it's fair to say we've become good acquaintances, and come to respect each other along the way," Williamson said. "If we didn't have each other's mutual respect, and dare I say trust, it wouldn't work."[22]

Certain issues are easily resolved. In 1996 negotiators for Bob Dole sought a position for their candidate on the left-hand side of the stage, because Dole's war injuries made gesturing with his right arm impossible. Clinton's negotiators dispensed with the usual coin toss and honored Dole's request. In 2004 representatives for Kerry and Edwards gave heart patient Dick Cheney his wish for a backstage holding room that did not require him to navigate any stairs. Negotiators for Obama agreed to McCain's request that the candidates have handheld microphones in the town hall.

Moments of cordiality notwithstanding, relations have not always been smooth. On rare occasions when campaigns cannot reach agreement, the disputes never do achieve reconciliation. In 1976 advisers for Ford and Carter battled for weeks over how blue the backdrop on the set ought to be, an argument that persisted even as the four-debate series was under way. According to Seltz and Yoakam, "The Carter people . . . wanted the background to be less blue—or warmer, as they put it. The Ford handlers wanted it to be more blue." Imero Fiorentino, a veteran lighting director hired by the League of Women Voters, ended up mediating the disagreement. Said Fiorentino, "The blueness of the background changed all the time. Now if there was anything that was of interest to the candidates' representatives, and befuddled me to death, it was the blue background."[23]

In 1984, podium placement generated sparks between the campaigns of Reagan and Mondale. Mondale's negotiators sought a particular angle that would allow their candidate to take a step away from the lectern, turn to his opponent, and address him directly in a dramatic on-camera maneuver dubbed "the pivot." According to debate coach Tom Donilon, the plan was to showcase Mondale by having him make a physical move that had never been tried in a presidential debate. "When you actually turn your body, the whole picture of the thing changes into a much more confrontational event," Donilon explained. "A little movement on television goes a long way."[24]

Democratic negotiators pressed hard on the matter of lectern placement, though they could not reveal their reason for doing so. Victoria Harian, debate coordinator for the League of Women Voters, recalled, "There was a lot of discussion about exactly how those [podiums] were going to be canted—what angle, how many inches, from what point were they going to be measured. It ended up being a very silly thing to have taken up so much time and to have become such a big deal."[25]

For the second debate of 1984, the flashpoint was lighting—the "battle of the bulbs," as the hometown *Kansas City Star* dubbed it in a news story devoted to the squabble. Mondale's people favored the lighting plot used in the previous debate in Louisville, where the Democratic nominee had been victorious; Reagan's people demanded changes. Reagan's team wanted, among other things, lights on the live audience. According to a spokesman for pool network CBS, the president's aides believed that lighting the audience would be less "stressful" for Reagan than "talking to a black hole."[26]

Eventually the Republicans got many of the changes they insisted on. Most significantly Michael Deaver, Reagan's television guru, made a last-minute alteration that worked to his candidate's benefit on the air. "I always lit Reagan from the top, never underneath," Deaver explained, "because you get that full head of hair, you don't get any lines in the face, and you get a line across the broad shoulders." Just before the debate, Deaver reconfigured the lighting according to this high-angle scheme—with the consent, he said, of the League of Women Voters and Mondale's campaign.

For Mondale, the results were disastrous: bags under the eyes, and a waxy pallor that added years to his appearance. "Mondale needed heavy lighting straight on," Deaver said, "and I had changed it, but I certainly didn't do it on purpose."[27] Frank Greer, Mondale's television consultant, later complained that the high angle of the lighting had been "extreme," and that the original setup would have been more advantageous to his candidate.[28] After this episode, campaigns took greater care to protect lighting schemes from tampering by the other side.

Twenty years later, it was timing lights, not stage lights, that ignited a predebate flare-up. Negotiators for George W. Bush had gotten John Kerry's campaign to accept the placement of warning lights on the candidates' lecterns, a provision that was then written into the debate contract. Republicans hoped to capitalize on Kerry's reputation for pro-lixity; they reasoned that timing lights visible to the viewing audience would accentuate Kerry's verbosity.

As a backup, Bush's negotiators also demanded a buzzer that would go off if the debaters continued speaking beyond their limits. "They wanted a loud buzzer," recalled Beverly Lindsey, on-site negotiator for Kerry's campaign. Ultimately, she said, both sides agreed to "a very soft buzz. We negotiated that down."[29] As it turned out, the buzzer never sounded in any of the actual debates.

Timing devices had long been used in presidential debates, but never had they figured so prominently in the camera shots as in 2004. In the opinion of Janet Brown of the debate commission, the lights and buzzer served no useful purpose: "But you know what? If at some point the candidates want to insist on features like that, our focus is on the substance of the debate, and you can't stop traffic because somebody decides they want to add, literally, bells and whistles to the podiums."[30]

Once at the debate venue in Miami, John Kerry and his top advisers expressed their displeasure with the placement and size of the light box. From an esthetic standpoint, the complaints were justified: the box looked like something constructed in a high school shop class, and its proximity to the debaters gave the production a game show quality. Hours before the program was scheduled to start, Kerry's aides demanded that the lights be removed from the lecterns, provoking a down-to-the-wire squabble with on-site representatives for Bush. A frantic call went out to Vernon Jordan, Kerry's original debate negotiator. "I had gotten to Miami," Jordan said, "and they still wanted to make some changes. So I just wouldn't take the phone calls—I couldn't be found. I was actually playing golf."[31]

In the end Bush's side won the battle but lost the war. John Kerry's answers during the debate consistently came in on time, depriving Republicans of their desire to see the Democratic nominee cut off in midsentence. The same light box was used in all of the subsequent debates, with no objections from Kerry's campaign. According to Beverly Lindsey, "we never negotiated it again."[32]

OTHER ON-SITE CHALLENGES

Sometimes the site itself exacerbates tensions between campaigns. The 1996 town hall debate in San Diego took place in a theater so cramped that it obviated a rule in the contract giving each candidate his own onstage "zone." Once the reality of the space became apparent, negotiators discussed a number of alternatives, including the possibility of painting a stripe down the middle of the set to create a border. In the end, against the wishes of Dole's camp, the concept of clearly delineated zones was abandoned.

"We spent more time on that than anything," said Beverly Lindsey, Bill Clinton's representative in the debates in 1996. "We wanted our candidate to be able to approach the audience on all sides, not just the side he was on." Dole's handlers, by contrast, feared that in so intimate a space the president might be tempted to instigate a confrontation. "I think they were concerned that Clinton would walk right up to Dole and put a finger in his shoulder or something," Lindsey said.[33]

In the end, the physical maneuvering in this debate proved to be one of its distinctive qualities. As Maureen Dowd wrote in the *New York Times*, "The president kept sliding out from behind his lectern, bearing down on Bob Dole and looking as if he were going to give him a good clip from the side."[34] At one point in the program, Dole stepped back, muttering, "I'm going to get out of your way here." Nothing, it appeared, could stand between Clinton and his need to bond with the studio audience.

A less successful maneuvering of town hall geography occurred in 2000, when Al Gore moved into George W. Bush's space as Bush was giving an answer. Though Bush used the moment to make Gore look silly, the experience left Republican negotiators wary when it came time for the town hall debate with John Kerry four years later. "Each candidate may move about in a pre-designated area," the memorandum of understanding in 2004 mandated, "and may not leave that area while the debate is underway. The pre-designated areas of the candidates may not overlap."[35]

At the debate site in St. Louis, the execution of this provision became contentious when Bush's negotiators insisted on a tape mark on the carpet to demarcate each candidate's boundaries. Democrats, fearful that borders would impede a feeling of openness, disparaged the layout as a "demilitarized zone." According to Kerry's media adviser Robert Shrum, "We finally came up with some kind of compromise so that if you went the Great Circle Route, you could get to talk to the people in the audience."[36]

Zone designations returned in the town hall debates of 2008 and 2012, although in practice the candidates largely ignored them. For the town hall in 2008, John McCain's area was marked with red tape and Barack Obama's with blue, but according to CBS's pool director Chip Colley, the boundaries may as well not have existed. "We were under the impression that the candidates were going to stay on their stools a little more and maybe stand up for emphasis," he said. "But from the moment it started, they just got up and started wandering around." Colley called the debate "one of the most challenging things I've ever directed in my life."[37] John McCain's meandering drew particular notice from journalists like John Dickerson, who wrote that "it looked like he was getting up to get a beer."[38] On *Saturday Night Live*, McCain was parodied as a doddering old man, cluelessly stumbling into and out of Obama's camera shot.

From year to year, one of the most heavily negotiated production points is the assignment of candidate holding rooms. As Democratic representative Brady Williamson said, "Not all space is equally desirable."[39] From the outset, debate sponsors have been sensitive to this issue. Back in 1960, ABC constructed identical "dressing room cottages" for Kennedy and Nixon on the studio set of the New York City debate. Although each cottage included its own sink, the candidates were expected to share a toilet.

Today's debaters no longer share much of anything. Backstage holding areas function as a traveling campaign headquarters, complete with private areas for the candidates and full-scale communications centers for the staff. Campaigns take extreme precautions to physically segregate the star participants from one another in the period before a debate begins. "You arrange their holding rooms so that they don't intersect each other's path," said debate consultant Robert Goodwin.[40] In some cases, curtains have been installed specifically to keep the competitors from catching an accidental glimpse of one another.

Just before the first debate in 1992 in St. Louis, Ross Perot violated this long-standing protocol by paying an impromptu social call at the dressing rooms of his surprised opponents. Brady Williamson remembered standing outside Clinton's holding room, when "out of the shadow comes this small figure and it's Ross Perot. He walks up to me and says, 'May I say hello to the governor?'" Overcoming his shock, Williamson went inside and got Clinton's approval, and Perot proceeded inside for a brief predebate chat. Perot, said Williamson, "didn't approach this thing quite the way the other two did."[41]

Perot's attempt to see President Bush was less successful. This time, the Reform Party candidate did not get past the holding room door.

On-site logistics may also extend to the candidates' spouses. For the debate in San Diego in 1996, Bob Dole's representatives unconditionally demanded that Elizabeth Dole be seated in her husband's line of sight during the telecast. This same request had been easily accomplished at the previous debate in Hartford, which took place in a standard auditorium. But in San Diego, with its theater-in-the-round setup, Mrs. Dole would have had to sit among the town hall participants, a position Democrats feared might influence the tenor of the questioning.

Negotiators struck a compromise: a platform was built above the last row of the audience where Elizabeth Dole would be visible to the senator but separated from the questioners; Hillary Clinton got an identical stand on her side of the house. During the debate, Dole's reason for wanting his wife in view became evident: her job was to smile at him, and thus remind him to relax. For the duration of the ninety-minute telecast, observers said, Mrs. Dole never stopped smiling.[42]

Despite the abundance of caution, one production detail cannot be completely controlled: the guests who are invited to attend the event live in the hall. Because each campaign is in charge of distributing its own tickets, opportunities for mischief arise. Before the final encounter in 1992, Democratic operatives got word that Bush's campaign was planning to seat Clinton's paramour Gennifer Flowers in the debate audience, next to Barbara Bush. "The notion was preposterous," wrote Jack Germond and Jules Witcover, "but the fact the rumor was circulating at all was an indicator of the high stakes in the debate."[43] In 1996 Bob Dole's campaign actually did plant an antagonistic figure in the audience: Billy Dale, who, in a minor dustup at the beginning of Clinton's presidency, had been fired from the White House travel office. Dale's presence at the Hartford debate was supposed to disconcert Clinton; in fact, the president had no idea what Billy Dale looked like.

The debates of 2004 brought two instances of audience-related psychological warfare, both instigated by the Democrats. At the first Bush–Kerry debate in Miami, Democratic National Committee chair Terry McAuliffe made a late arrival in the hall and slipped into an empty seat directly behind Laura Bush and the Bush twins. "Laura Bush turned around to see what had just sat down behind her and immediately wished she hadn't," wrote McAuliffe in his memoir. "It was like that scene in *The Shining* where Jack Nicholson cries out 'Here's Johnny!'" Secret Service agents asked McAuliffe to relocate. "I was disappointed I didn't get to sit up there, which would really have messed with Bush's head," he said.[44]

For the vice presidential debate, Democrats reserved a strategically placed second-row seat for Senator Patrick Leahy of Vermont, whom Vice President Dick Cheney had famously told to "go f——" himself on the floor of the U.S. Senate. The Cheney team interpreted Leahy's attendance as a not-so-subtle attempt to rattle the Republican candidate. "We had always thought that one of John Edwards's goals for the debate would be to try to get my dad to lose his temper," said Mary Cheney, the vice president's daughter and campaign aide. "Leahy's presence in the audience told us that we were right."[45]

In that same debate, Mary Cheney indulged in her own brand of impromptu audience participation. Cheney was seated in the front row next to her mother and sister, within the debaters' line of sight. When John Edwards complimented the vice president and his wife on accepting their daughter's homosexuality, Mary Cheney "mouthed a phrase that, coincidentally enough, my dad had acquainted Patrick Leahy with a few months earlier." The other Cheney women, meanwhile, "took a slightly higher road" and stuck out their tongues at Edwards. "I don't see how he could have missed us," Cheney said.[46]

In some cases, on-site logistics are determined by rank. When a sitting president debates a challenger, for instance, the president is always first to leave once the event ends. At the town hall in 2012, this became an aggravation for Mitt Romney, who after a less-than-stellar evening was eager to depart the venue at Hofstra University. An unhappy Romney had to wait impatiently for nearly half an hour as Barack Obama mingled with the audience in the hall.

PREDEBATE TECH CHECKS

On the afternoon of a presidential debate, several hours before broadcast, the on-site process culminates with each debater's final preshow technical check. As with other production particulars, the order of the candidates' arrival for the walk-throughs and how much time they are allotted on the set have been decided in advance. At the appointed hour, the hall is cleared of nonessential personnel, and the star and his entourage sweep in for a briefing session with producers and technicians.

In many ways this is standard show business procedure, like the sound check that takes place before a concert. In other ways the tech check preceding a presidential debate has no parallel, thanks to the uniquely bifurcated nature of the event, the weighty stakes involved, and the intensely felt pressure of the rival camps. For each side, the on-site walk-through represents one last opportunity to counteract any perceived inequities.

Even more important, the point of the exercise is to get the candidate as relaxed as possible in the crucial hours before the debate commences. Said Brady Williamson, "It's like trying on a new suit. You just want to make sure that you're comfortable, that it fits."[47] During the tech check, debaters receive their final instructions on such key production details as camera placement, timing, and how they will enter from offstage. Cueing devices and microphones are tested. Makeup and clothing are examined under television lights so advisers can preview the candidate exactly as he or she will appear on air. The last step, according to

Democratic debate coach Tom Donilon, is to go over ground rules with the producers, "to make sure they're not going to do anything that's not to your advantage. You want to be there with the stage manager, the camera people, the director."[48]

Technical checks may run smoothly, or they may fall victim to the intensity of the moment. Victoria Harian, debate producer for the League of Women Voters in 1984, described an unusually nerve-racking scene when Geraldine Ferraro came in for her walk-through before the vice presidential debate in Philadelphia. Campaign advisers were having "fits and tantrums" over a variety of minor matters, Harian said, "to the point you knew they weren't serving their candidate well. You could see Ferraro was getting too much exposure to all this nattering, and most of it was just absolutely a waste."[49]

Tech checks have always had the potential to harrow. Robert F. Kennedy, accompanying his brother to NBC's Studio A in Washington for the second debate in 1960, voiced objections on two counts: lighting and studio temperature. Standing at Nixon's podium, RFK demanded to know why the Republican side of the set seemed brighter than the Democratic side. The candidate himself asked if Nixon's people had arranged the lighting for both debaters. "There's only one light pointing over here [at Nixon's lectern]," JFK said. "Let's not have four lights in my eyes."[50] Technical director Leon Chromak agreed to reposition a stand light on the studio floor, in what he later called a "psychological lighting change" to appease the Kennedys.[51]

Mindful of Richard Nixon's on-camera perspiration in the first debate, Nixon's handlers had requested that the air conditioning be set at a cooler level in Washington. As John Kennedy entered the studio, he commented, "I need a sweater." Bobby Kennedy asked an aide, "What are they trying to do? Freeze my brother to death?" The Democrats insisted that adjustments be made, and the temperature came up a few degrees.[52]

For the transcontinental third debate of 1960, with Nixon in California and Kennedy in New York City, each candidate got his way: the temperature of Nixon's studio remained at fifty-eight degrees, while Kennedy's registered at seventy-two. Otherwise, ABC took great pains to create identical studio arrangements. The network purchased cloth for the two backdrops from the same mill run, in enough quantity to dress both sets. The same can of paint used on the New York set was hand-carried on a plane to Los Angeles so the colors would precisely match.

Even at that, physical distance and equal facilities did not prevent a long-distance tiff. After the debate, Republicans charged that JFK had violated an agreed-upon rule by bringing notes into the studio in New York. A few minutes before the program began, Nixon evidently caught a glimpse of Kennedy on a monitor shuffling papers at his lectern. Once the program went off the air, Nixon discussed the matter with journalists, as reported in the *New York Times*: "The vice president insisted, 'I'm not angry about it,' but his face was rigid, his lips taut, and his voice rose as he continued talking about the use of notes. 'I'm not complaining,' he told reporters in the ABC studio. 'I never complain about debates after they are over. But before the next debate we had better settle on the rules.' "[53]

This paranoia over bringing notes or other items onto the set eventually worked its way into the negotiated memorandum of understanding. The document of 2012, like most of its predecessors, specified that only blank paper and writing utensils could be placed on the candidates' lecterns. The memo of 2012 also outlined punitive measures for anyone who ran afoul of regulations: "If a candidate uses a prop, note, or other writing or other tangible thing during a debate, the moderator must interrupt and explain that . . . use of the prop, note, or other writing or thing violates the debate rules agreed to by that candidate."[54]

After the first debate of 2012, the liberal blogosphere briefly erupted over allegations that Mitt Romney had sneaked papers onto the set. "Hanky or Notes? Did Mitt Cheat?" asked a story in the *Daily Beast* that featured slow-motion video of Romney retrieving a flat white item from his pants pocket and placing it on his lectern at the start of the debate. Romney's campaign said the object was a handkerchief; this assertion is supported by subsequent camera shots in which the candidate is seen using the item to mop his mouth.[55]

LAST-MINUTE MANEUVERS AT THE DEBATE SITE

Over the years, technical walk-throughs have become increasingly off-limits to the media. Before the final Ford–Carter debate of 1976, Jimmy

Carter's closed rehearsal nearly became a news story when audio from inside the hall mistakenly found its way to the nearby press center. To make matters worse, Carter had decided to use his tech check to engage in a dry run, offering real responses to questions asked by advisers on topics like tax reform and foreign policy. NBC, the network in charge, spent the next several hours contacting people who might have heard the rehearsal, imploring them not to report it; apparently no one did.

At the site in San Diego in 1996, sponsors ejected an Associated Press photographer whom they discovered hiding under a canvas in the balcony during one of the technical checks. The photographer had concealed an automatic camera inside a curtain, and was snapping pictures of the rehearsal with a remote control device. The debate commission took away the man's credentials and banned him from the premises.

One reason campaigns do not allow press coverage of the tech checks is that the scenes can become volatile, in effect extending the bargaining into the hours immediately before the event. At the tech check preceding the first debate in 1976, President Ford roiled the waters by asking that the stool behind his lectern be removed. The League of Women Voters' production coordinator, "in the afterglow of meeting the president of the United States," honored this request, forgetting that campaign negotiators had spent hours haggling over the seating issue.

When Carter's people discovered the stool had been removed without their consent, they angrily demanded an explanation from the other side. "I got about thirteen phone calls in 45 minutes," recalled Ford's media adviser William Carruthers.[56] The stool was returned to Ford's lectern, but moments before the telecast began, the president again signaled Carruthers to strike it. Carruthers dragged the stool a few feet away from Ford, where it remained on the stage throughout the program, forlornly turning up in some of the two-shots of both candidates.

Stools recurred as a bone of contention sixteen years later in the three-way town hall debate in Richmond. According to director John Li-Bretto, at issue were the height and positioning of the seats, and whether each debater would have side tables to take notes on. "That seemed to take hours to figure out," LiBretto said. "I kept saying you can't have [the candidates] hindered in any way from getting up, they have to be able to get up easily from the chairs and walk around, but that just seemed to go on forever."

A couple of hours after the debaters had completed their tech checks, LiBretto said, representatives from both Bush's and Clinton's campaigns returned to the hall for yet another look at the floor layout. (Perot's people had pronounced themselves satisfied, even though the stools were too high for the diminutive Texan.) Concerned that the stools were still too close together, the handlers requested an adjustment. LiBretto tried adding space between candidates, but the repositioning adversely affected his camera shots. After about an hour of tinkering, the director and the handlers agreed to split the difference. "I can say that when we were done I had the chairs back where they started," LiBretto said. "I don't know they were even aware that I ended up with the chairs back on their original marks."[57]

According to Clinton's aide Paul Begala, at some point before airtime a Democratic handler surreptitiously replaced the official stools on the town hall set with the ones used in Clinton's prep sessions. "We wanted Clinton to be completely at ease in his surroundings," Begala said, "right down to his butt."[58]

The candidates themselves approach their tech checks with varying degrees of seriousness. Bill Clinton was renowned for being a highly engaged participant in his predebate walk-throughs. Before the town meeting in 1992, Clinton peppered director LiBretto with questions about the physical configuration of the set: "What if I did this, and what if I did that?" "Does this work?" "If I stand here and turn to the president, will that show on camera?" President Bush, LiBretto said, was far less interested in such arcana. "Bush hated that," confirmed aide David Demarest. "He no more would have done that than fly to the moon."[59] Ross Perot did not even attend his session, sending a surrogate instead.

For the town hall debate in San Diego in 1996, Clinton conducted a similarly thorough survey. "He got off the stage and walked the whole circumference of the theater," recalled Bob Asman, executive producer for the debate commission.[60] Bob Dole, by contrast, never left the stage. Where Clinton used most of his one-hour allotment of time, Dole made quick work of his on-site briefings, taking less than twenty minutes.

In 2008 it was candidate Barack Obama who took his tech check seriously, and John McCain who went through the motions. On-site observers at the first two venues recalled that Obama immediately engaged with the crew, asking detailed questions about camera setups and joking about his big ears. McCain "came in, saw it, said fine, and walked out," according to pool director Chip Colley. To John Reade, executive producer for the network pool, the difference between candidates was like "night and day." Obama "was vacuuming in information, not just to file but to use." McCain, on the other hand, spent more time talking with his makeup artist and his wife than with his handlers or the crew.[61]

Once tech checks are out of the way, candidates have several hours in which to rest, eat, practice, or exercise before they get dressed and made up. Different debaters have different rituals: some like to surround themselves with family members and campaign aides, while others prefer to spend the time alone, or exclusively with their spouse. The behind-the-scenes campaign documentary *Mitt* provides an unusually candid glimpse of candidate Mitt Romney in the hours before his first two presidential debates, chit-chatting with his wife and sons, eating Chinese take-out directly from the containers, and, in a profoundly strange moment, picking up garbage on his hotel balcony and carrying it out to the hallway while clad in his dress shirt and tie.[62]

In the moments just before a debate, Ronald Reagan liked to pray—or, as he put it, "have a word with the man upstairs." Backstage at the vice presidential debate in 2000, Joe Lieberman led his family in a sing-along of "This Little Light of Mine." George W. Bush also routinely prayed before his debates. Two days before his final match with Al Gore, Bush reached out to televangelist James Robison, a Texas-based anti-gay crusader, asking if they could pray together about the event. According to Robison, the two of them appealed to God over the telephone to grant Bush "calm, confidence, and the wisdom to know when to speak and when not to speak."[63]

Sarah Palin's predebate prayer ritual would prompt the candidate to criticize her handlers' insufficient religiosity. According to Palin's biographers Scott Conroy and Shushannah Walshe, in the minutes before her debate with Joe Biden, Palin prayed backstage with several staffers from McCain's campaign. A few months later Palin described the scene at a banquet of Alaska Republicans and claimed that she had been unable to find appropriate prayer partners: "The McCain campaign, love 'em, you know—there are a lot of people around me, but nobody I could find that I wanted to hold hands with and pray." Wrote Conroy and Walshe, "The remark drew laughter at the dinner but consternation among some former campaign aides, especially the ones who recalled that she had, in fact, deemed them worthy enough companions with whom to pray."[64]

Part of any predebate ritual involves traveling to the site. For the first debate of 2000, George W. Bush arrived by boat in order to avoid having to pass through anti-Bush demonstrations. "It was worth doing, if only to annoy the protesters who would have spent hours just waiting for a chance to yell when Bush drove by," said adviser Stuart Stevens.[65] The debate took place in a gymnasium at the University of Massachusetts in Boston, next door to the John F. Kennedy Presidential Library. The location had spooked Republicans; without the debates in 1960, would there have even been a JFK library?

Al Gore showed up later than scheduled for the debate in Boston, causing his makeup artist to rush through her task. "She'd be blamed for his 'orange' tint," wrote Gore's aide Robert Shrum. "But it wasn't her fault; she didn't have time to do her job."[66] A number of postdebate commentators mentioned Gore's garish cosmetics. "Did you see all the makeup Gore had on?" asked comedian Jay Leno on the *Tonight Show*. "In fact, today they fired his mortician."[67]

According to Shrum, Gore's immediate predebate regimen for the event in Boston included a heavy intake of energy-boosting food and drink. "Gore gulped down four or five diet colas and bolted down several protein power bars," he said. "It was a recipe for hyperaggression."[68]

VISUAL CAUTION IN PRESIDENTIAL DEBATES

The controversy over reaction shots in the first Kennedy–Nixon match initiated a tradition of visual caution in presidential debates that held sway for decades. Mindful of the widespread attention Nixon's cutaways had drawn in the opening encounter, the director of the second debate in 1960 pointedly timed each reaction shot with a stopwatch as campaign handlers looked on. The third meeting of Kennedy and Nixon, potentially a gold mine of contrasting images, was even more buttoned-down. This program had offered an unprecedented opportunity for experimentation: with Nixon in Los Angeles and Kennedy in New York, history's first and only split-screen presidential debate was, for its time, a technical tour de force. It took three studios to pull off the exercise, two in Los Angeles (one for Nixon, another for the panel) and a third in New York for JFK. ABC, the designated pool network, billed the production as "the most technically complicated broadcast in history."[69]

Oddly, in spite of the intricate set-up, viewers saw the split screen of both candidates only once, in the opening moments of the program before the men began speaking. Director Sonny Diskin (whose regular assignments included *The Fight of the Week*, ABC's Saturday night boxing show) explained afterward that he did not want the side-by-side shots to be "distracting."[70] Not coincidentally, the third debate is generally regarded as Nixon's best; with Kennedy a safe 3,000 miles away, the vice president managed to relax and deliver.

Since 1976, when debates moved out of the television studio and onto remote locations, the trepidation over cutaways has extended to reaction shots of the live audience. Throughout the history of television debates, campaigns have actively prohibited shots of spectators, fearful that such images might unduly influence the audience at home. In at least a couple of instances, entire rows of seats were removed from the debate hall in order to prevent audience reaction shots. Only during the town hall debates have on-site audiences been shown—and even in this format, campaigns have demanded visual proscriptions.

Carter's media adviser Barry Jagoda told *Newsweek* in 1976 that "one frown could color a whole public reaction."[71] Republican debate consultant William Carruthers, in a predebate strategy memo for Ford's campaign the same year, warned that a live audience represented "one of the most sensitive and potentially dangerous aspects of the debates. If there is any way we can preclude the appearance of an audience, we should do it."[72]

At the behest of the campaigns, the sponsoring League of Women Voters agreed to forbid spectator cutaways in the debates in 1976, a move that set off a nasty skirmish with the television networks. Likening the ban to censorship, the broadcasters contended they should be free to cover the debate as they would any bona fide news event. "If someone falls out of the balcony, boos or cheers, falls asleep, well, that's part of the event and we have a right to cover it," said Walter Pfister of the ABC Special Events unit, the group overseeing television pool coverage for the first debate.[73] After briefly hinting that they might refuse to carry the programs altogether, the networks backed down, and the series proceeded without audience reaction shots.

From a production standpoint, the effect of this prohibition was to artificially limit the way the event played out to viewers. As Seltz and Yoakam observed about the vice presidential debate of 1976, a television director operating without restriction might have cut to the audience when people in the hall laughed at Bob Dole's wisecracks. But rules imposed by the campaigns rendered this impossible. "To have faithfully reported the whole story of that debate," they concluded, "the director should have had the option of shooting the audience."[74]

A similar violation of visual grammar occurred in 1988, when Bernard Shaw asked Michael Dukakis the infamous question about the hypothetical rape and murder of his wife. For the program's director, the logical move would have been a reaction shot of Kitty Dukakis herself, seated in the audience only a few feet away. One could argue that such a cutaway, by adding visual context, might even have humanized her husband's clinical response. But the terms of that year's memorandum of understanding specifically forbade the possibility: "In no case shall any television shots be taken of any member of the audience (including candidate's family members) from the time the first question is asked until the conclusion of the closing statements."[75]

One of the boldest visual experiments in early presidential debates occurred in 1980, when CNN electronically inserted uninvited independent candidate John Anderson into the Reagan–Carter event. CNN, at that point an upstart operation with only 3.5 million subscribers, viewed the exercise as a publicity bonanza, though it turned out to be less a moment of glory than a technical farce.

As Reagan and Carter debated live in Cleveland, Anderson stood before CNN cameras at Constitution Hall in Washington, D.C., where an audience of 1,200 had gathered to watch him shadowbox the big boys. Four producers, camped in nearby production trucks, recorded the Reagan–Carter debate on as many videotape machines. These tapes were then played back in sequence, with Anderson's answers wedged in at the appropriate points. A stenographer listening to the live debate transcribed the panelists' questions from Cleveland, which were hand-delivered to CNN's moderator Daniel Schorr, who read them to Anderson in Constitution Hall.

Several times the audio either failed or fell out of synch with the video. Reagan was shown answering a question that had not yet been asked in CNN's version, and moderator Schorr understandably lost track of the complicated timing. In the *New York Times*, John J. O'Connor wrote, "The effort was extremely awkward. . . . But it was also an intriguing glimpse of a possible future when, armed with the multichannel capacities of constantly expanding cable, all third-party candidates will have access to a national forum that has proved impossible on limited over-the-air network television."[76]

Although time has not borne out O'Connor's prediction, recent cycles of presidential debates have introduced a number of pictorial innovations. The looser formats of the 1990s finally dragged debates into the modern era, particularly in the town hall forums, which, by definition, demand shots of candidates and audience members alike. Today's presidential debates are as visually sophisticated as almost everything else on television, with split screens, text graphics, animated graphics, real-time audience reactions, on-screen clocks, and the like.

Much of this pictorial layering is purely ornamental, but research by Harvard professors Todd Rogers and Michael Norton indicates a practical benefit as well: when text of the question is displayed on-screen while the debaters answer, the audience gains a mechanism for judging candidate responsiveness. "Our experiments show that this small visual tweak enables viewers to detect even the most artful dodges," they concluded.[77]

Debates have become more visually stimulating not because campaigns sought the change, but because the television networks that execute the programs ultimately control what goes out over the air. In the early rounds of presidential debates, only one version of the production was available to the various entities that carried it: the debate as directed by the designated pool network. Dissatisfaction with this practice dates back to 1976, when the sponsoring League of Women Voters refused to allow the broadcast networks to set up their own cameras in the debate hall. The pool was adopted as a practical solution to the problem of too much equipment competing for too little space.

Today, however, the pool network feeds not only its fully mixed version of the debate, with every shot selected by the director on-site, but also uninterrupted "unilateral" or "isolated" shots of the individual participants. This allows each outlet, in effect, to create its own visual rendering of the debate, including side-by-side split screens of both candidates at once. Although the contracts negotiated by the campaigns forbid reaction shots, the networks air them with impunity. In the final analysis, it is the television professionals, not the debaters, who determine which images get seen.

VISUAL MESSAGES IN PRESIDENTIAL DEBATES

One of the most storied of all presidential debate visuals materialized halfway through the first-of-its-kind town hall in Richmond in 1992, when George H. W. Bush glanced down at his watch. To many observers Bush appeared as though he was eager to leave. In an interview with Jim Lehrer in 1999, the former president confessed as much. "Now was I glad when the damn thing was over?" he asked. "Yeah, and maybe that's why I was looking at it—only ten more minutes of this crap."[78]

John LiBretto of NBC, who served as network pool director for the town hall in Richmond, considered himself free to call the camera shots as he saw fit. "I was cutting to him for a reaction shot," said LiBretto, "and as I cut to him he looked at his watch. I remember my reaction in the truck: What in the hell is he doing? That's exactly what came out of my mouth at that moment. The effect was devastating. I felt like here I just cut to a camera and cost the man the job, but I know that's not what happened."

LiBretto later wondered if he would have taken the shot had Bush looked at the watch *before* the camera change. "My instinct, especially as a sports director, is to go to that reaction shot," he said. "If it's there, if it's on camera, you go to it because you want to show everything that's going on."[79]

The visual imperative of presidential debates calls for the camera to focus on whatever is pictorially compelling, even when that image is unflattering. To an increasing extent, this means showing not just the person speaking, but also the reaction of the listener. "We want to give our viewers the opportunity to see both candidates as frequently as possible," said Sam Feist, Washington bureau chief for CNN, in 2012. "In a presidential debate, the image of the candidate who is listening is frequently as interesting as the candidate who is talking."[80]

In the first debate of 2004, the power of network producers to select their own camera angles proved devastating to George W. Bush. As in previous years, campaign negotiators had written into their memorandum of understanding a prohibition on reaction shots, though by now they realized that no such ban could be enforced. In advance of the debates, the television news networks made it clear they would ignore the restriction. "The campaigns have agreed to this—we haven't," Princell Hair, general manager of CNN, told the Associated Press. "We have access to these cameras and we're going to—as we would with any news event—decide which is the best way to broadcast this."[81]

"The best way" meant liberal use of split-screen reaction shots on all the networks—split screens that showed Kerry appearing confident and unruffled, blithely jotting notes while his opponent spoke. Bush, by contrast, served up a range of unflattering expressions and physical tics during Kerry's answers: scowls, knitted brows, mouth contortions, exaggerated blinks, hunched shoulders. The chief executive of the land came across like a child on the verge of a nasty tantrum. Reporter Ron Fournier of the Associated Press dubbed it "President Bush's pique performance—a flourish of fidgets, glares and grimaces." An undecided voter in Pennsylvania told the *Washington Post*, "Those looks of his drove me nuts. It was like Bush couldn't stand to hear the truth."[82]

Recognizing the potency of Bush's reactions shots, the Democratic National Committee hastily assembled a forty-five-second clip for its website called "The Faces of Frustration." The video showed the two debaters side by side, Kerry looking resolute and professional as Bush ran through the gamut of his goofy expressions. Upbeat jazz music accompanied the montage, no narration being necessary against such potent images. Edited into a compressed format, the shots of Bush were both comical and damning.

Republican officials scrambled to account for George W. Bush's testy performance, though their efforts at spin did not always align. "On his face, you could see his irritation at the senator's misrepresentations," said longtime handler Karen Hughes. "He was answering the senator with his face." But in the view of Karl Rove, "He was not looking irritated. I know irritated." Privately, members of Bush's campaign team realized their mistake in not stressing the importance of cutaways during the predebate practice sessions. According to media adviser Mark McKinnon, "In retrospect I think we should have been more focused on [the reaction shots] and better prepared for that outcome."[83]

As many commentators noted, the misfortune that befell Bush in the first debate of 2004 had also befallen Al Gore in the opening match four years earlier: both got nailed for their on-camera demeanor, especially during cutaways taken as their opponents were speaking. Something similar happened to John McCain in 2008, when his failure to look at Barack Obama became fodder for postdebate criticism. For presidential debaters, one television dynamic remains unchanged from the days of Richard Nixon: reaction shots send powerful, often unintentional, messages. Debaters should assume they are on camera at all times—because, in effect, they are.

Apparently this is a lesson that debaters must constantly relearn. In 2012 Barack Obama became the latest candidate to fall victim to the curse of the split screen. In his opening debate against Mitt Romney, Obama "soon began scribbling notes while his rival spoke, looking down and avoiding eye contact, even with the camera," wrote Alessandra Stanley in the *New York Times*.[84] Juxtaposed with images of a far more in-the-moment Romney, the shots of Obama cemented an impression of presidential disengagement. "We prepared for it," campaign manager David Axelrod said, "but obviously the split screen worked against us." Heading into the subsequent debate, he added, "We spent a lot more time on the whole reaction shot thing."[85]

GEORGE W. BUSH AND THE "MYSTERY BULGE"

In 2004, camera angles inspired a presidential debate mystery: the apparent presence in the first debate of a rectangular bulge situated under the back of George W. Bush's suit jacket. The issue quickly bubbled up via Internet postings by sharp-eyed viewers, who reported that in camera shots taken from behind, a boxy shape could be detected between Bush's shoulder blades. Early online speculation centered on the possibility that Bush had been wearing an electronic prompting device, a theory bolstered by the candidate's erratic performance and awkward timing.

The tale soon worked its way into the mainstream media, helped along by a series of less-than-persuasive clarifications from Bush's defenders. Presidential tailor Georges de Paris dismissed the bulge as a naturally occurring "pucker" that formed when the wearer shifted his posture. The White House seconded this hypothesis, with spokes-woman Nicolle Devenish calling the shape either a "wrinkle in the fab-ric" or a "rumpling." As Elisabeth Bumiller noted in the *New York Times,* "Ms. Devenish could not say why the 'rumpling' was rectangular."[86]

Excuses degenerated into scapegoating: on *Meet the Press* two weeks after the debate, Republican National Committee chair Ken Mehlman said, "I'm not sure what it was, but the gentleman responsible for the tailoring of that suit is no longer working for this administration." (In fact Mr. de Paris, suit-maker to every president since Lyndon Johnson, retained his job.) The White House's chief of staff Andrew Card echoed this talking point, blaming a "poorly tailored suit." George W. Bush himself, in an interview on *Good Morning America,* employed the same language—"I'm embarrassed to say it's a poorly tailored suit"—then pooh-poohed rumors that he had been receiving electronic signals: "I guess the assumption is that if I were straying off course they would, kind of like a hunting dog, they would punch a buzzer and I would jerk back into place. It's just absurd."[87]

For the most part, press coverage of Bush's bulge struck a lighthearted tone, reducing the allegation to an Internet conspiracy theory unwor-thy of serious inquiry. To some degree this was also the approach of Kerry's campaign. Appearing on the *Tonight Show,* vice presidential nominee John Edwards joked that he thought the object was Bush's battery and suggested that for the next debate, "John Kerry ought to pat him down."[88]

Online commentators were far more accepting of the story's legiti-macy. A website called isbushwired.com declared itself "a clearinghouse for discussion of whether President Bush uses an earpiece through which he's fed lines and cues by offstage advisers." Other sites soon followed, revisiting not just the debates but also previous instances in which Bush appeared to be taking cues from an unseen source.

The most dogged—and most credible—bulge investigator was Robert M. Nelson, a veteran photo-imaging specialist at NASA's Jet Propulsion Laboratory at the California Institute of Technology. Nelson, whose usual assignment was analyzing images from space probes, conducted an exhaustive visual dissection of the rear-angle shots of George W. Bush, enlarging the freeze frames and sharpening details. The results strongly suggested that an object had been present beneath Bush's suit coat during his first appearance with Kerry—and in the two following debates as well. "I am willing to stake my scientific reputation to the statement that Bush was wearing something under his jacket," Nelson told a reporter from the website *Salon*.[89]

Robert Nelson ended up sharing his photographic evidence with *Salon* after first attempting to interest major national news organizations in his findings. In fact he had begun working with two science reporters from the *New York Times* on an investigative story based on the photo enhancements; after several days the piece was spiked. According to executive editor Bill Keller, "In the end, nobody, including the scientist who brought it up, could take the story beyond speculation."[90] Minus the *Times* imprimatur, and amid the crush of preelection reporting, the national press corps soon lost interest in the saga of Bush's unexplained bulge. The moment had passed, except on the Internet, where questions resounded well past Election Day.

So what did account for the odd shape under Bush's jacket? The most benign theory is the official explanation: poor tailoring, though the freeze frames contradict this assertion. A report in the congressional publication *The Hill* suggested that Bush had been outfitted with a bulletproof vest,[91] an allegation the White House denied. Another strain of speculation, especially online, focused on the possibility that Bush might have been wearing some sort of medical device, such as a portable cardiac defibrillator, insulin pump, or back brace. Implicit in these claims was the cover-up of a presidential ailment.

Hard-core critics of George W. Bush never lost faith in the prompting device scenario. But the remote prompter hypothesis raised a number of counterarguments. First, in order to receive signals from an outside party, Bush would have needed some sort of earpiece, and none was discernible. Second, the danger involved in cheating during a live television debate far outweighs any potential benefit. Would a presidential contender in a neck-and-neck race really attempt such a risky stunt, knowing that its revelation would almost certainly cost him the White House? Finally, if Bush had been taking cues from an offstage source, puppet and puppet-master were completely out of synch: George W. Bush's delivery in Miami ranks among the worst debate showings by any presidential candidate since Nixon met Kennedy.

Questions about the bulge beneath George W. Bush's suit jacket have never been resolved. Whatever the explanation, a connection to the candidate's debate performance cannot be reliably established.

THE TELEVISION PROS TAKE OVER

Campaigns may function as executive producers of presidential debates, but once a program goes on the air, responsibility for its execution shifts from the political establishment to the television establishment. The advisers who draft the production agreements, plan the strategies, and oversee the on-site setup must now pass the baton to the television professionals, if only for the duration of the event.

The battle-zone atmosphere of the Kennedy–Nixon control rooms taught the networks to be wary of campaign interference while the program is on the air. The terms of the negotiated debate agreement provide for direct phone lines between campaigns and producers, and on occasion handlers have been allowed to sit in the control room for the broadcast. In practice, these arrangements are more perfunctory than hands-on; political operatives do not stand over the director's shoulder barking orders as he carries out his duties.

Nonetheless, there have been instances of campaigns expressing concerns while a debate is in progress. In the first presidential encounter in 1992, Bush's campaign chairman, James Baker, had one of his deputies telephone the control room with an urgent message for moderator Jim Lehrer. According to the language of the debate contract, the topic was supposed to shift from domestic to foreign policy halfway through the program; five minutes past this point, the switch had not occurred. Before the message could be communicated to Lehrer, the debate moved to foreign affairs anyway. Baker's phone call "didn't have any effect on what happened on the stage," Lehrer said.[92]

More typically, campaigns tend to back off during the actual telecast. For one thing, they know they are outmatched, not just by the professional experience of the crews but by the medium itself. A television production is an organic exercise, with its own energy and personality. Invariably, live programming overpowers the prescriptive words of a document. As debate producer Ed Fouhy put it, "Trying to micromanage a television program with a lot of lawyers is something that's not going to work."[93]

The negotiated documents that cause so much strife for the campaigns prior to the debate only indirectly affect the television crews who bring the program to life. John LiBretto, a director in 1992, said he did not even see the production guidelines that governed the town hall debate he directed in Richmond. "The 36-page documents are in the possession of the campaigns and in possession of the commission," said Janet Brown of the debate commission. "My sound guy who has done the Super Bowl and the Olympics and all this other stuff—trust me when I tell you he's not carrying a pocket copy of a 36-page thing, even though microphones are usually mentioned." Brown added that this does not mean sponsors willfully ignore the wishes of the campaigns: "It just means that it's a television event and you get on with doing the job."

The agreements spell out the specifics of camera shots in what Brown described as "excruciating detail." Instances have occurred during debates, she said, when campaign officials have complained that visual guidelines are being violated. "There are inevitably shots that end up mid-debate that some campaign guy, because he wants to sound important, is going to object to," Brown said. "Are you going to stop the debate and bring the director onstage and say, 'You abrogated the agreement'? I think not."

Brown notes that the highly skilled network directors chosen for this assignment understand and respect the seriousness of the occasion. From the beginning, presidential debates have been staffed with top-flight professionals who operate comfortably in the high-pressure setting of live, big-ticket television. They come from newscasts and magazine programs, talk shows, sports, even *Saturday Night Live*. Their mission is complicated: working within a tightly controlled political framework to create a television event that will enter the archives of American history.

"The quality of our production staff is without peer," says Janet Brown, citing the crews' experience in producing inaugural coverage and summit conferences, high-profile sporting events, and Academy Awards shows. "If there's something in television they haven't dealt with," she said, "I don't know what it is."[94] According to Bob Asman, a veteran of NBC who served as the debate commission's executive producer in 1996, the pool network takes pride in putting on a polished program, "so the tendency is to really use your best people."[95]

"I don't know how many times I went to meetings and demanded that the crew be absolutely the best crew NBC had," recalled Richmond's director LiBretto. "I told them about the sense of history I had about this—that we would be judged accordingly, and it had better be good. I insisted on an excellent crew and I got it."

Shortly before the groundbreaking debate, LiBretto and his team sat down for a group dinner. "It was the first time I've ever seen any of these guys nervous in all the years I've worked with them," he remembered. "Super Bowls, World Series—I've done major, major events with all these people."[96] Nothing in the world of television, he said, could quite match the pressure of a presidential debate.

PART III / REACTION

8 / SOCIAL MEDIA AND REAL-TIME REACTIONS

At 9:42 P.M. Eastern time, less than halfway into the first Obama–Romney debate of 2012, a nine-paragraph post appeared on the popular website BuzzFeed, headlined "How Mitt Romney Won the First Debate." "Romney's core success was that he won by not losing," wrote the story's author, BuzzFeed's political editor Ben Smith. "He has barely weathered a campaign that reduced him to a smaller figure than President Obama. On stage, they were roughly the same size."[1]

Smith's verdict quickly gained currency among his journalistic peers, cementing a narrative already taking root in real time on Twitter and other social media: Obama was tanking; Romney was clicking. In the crucial first half hour of the debate, momentum snowballed around Obama's dismal delivery. More rapidly and more conclusively than in any previous presidential debate, first impressions hardened into received wisdom. A new era had dawned in debates, one characterized by present-tense reactions, instantaneous judgments, and direct participation by the millions.

This tectonic shift in the way viewers consume debates makes 2012 a pivotal year in presidential debate history. In prior cycles, viewers and the media had to wait until after the program ended to render evaluations and compare notes. Now, thanks to innovations like Twitter, Facebook, Reddit, Xbox, and others, presidential debates generate real-time responses that add the voice of the public to the voice of the pundits. At least in theory, everyone with a computer or mobile device gets to comment on the debate, even as the event unfolds.

This development carries enormous implications for the candidates, for the press, for the electorate, and, at an existential level, for presidential debates themselves. Always risky, these high-stakes appearances now play out as collective national exercise of brief, sequential thumbs-up/thumbs-down judgments. With journalists and the public appraising debates on a statement-by-statement basis, candidates are under pressure to produce defining moments that dazzle the audience. As real-time reactions gain importance, debate narratives are evolving in quirky, unexpected ways: the same match that Obama so badly bungled also produced Mitt Romney's reference to the *Sesame Street* character Big Bird, a tossed-off one-liner that exploded on social media.

What is the net effect of this shift from postdebate, pundit-centric commentary to real-time reaction by the masses? Although the change remains too recent to be reliably understood, we can say with certainty that live televised debates are now scrutinized at a more granular level than ever, more immediately than ever, and by more arbiters than ever. For participants this raises the already perilous stakes: a debater's every word, gesture, and expression are under the microscope for the duration of the program and beyond. Audiences have always given presidential debates a close reading, but the relentlessness of social media considerably intensifies the level of observation—scrutiny on steroids, not just from the media but from the entire body politic.

EARLY REAL-TIME REACTIONS

Journalists and politicos have long been interested in measuring real-time responses to presidential debates. Campaign professionals were the first to commission focus groups to gauge live voter reaction during debates, arming an assortment of carefully selected citizens with handheld meters that register minute-by-minute responses to everything the debaters say and do. Intended exclusively for internal use, the results of these efforts have not been part of the general conversation.

News organizations have incorporated similar real-time survey techniques into their coverage—typically, dial groups of debate watchers who press buttons on handheld devices to express approval or disapproval of what they see and hear. For the second presidential debate of 1988, local station KHQ in Spokane, Washington, pioneered the technique on television, gathering a studio audience of ninety voters and displaying their live reactions by way of a superimposed graph.

CNN adopted the gimmick for its debate coverage in 1992, creating an animated "living graph" that showed the unfolding responses of un-committed voters on a moment-to-moment basis. Howard Rosenberg of the *Los Angeles Times* pronounced the technique "goofy," and said, "If you thought Perot was sidesplitting, then you should have caught CNN commentator William Schneider trying to explain what it all meant." Four years later NBC experimented with its own moment-to-moment graph, which *Washington Post* critic Howard Kurtz termed "incomprehensible."[2]

In Australia and New Zealand, this squiggly line at the bottom of the screen, dubbed "the worm," has been a hallmark of televised electoral debates since the 1990s. Inevitably its use provokes controversy. Critics charge that such on-screen displays wield a subtle but definite influence on viewers' perceptions of what they are seeing—at the very least, worms create a visual distraction. Apart from CNN, which continued to display running-reaction graphs in the debates in 2008 and 2012, the technique never really caught on among American television networks. Now, with social media producing broad-based, real-time data on citizen reaction, the need for focus groups of sample voters may have vanished.

Years before Twitter arrived on the scene, the Internet's capacity for supplying real-time information inspired an earlier and still viable out-let for instant reaction: live-blogging. Live-bloggers, both amateur and professional, provide a running commentary throughout the debate in the form of brief, continuously refreshed posts. Although the live blogs featured on traditional news sites tend more toward stenography than analysis, those written by opinion bloggers often bring fresh perspec-tives and valuable context to the debates. In that sense live-blogging pre-figures Twitter, and remains superior in its level of complexity.

For the past several election cycles, campaigns have assiduously courted influential bloggers, just as they court mainstream political re-porters. In 2004 John Kerry's team announced that debate bloggers would receive "special attention throughout the night with dedicated staffers providing them with rebuttals and fact checks." Additionally, both Kerry's and Bush's campaigns sent mass e-mails to millions of their supporters, urging them to talk up their candidate's performance in online polls, chat rooms, and discussion boards. As Republican strategist Mark Wallace explained, "There's primary, secondary, and tertiary spin."[3]

It was not until the presidential campaign of 2008 that social media began to assume a proactive role in debates. That season's presidential primaries introduced an array of experiments: the CNN/YouTube debate, in which viewers submitted videotaped questions for the candidates; instant messaging forums sponsored by MTV and MySpace; a "mashup" by the Huffington Post, Yahoo, and Slate that offered statements recorded by the candidates on various topics for remixing by the public; and 10Questions.com, a project of the website TechPresident that allowed citizens to vote on which questions should be asked in presidential debates.

Twitter, which was launched in 2006, inspired a forward-thinking experiment in the debates in 2008: "Hack the Debate" on Current TV, an independent cable and satellite network cofounded by former vice president Al Gore. As the centerpiece of its debate coverage in 2008, Current TV superimposed a continuous stream of tweets over the live exchanges between Barack Obama and John McCain. "One of the reasons we'll be layering tweets directly over the broadcast is to make a statement," wrote Current CEO Joel Hyatt. "Interactivity isn't an afterthought. The audience's voice matters. The presidential debates—and politics in general—should go two ways."[4]

Before displaying the tweets on screen, a team of editors and lawyers reviewed them for obscene language and copyright violations. Current TV ran an estimated 2,700 tweets for each of the Obama–McCain debates—about one every two seconds. "The effect of the set-up could be ghostly at times—it was like having a group of disembodied members of the community chiming in telepathically," wrote Sarah Lai Stirland of *Wired*. "But the hacked debate for the most part added a much-needed face-lift to a shopworn regime."[5]

The Current TV experiment raised several concerns at the time, concerns that four years later would seem quaint. The small pool of younger-than-average viewers who sent debate-related tweets favored Obama over McCain, giving Obama a distinct edge in the visual presentation. Some Current TV viewers complained that the running text flew by too fast, diverting attention from the debaters themselves. According to one academic study, "the tenor of the tweets during the debate was distinctly negative"—41.7 percent, compared with 25.1 percent positive tweets. A second academic study found that the tweets were more "reactionary and evaluative" than substantive. "The most frequent term during the opening segment from Twitter was 'drinking'—we assume people were inventing drinking games to play along with the debate," concluded the study's authors.[6]

"Hack the Debate" was seen by only a sliver of debate watchers in 2008. In the deafening crush of commentary surrounding the Obama–McCain debates, the experiment received remarkably little attention outside the tech-oriented press. But "Hack the Debate" pointed toward a future in which presidential debates would be driven as much by real-time voter reaction as by media punditry after the fact.

2012: THE YEAR OF TWITTER

The general election debates in 2008—three between Obama and McCain, one between Biden and Palin—generated a combined total of around half a million debate-related tweets. Four years later, the first Obama–Romney debate alone inspired 10.3 million tweets, making it the most tweeted-about event in American political history up to that point, and the fourth most tweeted-about telecast of any kind. By the time the series ended in 2012, some 27.5 million debate-related tweets had been sent—fifty-five times as many as in the previous presidential race.[7]

Impressive as these statistics are, they tell only part of the story. The explosive growth of Twitter brought not just a dramatic increase in the number of users in 2012 but also a radical shift in the way presidential debates are viewed, critiqued, won, and spun. By exponentially broadening the conversation, Twitter, along with other social media, forced campaigns and the press to reconfigure their approach to debates.

A key effect of Twitter was to transplant the locus of debate reaction from after to during the event, with live responses delivering an ongoing nationwide verdict. According to Democratic debate adviser Ron Klain, "It definitely moves the power over how this event is interpreted from a postdebate spin game to an in-the-debate Twitter game."[8] What was once a closed loop—journalists covering the debate, campaigns seeking to influence that coverage—is now open to the public at large. And the public has eagerly jumped on board.

"Twitter has become the natural companion to the televised experience," according to Adam Sharp, head of government and elections for Twitter in Washington, D.C. "It has taken us back to the idea of everybody gathering together on the couch to share the experience of watching this pivotal event in history—but now, that couch is big enough to fit the whole country."[9]

Shortly after the first Obama–Romney debate, Dashiell Bennett of the *Atlantic* summed up the shift in an online post entitled "Twitter Won the Presidential Debate." "The idea of watching such a key national event without the instant reactions of your fellow tweeters has become almost unthinkable," Bennett said. "If you're just watching on TV and not taking part in (or at least following) the simultaneous online conversation, then you might as well not even be paying attention at all."[10]

Debate reaction on Twitter and other social media took some unforeseen turns. Bluefin Labs, a social analytics company in Cambridge, Massachusetts, conducted a study of social media conversations as part of its Crowdwire initiative, which focused on the presidential election of 2012. According to Crowdwire, more women than men commented about the first debate by a margin of 55 percent to 45 percent. "It pulled in a lot of women who don't typically talk about political shows," Crowdwire concluded; "younger women in particular." Over the course of the remaining debates, women continued to outnumber men as social media commenters.

Researchers found that nearly one in ten of those who wrote on social media about the opening Obama–Romney debate were tweeting or posting about a televised event for the first time. "The Super Bowl and several entertainment-awards shows have drawn responses from large numbers of newbies," according to Crowdwire. "But this is the first time a political event has sparked such a large influx."[11]

To a great extent, debate reaction on Twitter centered upon specific phrases and moments. Mitt Romney's reference to Big Bird inspired more than 250,000 tweets. President Obama's "horses and bayonets" line sparked more than 105,000, and Joe Biden's use of the word *malarkey* produced 30,000. Romney's oddly constructed phrase "binders full of women," intended to accentuate his commitment to gender diversity, rose to number one on Twitter's trending topics. Each of these examples became amplified both during and after the debates in parody accounts, Facebook groups, web searches, and visual spoofs.

Twitter users also opined vigorously about the moderators. In the first debate, when Mitt Romney requested a topic change and Jim Lehrer quipped "Let's not," Twitter lit up with 158,690 tweets per minute—the biggest response of the night. Several hours before the second Obama–Romney debate, Adam Sharp of Twitter noted in an online preview post that "Twitter conversation about [moderator Candy] Crowley is already crescendoing. Her role is also sparking discussion given the high level of conversation and opinion about the two moderators to date, Jim Lehrer and Martha Raddatz."[12]

Twitter applied its "Twitter Political Index" to the debate moderators in 2012, tracking their standing among users of the service before and after each debate—just as it rated the candidates themselves. Lehrer dropped nine points after moderating the first Obama–Romney match; after the vice presidential debate, Raddatz saw her number rise by twelve.

Which is not to suggest that Twitter users were concerned exclusively with performance critiques and one-liners. Substantive matters also resonated—150,000 tweets per minute in the first debate on the topic of Medicare, to cite one example. Even viral catch-phrases like "Big Bird" and "horses and bayonets" led to serious exchanges about the funding of public television and the shifting priorities of military spending. "That moment that may have gotten all the buzz is still really just a fraction of what people are talking about," said Twitter's Adam Sharp. "The bulk of the audience is interested in substantive issues. You don't get to a tweet volume around the 2012 debates that exceeded that of the Olympics and the Super Bowl just on frivolous reactions."

As for Twitter's political effects, early research suggests that debate-tweeting may be a case of preaching to the choir. After the Biden–Ryan vice presidential match, the social media marketing company SocialFlow compiled tweets that conclusively declared one or the other candidate as having won—an almost even number. Researchers found a striking degree of polarization between the two camps: those who thought Biden won followed an entirely different group of Twitter sources than those who thought Ryan won, with virtually no overlap between the two. "The narrative is that technology is the great democratizer," said Social-Flow executive Gilad Lotan, "yet we are divided as ever into our familiar neighborhoods."[13]

TWITTER'S EFFECT ON NEWS COVERAGE

"Walk into the filing center at a presidential debate and you'll see hundreds of reporters seated at tables doing two things: Watching the action on TV and monitoring Twitter on their laptops," wrote Dana Milbank of the *Washington Post* during the presidential campaign of 2012. "They are hard at work on one of the most elaborate exercises ever undertaken in groupthink."

In Milbank's view, the promise of Twitter and other social media—to diversify the debate conversation by adding new voices to the mix—got subverted. Instead of an array of perspectives, the shared conversation on Twitter produced a monolithic, self-reinforcing response, especially from journalists. "Not too long ago, the wire services, broadcast networks and newspapers covered major political events differently," Milbank said. "Each outlet had its own take and tidbits. But now everybody is operating off the same script and, except for a few ideological outliers, the product is homogenous."[14]

Similar misgivings were expressed by Peter Hamby, a political reporter for CNN who after the election of 2012 spent a semester at Harvard debriefing journalists and political professionals about the campaign. "No one is complaining about the revolutionary gateway to news and information that Twitter provides," Hamby concluded. "But plenty of people in politics are anxious about the way the Twitter conversation thrives on incrementalism, self-involvement and snark."[15]

As Milbank and Hamby observe, Twitter prizes the pithy riposte over the nuanced observation, the freeze frame over the big picture. A Pew Research Center study of two months of media coverage of the general election presidential campaign of 2012 found Twitter to be the "most negative" of all the news platforms analyzed. "Every week on Twitter resembled the worst week for each candidate in the mainstream press," wrote the study's authors.[16] Inevitably this negative tone attached itself to the debates, whose competitive stakes and high visibility intensify already passionate viewership.

Twitter's influence in the debates of 2012 extended not just to journalists and other users of the service, but to traditional audiences watching the programs on television. During the live telecasts various networks displayed on-screen tweets, just as Current TV had done four years earlier. As before, the tweets competed for attention with the words of the debaters. Stephen Kurczy, in the online publication *Construction Magazine*, described watching the first Obama–Romney debate as one of several hundred spectators at a performing arts venue in Brooklyn, where "the laughter from some tweets actually drowned out the candidates." At first, Kurczy found himself annoyed. "Then, as I grew frustrated with Mitt Romney's jiving around his $5 trillion tax gap and confused with Barack Obama's stuttering responses, I realized that the most interesting thing on TV was Twitter."[17]

In partnership with Twitter, Fox News in 2012 displayed an on-screen graphic that measured the volume of Twitter conversation moment by moment for the duration of the live event. A counter at the bottom of the screen tracked the number of tweets per minute, giving television viewers a clear visualization of how the debate was playing in real time, and which comments were hitting home with the tweeting public.

This citizen response, in turn, influences professional debate assessments. According to Adam Sharp of Twitter, "journalists can be even more forceful in their follow-up because they are backed by this demonstrated public sentiment as opposed to the whims of one person sitting in the studio." In Sharp's view, the wisdom of the crowd as expressed on Twitter gives reporters "an opportunity to be a more effective proxy for the public interest."

TWITTER'S USE BY THE CAMPAIGNS

Like journalists, campaign professionals have also embraced Twitter. "I think the challenge of 2012 was that Twitter adoption was probably exceeding our comprehension of how to use it," said Zachary Moffatt, digital director of Romney for President.[18] Unlike Obama's campaign, Romney's team had gained invaluable experience with the platform during the long and grueling Republican primary season. "I think that was probably an advantage we had over the Obama group, because they hadn't done twenty primaries like we had," Moffatt said. "We learned what you had to have."

The debate preparations by Romney's campaign included a 179-page document organized by topic that itemized potential responses to be tweeted during the debate. "Literally as Obama was saying something, then we would have a tweet pre-approved, plus or minus a few words, and a graphic that went with it," according to Moffatt. "We were doing test runs on the debates every weekend for five weeks before, so we would be ready for debate night."

By contrast, Obama's forces were caught flat-footed in the first debate by the groundswell of tweets criticizing the president's performance. "Even the Obama rapid response team appeared at a loss on exactly how to fire back, sending five or so press releases that didn't stick," wrote BuzzFeed's Michael Hastings. About the only break Obama caught on Twitter during the opening debate came from Mitt Romney's ill-advised reference to Big Bird, which diverted the spotlight from Obama to Romney. (Two days after the debate, Obama's campaign dispatched a costumed Big Bird to a rally for Mitt Romney, bearing the placard "Crack down on Wall Street, not Sesame Street.")

For the subsequent debates, Obama's campaign command considerably beefed up its Twitter efforts. Hoping to persuade journalists that the first debate had been an aberration, the president's strategists pushed a comeback narrative. From the opening minutes of the second program, it was clear that Obama would assume an aggressive posture; in his first two answers, Obama essentially called his opponent a liar, and the mood did not lighten from there. As part of its Twitter strategy, Obama's campaign also urged supporters to send positive tweets, force-multiplying the drama that played out onstage.

For the third debate, Obama crafted a line specifically to capitalize on Twitter's appetite for the clever turn of phrase: "horses and bayonets," a vivid image deployed by the president to emphasize his opponent's outmoded thinking on military spending. According to Obama's adviser Ron Klain, "We came up with the horses and bayonets line because we thought that would be a hashtag on Twitter. We thought it would drive the Twittersphere." Before the debate, Obama's prep crew alerted the campaign's social media team that "horses and bayonets" was looming on the horizon. "There's a part of deb prep that's about getting ready for the post-debate period," Klain said, "and up until 2012 it was all about getting ready to prove your candidate is right, lining up the points for the spinners. But in 2012 that morphs into a conversation with your digital media and your social media team about what kind of things to drive on Twitter."

As part of their response, both presidential campaigns purchased trending Twitter terms as advertising vehicles while the debates were still under way. According to Adam Sharp of Twitter, "Less than 30 seconds after Mitt Romney uttered the words 'binders full of women,' the Obama campaign had an ad running on Twitter against that particular search phrase. Likewise the Romney campaign was up in less than 30 seconds when Biden said 'malarkey.'" This stepped-up pace, Sharp said, represents a dramatic change in the way campaigns seek to leverage specific debate moments. "If you think about the cycle in years past, of how long it would have taken a campaign to take an opponent's sound bite in a debate, package that into an ad, and get it onto the air in front of a few million people, you would have been talking about a cycle of days. And now from start to finish that cycle was complete in less than a minute."

In less revolutionary ways, the campaigns also used Twitter for promotional purposes. During the vice presidential debate, Obama's aides tweeted a photo of the president on board Air Force One watching Joe Biden and Paul Ryan in action. For that same debate, Romney's campaign tweeted pictures of the Republican candidate sharing pizza with the winner of a "Win a Bite with Mitt" contest; the woman, identified only as "Christine B," had donated fifteen dollars in order to compete for a chance to watch Biden–Ryan alongside the nominee. A few hours before the debate, Paul Ryan tweeted a shot of himself with his seven-year-old son, Sam. The caption: "Great pep talk with one of my most trusted advisors."

DUAL-SCREEN VIEWERSHIP AND OTHER REAL-TIME REACTIONS

Heading into the general election debates in 2012, the telecommunications company Verizon commissioned a poll to see how Americans intended to view the events. The poll found that 65 percent of the voters surveyed planned to watch the debates on live television with a computer, smartphone, or media tablet in their hands. This "second-screen" phenomenon was expected to manifest itself in several key ways: to follow and post reactions on social media, to fact-check candidates' claims, and to track what comedians were saying.[19]

The actual number of dual-screeners appears to have fallen a good deal short of what the Verizon poll predicted. After the first debate, a Pew Research Center study found that only one in ten viewers had watched on more than one screen. Among those under the age of forty, however, that rate was considerably higher: nearly one-third (32 percent) experienced the Obama–Romney match via a combination of television plus a second device, and 10 percent of under-forty debate watchers followed the program exclusively on a computer or mobile device.[20] The message is clear: debates may still be predominantly television events, but an ever-increasing portion of the audience is either watching on more than one screen or watching solely online.

This comports with a broader trend in electoral politics, in which social media have inspired a stepped-up level of public engagement. "People like talking about politics, and [social media are] another venue for them to share their excitement," said Aaron Smith, a Pew research scientist who studied political engagement and social media in the campaign of 2012. "A small number of really engaged people can in many instances, at least from the point of an election campaign, be more powerful than a large number of people who are either passively engaged or are only marginally interested."[21]

Such was the case with the debates in 2012. Although real-time reactions on social media reflected the views of a relatively limited number of voters, the fervor and energy of those reactions had a multiplying effect—in the media, the public, and the campaigns. "You need a strategy to deal with the second screen," acknowledged Ron Klain of Obama's campaign. "It changes how the debates are seen; it changes how they're understood."

Already dual-screen viewership has altered the time-honored practice of fact-checking. In 2012 both Romney's and Obama's campaigns set up microsites and Twitter accounts dedicated to debunking dubious statements uttered during the debates. According to Zac Moffatt of Romney's campaign, "We have the expertise with all the research in place, so when he says 'I say X,' and we have him on the record saying 'Y,' we have that video already cut, we have that graphic ready to go."[22]

For candidates these online fact-checking efforts are useful, because they serve as informational footnotes that free them from having to debunk claims during the program itself. "There are a lot of ways to get content to people that don't involve it coming out of your candidate's mouth," said Klain. "So we made a decision in the third debate to basically have Obama say, Romney's just wrong, here's my point, and let others fill in on why. You're not wasting debate time."

As in election cycles past, a number of media outlets also set up operations devoted to fact-checking the candidates' assertions. The website PolitiFact.com had a staff of about ten reporters and editors on duty for each of the events; given the time constraints of a live debate, much of their work involved linking to previously scrutinized claims. During the campaign in 2012, PolitiFact saw a sizable uptick in web traffic. According to founder and editor Bill Adair, "It's just gone off the charts on debate nights."[23]

FactCheck.org, a project of the Annenberg Public Policy Center at the University of Pennsylvania, offered a similar service, as did the Sunlight Foundation, a nonprofit organization that advocates for government transparency through the use of technological tools. Traditional news organizations like the Associated Press, major newspapers like the *New York Times* and *Washington Post*, and the national television networks ran fact-checking operations of their own, allowing viewers to judge the veracity of the candidates' statements during and after the debate.

It bears mention that Twitter, despite its outsized role in the debates in 2012, presented only a limited mechanism for live fact-checking. Research published in the *International Journal of Press/Politics* found that political reporters on Twitter tended to repeat the candidates' assertions more than challenge or contextualize them. "For all the talk of Twitter as a revolutionary tool, what we and others have found is that political journalists tend to use it simply to snark, talk strategy, and link to their work," said the study's lead author, Mark Coddington. "Those are all fine ways to use Twitter, but that's a big journalistic whiff if it's not being used for anything more substantial than that."[24]

Although Twitter dominated real-time debate reaction in 2012, other social media platforms drew their share of users as well. According to the social analytics company Attention, 77 percent of the online conversation after the first Obama–Romney debate took place on Twitter, as opposed to 7 percent for blog posts and 6 percent each for Facebook and Tumblr. For the second debate, however, Facebook caught up to Twitter, with each accounting for about 40 percent of the conversation. "Since messages on Twitter tend to be one-sided and immediate, it is harder to engage with in a meaningful way," Attention's analysis concluded. "The increased mentions on Facebook indicates conversations and, accordingly, debates."[25]

Facebook's increased prominence in the second presidential debate stemmed partly from the runaway success of a "Binders Full of Women" page, created in response to Mitt Romney's ham-handed attempt to depict himself as a champion of hiring females. Within twenty-four hours, the "Binders Full of Women" Facebook page had gotten nearly 300,000 "likes."[26] As with other debate-inspired memes, "Binders" stands as an example of the power of the crowd to elevate isolated, seemingly trivial debate moments to matters of national consequence.

According to Zac Moffatt of Romney's campaign, in the context of presidential debates, social media can be plotted on a time-based continuum. "On the far end, in real time, would be Twitter, because that's how instantaneous determinations are being made, and also it's the primary means of communication for reporters," Moffatt said. Because of its popularity with journalists, Twitter carries "disproportional value." Facebook, according to Moffatt, "probably has the furthest reach because it has a far higher adoption rate, it's far more visual, it has larger audiences so you can do more with it." On the timeline, Facebook occupies the middle spot. After Twitter and Facebook comes the final phase of the continuum, the Google search. "Twitter's in real time, Facebook is probably on a three-to-six-hour lag, and Google the next morning puts structure to all the conversations that occurred the night before," Moffatt said.

Both during and after the live events, Google searches provide a clear sense of what viewers are interested in. For all but one of the debates in 2012, the most popular real-time search term was "Who is winning the debate?," an indication that media pundits are not the only ones obsessed with the horse race. Predictably, sound bite terms like "Big Bird," "horses and bayonets," "binders full of women," and "malarkey" trended on Google, but so did policy-oriented topics such as the Dodd–Frank law, the Simpson–Bowles debt plan, and the war in Syria.

A hallmark of the 2012 presidential debates was the panoply of choices audiences had for seeing and reacting to the event. Beyond traditional television, viewers could watch live-streams on YouTube, Hulu, Ustream, and the websites of major news outlets, where real-time interactivity accompanied the experience. Smartphone users could register live feedback via mobile apps such as Peel and Ponderoo. Spanish-speakers could catch a live translation of the debates on Univision.

Tumblr, the popular blogging site and social networking platform, covered the debates with a string of rapidly produced GIF (graphic interchange format) animations—freeze-framed images looped together to create the illusion of motion. In a press release announcing its plans, Tumblr poked fun at its unorthodox approach: "Elevating the discourse as only Tumblr can, we'll have a crack team of GIF artists cranking out instant animations of the best debate moments, from zingers to gaffes to awkward silences."[27] As promised, the animations commemorated everything from Big Bird and binders full of women to Joe Biden's facial expressions during the vice presidential debate—a social media version of political cartooning.

In 2012 the video game industry also stuck its oar in the water. Microsoft's Xbox Live service offered subscribers the opportunity to watch and respond to the debates on their game consoles; the final two Obama–Romney debates attracted some 100,000 viewers each on Xbox. In partnership with the market research firm YouGov, Xbox live-polled its users on a range of issues raised in the debates, generating tens of thousands of answers.[28]

Matt Peckham, author of *Time* magazine's *Techland* blog, described the experience of watching the final presidential debate on Xbox and taking part in the polling. Like other multiscreeners, he did so while simultaneously monitoring Twitter and Facebook. "It's what we do these days, often vamping and cracking jokes as events occur," Peckham wrote. "But is all this interaction coming at a cost? Are we too distracted to properly analyze what we're hearing, especially in a debate where many of the responses were complex or wide-ranging?"[29]

Technology may be revolutionizing presidential debates, but not everyone is ready to jump on the bandwagon. For the first Obama–Romney match, columnist Ken Wheaton of *Advertising Age* made a conscious decision to tune in the old-fashioned way, "without the so-called benefits of social media." He put away his phone and computer and experienced the debate the way voters did in the era of Kennedy–Nixon: as a television program. At the end of the debate, after coming to his own decision about what he had seen, Wheaton went online to discover how the event was playing on social media. The tsunami of reaction instantly turned him off. Social media, he said, "sounded like an unfortunate hybrid between the vapidity of traditional political media and the hysteria of sports fanatics."

Wheaton identified three ways in which debate watchers were using social media: "(a) looking for comments that you agree with to shore up your position, (b) looking for comments you disagree with in order to fight, (c) snarking on one or both sides because you're a funny guy." Such reactions might be appropriate for an entertainment event, he said, but "not so much for focusing on the actual debate and arriving at your own conclusions based on what either candidate is saying."

Wheaton's verdict: "It's much easier to listen to the candidates if you're, you know, listening to the candidates."[30]

9 / POSTDEBATE NEWS COVERAGE

When the first Kennedy–Nixon debate signed off the air at 10:30 P.M. Eastern Daylight time on September 26, 1960, the broadcast networks did not follow the event with news analysis. Instead, they resumed regular programming: the *Original Amateur Hour* on ABC; *Jackpot Bowling with Milton Berle* on NBC; and, on CBS, a prerecorded interview between Walter Cronkite and Lyndon Johnson. For the duration of the debates in 1960, television scrupulously refrained from instant commentary and postevent news specials. Remarkable as it may seem to contemporary audiences, the millions of Americans who tuned in for the debates in 1960 had to wait until the next morning's newspapers to catch the reviews.

In 1976 this programming isolation ended, and today no presidential debate exists in a vacuum. Starting with the Ford–Carter matches and continuing to the present, a live debate has come to represent only the centerpiece of the larger media marathon that begins weeks before air time and ends well after the program fades to black. In the aftermath of a presidential debate, two things happen: initial impressions settle into conventional wisdom, and the ninety-minute event is reduced to a collection of highlight clips that serve as a shorthand for the program in full. A parallel version of the debate thus emerges, one that may overtake viewers' original perceptions of what they saw.

This was hardly the case in 1960. That year, for the first and last time, the debate story belonged almost exclusively to the pencil press, whose visual limitations and slower deadlines meant subdued coverage. At the time of the Kennedy–Nixon debates, television news scarcely registered in the national consciousness, much less as the country's primary conduit of campaign journalism. The day after the first event, none of the three network newscasts led with the debate. CBS ran only a brief mention of the joint appearance as the tenth story in its lineup, after such items as the arrival of Japanese royalty in Washington, Nigerian independence preparations, and a plane crash in Moscow.[1]

Television news outlets approached the debates in 1960 warily, perhaps because the programs were produced and sponsored by the very networks that would then have to provide objective coverage. By today's standards, television's underplaying of the events seems almost irrationally circumspect. Not a single newscast excerpted sound bites from the Kennedy–Nixon broadcasts. Neither the candidates nor their surrogates came forth with any on-camera spin, and anchormen and reporters studiously avoided anything but the most cursory references to the debate.

Newspaper accounts were decidedly less diffident. Richard Nixon's anemic performance handed print reporters a story line that would sustain momentum for the remainder of the series. The morning after the debate in Chicago, the *Christian Science Monitor*'s Richard Strout was among the first to assess the effect of the reaction shots: "The cameras showed close-ups of the listening candidate's face while the other talked. . . . Nixon looking to many weary from endless campaigning, with chin perspiring under the hot TV lamps." Peter Lisagor, in the *Chicago Daily News*, wrote that Nixon's face "looked drawn, and beads of perspiration on his chin were plainly visible as he spoke." The *Boston Globe*'s Percy Shain also used the word "drawn" to describe Nixon, and added, "Kennedy was almost chubby by contrast."[2]

In the days that followed, journalists had no difficulty keeping this tale alive. Nixon's people did their part by issuing hasty proclamations of their candidate's vitality. Press secretary Herbert Klein announced that "Mr. Nixon is in excellent health and looks good in person." Pat Nixon told a reporter she didn't know if her husband had lost weight "because Dick and I aren't the types who weigh in every day." Nixon himself said, "I think I lost a couple of pounds and it may show up in my face."[3]

Three days after the first debate, the *Chicago Daily News* goosed the narrative with a copyrighted front-page article that ran under the headline "Was Nixon Sabotaged by TV Makeup Artist?"[4] The story quoted an official from the makeup artists and hair stylists union in New York as saying he believed Nixon had been worked on by a Democrat. "They loused him up so badly that a Republican couldn't have done the job," the union rep alleged. Although no evidence was advanced to support this claim, the *Daily News* nonetheless used the quote to trump up the possibility of a conspiracy. Network officials denied the charge, and the vice president's aides stepped forward to admit they had done their own cosmetic work.

The matter of Nixon's camera presence snowballed in the press. By the time the weekly news magazines published their accounts of the first debate, the received wisdom had been set in concrete. "Within minutes after the candidates went off the air," wrote *Newsweek*, "the whole country seemed to be chattering about who did what to whom. But the one question that was on almost everyone's lips was: Why did Nixon look so haggard, so worn, and so grim?"[5] Even Nixon himself got into the act. During a visit to the set of the television series *77 Sunset Strip*, the vice president joked to actor Efrem Zimbalist Jr., "How come you look like yourself with makeup and I don't?"[6]

The tale of Richard Nixon's on-camera visage illustrates the highly self-referential nature of postdebate news coverage. Today, as in 1960, the cumulative effect of journalistic reporting is to reinforce existing perceptions and perpetuate particular story lines. In each debate, reporters hope for an angle that will provide grist for the news mill; the best stories are those with a whiff of controversy and a prolonged shelf life. In Nixon's visual misfortune, the political press corps of 1960 found a narrative thread with which to weave a veritable tapestry. Even now, decades after the fact, the disparity in appearance between Nixon and JFK stands as a lasting legacy of history's first televised debate.

But an even bigger headline to come out of the debates in 1960 is one that eluded the news media of the day, probably because the story was too close at hand to be grasped. Russell Baker, who covered the Kennedy–Nixon debates for the *New York Times*, would write nearly thirty years later of the significance of the first broadcast. "That night," Baker said, "television replaced newspapers as the most important communications

medium in American politics."[7] Indeed, few such transitions in the nation's history have been so clearly demarcated. Not only newspapers
were knocked off their throne; so was radio. So, for that matter, was the
accepted formula for waging a presidential campaign.

At the time, only a few journalists sensed the shifting ground beneath
their feet. "Both sides have found that television has added a new element to politics—one that is not yet fully appraised," wrote *U.S. News &
World Report.*[8] The *Atlanta Constitution*'s publisher, Ralph McGill, confessed, "We and the candidates are up against the fact that we do not
understand all we would like to know about the impact of television."
McGill recounted the outcome of an informal experiment he had conducted, one that would quickly enter the lore of presidential debates. He
had arranged for "a number of persons" to listen to the first Kennedy–
Nixon debate on radio, to see if they would react differently than television viewers. "It is interesting to report they unanimously thought
Mr. Nixon had the better of it," McGill concluded.[9]

McGill's poll, specifying neither sample size nor methodology, reflects
the casual approach the news media of 1960 took toward the audience
reaction story. Instead of slavishly collecting and reporting survey data,
journalists favored the anecdotal response.

The *New York Times*, for example, contacted a Mr. and Mrs. John F.
Kennedy of Stuyvesant Town, New York City, for their comment on the
big event: "What show you talking about?" asked Mrs. Kennedy. "Oh,
the television show. We didn't get around to it. We were out visiting."[10]
This quote, included in a larger roundup of viewer opinion, typifies the
down-home nature of audience reaction coverage in 1960.

The *Los Angeles Times* published one of the more commendable examples of this genre, devoting a full page to viewers' responses the morning after the first debate. Next to each comment, the article featured a
photo of the interviewee watching television. A brief introduction
stressed that "in this effort to learn what people said and thought during and after the first of the Great Debates, the *Times* deliberately ignored political leaders, candidates, and active party workers."[11]

In years to come, this same constituency that the newspaper so
assiduously shunned would be dubbed "spinners," and their comments,
along with those of the journalists themselves, would dominate the

postdebate agenda. Sixteen years after the Kennedy–Nixon debates, when television news had grown up, debate coverage underwent a radical change. Presidential debaters no longer played to win just the audience at home; they played to sway the media as well.

THE BIRTH OF INSTANT ANALYSIS

In a wholly unplanned way, the twenty-seven-minute audio gap that interrupted the first presidential debate of 1976 begat the era of punditry that viewers now take for granted. Network anchors and reporters, desperate to plug the hole caused when the sound failed, started their coverage with predictable filler: sketchy statements about the technical problem and cautiously worded, well-balanced summaries of the debate to that point. But as the minutes ticked on, the on-air personnel found themselves drifting further into uncharted waters, babbling to stay afloat.

A review of NBC's coverage during the audio gap demonstrates the pitfalls of off-the-cuff reporting. A few seconds after the problem arises, David Brinkley comes on-screen to repeat the obvious: The cause of the failure is unknown. After a bit of vamping, Brinkley throws to reporter Douglas Kiker inside the debate hall, and the two of them kill time. Brinkley asks if his colleague has a screwdriver and a pair of pliers, and Kiker launches into a lengthy recap of the debate, which ends when Ford's press secretary Ron Nessen steps into the lobby where Kiker is standing. Kiker collars Nessen for an impromptu interview, asking, "How is your guy doing so far?" "It's a clear-cut victory for the president," Nessen says, adding that Ford had come across as "being in command of the situation, being in control." Kiker, trying to soften Nessen's partisan tone, points out that the same could be said of Carter.

Next, Kiker insinuates himself to a nearby interview in progress between CBS's Lesley Stahl and Democratic national chairman Robert Strauss, who calls it a "good night for the American people and a great night for Jimmy Carter." Kiker listens, then grabs Strauss for himself. A few seconds into the questioning, Kiker gets a cue to return to the candidates. Announcing that the audio is back, he throws to the debate stage, where in fact the problem has not been fixed.

David Brinkley reappears and, continuing to improvise, adds his judgment to that of the campaign managers. Brinkley calls it a "pretty lively debate, each one landing a few blows on the other, though I don't think anyone was permanently disabled, politically speaking." After yet another recap, Brinkley tosses back to Douglas Kiker, who interviews Republican adviser James Baker about Ford's debate preparations. Baker tells Kiker, "I think the president did an excellent job."

Kiker then commandeers Carter's press secretary Jody Powell, again away from Lesley Stahl. Kiker follows up Powell's pro-Carter spin by asking if he knows why the microphones went dead. Powell demurs: "I assume it was a technical problem, as sometimes happens." Strangely, Kiker then proceeds to raise the possibility of "a conspiracy at work," telling Powell, "It's been my experience in a situation like this that there's always a theory held by a lot of people that, oh, there was a conspiracy to cut him off. We have no proof of that, it was just simply a technical foul-up as far as we can determine, isn't that correct?" Powell's comeback is biting: "Not only do you have no proof, but nobody's brought up the subject that I know of, have they?"[12]

The audio gap of 1976, with its twenty-seven minutes of ad hoc political spin and reporter commentary, marks a turning point in media coverage of presidential debates. Even without the technical malfunction, however, change was poised to happen. The networks that had been so averse to postdebate programming in 1960 now inaugurated a tradition from which there would be no retreat: instant analysis.

Roger Mudd of CBS was among the first reporters to offer his opinion when the opening Ford–Carter debate came to an end. "It certainly wasn't the most scintillating television that we've ever witnessed," Mudd declared. "In fact, I think we could honestly call it dull." Though the television pundits of 1976 were willing to pass general judgments of this sort, they steered clear of outright proclamations of winners and losers. "To some measure," said Walter Cronkite in a characteristically tactful observation, "each probably succeeded."[13]

In the years since the Ford–Carter debates, journalists have overcome their shyness about calling victors. Even though presidential debates are nowhere near as conclusive as athletic events or awards shows, the press cannot resist the impulse to attach resolution to conflict, to wrap up the yarn with a definitive ending.

DECLARING WINNERS AND LOSERS

According to political reporter David Broder, the problem with declaring winners and losers in presidential debates is that more often than not, the outcome is murky. "I thought that Clinton in [the 1992 town hall debate in] Richmond was an easy one to be confident about," Broder said, "although by way of self-criticism I did not notice and therefore did not remark upon what everybody remembers from that debate, which was George Bush looking at his watch. That went right by me."[14]

As this comment of Broder's points out, even seasoned observers can miss things. In his book *Behind the Front Page*, Broder outlined the difficulties of rendering postdebate judgments:

A reporter has to jump three hurdles to handle the debate assessment well. We are trained to make a balanced judgment, so we score the debate by rounds, as if it were a prize-fight: we say A did well on Points one, four, six and seven, but B probably came out ahead on Points two, three, five and eight. As a result our verdicts tend to be cautious and fuzzy.

Second, being somewhat familiar with the issues, we are inclined to give some weight—perhaps undue weight—to the candidates' accuracy and skill in answering policy questions. Ironically our performance as instant analysts is handicapped by qualities our critics say we lack: a desire to be fair and an interest in substance.

The third point—which took me a long time to understand—is that our overall assessment of the debate must be based on who seems more in command. That is the test. And if you realize that television news shows will quickly capsulize the whole debate into that moment or two when one candidate or the other takes command, your attention can focus on recognizing that moment and can put it into the context of the campaign situation.[15]

As Broder indicates, the ethos of objective journalism makes reporters uneasy about reaching clear-cut verdicts, at least in the first blush of postdebate coverage. "The most common result of debates," said political columnist Roger Simon, "is no hits, no runs, no errors. Nobody really won, nobody really lost, nobody really made a huge mistake." But because journalists must come up with a specific angle in recounting the tale, he added, they are "looking for small things. They're looking for anything which will give a focus to the story."[16]

Opinions vary as to the appropriateness of journalists declaring winners and losers. To critics the media's propensity for crowning a champ reduces serious political discourse to mindless sport. Yet politics *is* a sport, and audiences inevitably watch debates with a heightened sense of competition. According to James Fallows, who has written extensively about presidential debates, the win-loss emphasis is "not such a bad thing, since from the public's point of view that's really what is going on here. There is a kind of primal sizing-up under way."[17]

Researchers like Diana Carlin of the University of Kansas have noted that journalists evaluate debates differently from regular viewers. "Many of the people who do the critiquing of debates . . . are far more knowledgeable and involved than the average voter," Carlin said at a symposium in 1992. "Most voters are not that intimately involved in the process until the last few weeks. So for most . . . this is the first time they really know what someone's position might be."[18]

The audience's perception of debates as informational would appear to conflict with the criteria by which reporters pass postdebate judgments. As Bob Schieffer of CBS explained, "The first thing I always try to do is see if there's any news there. Did one of these candidates say something he hadn't said before? Next you ask, did one guy get the better of the other one, and how's this going to play on the eleven o'clock news, and what impact is it going to have on the campaign?"[19] The general public may watch for information, but journalists watch for different things: strategic maneuvers and departures from the norm.

According to Blake Zeff, a former campaign aide to Hillary Clinton and Barack Obama, the predictability of postdebate news coverage hands candidates a template for grabbing headlines. "Want to dominate the TV news packages and internet wrap-ups? Unleash a zippy zinger or gimmick that can be recounted in 20 seconds (or 140 characters or less). Want to get the fourth estate buzzing? Issue a new attack—or piece of opposition research—during the affair that reporters haven't seen before," Zeff advised in a BuzzFeed post in 2012. "Satisfying the viral, hyper-speed media beast hinges less on a thorough 90-minute performance . . . and more on the quick recounting of the night."[20]

In its quest for a good story, the press glorifies colorful characters and punishes dullards. Sober-minded debaters operate at an automatic disadvantage in such a universe, where winning smiles and clever ripostes are the coin of the realm. Reporters prefer their candidates to fall into brasher, more stereotypical categories: stars (JFK, Reagan, Clinton), buffoons (Quayle, Bush 43), or star-buffoons (Perot, Palin). Debaters who are unusually gifted or unusually bad make juicier copy than those of average ability.

Increasingly, reporters have prized performance over substance in their coverage of debates. Communication scholar James Lemert found that 38 percent of postdebate journalistic statements in 1976 about the first two Ford–Carter encounters pertained to issues. Four years later, that percentage decreased by more than half. By 1988 the percentage of content coverage had dipped to less than 10 percent of all the postdebate reporting on television news. Over the same period of time, the number of references to performance and tactics rose dramatically.

Lemert made a second interesting observation: In 1976 and 1980, the networks followed the debates with only brief remarks from the anchors, waiting until after local newscasts had aired to run their own programs of postdebate commentary.[21] Since that time, the pace and intensity of postdebate coverage have accelerated considerably. In the era of Twitter and live-blogging, journalists now report the story as it happens, with virtually no time for contemplation. The dizzying rhythm of modern journalism demands glib, off-the-cuff verdicts.

Debate reporting that fixates on candidate performance and campaign strategy may suit the media's needs, but it offers limited nutritional value to the body politic. In 2012, as in previous election cycles, the Pew Research Center conducted a study of how news media covered the presidential election. Among its findings: the three-week period encompassing the general election debates saw a stepped-up emphasis on horserace coverage; nearly half the stories within that window of time dealt with competitive ups and downs. "Rather than a window to examine the candidates' ideas at more length, the debates became a frame about campaign momentum to a greater degree than the rest of the campaign," the study's authors concluded.[22]

In some measure, the herd mentality of debate reporting reflects logistical realities. Journalists who cover presidential debates on-site do so in multitudes, working from cavernous press filing centers in which viewing conditions are less than ideal. Because these reporters typically see only the official program feed, not the network-directed versions that provide multiple camera angles, they may not be watching the same debate that viewers see at home. Just as David Broder did not catch George H. W. Bush glancing at his watch in 1992, so did reporters in the press center fail to note George W. Bush's facial contortions twelve years later. "Bush's scowls were at first overlooked by many of the people covering the event," wrote Dana Milbank in the *Washington Post*. "In the press room at the debate site at the University of Miami, the direct television feed of the debate did not have the telltale split screens and reaction shots that most Americans saw at home."[23]

This limitation notwithstanding, campaign journalists cite various reasons for attending debates in person. Perhaps the most straightforward justification comes from Roger Simon: "I'm still 'old-school' on this kind of thing. If, God forbid, something awful were to happen, you've got to be there. It's our job."[24]

THE EARLY YEARS OF POSTDEBATE SPIN

In the hours after the first debate in 1960, Nixon's press secretary Herbert Klein gathered a handful of aides and made the rounds of Chicago's hotel bars to talk with some of the reporters who had covered the event for the morning papers. "I thought it was highly important to put on a confident front and to find out what they really thought," Klein wrote. "Most of them had concentrated so much on the content of the debate that they offered few opinions on the outcome, and the initial stories generally treated the 'joint appearance' with balance."[25] Interestingly, Klein and his team made no attempt to directly influence journalistic opinion; by the time the conversations took place, the reporters had already filed their stories.

Compared with today's tarantella of spinning, the political establishment of 1960 exercised admirable restraint in its postevent dealings with the press. Of course, the absence of follow-up programming by the television networks erased the need for on-air spinners. The reaction story belonged to newspapers, which focused on matters other than how campaign aides felt their candidates had fared. For the most part, journalists and handlers maintained a respectful distance from one another.

In the *New York Times*'s morning-after account of the first debate, an unusual sidebar story on page 30 did deal with reactions from Kennedy's and Nixon's camps. JFK's brother and campaign manager, Robert F. Kennedy, said Kennedy's team had been "tremendously pleased," while Nixon's press secretary Klein allowed that the vice president "presented the issues, and when he does that he always comes out very well." The story went on to note, "Some Kennedy aides, asking not to be quoted, said they felt their candidate had scored more points and over-all had made the best impression."[26] The air of modesty conveyed in this sentence would soon become a relic of the past.

The candidates themselves offered virtually no comment in the press about their debate performances, leaving behind a woefully slim record for historians. After the first debate, Kennedy was quoted only as saying that the exchange had been "very useful." Nixon told reporters, "A debater never knows who wins. That will be decided by the people November eighth. I thought he presented his case very well."[27] Later debates in the series in 1960 produced similarly tepid reactions to the candidates in the media or no reactions at all.

Over the years, the public has come to expect its presidential debaters to deliver a pithy postevent sound bite, either at a rally that evening or the next day on the campaign trail. At the end of the first debate in 1996, NBC's Tim Russert conducted the fastest postdebate interview in history by nabbing Bill and Hillary Clinton just seconds after the program concluded. Materializing at the apron of the stage, Russert stuck a microphone in the president's face and asked for a self-assessment. "I did the best I could," said the grinning Clinton. Russert then asked the first lady how the next day's headlines would read. "President Outlines His Vision for America in the 21st Century," Hillary Clinton replied. A few minutes later, Russert returned with Bob and Elizabeth Dole, but because of technical problems only Elizabeth's comment made it on the air.[28]

Russert's postdebate floor interviews touched off an angry protest from campaign representatives and competing journalists, who complained that NBC had violated the ground rules—as, in fact, it had. Without permission from the sponsors, technicians had strung an audio cable from backstage to the front of the house, where Russert was seated. Just as the debate went off the air, a crew member hooked up the microphone and handed it to Russert. "In the annals of spin," wrote media critic Howard Kurtz, "this was a new indoor record."[29]

In 1976, when the Ford–Carter audio breakdown prematurely initiated the practice of organized spin, the two campaigns were well positioned to supply representatives to plug the silence. As part of their press strategies, both operations had assigned key individuals to appear on the networks' postdebate specials with the goal of creating positive buzz. According to Ford's press secretary Ron Nessen, Republican aides held a conference call before the debate ended to agree on a "line" they would follow in talking to reporters: "We decided to declare flatly that the president was the clear winner—decisive, specific, in control of the situation and in command of the facts. Our theory was that our own enthusiasm would sway the judgments of voters and press commentators trying to decide who won."[30]

Larry Speakes, press secretary to the Republican vice presidential candidate in 1976, Bob Dole, deployed a trio of spinners to go on the networks immediately after the Dole–Mondale debate: the candidate's wife, Elizabeth; Texas governor John Connally; and Vice President Nelson Rockefeller. "As the debate ended they were to get out of their front-row seats, go straight to an assigned camera, beating the Mondale aides to the airwaves," Speakes wrote. "Each one claimed debate victory for Dole on each of the three networks, so we had nine at-bats."[31]

Speakes and his team also contrived a made-for-television telephone call in which President Ford publicly congratulated Bob Dole on his performance. Dole took the call in his backstage holding room, where network cameras had been set up. Ford's side of this stage-managed conversation, heard but not seen by television viewers, is a classic of transparent postdebate spin:

Ford: Bob?

Dole: Yes, Mr. President?

Ford: You did great. And Betty and I on our anniversary are very, very grateful for the anniversary present because your performance was superb and we all are applauding and very, very proud of your accomplishments.

Dole: Well, I'm very proud of you, Mr. President. I hope I did a good job. I had a bad cold, but I guess my voice held out long enough.

Ford: You were confident, you hit hard but hit fairly and you differentiated the issues, I think very effectively between their platform and ours, between our promises and theirs, where we have consistently said that taxes ought to be reduced and they have, as we all know, played both sides of the street. You've done a fine job in showing that they're the big spenders and we're the ones that think we should spend responsibly and effectively.

As Walter Cronkite reported at the end of the exchange, "President Ford, in congratulating him, got in some more campaign licks of his own tonight."[32] Meanwhile, ABC's Hal Bruno was among the reporters present in Dole's green room during the call. "They hung up," Bruno recalled, "and Dole turned to me and said, 'I wonder what *he* was watching.'"[33]

By contemporary standards the spinning in 1976 seems measured, balanced, and lacking in the desperation that makes later political reaction so excruciating to endure. Audiences today are accustomed to shameless ballyhooing by everyone from running mates and spouses to lowly aides and obscure public officials. But spinners did not burst onto the scene fully formed; instead, their profile as players in the postdebate drama advanced incrementally. "We had three or four people who'd go out and talk to the media afterward," said Michael Deaver of the campaigns of 1980 and 1984, in which he served as an aide to Ronald Reagan, "but it was nothing like it is now."[34]

As early as the Reagan–Mondale debates of 1984, television analysts had begun to openly disparage spinning, even as they gave it a thorough airing. NBC's postevent coverage of the Bush–Ferraro vice presidential debate in 1984 featured a three-way interview between Roger Mudd and a handler from each of the two campaigns that began with Mudd asking his guests to "raise your right hands and swear to tell the truth, the whole truth, and nothing but the truth." After dutifully complying, the predictable propaganda kicked in. At the end of the chat, Mudd said, "I'm going to get indictments of perjury on you two guys," and the three shared a laugh, united in appreciation of the

fatuousness of postdebate gamesmanship yet unwilling to break themselves of the habit.[35]

THE PROFESSIONALIZATION OF POSTDEBATE SPIN

Although the word *spin* appears to have come into common use around
1984, the Bush–Dukakis election of 1988 is generally considered the
"year of the spin doctor." Media researcher James Lemert and colleagues
found a threefold rise in spin doctor references between 1984 and 1988,
reflecting the increased presence of partisan surrogates at debate venues.[36] As Tom Brokaw said on NBC after the vice presidential debate in
1988, "There was so much spinning going on here tonight it's a wonder
that the Omaha Civic Auditorium didn't lift off into orbit."[37]

Not all of the spin was verbal. After the vice presidential debate in
1988, Dukakis's campaign manager Susan Estrich arrived at the press
center wearing a "President Quayle?" button. Other Democratic spinners wore buttons showing an EKG graph and the slogan "Quayle—A
Heartbeat Away." Both campaigns applied military-style tactics to their
postdebate spin efforts. David Demarest of Bush's team dispatched his
surrogates into the press room in waves, holding back top-tier spinners
in order to draw maximum media interest—"almost like if you threw
fish food into an aquarium and the fish food was the surrogates."[38]

In an article about the spinners of 1988, reporter Michael Oreskes of
the *New York Times* wrote that the campaigns "spent almost as much
time and effort trying to influence what was said after the debate as they
spent deciding what [the candidates] should say in the debate." Oreskes
likened the spinners' arrival in the press facility at the end of the program to an "invasion landing force," and added, "A decade ago campaign
staff members were evicted from press rooms on occasion for interfering with reporters at work on debate stories. But tonight they were
quickly surrounded by reporters, cameramen and photographers record-
ing their views."[39] As Oreskes's comment suggests, the collusionary aspect of postdebate spin is what makes the custom so creepy.

So why does the press play along? According to political journalist
Roger Simon, "Spin fulfills two essential purposes: It fills stories with

official 'react,' and it is an excuse for reporters to leave home."[40] Spin Alley does offer journalists certain advantages. Garrett Haake, a reporter for NBC embedded with Romney's campaign in 2012, found postdebate chatter by campaign surrogates to be of little value, "but as Spin Alley wound down it was a good opportunity to talk to advisers you didn't typically see in person on background or off-the-record, and get actual insight into what was going on."[41] Furthermore, Spin Alley has tradition-ally functioned as a launching pad for new political talent, giving re-porters a chance to interact with rising stars. In the final analysis, as Mark Leibovich of the *New York Times* observed, "Probably the best way to answer the question 'Why spin rooms?' is with the question 'Why turkey on Thanksgiving?' It's tradition."[42]

With every election cycle, the media filing center undergoes a popu-lation increase. For the first debate in 1960, 200 reporters were expected at WBBM; 380 showed up, and a second press room had to be installed in an adjacent studio. By the 1980s each presidential debate could ex-pect to draw as many as 1,500 accredited journalists. In 1996 that fig-ure topped 2,000, and in 2012 as many as 3,000 press credentials were issued, about a quarter of them to international news organizations.

In rare instances, when it is used to counteract damage incurred dur-ing the live broadcast, postdebate spin may genuinely qualify as news. Gerald Ford's verbal slip about Eastern Europe taught campaigns the value of rectifying a candidate's misstatements as quickly as possible. During the first debate of 1988, George Bush implied that women who obtained illegal abortions might be considered criminals; the next day, campaign manager James Baker appeared on the morning news shows to announce that after reconsidering, Bush did not equate abortion with criminality. As Brit Hume said on ABC, "This was fast action to head off political trouble, something this campaign is good at."[43]

Handlers face a more daunting hurdle when a good face must be put on a bad performance. In the wake of Ronald Reagan's staggering loss in the first debate of 1984, Baker did a live interview with Roger Mudd on NBC in which Mudd suggested that "the president was off his form. . . . At times he seemed to get lost and he was not as sharp as past debate experience would have led us to believe." Baker, without missing a beat, replied, "All of us felt unanimously that he was relaxed, confident, in command both of the issues and the debate." Four years later Dan Quayle's abysmal showing in the vice presidential debate of 1988 was too much even for the silver-tongued Baker. "When you think about what could have happened," Baker said on CNN, in a remarkably unguarded comment, "we have to be pretty happy."[44]

The campaign documentary *The War Room*, by D. A. Pennebaker and Chris Hegedus, offers a rare behind-the-scenes journey into one of the most impressive of all spin machines, the Clinton operation in 1992. In the film, Clinton's aide George Stephanopoulos is seen sprinting toward Spin Alley to join the postevent feeding frenzy just as one of the debates is wrapping up. Poking his head into a backstage staff room, he energetically exhorts aides to remember the party line: "Bush was on the defensive. Keep repeating, 'Bush was on the defensive.'" When Stephanopoulos finally makes his way onto the set and goes on air, the first words out of his mouth are, "Bush was on the defensive all night long."[45]

Shortly after the election of 1992, at a debate postmortem at Harvard, Stephanopoulos admitted that "one of the lessons we learned from this campaign is that spin after debate doesn't matter because of the preponderance of polling and focus groups." In the future, he said, spin "may not matter at all."[46]

To some extent, Stephanopoulos's prediction has come true. Changes in technology have diminished the importance of Spin Alley and shifted the locus of campaign spin to other, less insular arenas. "Twitter's centralized conversation, rapid-response emails, and instant, televised focus groups have largely superseded [the spin room] in expressing and forming the reactions of the television producers and writers who tell the debate's story to Americans who didn't see it," wrote Zeke Miller in a BuzzFeed column in 2012. Spin Alley, formerly ground zero for postdebate reaction, now serves a different purpose, Miller said. "The news cycle moves so fast now that the spin room is where you find a counterintuitive take to instant conventional wisdom, and a response to whatever critique appears to be sticking."[47]

The campaigns themselves have likewise reduced their reliance on Spin Alley in shaping postdebate reactions. According to Ron Klain, Obama's campaign invested less in on-site spin efforts in 2012 than in previous cycles, flying in a handful of "mid-level" surrogates instead of the big names who had populated earlier spin rooms. Explained Klain: "You're spinning on e-mail, you're spinning on Twitter, you're spinning in a lot of ways that don't involve standing up in some room."[48]

KEEPING THE STORY ALIVE: FORD AND THE EASTERN EUROPE GAFFE

Reporters covering presidential debates pray to the news gods that the encounter will produce a follow-up story that extends into the days beyond. The shelf life of most debates is around twenty-four hours; they then vanish into the mists of history, memorable only if they contain a transcendent clip for the "greatest hits" reel. As with so many big-ticket television events, like lackluster Super Bowls and long-winded Oscar shows, presidential debates often deliver less than they promise.

In 1960 and again in the first debate of 1976, production problems—Richard Nixon's appearance, the audio gap—dominated postdebate coverage. The first major *performance* story to break from a televised presidential debate was Gerald Ford's Eastern Europe gaffe, committed in the second program of 1976 and kept alive by a combination of Ford's stubborn refusal to retract the misstatement and media demands for an apology.

In the initial postdebate television coverage, commentators were slow to recognize the error. On CBS, Walter Cronkite's first summation of the event failed to note what *Time* magazine would call "the blooper heard round the world." Harry Reasoner also ignored the issue in his close-of-program remarks on ABC. Only during the later news specials did the subject crop up. CBS's diplomatic correspondent Marvin Kalb held that the president's comment would "come as a great surprise to the people in Eastern Europe," while Bob Schieffer called it "a major blunder." David Brinkley of NBC speculated that Ford's "rather curious statement . . . may have been a slip of the tongue. We think he may have meant Western Europe."[49] As Brinkley's line suggests, reporters at this point were more baffled than derisive.

In the next morning's newspapers, the story evolved from curiosity to folly. The *New York Times* devoted a front-page sidebar exclusively to Ford's slip of the tongue. The *Boston Globe* quoted Carter's exultant aides, one of whom described it as an "incredible statement." An account in the *Washington Post* included a prescient observation from Hamilton Jordan, Carter's campaign manager, who said of the error, "You will hear a great deal about that in the next few days."[50]

Just as Jordan forecast, within twenty-four hours the story had exploded. The gaffe dominated newscasts the evening after the debate, leading all three networks. Coverage was extensive, including reaction stories from Eastern European ethnic communities in the United States, as well as response from around the world. Jimmy Carter used the occasion to say his opponent had "disgraced our country," and running mate Walter Mondale joked that after the telecast he had gone looking for a Polish bar, certain that drinks would be on the house for Democrats.[51]

The day after the debate in San Francisco, Ford embarked upon an ill-fated odyssey of clarification that for the better part of a week effectively subsumed his campaign. At an event at the University of Southern California, the president offered a lukewarm amendment to his original declaration. "Last night in the debate I spoke of America's firm support for the aspirations for independence of the nations of Eastern Europe," Ford stated, then added that the United States "has never conceded and will never concede their domination by the Soviet Union." As Marilyn Berger said on NBC, "It was a stab at correcting a costly impression."[52]

For the news media, it was also insufficient. Again the next day, Ford labored to explain himself, first at a breakfast appearance before business supporters in Los Angeles. Recalling a trip to Poland he had made in 1975, the president said Polish citizens "don't believe they are going to be forever dominated—if they are—by the Soviet Union. They believe in the independence of that great country and so do I. We're going to make certain, to the best of our ability, that any allegation of dominance is not a fact."

Things got even fuzzier with an impromptu statement to journalists a few hours later, just after a midday rally in Glendale. In a bizarre arrangement, Ford read his explanation into a walkie-talkie transmitted to press buses via walkie-talkies belonging to campaign handlers. Speaking in the third person, Ford said, "President Ford does not believe that the Polish people over the long run—whether they are in Poland or whether they are Polish-Americans here—will ever condone domination by a foreign force."[53]

Finally, on October 12, six days after the debate, a chastened Ford flatly admitted, albeit off-camera, that he had made a mistake. In a meeting with ethnic leaders at the White House, the president finally spoke the words the news media had been clamoring to hear. "Let me be blunt," he said. "I did not express myself clearly when this question came up in the debate. The countries of Eastern Europe are, of course, dominated by the Soviet Union."[54] The apology was duly reported, and the press moved on to greener pastures.

Why did Ford take so long to perform his ritual act of contrition? According to press secretary Ron Nessen, advisers urged the president the morning after the debate to acknowledge that he had misspoken, but he refused. "I can be very stubborn when I think I'm right," Ford wrote in his memoir, "and I just didn't want to apologize for something that was a minor mistake."[55]

On the same day he issued his final apology, Ford took the press to task in a meeting with newspaper and broadcasting executives, lamenting that 90 percent of reporting on the debate held in San Francisco involved the single remark about Soviet domination. "There was such a concentration on that one point, ignoring virtually everything else, that I think the news media didn't give a full and accurate picture of the substance in many of the questions and many of the answers," Ford said.[56]

What may at first appear to be an effort to shift blame is, upon closer inspection, a legitimate complaint. Why should journalists have fixated on Ford's mistake to the exclusion of almost everything else? Why was the president of the United States hounded into issuing an apology when he felt none was required? Is it the proper function of the news media to demand atonement from public figures? As political scientist Thomas Patterson noted, "The candidate usually has no choice but to respond to the press's demands for a mea culpa. The price of silence is crippling news coverage for days on end." Ford's aide and future vice president, Dick Cheney, described the incident of 1976 as a case of reporters extracting their "pound of flesh."[57]

Media coverage of Ford's gaffe offers a case study in the power of the press to alter perceptions. Right after the debate, between eleven at night and one o'clock the next morning, Republican pollster Robert Teeter conducted a poll of viewers who named Ford the winner by a percentage point. After news reports of the mistake appeared the next day, the surveys began to reflect a downward trend; Teeter's poll showed that 62 percent of those queried between 5:00 P.M. and midnight the day after the debate thought that Carter had done the better job, compared with 17 percent for Ford. "Reports of the debate had reemphasized the president as a mistake prone, inept bumbler, exactly what we had spent six or seven weeks trying to get away from," Teeter said.[58]

"The volunteered descriptions of the debate by voters surveyed immediately after the debate included no mentions of Ford's statement on Eastern Europe," wrote researcher Fred Steeper of the Republican study. "Not until the afternoon of the next day did such references appear, and by Thursday night they were the most frequent criticism given of Ford's performance." A voter who participated in a different research study said: "I thought that Ford had won. But the papers say it was Carter. So it must be Carter." As Ford's press secretary Ron Nessen put it, "The average guy in his living room watching the debate didn't see the Eastern European comment as a monumental mistake. But after 24 hours of being told how bad a mistake it was, people changed their minds."[59]

REAGAN AND THE "AGE ISSUE"

The first presidential debate of 1984 ignited one of the biggest follow-up stories in debate history: was Ronald Reagan competent to lead the country? Like the Ford gaffe, the matter did not fully surface in the program's immediate aftermath. Bruce Morton, on CBS, hinted at a problem, saying that Reagan "floundered" more than usual and appeared "ill at ease." John Chancellor, on NBC, asserted that "the president got very tired at the end and seemed quite disorganized in his closing statements."[60] But none of the analysts came close to questioning Reagan's fitness for office.

Morning-after newspaper accounts also noted President Reagan's tentative delivery without linking the debate to a discussion of jobworthiness. "Mr. Reagan appeared less confident than he customarily does on television," wrote Howell Raines in the *New York Times*, in a typically subdued comment, while Tom Shales in the *Washington Post* joked, "Obviously, it's back to the old briefing books for the Reagan team."[61]

Ronald Reagan's inferior performance did not morph into the "age issue" until two mornings after the debate, when the *Wall Street Journal* ran a story with the headline, "New Question in Race: Is Oldest U.S. President Now Showing His Age?" The article, by Rich Jaroslovsky and James Perry, got to the point in its fourth paragraph: "Until Sunday night's debate, age hadn't been much of an issue in the election campaign. That may now be changing. The president's rambling responses and occasional apparent confusion injected an unpredictable new element into the race."

The story went on to quote from a psychologist and supporter of Reagan who said: "I'd be concerned to put him in a corporate presidency. I'd be all the more concerned to put him into the U.S. presidency." Democratic congressman Tony Coelho of California told the *Journal*: "He created an issue that has not yet come in this campaign—age. He looked old and acted old." The piece ended with thoughts on how other presidents had aged in office, interviews about the warning signs of mental deterioration, and a reminder that candidate Reagan in 1980 had pledged to undergo regular tests for senility if he became president.[62]

The same day the story by Jaroslovsky and Perry ran, the *Washington Post* carried an op-ed column by influential political writer David Broder. Broder also candidly addressed the broader implications of the president's performance, saying Reagan had "let the age issue emerge as it had not done in any of his previous campaigns." Broder called the physical contrast between Mondale and Reagan "the most startling" since Kennedy and Nixon.[63]

The combination of the article in the *Journal* and Broder's column seemed to unleash pent-up energy in the press, legitimizing the age issue for media scrutiny. "It was as if the men and women of the press felt they needed permission before they could truthfully describe what they had seen the night before," wrote Mark Hertsgaard. Hertsgaard castigated journalists for "poaching" off the *Journal*'s story instead of undertaking their own investigations into Reagan's health.[64]

The same day the newspaper pieces ran, the networks scrambled to air television versions of the story. "This was one of those rare days in schizophrenic Washington when the whole town seemed to focus on one thing—Ronald Reagan's age," said Jim Wooten on ABC. Wooten's piece included a series of unflattering shots: a debate sound bite in which Reagan sputtered and stumbled, a clip that showed the president nodding off during an audience with the pope, and an excerpt in which First Lady Nancy Reagan appeared to be prompting her husband in response to a reporter's question.[65]

CBS ran a similar montage, a "worst-of" collection of Reagan bloopers that included some of the same moments ABC had used. As Thomas Rosenstiel wrote in the *Los Angeles Times*: "The abbreviated tape clips had an impact far beyond what they had in their original context. Reagan's debate fumbles in clip form seemed more drastic than they did live during the debate."[66] The networks also interviewed doctors and psychiatrists about the effects of aging on mental acuity.

At first the president's vaunted team of public relations experts appeared caught off-guard by the barrage of bad press. "I'll challenge him [Mondale] to an arm-wrestle anytime," Reagan told reporters on the day the *Journal*'s and Broder's stories ran,[67] but for once the wisecrack rang hollow. The White House came back the next day with a statement about the president's physical health that said, "Mr. Reagan is a mentally alert, robust man who appears younger than his stated age." Reagan's personal physician, Dr. Donald Ruge, was trotted out to describe his patient as being in "excellent" health, though when asked if Reagan had lost any of his stamina over the past four years, the doctor replied, "I don't know, you have to ask him."[68]

"I wasn't tired," Reagan informed the press corps, and to underscore the point, Republican strategists made sure their candidate was photographed getting out of his limousine at a campaign stop and taking an "impromptu" on-camera stroll. "The White House today did everything but put a Superman cape on President Reagan as it wrestled with questions about his age and fitness," said Tom Brokaw on NBC.[69]

The relentless coverage took an obvious toll on Reagan. Displaying an uncharacteristic testiness, the president grumbled about his opponent, "If I had as much makeup on as he did, I'd have looked younger too." Reagan insisted to reporters that he never wore makeup, even as an actor. This claim prompted a *Los Angeles Times* story that quoted one Hollywood makeup artist as saying Reagan had used cosmetics on television's *General Electric Theater*, and another from the Warner Brothers film studio who said Reagan avoided makeup in the movies. Mondale himself joined the dialogue, telling a crowd in Pittsburgh, "Mr. President, the problem isn't makeup on the face, it's the makeup on those answers that gave you a problem."[70]

Just as media reaction upended voter opinion after Gerald Ford's gaffe about Eastern Europe, so did coverage of the "age issue" realign public thinking about the first debate of 1984. "The initial public response was that Reagan had won; with the passage of time and news media spin, his early victory turned into something approaching a historic defeat," wrote political scientist Austin Ranney. The first poll on ABC, taken during the final minutes of the telecast, had Reagan in the lead by three points. An hour later, after negative reviews came in for the president, the edge had shifted to Mondale by a point. Two days after the debate, a CBS News–*New York Times* poll showed a lead for Mondale of forty-nine points.[71] The unceasing media focus on the "age issue" had reversed public opinion about who won the match.

GORE AND THE "TRUTH ISSUE"

Was Al Gore a serial fabricator, or a politician of average truthfulness who got nailed by a hostile press corps for minor misstatements of fact? When questions about Gore's veracity arose in his first debate of 2000 with George W. Bush, it fit neatly into a framework that the media had already constructed around the vice president. Like Ford's gaffe about Eastern Europe and Reagan's befuddlement, the "truth issue" reinforced an existing journalistic trope about the candidate. Unlike Ford's and Reagan's episodes, however, this story was largely the handiwork of political operatives. Bush's campaign hatched Al Gore's "truth issue" as part of an overall strategy, then successfully seeded it into news coverage through the machinations of opposition researchers.

Postdebate reporting centered on two comments Gore made during the telecast. The first involved a high school student in Sarasota, Florida, who the vice president said "has to stand" in science class because of overcrowding at the school. Gore had taken his information from a letter written to him by the girl's father, who enclosed a photo from the local newspaper that showed her standing in the classroom. As it turned out, although the essence of Gore's statement was correct, he got his verb tense wrong. The girl had had to stand at the beginning of the term, but by the time of the debate the problem had been rectified.

The second factual error stemmed from a trip Gore took to Texas to survey wildfire damage. In describing his tour, Gore said he had been accompanied by James Lee Witt, head of the Federal Emergency Management Agency. The vice president had made more than a dozen such excursions with Witt, but on the date in question they did not travel to Texas together.

Bush's campaign seized upon both discrepancies, linking them to a larger effort to portray Gore as untrustworthy. As the live debate entered its final stretch, the Republican high command met to review talking points before descending upon Spin Alley. "The key offense against Gore," recalled Bush's media adviser Stuart Stevens, "was to hit him on the distortions and on his inability to tell the truth."[72] According to Carl Leubsdorf, Washington bureau chief for the *Dallas Morning News*, "I can tell you that one minute after that debate ended Karl Rove was over at the *Dallas Morning News* workstation, telling our correspondent who was covering Bush [that Gore had not traveled with Witt]."[73]

A BBC documentary called *Digging the Dirt*—not seen in the United States—presented viewers with a remarkable portrait of Bush's opposition research team in action during the first debate of 2000. From the moment Gore begins his opening remarks, researchers in the Republican National Committee "Oppo Room" in Washington are shown scouring computer databases in search of inconsistencies between the vice president's words onstage and his extensive public record. "We think of ourselves as the creators of the ammunition in a war," RNC researcher Tim Griffin tells a BBC interviewer. "We make the bullets."

As the debate progresses, the researchers peddle their ammo to a bloodthirsty press corps. After Gore makes the reference to James Lee Witt, Tim Griffin is seen on the phone describing his plan to "get one of these AP [Associated Press] reporters or somebody on it for the next few days and then we get a lie out of it and roll a few days with a new lie." Another RNC researcher brags to the BBC camera, "It's an amazing thing when you have top line producers and reporters calling you and saying, 'We trust you, we need your stuff.' "[74]

Do journalists cross a line of impropriety in accepting blatantly partisan information from the campaigns' opposition research teams? In the view of columnist Martin Lewis, writing about the BBC documentary for Time.com, "The research offered by both sides is so intensively fact-checked and triple-checked that (reporters) can safely accept the word if offered by the oppo experts." But Lewis added this caveat: "The problem lies not in the veracity of the information per se—but in the significance and disproportionate magnification that is then placed on the information—and how its disbursement reinforces other themes in the campaign gameplans."[75] In other words, consider the source.

For Republicans the attack on Gore's veracity reaped a bountiful harvest: several days of stories in mainstream news outlets and, in the tabloid *New York Post*, a front-page headline straight out of Bush's playbook: "GOP's New Battle Cry vs. Gore: Liar! Liar!"[76] Although initial postdebate polls gave the win to Vice President Gore, the drumbeat of chatter brought a shift in public opinion. A USA Today/CNN/Gallup poll taken several days after the debate found that respondents, especially men, considered Bush more "honest" than Gore. "The fallout from last week's presidential debate shows that Democrat Al Gore just might have lost by winning," wrote Richard Benedetto in an accompanying article in *USA Today*.[77] As political communication scholars Kathleen Hall Jamieson and Paul Waldman concluded, "Post-debate coverage seems to have had a significant effect in altering people's judgments."[78]

What explains journalists' complicity in promulgating a Republican caricature of Al Gore? Some of the credit can be attributed to Gore's unpopularity among the reporters who covered him. This feeling was summed up by *Time* columnist Margaret Carlson, who told radio host Don Imus, "It's really easy, and it's fun, to disprove Gore. . . . As sport, and as our enterprise, Gore coming up with another whopper is greatly entertaining to us."[79] That this came from a *liberal* journalist underscores Al Gore's low standing with the Washington press corps.

The candidate gave his detractors plenty to complain about. The first debate with Bush was the so-called sighing debate, in which Gore emitted a series of audible sighs and exaggerated facial expressions during his opponent's responses. Gore's performance was condescending both to Bush and to the audience, handing the media a ready-made context for negative evaluations. Furthermore, as coverage of the misstatements snowballed, the vice president seemed unable to mount an effective defense. During a conference call with journalists several days after the debate, he could not resist highlighting two factual errors Governor Bush had made. As the *New York Times* noted, "Even as he pointed out Mr. Bush's 'mistakes,' Mr. Gore said he was not denigrating his rival's character." "These are negative personal attacks of the kind I simply do not engage in," Gore told the reporters.[80]

A few days later, Al Gore used the second debate to issue a smarmy apology for mistakes he had made in the first. "I got some of the details wrong last week in some of the examples that I used," he said, "and I'm sorry about that. And I'm going to try to do better." Instead of pointing out the absurdity of the charges against him—an incorrect verb tense and an erroneous date—Gore entered a plea of guilty.

Whatever the mitigating circumstances, it is the press that bears ultimate responsibility for distorted coverage of the first Gore–Bush debate. In recounting the story, reporters fell for a cleverly packaged scenario that made mountains of molehills. "Journalists are looking for a story line, a narrative device, that plays out over weeks and months," said Tom Rosenstiel, director of the Project for Excellence in Journalism, "and there's nothing wrong with that. The problem is if they let the narrative overwhelm the facts, then it becomes a distorting lens. It can lead journalists to ignore and mischaracterize facts as they try to fit them into the story."[81] In the case of Al Gore, adherence to the preordained narrative caused reporters to inflate trivial mistakes into broader character flaws.

OBAMA AND THE DISASTER IN DENVER

Heading into the first presidential debate of 2012, a poll conducted by the Pew Center showed that by a 51-to-29 margin, most Americans expected Barack Obama to beat Mitt Romney in their opening encounter. After the debate, a survey by Gallup found that 72 percent considered Romney the winner, as opposed to 20 percent for Obama.[82] Over the course of ninety minutes, in a transformed hockey arena at the University of Denver, Barack Obama lost the debate by a larger margin than any previous candidate in American history, handing the media an un-anticipated plot twist that dominated campaign coverage in early October.

Obama's loss may have been unprecedented, but so was the environment in which it occurred. For the first time, the influence of social media recast the usual win–loss conversation from a postdebate exercise to a real-time judgment call. Unprepared for the demands of this new environment, Obama fell victim to it, immediately and profoundly.

Criticism of the president's performance was particularly harsh on Twitter, but the flavor of the commentary was perhaps best captured by Andrew Sullivan, a staunch supporter of Obama who live-blogged the debate on his website *The Dish*. Sixteen minutes into the program, Sullivan wrote, "Romney is kicking the president's ass." Eighteen minutes in: "Obama is professorial and wonkish. He's on defense." Forty-two minutes in: "This is a rolling calamity for Obama." Sixty-three minutes in: "He is leaving argument after argument on the table." At 10:31 P.M., just as the debate ended, Sullivan called it a "disaster" that had done "extensive damage" to the president.[83]

Just as Sullivan was rendering his final verdict, the television pundits began offering their on-camera assessments. "Where was Obama tonight?" barked MSNBC's Chris Matthews, another reliable supporter of the president. "What was he doing tonight? He went in there disarmed!" On CNN, James Carville hit the nail on the head: "It looked like Romney wanted to be there and President Obama didn't want to be there."[84]

Two former debaters weighed in with theories of their own. Sarah Palin, on Fox News, thought that Obama had been exposed as an emperor with no clothes. "He didn't have his buddy, the teleprompter, in front of him writing out what somebody had written out for him in all these years of being a candidate and the president—the answers," she said. On Current TV, Al Gore, the network's co-owner and commentator, advanced a different explanation. "I'm going to say something controversial here," Gore began. "Obama arrived in Denver at two P.M. today, just a few hours before the debate started. Romney did his debate prep in Denver. When you go to 5,000 feet, and you only have a few hours to adjust—I don't know . . ."[85]

Reporters in the media filing center made much of the fact that after the debate ended, Obama's campaign officials waited several minutes before entering the spin room. Olivier Knox, chief Washington correspondent for Yahoo! News, tweeted, "Not one Obama surrogate in the 'spin room' right now. Emergency talking points meeting?" Behind the scenes, just such a conversation was taking place among Obama's high command. "None of the advisers fooled themselves into thinking it was anything but a disaster," the *New York Times* would report a few days later. "Instead they scrambled for ways to recover."[86]

Those ways included an effort to depict Mitt Romney as having been less than truthful in his remarks during the debate. In a conference call with reporters the next day, senior White House adviser David Plouffe made a dozen references to Romney's lack of veracity. Senior aide David Axelrod said on the Sunday talk show *Face the Nation* that the president had been "taken aback by the brazenness of Romney's statements." According to Axelrod, Romney's performance "was completely unrooted in the positions he's taken before."[87]

Obama himself chimed in, telling radio interviewer Tom Joyner a week after the debate that he had been "just too polite" and that "it's hard to sometimes just keep on saying 'and what you're saying isn't true.' It gets repetitive." That same day, in an interview with Diane Sawyer, anchor for ABC News, Obama likened his debate loss to an athletic competition: "If you have a bad game, you just move on. You look forward to the next one. And it makes you that much more determined." The president also struck a self-deprecating note, remarking at a fundraising concert in Los Angeles that the evening's musical acts "just perform flawlessly, night after night." After a beat, he added. "I can't always say the same."[88]

The Obama damage control efforts also enlisted Big Bird, the Sesame Street character who had emerged as one of the debate's inadvertent stars. A Big Bird ad put together by the digital media team drew more than three million views on YouTube. At a rally the day after the debate, Obama picked up the theme, delivering the rejoinders he had neglected in the actual debate. "Thank goodness somebody is finally getting tough on Big Bird," he said. "We didn't know that Big Bird was driving the federal deficit."[89]

However gamely they tried, Obama and his staff could not paper over what had happened during the debate. Their efforts were hampered by the calendar, which kept the story alive for two more weeks until the candidates met for their next encounter. But although initial polls showed a tightening of the race after the debate that was held in Denver, the numbers soon stabilized, with strong follow-up performances by Obama and Joe Biden helping to right the ship.

In a perverse way, Obama's loss bore positive fruit, not in the media but among his supporters. "One of the counterintuitive impacts of the Denver debate was that the complacency people felt about the election disappeared," David Axelrod said at a Harvard University campaign postmortem. "That went away overnight, and we had a huge bump in volunteer activity." One day after the debate, Priorities USA, the pro-Obama super PAC, saw a $7 million infusion of donations, its best single-day showing of the campaign.[90]

OTHER POSTDEBATE STORY LINES

The drubbing of Dan Quayle in the debate with Lloyd Bentsen in 1988 sparked a narrative line that would sustain several days of lively coverage. The specific impetus for the story was Bentsen's "You're no Jack Kennedy" sound bite, an irresistible video snippet that was like catnip to television news producers. As Bob Schieffer predicted on CBS immediately after the broadcast, this was the bite the whole country would see, even those who had not watched the debate. When ABC's *Nightline* came on the air half an hour after the debate, the program opened with the clip. The next day, NBC aired the exchange four times on its morning show, and all three major networks repeated it in their evening newscasts.[91]

Intentionally or not, George Bush exacerbated Quayle's problems by not appearing in public with his running mate the day after the debate, as Michael Dukakis did with Lloyd Bentsen. Damage control instead fell to President Reagan, who called Bentsen's line a "cheap shot and unbecoming to a senator of the United States." Quayle himself attempted a belated response to the question about his qualifications for office.

"There is no doubt I would maintain and build on the excellent policies of a President George Bush," Quayle declaimed at a rally the next day in Joplin, Missouri.[92]

Meanwhile, in half a dozen postdebate appearances, Bush failed even to mention his running mate, an omission that did not go unnoticed by the press. Two days after the event, reporters were still waiting for Bush to endorse Quayle's performance. Finally the vice president had little choice but to issue a statement of support. "The concept that I see in some of these reports that I am not supportive of Dan Quayle are absolutely ludicrous," Bush told a group of journalists outside his Washington home. "They are ridiculous. He did well in that debate, he has my full support, and he is getting strong support since the debate and before around this country."[93]

The postdebate journey of Dan Quayle then veered off in a new direction. Angry at what he perceived as a lack of support from Bush's insiders, Quayle made a display in the press of taking charge of his own fate—and, not coincidentally, seizing control of the narrative. "I got tired of all the publicity," Quayle told ABC's Jackie Judd on board his campaign bus. "I figured it couldn't get any worse, and I was going to take over." Quayle declared that from now on, "I'm the person that's going to do the spinning." Bob Schieffer, in a report on CBS, questioned this new tactic: "It was all so unexpected, some wondered if Bush aides had planned the whole thing to show Quayle was his own man."[94]

Ultimately the criticism seemed to liberate Dan Quayle. As B. Drummond Ayres wrote in the *New York Times*, "Something happened to Dan Quayle in Omaha, or shortly thereafter, something besides that 'You're no Jack Kennedy' verbal leveling administered by Senator Bentsen. Mr. Quayle came away a changed campaigner."[95] At the very least, the news media *perceived* him as a changed campaigner. Once he had acted out his little role in the drama and obliged reporters by offering up a fresh angle on the story, Dan Quayle started getting better press.

One week after Quayle's devastation in the vice presidential debate of 1988, Michael Dukakis suffered a mortal blow of his own at the hands of Bernard Shaw. Just as Dan Quayle continued to address the bungled question about qualifications in his postdebate appearances, so did Dukakis take to the airwaves to recast his response to Shaw's hypothetical about capital punishment. As both candidates proved, a debater's second crack at a question cannot always undo the original answer.

Several days before Election Day in 1988, Dukakis appeared in a CNN interview with Shaw, arranged at the request of Democratic handlers. Early in the exchange, before the anchorman had a chance to mention it, Dukakis brought up the notorious opening volley. Assuring Shaw that the question had been fair and reasonable, Dukakis added that he had been thinking about his response, and how he might better have stated it.

> *Dukakis*: Let me just say this: Kitty is probably the most—*is* the most—precious thing, she and my family, that I have in this world. And obviously, if what happened to her was the kind of thing that you described, I would have the same feelings as any loving husband and father.
>
> *Shaw*: Would you kill him?
>
> *Dukakis*: I think I would have that kind of emotion. On the other hand, this is not a country where we glorify vengeance.[96]

As journalist Roger Simon observed, "This is what campaigning had come down to. Anyone who wanted to be the leader of a great nation and do great things . . . had to show emotion. And in order to be likable, he had to tell people that, yes, he would want to take a human life."[97]

After three strong performances against George W. Bush in 2004, John Kerry saw the media conversation divert from his winning streak to an ill-considered remark he made about Mary Cheney, the gay daughter of the vice president. When Bob Schieffer, moderator of the third debate, asked the candidates if they considered homosexuality a choice, Kerry responded, "We're all God's children, Bob. And I think if you were to talk to Dick Cheney's daughter, who is a lesbian, she would tell you that she's being who she was." Although Kerry and his campaign later insisted that the comment had been both unplanned and intended as a compliment, the reference seemed oddly gratuitous. Adding to the awkwardness, Kerry's running mate, John Edwards, had also broached the matter of Mary Cheney's homosexuality in the vice presidential debate a week earlier.

But the inappropriateness of Kerry's remark could not have gained traction without a concerted effort by Republicans to depict Cheney's entire family as victims of a grievous injustice—a portrayal the Cheneys themselves eagerly promoted. Reaction to the comment came almost immediately after the debate, and in a predictable venue: the pro-Bush precincts of the Fox News Channel, where pundit Mort Kondracke denounced the "underhanded outing" of Mary Cheney, conveniently ignoring the fact that Ms. Cheney had long been open about her homosexuality. In a Spin Alley interview, also on Fox, Kerry's campaign manager Mary Beth Cahill tossed fuel on the fire by calling Mary Cheney's sexuality "fair game."[98] (Mary Cheney was an official in her father's campaign, which had taken a number of anti-gay positions.)

Choreographed outrage quickly issued from the Republican camp, with enough force to propel several days of press commentary, most of it critical of John Kerry. "I thought it was totally inappropriate and, frankly, I was surprised he would do something like that," Dick Cheney told an interviewer.[99] Lynne Cheney, the vice president's wife, paraded her wrath before cheering crowds at a postdebate rally, concluding of Kerry, "This is not a good man. What a cheap and tawdry political trick." Lynne Cheney's assessment of the situation might have been even blunter; originally she had planned to denounce Senator Kerry as "a man with a dark hole in his soul. . . . Deep down inside, he's rotten."[100]

Although publicly Mary Cheney remained above the fray, she approved her parents' strategy of retaliation, instructing her father to "make it hurt."[101] For several days the story stayed in the headlines, all but overshadowing the final debate itself. "Here's the impact it had," said Joe Lockhart, a senior adviser to Kerry's campaign. "Two days of nonstop cable talk about how Bush lost the debate was avoided for them. . . . They lost the debate and they scrambled and they came up with the best hand they had."[102]

Did John Kerry's reference to Mary Cheney damage his electoral chances? At a minimum, it deprived the candidate of a well-deserved postdebate victory lap. The press had chanced upon a sidebar that played better than the main story, and suddenly the footnote became the headline. Republicans would coin a descriptive term for the episode's effect: *the Mary bounce*, in recognition of the unexpected boost George W. Bush received at a critical point in the campaign.

We conclude our survey of postdebate media coverage with two tempest-in-a-teapot incidents that spawned a flurry of tongue-in-cheek reporting: President Carter's reference during the debate of 1980 to his daughter, Amy, and Vice President Bush's assertion after the match with Ferraro in 1984 that he had "kicked a little ass."

The so-called Amy gaffe, in which Carter recounted a conversation with his daughter on the topic of nuclear weapons, provoked an immediate wave of ridicule in the media. In ABC's postdebate special, Barbara Walters, who had moderated the debate, named Amy the winner of the match, and said, "I'm going home to my child, who's the same age as Amy, and if she doesn't tell me that nuclear proliferation is the major concern on her mind, she's going to hear it from her mother." Former Secretary of State Henry Kissinger told a reporter, "I gag at that kind of stuff in general, although I like Amy."[103]

The next day, ABC's reporter Bettina Gregory turned up at Amy's school in Washington and conducted an ambush interview with the thirteen-year-old first daughter. Amy confirmed to Gregory and several other reporters that she and her father had discussed nuclear war. From there, the conversation degenerated:

> *Reporter*: Does he talk to you often about your opinions?
> *Amy*: Yeah.
> *Reporter*: What else is important?
> *Amy*: I don't know.
> *Reporter*: Were you surprised to hear him mention that he had talked to you about it in the speech?
> *Amy*: Yeah, kind of.[104]

Four years later, in the Bush–Ferraro episode, it was an indiscreet remark to a group of New Jersey longshoremen that got the media clucking. "We tried to kick a little ass last night," George H. W. Bush told the dockworkers the morning after the vice presidential debate of 1984, just in time to notice that a sound man from a local television station was standing nearby with a boom microphone. "Whoops—oh, God, he heard me!" Bush cried, then implored the news crew to "turn that thing off!" As the *Washington Post* pointed out, "Minutes earlier, Bush had described Ferraro to reporters as 'gracious' and declined to declare himself the winner."[105]

After videotape of the putdown was made available to journalists, Bush called a news conference to extinguish the media brush fire. The vice president defended his comment as an "old Texas football expression," adding that he had no intention of apologizing. "I stand behind it, I use it all the time," he said. "My kids use it, everybody who competes in sports uses it. I just don't like to use it in public." The story led two of the network newscasts and ran prominently in the next morning's newspapers, though the *New York Times* primly identified the phrase only as a "locker room vulgarity." In an interview on NBC, Ferraro told Tom Brokaw, "I think Mr. Bush was about as accurate in his assessment of the result of the debate as he was in the facts and figures he put forth during the debate."[106]

Bush never did apologize, but in the context of other anti-Ferraro rumblings from the Republican camp, the slur seemed curiously ill-advised. *Time* magazine called it "one of the silliest blunders of the campaign,"[107] as it most certainly was. What *Time* failed to add was that for the news media, silly blunders are manna from heaven.

10 / DEBATES AND VOTERS

The one undisputed fact about presidential debates is their popularity. From the outset, the public has shown a willingness, even an eagerness, to pay attention to these programs. The 70 million Americans who watched the first Kennedy–Nixon broadcast inaugurated a tradition of high viewership that has never abated.[1]

The single meeting between President Jimmy Carter and challenger Ronald Reagan in 1980 drew between 80 and 100 million people, making this the most-watched presidential debate—and one of the most-watched television shows—of all time. The second highest-rated debate, the final match between Clinton, Bush, and Perot in 1992, attracted between 70 and 90 million. More typically debate viewership ranges from 50 to 70 million for presidential debates, 30 to 50 million for the vice presidentials. (The vice presidential exception is Biden–Palin in 2008, seen by some 70 million.)[2]

By any standard the ratings for presidential debates are extraordinary. To comprehend the significance of these numbers, it is useful to compare debates to other productions on the list of top-ranked television programs. Traditionally the two highest-rated shows of any year in the United States are the Super Bowl and the Academy Awards. Super Bowl audiences regularly top the 100 million range, and Oscar telecasts pull in around 40 million. On the blockbuster scale, presidential debates fall somewhere in between.

Debates also correlate to another type of programming on the most-watched list: special episodes of television series and miniseries. In this category the final broadcast of *M*A*S*H* (1983) holds the ratings record of 105 million people, followed by 83 million for the "Who Shot J.R.?"

installment of *Dallas* (1980), and around 80 million for the conclusion of *Roots* (1977). The farewell episode of NBC's *Seinfeld* (1998) reached 76 million people, slightly fewer than the 80 million who saw the finale of *Cheers* (1993). The last show of *Survivor*'s first season drew 51 million (2000), about the same number as the *Friends* conclusion (2004).[3]

This roster of television's highest-rated shows spans a wide range of programming, and audience enthusiasm can be attributed to a variety of factors. But particularly among the live telecasts, common bonds exist: big names, high stakes, competition, spontaneity, and hype. To one degree or another, presidential debates borrow these ingredients from the sports spectaculars and entertainment extravaganzas and refashion them into a political event that is sui generis. In this unique hybrid of show biz and civics, audiences find a television genre that effectively mixes entertainment with information.

To what can we attribute the staggering popularity of presidential debates? Why, in an age of apathy and cynicism toward politics, do viewers continue to pay heed? What are the benefits and limitations of these programs? And what influence, if any, do debates have on voter decision making? Let us explore the relationship of debates to the people who watch them.

THE DRAMATIC APPEAL OF TELEVISION DEBATES

Presidential debates represent a highly personal transaction between candidates and voters—or, to view it another way, between stars and an audience. A debate is human drama at its most raw: the obvious drama between the participants onstage but also the more subtle and complex drama that unfolds between presidential contenders and the citizens passing judgment on them. The *New York Times*'s columnist William Safire called presidential debates "political-emotional events . . . great moments in American life when the nation comes together to share an experience neither frightening nor artificial."[4]

It is the visceral nature of these programs that sets them apart from other highly watched television shows. Debates, said Walter Mondale, "go to this mysterious, primal question of who's ready to be president, who's presidential, who's got stature. That is not a technical question, it's a deep, emotional issue." According to Mondale, debates appeal to the public because they exist in a "kind of environment that people remember: combat. It's not giving a speech. This was real war, and people find it credible."[5]

Live televised debates teem with dramatic conflict: interpersonal conflict between candidates; intrapersonal conflict within a debater's psyche; the conflicts between expectation and performance, preparation and spontaneity. These juxtapositions make irresistible television, for conflict is the engine that propels all narrative, be it political, journalistic, dramatic, or athletic. Television, with its hunger for personalities and its compulsion to reduce abstractions to particularities, is especially well suited to the mano-a-mano clash of presidential debates.

"Straight exposition in any form is always the most difficult way to engage and hold the attention of anyone," wrote CBS's Frank Stanton after the Kennedy–Nixon debates. "Conflict, on the other hand, in ideas as in action, is intriguing and engrossing to great numbers of people. Drama has always got more attention than essays."[6] As Stanton's comment suggests, debates entice audiences because they are formatted as duels. No other televised political event presents such a strong structural incentive to watch.

Conflict that is live and unedited further compels viewership. By definition, live encounters are fragile. In this sense, presidential debates parallel other high-powered "event programming" like the Super Bowl or major awards shows. In each case, an ending cannot be scripted in advance. Audiences watch in the knowledge that vast stretches of boredom await; still, until the final second, some unforeseen plot twist could come rocketing off the screen to justify the investment of time.

As live television, presidential debates are a good example of the contradiction being contained within itself: these are simultaneously the most unpredictable and most ritualized of events. No matter what protective measures the campaigns take, a televised debate cannot be completely domesticated. With the race for the White House becoming ever more sanitized and risk averse, presidential debates represent a rare walk on the wild side.

Before the joint appearances in 1992, the *New York Times*'s television critic Walter Goodman wrote, "In a season of set pieces, a television debate could offer one of the few hopes of unprogrammed revelation."[7] If we accept the analogy of presidential debates as job interviews, the question of the "unprogrammed revelation" becomes all the more significant. As in any job interview, what is most interesting is not the applicant's carefully constructed facade, but the reality lurking behind the mask.

Beginning with the first Kennedy–Nixon broadcast in 1960, debates have had a way of delivering inadvertent messages to the audience, providing viewers with insights both large and small. As Norman Cousins, editor of the *Saturday Review*, observed after the forums of 1976, "The strength of the TV debates derives less from what is hidden than from what is impossible to conceal."[8]

Richard Nixon could not conceal the fact that he was uncomfortable in his own skin. Jimmy Carter and Gerald Ford could not conceal their inflexibility when faced with an unexpected technical snafu. Ronald Reagan could not conceal his befuddlement in the debate in Louisville with Walter Mondale. George H. W. Bush could not conceal a patronizing attitude toward Geraldine Ferraro, nor Dan Quayle a lack of gravitas. Al Gore could not conceal his pomposity, George W. Bush his thin skin, nor Barack Obama his aloofness. The list goes on. In each situation the inadvertent message shines through, contributing to our understanding of the debaters as human beings.

Do such unplanned episodes give voters legitimate reasons to accept or reject a particular candidate as president? Generally not, though the most sobering instance—Reagan's addled performance in the opening match of 1984—presents a possible exception. That debate, remarkable for the degree to which it diverged from the preordained script, alerted the public to an issue the Washington press corps had neglected to report. If only for a moment, the significance of this information caused voters to question Reagan's fitness for the job.

In retrospect, one wonders if the message of the first debate of 1984 ought not to have been more closely heeded, by both the media and the public. Charles Pierce, a journalist who began writing about Alzheimer's disease when it struck his father, is one of many observers who saw evidence in Reagan's performance of the illness that would not be officially acknowledged until 1994. Early Alzheimer's patients, Pierce said, "can waver between clarity and startling blankness," remembering events from the distant past, but not what happened yesterday. "That night in Louisville, Reagan passed in and out of himself, like a broad-cast signal filtered through mountains," Pierce wrote in a *Boston Globe* essay fifteen years after the debate. "He was lucky none of the panelists asked him where he was."[9]

If the images emanating from the screen in 1984 were trying to tell the audience that its leader was in an early stage of mental decline, then television debates were doing their job, even if the news did not fully register. Although it is important not to overconclude from presidential debates, inadvertent signals deserve to be listened to, particularly in a campaign environment dominated by manufactured messages and masked realities. At their best, debates reflect what Walter Lippmann called television's capacity to serve as a "truth machine";[10] viewers who pay close attention are bound to spot the chinks in a candidate's armor.

Consider the case of George H. W. Bush stealing a glance at his wrist-watch in the town hall in 1992. Bush's obvious desire to be done with the debate came across as an expression of rudeness—or at minimum a lack of interest. Although Republican handlers attempted to contain the damage by insisting that he had been checking to see if his opponents were running past their allotted time, viewers had perceived something entirely different.

Moments like this burst through the veneer of campaign control much as Toto pulls back the curtain to reveal the Wizard of Oz. In a live debate, no matter how the deck has been stacked, little arrows of verisi-militude manage to shoot from the screen into the living rooms of Amer-ica. Lawrence Spivak, the creator and for many years host of NBC's *Meet the Press*, came to honor television's ability to act as a magnifying glass. "Television has an awesome facility for showing up sincerity as well as insincerity," Spivak said. "So if a man is honest and knows his stuff, he'll emerge with his proper stature. By the same token, so will a phony."[11] Apply this scrutiny to candidates over the length of a ninety-minute debate, and audiences cannot help but acquire valuable information.

Another, less high-minded explanation for the high ratings of presi-dential debates merits passing mention. Viewers tune in for voyeuristic reasons; there is, after all, a certain sadistic pleasure to be taken from watching fellow human beings, politicians in particular, operating under duress. Journalist Valerie Helmbreck, who has regularly covered the Miss America pageant, drew a parallel between beauty pageants and debates.

"What both things are about," she said, "is seeing how poised people can look in a ridiculous situation."[12] Helmbreck's analogy stands to reason: the sheer audacity of debates, their high-wire daringness, virtually defies the public not to watch.

BENEFITS OF PRESIDENTIAL DEBATES

An underappreciated attribute of televised debates is their insulation from the financial machinery that drives contemporary American elections. Debates, unlike virtually everything else on the presidential campaign trail, are untainted by money. No infusion of cash can upgrade a candidate's performance; no deep-pocket donation can buy a more favorable set of ground rules. By any index, presidential debates are financially incorruptible.

It is true that recent rounds of debates have had corporate underwriters—Anheuser-Busch, Philip Morris, and AT&T among them—but this is an arrangement with the debate commission, not the candidates. Critics like George Farah have decried the influence of corporate donors on the Commission on Presidential Debates (CPD), the body that has produced every general election debate since 1988. "Under the auspices of the CPD, debate sites have become corporate carnivals, where sponsoring corporations market their products and propaganda to influential journalists and politicians," Farah wrote in his anticommission screed *No Debate*.[13] While the point may be valid, corporate involvement has had no discernible effect on the debaters themselves—nor is such a possibility plausible.

Because presidential debates are not about money, they pose a striking contrast to campaign commercials. In political advertising, the candidate with the most cash has the loudest voice; debates are a meritocracy in which each participant stands before voters on an equal footing. Messages in campaign ads must be stated briefly, and are selected by political pros; debates allow for a more thorough discourse, on topics chosen by voters and their representatives in the press. Most important, disembodied advertisements encourage negative campaigning, while face-to-face debates hold candidates personally accountable.

For the networks, too, presidential debates represent an uncommon departure from the usual bottom-line mentality. Unlike other "event programming"—sports, entertainment specials, and awards shows—general election debates are not given over to advertising. Far from producing revenue, they cut into profits.

Consciously or not, these distinctions enhance the standing of presidential debates with the public. Alone among television spectaculars, debates carry an aura of civic virtue. Without the participation of the citizenry, these events are meaningless, which distinguishes them from football games, where professional athletes determine the outcome, or the Oscars, which are voted on exclusively by members of the film industry. In a presidential debate the folks at home decide who takes home the prize. As an Arizona man said in a focus group study, "I think debates are one of the good old American ways to do it."[14]

Communication scholar Robert Meadow has written that debates "offer the viewers a chance to observe 'history,' be it the event itself as history or the possibility that a candidate will make a verbal error, stumble, or otherwise appear less than presidential."[15] To pass up such an occasion is to deprive oneself of both entertainment and duty. Debates provide a sense of connectedness, granting individual viewers a voice in the collective discourse. In contemporary America, to miss a presidential debate is a violation of the societal norm.

For most Americans, debates are also educational. Political scientist Doris Graber said that presidential debates serve as a "last-minute cram session for preparing the voting public,"[16] a point reinforced by other researchers. "The ability of viewers to comment sensibly on the candidates and their stands on issues increases with debates," wrote Kathleen Hall Jamieson and David Birdsell. The professors describe the informational impact of debates as "surprisingly wide," cutting across differences of class, race, income, and education level.[17] A poll conducted by the Pew Research Center after the election of 2008 found that 77 percent of those who watched the debates found them interesting; 70 percent described them as informative.[18]

As always with presidential debates, matters of content and delivery become inextricably linked. According to Republican strategist Karl Rove, a candidate's platform accounts for only part of what voters are learning. "It's the mix of the individual's persona and the issues that together meld the view of how this person will be as a leader," Rove said after the election of 2000. "Debates should not be taken lightly as just simply exchanges on, I'm going to lay out my policy position, you're going to lay out yours, and let the American people compare them." Audiences watch, he said, to see "how these people handle themselves under fire."[19]

Another intangible benefit of presidential debates is that they preview how a candidate is likely to use his bully pulpit. This is no small matter. When a chief executive pleads the case for war or consoles the nation in time of tragedy, he does so through the medium of television. Debate performance foreshadows the communication style a candidate will bring into office. John F. Kennedy's fluid presentation in the joint appearances of 1960 flowed directly into his live televised press conferences as president. Ronald Reagan's lofty language in the debate in 1980 became a familiar rhetorical device over the next eight years. Bill Clinton's empathy with the citizen-questioners in the town hall forum of 1992 presaged his touchy-feely style in office. Barack Obama's air of detachment followed him to the White House. Debates allow us to see whether the person we are inviting into our lives speaks a language we respond to.

The public seems to appreciate this chance to examine candidates with the usual filters removed. At least for the duration of the live event, viewers can apply their own criteria and reach their own decisions about the individuals seeking office. The protective layers in which presidential contenders so carefully wrap themselves fall away, if only fleetingly. Handlers and journalists step aside; what matters is the interplay of candidates and citizens.

According to Diana Carlin, an academic who has conducted extensive research on debate audiences, joint appearances between presidential nominees offer voters several key advantages. First, debates present an opportunity to measure the candidates side by side. Second, because debaters address the same topics, comparisons on positions can be easily drawn. Third, viewers can assess the candidates' statements in an overall context, not as a disparate collection of media-selected sound bites.[20] On all these points, the body politic exhibits its understanding of presidential debates as programming that requires the audience's active engagement.

"One thing the debates do is put the candidates on an equal plane," a Texas woman told one of Carlin's focus groups of 1992. "They are right there. Both of them together at the same time, same situation, with the same questions."[21] In the absence of face-to-face contact between candidates and voters, television debates serve as a substitute mechanism for rendering judgments. They allow the audience to evaluate not just statements but also nonverbal signals—the facial expressions and body language that lawyers call "demeanor evidence."

As debate scholar Allan Louden put it, candidates "communicate their relational status with every interjection" in debates. "Voters inherently assess how candidates treat each other and hosts. Viewers' evaluations are not limited to character and policy, they also are informed by the ways those on stage interact. This element becomes more than speculation when contestants are uniquely side by side."[22]

Debates are valuable not just to voters but to the candidates who take part in them. As one of history's most successful practitioners of the art, Bill Clinton stands as a positive role model for his fellow debaters—and a reminder that debates need not inspire dread. Clinton identified several benefits to participation: First, "you're forced to learn the things that you ought to know anyway about issues that you may not be all that interested in, or you didn't have time to deal with" during the presidential primary season. Second, "they force you to come to terms with what you really believe." And finally, "these are contests of ideas, as well as political positioning . . . there is some substance; there is some meat there." Said Clinton, "I am convinced that the debates that I went through, especially those three in 1992, actually helped me to be a better president."[23]

LIMITATIONS OF PRESIDENTIAL DEBATES

Do presidential debates make a valuable contribution to voter enlightenment, or do they reduce the campaign to a political beauty contest? From 1960 on, observers have criticized television debates for putting image before issues, style ahead of substance. The genre has been dismissed as contrived, counterfeit, even countereducational.

The objections coalesce around several points. After the Kennedy–Nixon telecasts, historians derided debates on conceptual grounds, defining them as fundamentally flawed in both structure and objective. Henry Steele Commager, in a widely circulated magazine piece that ran just before the election in 1960, argued that America's greatest presidents—Washington, Jefferson, Lincoln, and Wilson—would all have lost television debates. Commager condemned the programs for prizing "the glib, the evasive, the dogmatic, the melodramatic" over "the sincere, the judicious, the sober, the honest in political discussion."

Like other critics, Commager feared that the institutional strictures of television made political debates not just ineffective but downright disinformational. The process, he wrote, "encourages the American public to believe that there are no questions, no issues before us that are so difficult that they cannot be disposed of in two or three minutes of off-the-cuff comment." Television itself was not to blame for this failing, Commager wrote. "It would be imbecility not to take full advantage of television in this and future campaigns. The trouble is that we are not taking advantage of it at all, but permitting it to take advantage of us."[24]

In his classic book *The Image* (1964), historian Daniel Boorstin intensified the reproach, calling the Kennedy–Nixon debates "remarkably successful in reducing great national issues to trivial dimensions." Boorstin cited presidential debates as a "clinical example" of his new coinage, the "pseudo-event": "Pseudo-events thus lead to emphasis on pseudo-qualifications. Again the self-fulfilling prophecy. If we test presidential candidates by their talents on TV quiz performances, we will, of course, choose presidents for precisely these qualifications. In a democracy, reality tends to conform to the pseudo-event. Nature imitates art."[25]

To some extent, the damning of presidential debates by Commager and Boorstin reflects the fears of an era now past. Television in 1960 was far less a medium of information than a medium of entertainment; much of the early trepidation stems from the very real concern that the values of commercial television would infect those of electoral politics. This is, of course, essentially what happened, and presidential debates had a hand in facilitating the shift.

Harvey Wheeler, another critic of the debates of 1960, worried that John Kennedy's physical attractiveness—his resemblance to "a composite picture of all the good stereotypes television has created"—may have unduly influenced audience reaction. Wheeler cautioned that a potentially dangerous dynamic could develop in presidential debates, with viewers swayed by "invisible visual values" that preempted their conscious desires. "It seems likely that in the future one of the tests of a candidate's 'availability' for political nomination will be his correspondence with the then current image of the good guy," Wheeler wrote.[26]

Though Wheeler's prophecy has not come to pass, it does merit consideration. By substituting televisual talent for facial attractiveness, we can argue that debate audiences may indeed be responding to a set of "invisible values," imposed by the camera and bearing more on stylistic fluency than intellect or ability. Don Hewitt of CBS, who produced and directed history's first television debate, began almost immediately to question the value of the matches, wondering if too much emphasis had been placed on performing prowess. "When it was over, I remember thinking there's something wrong here," Hewitt recalled. "We may have made the right choice, but it worried me that it might have been for the wrong reasons. We were electing a matinee idol."[27]

Critics of presidential debates have long bemoaned television's weakness for glittering personalities. Not surprisingly, Richard Nixon added his voice to this chorus, writing after the Ford–Carter debates in 1976, "I doubt that they can ever serve a responsible role in defining the issues of a presidential campaign. Because of the nature of the medium, there will inevitably be a greater premium on showmanship than on statesmanship."[28]

Undoubtedly candidates who play well on camera hold an advantage in live televised debates. Kennedy proved this, as did Reagan and Clinton. In each case, superior performing skills strongly accrued to the individual's benefit. But telegenic gifts in themselves may not be enough to satisfy a debate audience.

A useful case study in this regard is Ross Perot, who in 1992 illustrated the pros and cons of coming across as a colorful character. Perot's initial appearance in the three-way debates with Clinton and Bush brought something revolutionary to presidential debates: an endearing, and genuine, sense of humor. But audience surveys found that even as viewers responded favorably to the comic relief, they also dismissed Perot as shallow. Similarly, although the camera-friendly Sarah Palin outperformed expectations in her vice presidential debate in 2008, she could not establish herself as adequate to the job she sought. It is possible, in other words, for a debater to be interesting and unpersuasive at the same time.

Still, one wonders how a charismatic candidate without the negative baggage of Perot and Palin might fare in a presidential debate. Could a more polished practitioner of the television arts, someone better versed in the principles of rhetoric and timing and drama, use these skills to win a debate on superficial criteria? In a close election, could the scales tip in favor of the candidate who puts on the more entertaining show? Might a candidate who is trailing in the polls misappropriate the innate instability of a live debate to advance his or her cause?

During the campaign of 1992, Elizabeth Drew wrote that debates reward "wrong, or irrelevant, qualifications." She called them a "false test" for the presidency,[29] an opinion widely shared by critics. As academic researcher Stephen Mills noted, "Debating requires brevity, consistency, extensive briefing, and constant rebuttal of the opponent. Governing requires more time, perhaps some inconsistency, improvisation, and compromise with opponents." Mills said debates emphasize *individual* performance, a structure at odds with the collegial functioning of the executive branch. "Governing requires skillful management of a team of advisers," he wrote. "Debating, in contrast, focuses on the presidential candidates in isolation."[30]

The argument that debates have limited relevance to the presidency has not been lost on political professionals. After Ronald Reagan's debacle in the first debate of 1984, Republican strategist Lee Atwater devised a contingency plan in case Reagan went on to a second flop. In an internal memo known as "The Great American Fog Machine," Atwater proposed a set of media talking points: spinners would dismiss debates as "artificially contrived 'pressure cookers' which do not coincide with the actual pressures that confront a president." Debates would be called "fundamentally degrading," and a "bizarre ritual."[31]

Because the age joke put Reagan back on track, Atwater's plan never came to fruition. As long as the "bizarre ritual" of presidential debates did not harm the candidate, it would be allowed to endure.

THE INFLUENCE OF DEBATES ON VOTING

"Debates are to elections what treaties are to wars," according to political scientist and Democratic debate adviser Samuel Popkin. "They ratify what has already been accomplished on the battlefield."[32] Experts agree that joint candidate appearances move perceptions more than votes. Evidence from numerous academic studies and political surveys indicates that despite their high profile, presidential debates are but one of many factors considered at the ballot box. To further muddy the question, it is virtually impossible to isolate debates from other influences on voters' decisions.

The mythos of presidential debates would have us believe that Kennedy won election because he looked better on television than Nixon; that Ford's gaffe about Eastern Europe cost him the White House; that Reagan's "There you go again" was the coup de grâce that finished Carter's presidency. As with most legends, these assertions reflect at least a kernel of truth. But contrary examples make the opposite case.

In 1984 an exceptionally bad debate did not stop Ronald Reagan's electoral landslide, while an exceptionally good one did not help Walter Mondale. If debates were determinative, Reagan's wobbly performance in Louisville ought to have inflicted more damage. Ditto for Barack Obama in the first debate in 2012 and George W. Bush in 2004.

"One reason that presidential debates have not necessarily vaulted the underdog to victory is that a single debate victory has not been enough," wrote political scientists John Sides and Lynn Vavreck. "Other debates have followed, and it has proven difficult to run the table and win them all." Evidence suggests that debaters who succeed early in a series tend to fare worse later on, and vice-versa—like Romney and Obama in 2012.[33]

It speaks well of the audience's common sense that although debates have been highly watched, they have not been excessively influential. Voters regard live television debates as only one device for evaluating candidates—and an imperfect one at that. After fifty-plus years of exposure, Americans have reached a sophisticated understanding of what presidential debates can and cannot do.

With each new series, the electorate's frame of reference expands. Increasingly viewers recognize the coaching, the planted one-liners, the jockeying for narrative control, and the expectations-setting that color the televised encounters. Audiences for the Kennedy–Nixon broadcasts approached the "Great Debates" with relatively few preconceptions; today's public watches with a deeper awareness of the tactical considerations at play.

Researcher Diana Carlin has found audiences to be fully cognizant of the artifice of debates, and equally quick to dismiss it. "We often misjudge what the general public does and doesn't understand, or why they are or aren't interested, and we often attribute motives that are very different from reality," Carlin said. "They're on to the sound bites, they're on to when candidates are avoiding, they're on to strategies."[34]

One solid conclusion can be drawn about debate viewers: they are as unpredictable as the programs themselves. To the chagrin of political strategists, conventional wisdom formed in one debate season cannot accurately foretell what will happen in the next. Because public reaction is a constantly moving target, the lessons of history will inevitably lack definition.

"Perhaps we have not yet witnessed enough presidential debates to determine which are the rules and which are the exceptions," wrote debate scholars David Lanoue and Peter Schrott in the wake of the election of 1988, and the statement remains valid many cycles later. "Perhaps viewers' reactions to each individual encounter are more idiosyncratic than we would like to think."[35] If so, the crowd may once again be demonstrating its wisdom. For an idiosyncratic response keeps candidates on their toes—and vests the power of presidential debates with the people.

CONCLUSION

The Globalization of an American Tradition

The meeting of John F. Kennedy and Richard Nixon in a Chicago television studio in September 1960 begat a campaign tradition that reconfigured the electoral landscape—not only in the United States but around the world. In the decades since that historic night, more than seventy-five countries have integrated into their elections televised debates among candidates for national leadership. In every part of the globe, under a vast variety of political systems and circumstances, debates have entertained and enlightened voters.

This most American of television genres qualifies as a worldwide hit. Just about everywhere debates occur, audiences sit up and take notice. The *face-à-face* in 2012 between French presidential contenders Nicolas Sarkozy and François Hollande attracted nearly 20 million viewers— almost one-third of France's entire population. Audience shares for presidential debates in Spain have topped 50 percent of the viewing audience. Ratings data from other nations are correspondingly impressive. Why? Because people recognize television debates as rare and genuine moments of high drama. In an era in which political campaigns around the world seem risk averse and out of touch, live debates stand out for their power to reach the electorate in direct and sometimes surprising ways.

The momentousness of debates virtually compels voters to watch—if they fail to do so, they might miss history in the making. The groundbreaking debate in 1994 between South African presidential candidates Nelson Mandela and F. W. de Klerk drew millions of viewers, both domestically and internationally. Seizing the moment, Mandela clasped his opponent's hands and spoke of their shared goals as citizens of the same country. This unexpected gesture of conciliation spoke volumes about the transformation of postapartheid South Africa, riveting everyone who watched. Recent televised debates in Egypt, Iran, and Afghanistan have similarly affirmed a shift in those countries toward more transparent elections—baby steps, perhaps, but steps in the right direction.

Because live debates are so perilous for their participants, candidates everywhere either sidestep them or approach with trepidation. Italian prime minister Silvio Berlusconi initially refused to debate his opponent in 2006 unless the event would be followed by a press conference—a press conference featuring Berlusconi alone. The prime minister reasoned that his incumbent status accorded him this right; only after strenuous opposition from his competitor did he back down.

In Russia both Vladimir Putin and his handpicked successor Dmitry Medvedev have refused to take part in televised debates. So have Hugo Chávez of Venezuela and Evo Morales of Bolivia, among numerous others. Their excuses follow predictable lines, usually involving a disparagement of the debate institution itself. The "real debate," a spokesman for Morales said in 2014, is "with the people, not with candidates who represent only themselves." Colombian president Álvaro Uribe, dismissing calls for a debate in 2006, reasoned that "in order to sell your own *panela* (concentrated sugarcane juice), you do not have to discredit the *panela* of your neighbor." An early attempt to schedule debates between candidates for chancellor of West Germany elicited an even more blatantly self-interested rejection from Christian Democratic Union party leader Georg Kiesinger. "It misbecomes a chancellor," Kiesinger said, "to sit on a chair and wait until he is allowed to speak."[1]

Organizers of debates routinely meet resistance from candidates, and in countries all over the globe, debates have been canceled when participants failed to show up—sometimes even after they have agreed to attend. In 2008 Paraguayan candidate Fernando Lugo gave producers one hour's notice that he would not appear in a nationally televised debate; the program went on without him, an empty chair representing the missing-in-action Lugo. Mexican presidential contenders are obligated by law to take part in televised debates, though the candidates and their advisers exercise a great deal of control over matters of format, scheduling, and staging. Legislators in other countries have also considered mandating debates as an electoral requirement.

A long history of strong-arm tactics by politicians seeking to protect themselves underscores the need for strong, autonomous debate sponsorship. On this question, the United States serves as a positive role model for the rest of the world. America's independent Commission on Presidential Debates (CPD) is much admired by debate producers internationally, who regularly turn to the CPD for advice. Several years ago, Jamaica established its own such body, the Jamaica Debates Commission, which in addition to sponsoring several rounds of national debates has published an excellent handbook for staging them.[2]

Elsewhere, debate sponsorship takes various forms. Journalists organized Australia's first debates in 1984, but after that initial round, politicians co-opted the process and began setting the rules and conditions themselves. In Canada and Germany, a consortium of television networks traditionally produces the debates, albeit with extensive input from the political parties. A similar arrangement can be found in the United Kingdom, where debates came into being only in 2010. A frequent debate sponsor in Latin America has been the Spanish-language television news network CNN en Español, which partners with local broadcast entities to produce and televise candidate forums in the host country. Recent presidential debates in Spain have been sponsored and executed by the Academia de las Ciencias y las Artes de Televisión (Academy of Television Arts and Sciences), a highly respected organization made up of broadcast professionals who bring to the task formidable production skills.

Mexican presidential debates fall under the purview of the Instituto Federal Electoral (IFE), an autonomous agency funded by the national government and charged with overseeing various aspects of federal elections. IFE's debates have not been without controversy: following a presidential debate in 2012, the agency had to issue an apology for featuring a provocatively clad former Playboy model who kicked off the program with a drawing to determine the candidates' speaking order. IFE's productions have also been criticized for their lack of spontaneity and for their restrictive rules, including prohibitions on camera shots of debaters who are listening rather than talking.

Successful sponsorship hinges largely on clout. Can sponsors and candidates engage as equals? At a minimum, do sponsors wield sufficient leverage to bring a debate to fruition? Internationally, experience suggests that campaign debates are almost as likely to be canceled as to occur, or to be held minus the participation of leading players. In every corner of the planet, politicians share a common trait: they do what is best for themselves, especially when running for election. Debate negotiators for the American television networks discovered this in 1960, and the pattern has not failed to repeat itself across geography and time.

It bears mention that politicians outside the United States subject themselves to conditions that American candidates would never accept. A debate in Ecuador in 2006, for instance, ran for three hours and thirty minutes, more than twice the length of the longest U.S. presidential debate. In nocturnal Brazil, a debate that same year did not go on-air until 10:30 P.M. and lasted until well past midnight (skeptics saw the timing as a ploy by the campaigns to reduce viewership). Finnish candidates have been known to extend their debates over two consecutive nights. Canadian party leaders debate not only in English but also in French.

A wide variety of debate formats exists internationally, from press panels to town hall forums to sit-down conversations. Party leaders in New Zealand have answered questions submitted by voters via YouTube; Colombian presidential candidates took part in a similar exercise, entitled "Yo Pregunto" (I'm Asking). But to a great extent, debate formats around the world are cautious to the point of dullness, and overly deferential in tone. Candidates in young democracies in particular tend to steer clear of confrontation and controversy.

In Asian countries like South Korea and Taiwan, debates have been moderated by academics, whose questions can be weightier than the topics raised by journalists. In 2002, for example, the moderator of all three South Korean debates was Jaeho Yeom, a professor of political science at Korea University who received his doctorate at Stanford. The presidential debates in Costa Rica in 2014 incorporated questions crafted by experts from academia and the professional community.

Internationally as in the United States, however, journalists predominate as debate interrogators, and on occasion their questions rankle the participants. In the party leaders' debate of 1999 in New Zealand, the journalist-moderator asked if the candidates had ever smoked marijuana. Soon-to-be prime minister Helen Clark batted the question right back, responding, "Do you want to bring politics to this level?"[3]

As this example indicates, debaters the world over have mastered the art of press-bashing.

Perhaps the most rigorous of all formats, at least from the candidates' perspective, is one that television broadcasters in the United States originally sought for the Kennedy–Nixon series: a "direct confrontation" or "Oxford"-style debate, in which the participants question each another directly, with minimal input from a moderator. This setup, rejected by campaign negotiators in 1960, remains the holy grail of American presidential debate formats, regularly promoted by sponsors, scholars, and pundits, and just as regularly swept off the bargaining table by hypercautious candidates.

In France presidential debates have faithfully—and successfully—followed this format since the country's inaugural television joust between François Mitterrand and Valéry Giscard d'Estaing in 1974. French debates demand a great deal of their participants, for direct confrontation forces an intense interpersonal dynamic that keeps debaters poised on the razor's edge from start to finish. For viewers, this provides a compelling structural incentive to watch. But without the intercession of a moderator or other external questioners, the lead actors have perhaps too much latitude for grandstanding, obfuscation, and evasion. As a format, direct confrontation runs the risk of becoming excessively candidate-centric.

How should topics in a debate be introduced, and who should be tasked with the questioning? These matters have long vexed debate planners, in the United States and around the world. In the first Obama–Romney encounter in 2012, moderator Jim Lehrer came under fire for laying out subject areas, then stepping back. In the second encounter, moderator Candy Crowley came under fire for participating too directly. When panels of journalist asked questions in American debates, complaints abounded about the journalists, and when town hall audiences joined the debate mix, their questions sparked criticism as well.

No ideal debate format exists. Each arrangement has its advantages and disadvantages; even the best formats can be undermined by rules that are too rigidly defined or that favor the interests of politicians over the interests of voters. This is why it makes sense to vary structures within a series, as in recent American presidential debate cycles. Even within a single debate, it is possible to mix formats—combining town hall participation with questions from a solo moderator, for instance, or live questions with recorded questions. Costa Rica's official debates in 2014 were divided into three segments: one round featuring questions prepared by experts, one round of questions submitted by social media users, and one round in which the debaters queried each another.

A number of interesting ideas are finding their way into televised debates globally. Candidates have taken part in thematic debates, as in the Netherlands, where party leaders debate before an audience of children and adolescents, or Denmark, where candidates have held single-topic discussions of health care. In Indonesia the presidential and vice presidential contenders have engaged in team debates against their rivals, and in Brazil the Catholic Church has hosted religiously themed presidential debates, with questioning by local bishops.

As live television events, debates in all countries have the potential to veer in unforeseen directions. During an encounter in Mexico in 2000, candidate Francisco Labastida complained that his opponent, Vicente Fox, had referred to him on the campaign trail as "shorty," "henpecked," and "a queer." "It's not that it offends me," Labastida insisted, "it's that it offends Mexican families." Yet instead of gaining sympathy as the aggrieved party, Labastida struck audiences as whiny, especially after Fox's quick-witted rejoinder: "Some day I'll stop being crude, but you guys will never stop being devious, bad governors, and corrupt."[4]

In rare instances campaign debates have turned physical. Consider the case of Azerbaijan, where in 2003 a live televised forum degenerated into the functional equivalent of a barroom brawl. After two of the debaters began exchanging insults and hurling bottles of water at each other, producers hastily yanked the program off the air. Ten years later, another Azerbaijani presidential debate fell apart after one candidate threw a water bottle at a rival and several of the participants stormed out.

American debates, by contrast, are positively staid.

Wherever they take place, campaign debates must first and foremost serve the needs of the electorate, a goal more easily articulated than accomplished. Much has been made in recent years of the power of social media to reshape debates by casting voters as participants rather than spectators. A Twitter experiment called "#Answer or #Dodge," for example, allowed viewers of an American primary debate in 2012 to weigh in on whether the participants were being sufficiently responsive. Imagine a scenario in which a debate moderator could use such results to press for more satisfactory answers even as the event is under way. From a technological standpoint, interactivity between citizens and debaters presents intriguing possibilities for reform.

Yet the simplicity of debates—the high drama of two or three competitors answering questions in real time, unadorned, in front of cameras—may be fundamentally resistant to a radical overhaul. "There is still a school of thought that the elegance and focus of these debates need to be retained," said Janet Brown, executive director of the CPD. "For all the talk of new media, the question is how do you use that to make a debate better?"[5] Instead of altering the basic structure of debates, social media may best serve as a participatory adjunct to the main event, with voters interpreting and sharing the experience on a parallel track.

As televised campaign debates take root around the world, format innovations and increased levels of interactivity will inevitably breathe new life into the institution. A political genre launched more than half a century ago, in a now-antiquated media environment, has no choice but to change and grow. Yet whatever form debates take, in whatever society, these events rest upon a straightforward, irresistible premise: verbal and visual combat between the men and women who seek to lead their countries. Kennedy and Nixon could scarcely have foreseen that their television experiment on September 26, 1960, would give rise to America's most popular political export.

SCHEDULE OF TELEVISED PRESIDENTIAL AND VICE PRESIDENTIAL DEBATES, 1960–2012

1960

JOHN F. KENNEDY AND RICHARD NIXON
September 26, 1960: Chicago
October 7, 1960: Washington, D.C.
October 13, 1960: Los Angeles (Nixon) and New York City (Kennedy)
October 21, 1960: New York City

1976

JIMMY CARTER AND GERALD FORD
September 23, 1976: Philadelphia
October 6, 1976: San Francisco
October 22, 1976: Williamsburg, Virginia

WALTER MONDALE AND BOB DOLE
October 15, 1976: Houston

1980

RONALD REAGAN AND JOHN ANDERSON
September 21, 1980: Baltimore

RONALD REAGAN AND JIMMY CARTER
October 28, 1980: Cleveland

1984

RONALD REAGAN AND WALTER MONDALE
October 7, 1984: Louisville
October 21, 1984: Kansas City

GEORGE BUSH AND GERALDINE FERRARO
October 11, 1984: Philadelphia

1988

GEORGE BUSH AND MICHAEL DUKAKIS
September 25, 1988: Wake Forest, North Carolina
October 13, 1988: Los Angeles

DAN QUAYLE AND LLOYD BENTSEN
October 5, 1988: Omaha

1992

BILL CLINTON, GEORGE BUSH, AND ROSS PEROT
October 11, 1992: St. Louis
October 15, 1992: Richmond
October 19, 1992: East Lansing, Michigan

AL GORE, DAN QUAYLE, AND JAMES STOCKDALE
October 13, 1992: Atlanta

1996

BILL CLINTON AND BOB DOLE
October 6, 1996: Hartford
October 16, 1996: San Diego

AL GORE AND JACK KEMP
October 9, 1996: St. Petersburg, Florida

2000

GEORGE W. BUSH AND AL GORE
October 3, 2000: Boston
October 11, 2000: Wake Forest, North Carolina
October 17, 2000: St. Louis

DICK CHENEY AND JOSEPH LIEBERMAN
October 5, 2000: Danville, Kentucky

2004

GEORGE W. BUSH AND JOHN KERRY
September 30, 2004: Coral Gables, Florida
October 8, 2004: St. Louis
October 13, 2004: Tempe, Arizona

DICK CHENEY AND JOHN EDWARDS
October 5, 2004: Cleveland

2008

BARACK OBAMA AND JOHN McCAIN
September 26, 2008: Oxford, Mississippi
October 7, 2008: Nashville
October 15, 2008: Hempstead, New York

JOE BIDEN AND SARAH PALIN
October 2, 2008: St. Louis

2012

BARACK OBAMA AND MITT ROMNEY
October 3, 2012: Denver
October 16, 2012: Hempstead, New York
October 22, 2012: Boca Raton, Florida

JOE BIDEN AND PAUL RYAN
October 11, 2012: Danville, Kentucky

NOTES

INTRODUCTION

1. David Halberstam, "President Video," *Esquire*, June 1976, 130.

2. On September, 26, 1985, the Museum of Broadcast Communications in Chicago held a live event called the "Twenty-Fifth Anniversary Gala," which brought together many of the surviving principals involved in the first Kennedy–Nixon debate to share recollections of their experience. The event took place in Studio One at WBBM, the site of the debate.

3. Rogers was interviewed on the *Lee Phillip Show*, WBBM, Chicago, September 22, 1985.

4. Jules Witcover, "The Bottom Line Is Style," *Washington Post*, September 19, 1976, A4.

5. Howard K. Smith, *Events Leading Up to My Death: The Life of a Twentieth-Century Reporter* (New York: St. Martin's Press, 1996), 263; Rogers, *Lee Phillip Show*.

6. Footage and sound from Kennedy and Nixon in the WBBM studio were taken from recordings screened at the Museum of Broadcast Communications in Chicago. These include *The Great Debate*, a twenty-fifth anniversary retrospective that aired on WBBM in September 1985, and "The Twenty-Fifth Anniversary Gala."

7. Rogers was interviewed for the PBS *American Experience* documentary *Nixon*, which originally aired on October 8, 1990.

8. Christopher Matthews, *Kennedy and Nixon: The Rivalry That Shaped Postwar America* (New York: Simon and Schuster, 1996), 145.

9. Ibid., 149.

10. Sig Mickelson, *From Whistle Stop to Sound Bite: Four Decades of Politics and Television* (New York: Praeger, 1989), 123.

11. Mary Cremmen, "Listening Party," *Boston Globe*, September 27, 1960, 1, 9.

12. Earl Mazo, Malcolm Moos, Hallock Hoffman, and Harvey Wheeler, *The Great Debates* (Santa Barbara, Calif.: Center for the Study of Democratic Institutions, 1962), 4; J. Leonard Reinsch, *Getting Elected: From Radio and Roosevelt to Television and Reagan* (New York: Hippocrene, 1988), 143.

13. Halberstam, "President Video," 132.

14. Theodore White, *The Making of the President 1960* (New York: Atheneum, 1961), 288–89.

15. Erik Barnouw, *The Image Empire: A History of Broadcasting in the United States from 1953* (New York: Oxford University Press, 1970), 164.

16. Terry Turner, "What 'Debate' Didn't Show," *Chicago Daily News*, September 27, 1960, 35.

17. Mickelson, *From Whistle Stop to Sound Bite*, 122.

18. White, *Making of the President 1960*, 285.

19. Debate transcriptions used throughout this book were prepared by the Commission on Presidential Debates. They are available on the commission's website (www.debates.org).

20. Fawn Brodie, *Richard Nixon: The Shaping of His Character* (New York: Norton, 1981), 427.

21. Kenneth P. O'Donnell and David F. Powers, with Joe McCarthy, *Johnny, We Hardly Knew Ye: Memories of John Fitzgerald Kennedy* (Boston: Little, Brown, 1972), 213.

22. William Braden, "Some Tidbits for Posterity," *Chicago Sun-Times*, September 27, 1960, 18.

23. Hewitt made this remark at the "Twenty-Fifth Anniversary Gala."

24. Cremmen, "Listening Party," 9.

25. Emilie Tavel, "Back at Hyannis Port . . . ," *Christian Science Monitor*, September 27, 1960, 6.

26. Richard Nixon, *Six Crises* (Garden City, N.Y.: Doubleday, 1962), 340.

27. "Pat Sees Nixon 1st Time on TV: 'Looked Great,'" *Boston Evening Globe*, September 27, 1960, 9; Richard T. Stout, "Nixon Aides Admit Makeup Job," *Chicago Daily News*, September 30, 1960, 4.

28. White, *Making of the President 1960*, 291; and "The Campaign: Candid Camera," *Time*, October 10, 1960, 20.

29. Todd Gitlin, "Bites and Blips: Chunk News, Savvy Talk, and the Bifurcation of American Politics," in *Communication and Citizenship: Journalism and the Public Sphere in the New Media Aged*, ed. Peter Dahlgren and Colin Sparks (London: Routledge, 1991), 132.

30. Polsby quoted in George J. Church, "Debating the Debates," *Time*, October 29, 1984, 31.

1. THE PREDEBATE DEBATE

1. David Halberstam, "President Video," *Esquire*, June 1976, 134.

2. Ibid., 94.

3. Transcript of "Debating the Debates: Defining Moments in Presidential Campaigns," a symposium presented by the Ronald Reagan Center for Public Affairs, October 15, 1996, 31; Herbert G. Klein, *Making It Perfectly Clear: An Inside Account of Nixon's Love-Hate Relationship with the Media* (Garden City, N.Y.: Doubleday, 1980), 103.

4. Earl Mazo, "The Great Debates," in Earl Mazo, Malcolm Moos, Hallock Hoffman, and Harvey Wheeler, *The Great Debates* (Santa Barbara, Calif.: Center for the Study of Democratic Institutions, 1962), 3.

5. Walter Lippmann, "Today and Tomorrow: The TV Debate," *Washington Post*, September 29, 1960, A23; Sig Mickelson, *From Whistle Stop to Sound Bite: Four Decades of Politics and Television* (New York: Praeger, 1989), 134.

6. Goldwater's quote was replayed in an obituary of the Arizona senator that aired on *The NewsHour with Jim Lehrer*, PBS, May 28, 1998. See also two autobiographical books by Goldwater: *The Conscience of a Majority* (Englewood Cliffs, N.J.: Prentice-Hall, 1970), 37; and *With No Apologies: The Personal and Political Memoirs of United States Senator Barry M. Goldwater* (New York: Morrow, 1979), 156.

7. Newton Minow, J. B. Martin, and Lee Mitchell, *Presidential Television* (New York: Basic Books, 1973), 54.

8. Edward Walsh, "Ford Picks Dole for No. 2 Spot, Challenges Carter to a Debate," *Washington Post*, August 20, 1976, 1.

9. Jonathan Moore and Janet Fraser, eds., *Campaign for President: The Managers Look at '76* (Cambridge, Mass.: Ballinger, 1977), 122.

10. Anthony Corrado, "Background Paper," in *Let America Decide* (New York: Twentieth Century Foundation, 1995), 117.

11. Walter Fisher, "Soap Box Derby," *University of Southern California Chronicle*, October 1980, 3.

12. Pat Oliphant, *Washington Star*, September 11, 1980, A17; Robert G. Kaiser, "Carter Winning Gamble on Debates," *Washington Post*, September 18, 1980, A1.

13. Godfrey Sperling Jr., "The 2/3 Debate: Whose Risks Are Greatest?," *Christian Science Monitor*, September 19, 1980, 3.

14. Jimmy Carter, *Keeping Faith: Memoirs of a President* (New York: Bantam, 1982), 543.

15. Hamilton Jordan, *Crisis: The Last Year of the Carter Presidency* (New York: Putnam, 1982), 353; Elizabeth Drew, *Portrait of an Election: The 1980 Presidential Campaign* (New York: Simon and Schuster, 1981), 410. Patrick Caddell's "Debate Strategy Memorandum," reprinted in its entirety (410–39), offers interesting insight into the strategic thinking by Carter's camp before the debate in 1980.

16. Michael Deaver, interview by author, June 17, 1998.

17. Richard Wirthlin, interview by author, September 2, 1998.

18. Rowland Evans and Robert Novak, "The Decision to Debate," *Washington Post*, October 20, 1980, A21.

19. Myles Martel, *Political Campaign Debates: Images, Strategies, and Tactics* (New York: Longman, 1983), 18.

20. NBC News "Postscript," October 28, 1980.

21. William F. Buckley Jr., "When I Debated Reagan," *New York Times*, September 11, 1984, A23.

22. Deaver, interview.

23. Bush's draft reference was to Bill Clinton's military inexperience; "Arkansas River" apparently referred to water pollution caused by the chicken-processing industry in Clinton's home state.

24. Dan Routman, interview by author, August 31, 1998.

25. CBS News *Morning Show*, September 6, 2000.

26. Karl Rove, *Courage and Consequence: My Life as a Conservative in the Fight* (New York: Simon and Schuster, 2010), 179.

27. Stuart Stevens, *The Big Enchilada: Campaign Adventures with the Cockeyed Optimists from Texas Who Won the Biggest Prize in Politics* (New York: Free Press, 2001), 204.

28. Bill Carter, "The Viewers; Debates Picked by Bush Would Draw Small Audiences," *New York Times*, September 7, 2000, A25.

29. Paul G. Kirk Jr., interview by author, April 10, 2007.

30. *Larry King Live*, CNN, August 12, 2004.

31. James A. Baker III, *"Work Hard, Study . . . and Keep Out of Politics!": Adventures and Lessons from an Unexpected Public Life* (New York: Putnam, 2006), 393.

32. NBC *Saturday Night Live*, September 27, 2008.

33. Beth Fouhy, "Obama Rebuffs McCain's Call to Delay Debate," Associated Press, September 24, 2008; Dana Bash, "McCain Camp to Propose Postponing VP debate," *Political Ticker* (blog), CNN, September 24, 2008, http://politicalticker.blogs.cnn.com/2008/09/24/mccain-camp-to-propose-postponing-vp-debate/.

34. Nedra Pickler, "McCain to Attend Debate Even Without Bailout Deal," Associated Press, September 26, 2008; Adam Nagourney and Elisabeth Bumiller, "McCain Leaps into a Thicket," *New York Times*, September 26, 2008, A1, http://www.nytimes.com/2008/09/26/us/politics/26campaign.html.

35. Janet Brown, interview by author, February 5, 2014.

36. Ron Klain, interview by author, February 4, 2014.

37. David Plouffe, *The Audacity to Win: The Inside Story and Lessons of Barack Obama's Historic Victory* (New York: Viking, 2009), 340.

38. Letter, John McCain to Barack Obama, June 4, 2008, https://newrepublic.com/article/42214/mccain-calls-joint-town-hall-meetings; Jim Tankersley, "Trav-

eling Debates for McCain, Obama?," *The Swamp* (blog), *Chicago Tribune*, May 11, 2008, http://weblogs.chicagotribune.com/news/politics/blog/2008/05/traveling _debates_for_mccain_o.html.

39. Jim Rutenberg, "McCain and Obama Agree to Attend Megachurch Forum," *New York Times*, July 21, 2008.

40. "Democratizing the Debates: A Report of the Annenberg Working Group on Presidential Campaign Reform," June 17, 2015, http://www.annenberg publicpolicycenter.org/democratizing-the-debates/.

41. Anita Dunn, interview by author, June 24, 2014.

42. Baker, *"Work Hard, Study . . . and Keep Out of Politics!,"* 111.

43. "Twenty-Fifth Anniversary Gala," Museum of Broadcast Communications, September 26, 1985.

44. Herbert A. Seltz and Richard D. Yoakam, "Production Diary of the Debates," in *The Great Debates: Background, Perspective, Effects*, ed. Sidney Kraus (Bloomington: Indiana University Press, 1962), 122.

45. Memorandum, Stephen M. Travis to Stuart E. Eizenstat and Al Stern, August 27, 1976, Domestic Policy Staff: Stern box 1, folder "Debates—Carter/Ford," Jimmy Carter Presidential Library.

46. Jody Powell, "When We Organized the Debates," *New York Times*, September 11, 1984, A23.

47. Institute of Politics, Harvard University, ed., *Campaign for President: The Managers Look at 2000* (Hollis, N.H.: Hollis, 2002), 176.

48. Ibid., 179.

49. Jay Rosen, "Ungovernable Reality, not Candy Crowley, Threatens Obama and Romney," *Guardian*, October 16, 2012.

50. Frank Fahrenkopf Jr., interview with author, March 13, 2014.

51. Clay Mulford, interview by author, August 28, 1998.

52. Memorandum of Understanding, 1992, 5, 31.

53. Paul Kirk, interview by author, April 10, 2007.

54. Aaron Zelinsky, "A Secret Memo Controls the Rules of the Presidential Debates—Should It?," *San Francisco Chronicle*, October 14, 2008, B7.

55. James A. Baker 3d, interview with author, September 4, 1998.

56. Lou Cannon, *Reagan* (New York: Putnam, 1982), 295.

57. Jack W. Germond and Jules Witcover, *Blue Smoke and Mirrors: How Reagan Won and Why Carter Lost the Election of 1980* (New York: Viking, 1981), 276.

58. Terence Smith, "Presidential Debate Format Set; Camps Differ on Time and Place," *New York Times*, October 21, 1980, A1.

59. David Hoffman, "At Least One Debate by Reagan, Mondale Agreed to by Aides," *Washington Post*, September 1, 1984, A4.

60. Elizabeth Drew, *Election Journal: Political Events of 1987–1988* (New York: William Morrow, 1989), 283.

61. Robert Goodwin, memorandum of conversation, written after the negotiating meeting on October 1, 1992, and provided to the author by Goodwin.

62. David Von Drehle, "Punditocracy Faces Dizzying Spin Cycle," *Washington Post*, October 3, 1992, A1.

63. Roger Simon, *Show Time: The American Political Circus and the Race for the White House* (New York: Times Books, 1998), 278.

64. Institute of Politics, *Campaign for President 2000*, 162, 167, 175.

65. James A. Baker 3rd, interview by author, April 19, 2007.

66. Klain, interview.

67. Kathleen Hall Jamieson and Paul Waldman, *Electing the President 2004: The Insiders' View* (Philadelphia: University of Pennsylvania Press, 2006), 123.

68. Joan Quigley, *What Does Joan Say? My Seven Years as White House Astrologer to Nancy and Ronald Reagan* (Secaucus, N.J.: Birch Lane, 1990), 92.

69. Deaver, interview.

70. Klein, *Making It Perfectly Clear*, 103.

71. Richard M. Nixon, *Six Crises* (Garden City, N.Y.: Doubleday, 1962), 324.

72. Richard C. Leone, interview by author, April 6, 1998.

73. Robert W. Sarnoff, "An NBC View," in Kraus, *Great Debates*, 61.

74. Nancy Reagan, *My Turn: The Memoirs of Nancy Reagan* (New York: Random House, 1989), 266.

75. Elizabeth Drew, *Campaign Journal: The Political Events of 1983–1984* (New York: Macmillan, 1985), 691–92.

76. Douglass Cater, "Notes from Backstage," in Kraus, *Great Debates*, 129.

77. B. Drummond Ayres, "Bush Rejects Panel's Plan for 3 Debates," *New York Times*, September 4, 1992, A13.

78. Mickey Kantor, interview by author, July 20, 1998; Charles T. Royer, ed., *Campaign for President: The Managers Look at '92* (Hollis, N.H.: Hollis, 1994), 254.

79. Edward M. Fouhy, "The Debates: A Winning Miniseries," *Washington Journalism Review*, December 1992, 28; Baker, 1998 interview.

80. Fouhy, "Debates," 28.

81. Richard L. Berke, "Debating the Debates: John Q. Defeats Reporters," *New York Times*, October 21, 1992, A19.

82. J. Leonard Reinsch, *Getting Elected: From Radio and Roosevelt to Television and Reagan* (New York: Hippocrene, 1988), 137.

83. Herbert A. Seltz and Richard D. Yoakam, "Production Diary of the Debates," in *The Great Debates: Carter vs. Ford, 1976*, ed. Sidney Kraus (Bloomington: Indiana University Press, 1979), 98.

84. Transcript of "Debating the Debates: Defining Moments in Presidential Campaigns," 76.

85. Vernon Jordan, interview by author, July 11, 2007.

86. Baker, 2007 interview.

87. Mark Wallace, interview by author, February 28, 2006.

88. Brett O'Donnell, interview by author, February 24, 2006.

89. Klain, interview.

90. Brown, 2014 interview.

91. James Dao, "The 2000 Campaign; the Texas Governor; Prime Time Fine, Bush Says, for 3 Presidential Debates," *New York Times*, August 30, 2000, A20.

92. Josh Voorhees, "The Town Hall Debate Was One Giant Rule Violation," *Slate*, October 17, 2012, http://www.slate.com/blogs/the_slatest/2012/10/17/town _hall_debate_rules_candy_crowley_barack_obama_mitt_romney_throw_rule .html.

93. David M. Alpern, "The Debates," *Newsweek*, September 27, 1976, 28.

94. Baker, 1998 interview.

95. Baker, *"Work Hard, Study . . . and Keep Out of Politics!"*, 112.

96. Stevens, *Big Enchilada*, 222.

97. Robert Ajemian, "Jostling for the Edge," *Time*, September 27, 1976, 11.

98. Memorandum, Greg Schneiders to Jerry Rafshoon, August 1980, Press Powell, box 8, folder "Debate Invitations, 8/25/80–9/24/80," Jimmy Carter Presidential Library.

99. Memorandum of Understanding, 2004, 1, 4, 7, http://www.gwu.edu /~action/2004/deb04main/debateagreement.pdf.

100. *Inside Politics*, CNN, September 27, 2004.

101. John Tierney, "Political Points: The Debates' Greatest Hits," *New York Times*, October 17, 2004, 30.

102. Bill Keller, "League Irate as Campaigns Select 3 Panelists," *New York Times*, October 7, 1984, 33.

103. Victoria Harian Strella, interview by author, April 2, 1998; Dorothy Ridings, interview by author, April 2, 1998.

104. Eleanor Randolph, "Journalists Deplore 'Blackballing' of Prospective Debate Panelists," *Washington Post*, October 8, 1984, A16.

105. Baker, 1998 interview.

106. Janet Brown, interview by author, May 18, 2007.

107. Paul Taylor, "Democrats Pledge Aggressive Debate," *Washington Post*, October 6, 1984, A3.

2. PREDEBATE STRATEGY

1. Kathleen Hall Jamieson, *Eloquence in an Electronic Age: The Transformation of Political Speechmaking* (New York: Oxford University Press, 1988), 51.

2. Transcript of "Debates '92: A Symposium," presented by the Commission on Presidential Debates, May 9, 1990, 38.

3. Lou Cannon, *Reagan* (New York: Putnam, 1982), 297.

4. Myles Martel, "Debate Preparations in the Reagan Camp: An Insider's View," *Speaker and Gavel* 18 (1981): 44.

5. Ronald Reagan, *An American Life* (New York: Simon and Schuster, 1990), 221.

6. Ibid., 329.

7. Richard Wirthlin, interview by author, September 2, 1988.

8. David S. Broder, "Encounter Leaves Reagan on Course," *Washington Post*, October 22, 1984, A1.

9. Roger Simon, *Road Show: In America, Anyone Can Become President. It's One of the Risks We Take* (New York: Farrar, Straus and Giroux, 1990), 271.

10. Richard Stengel, "Ninety Long Minutes in Omaha," *Time*, October 17, 1988, 21.

11. *This Week with David Brinkley*, ABC, October 6, 1996.

12. Jonathan Moore, ed., *Campaign for President: The Managers Look at '84* (Dover, Mass.: Auburn House, 1986), 218–19; David R. Runkel, ed., *Campaign for President: The Managers Look at '88* (Dover, Mass.: Auburn House, 1989), 221.

13. Michael Deaver, interview by author, June 17, 1998.

14. Ron Klain, interview by author, February 4, 2014.

15. Bill Clinton was interviewed by Jim Lehrer on August 11, 2000, for the PBS documentary *Debating Our Destiny*.

16. Jack Hilton, "10 Guidelines for Scoring the Debate," *Washington Post*, October 26, 1980, C2.

17. Christine M. Black and Thomas Oliphant, *All by Myself: The Unmaking of a Presidential Campaign* (Chester, Conn.: Globe Pequot, 1989), 269.

18. David S. Broder, "Scoring the Debates," *Washington Post*, October 1, 2000, B7.

19. Robert V. Friedenberg, "Patterns and Trends in National Political Debates: 1960–1992," in *Rhetorical Studies of National Political Debates 1960–1992*, ed. Robert V. Friedenberg, 2d ed. (Westport, Conn.: Praeger, 1994), 243.

20. Deaver, interview.

21. *Tonight Show*, NBC, October 1, 2008.

22. Austin Ranney, *The American Elections of 1984* (New York: American Enterprise Institute, 1985), 197.

23. Elizabeth Drew, *Portrait of an Election: The 1980 Presidential Campaign* (New York: Simon and Schuster, 1981), 411–12.

24. Jimmy Carter was interviewed by Jim Lehrer on April 28, 1989, for the PBS documentary *Debating Our Destiny*.

25. Ron Nessen, *It Sure Looks Different from the Inside* (Chicago: Playboy Press, 1978), 261–62.

26. Drew, *Portrait of an Election*, 426.

27. Wirthlin, interview.

28. Jack W. Germond and Jules Witcover, *Mad as Hell: Revolt at the Ballot Box, 1992* (New York: Warner, 1993), 465.

29. Clinton, *Debating Our Destiny.*

30. Michelle Cottle, "Prepping Obama for Debates," *Daily Beast*, September 24, 2012, http://www.newsweek.com/prepping-rusty-obama-debates-64701.

31. Mike Allen, "Bush's Isolation from Reporters Could Be a Hindrance," *Washington Post*, October 8, 2004, A9.

32. Kathleen Hall Jamieson and David S. Birdsell, *Presidential Debates: The Challenge of Creating an Informed Electorate* (New York: Oxford University Press, 1988), 218.

33. Memorandum, Ted Sorensen to Stu Eizenstat, August 27, 1976, Domestic Policy Staff: Stern box 1, folder "Debates—Carter/Ford," Jimmy Carter Presidential Library.

34. Martel, "Debate Preparations in the Reagan Camp," 42.

35. Walter Mondale was interviewed by Jim Lehrer on May 25, 1990, for the PBS documentary *Debating Our Destiny.*

36. Jack W. Germond and Jules Witcover, *Wake Us When It's Over: Presidential Politics of 1984* (New York: Macmillan, 1985), 497.

37. Elizabeth Drew, *Campaign Journal: The Political Events of 1983–1984* (New York: Macmillan, 1985), 688–89.

38. Jack W. Germond and Jules Witcover, *Whose Broad Stripes and Bright Stars? The Trivial Pursuit of the Presidency 1988* (New York: Warner, 1989), 10.

39. Runkel, *Campaign for President*, 68.

40. Charles T. Royer, ed., *Campaign for President: The Managers Look at '92* (Hollis, N.H.: Hollis, 1994), 251.

41. Charles McCarry, "The Unasked Question," *U.S. News & World Report*, October 28, 1996, 7.

42. Katharine Q. Seelye, "Searing Images from Debates Past Are Continuing to Haunt Dole," *New York Times*, October 17, 1996, B11.

43. Joe Klein, "Learning to Run," *New Yorker*, December 8, 1997, 53.

44. Jonathan Alter, *The Center Holds: Obama and His Enemies* (New York: Simon and Schuster, 2013), 326.

45. Karl Rove, *Courage and Consequence: My Life as a Conservative in the Fight* (New York: Simon and Schuster, 2010), 392.

46. John Dickerson, "Tie Goes to Obama," *Slate*, September 27, 2008, http://www.slate.com/articles/news_and_politics/politics/2008/09/tie_goes_to_obama.html.

47. ABC News, *This Week*, September 28, 2008.

48. Tom Shales, "McCain's High Horse Meets Obama's High-Mindedness," *Washington Post*, September 27, 2008, C1.

49. Jim Lehrer, *Tension City: Inside the Presidential Debates* (New York: Random House, 2011), 152.

50. Arnab Datta, "Debating McCain Reference to 'That One,'" ABCNews.com, October 7, 2008, http://blogs.abcnews.com/politicalradar/2008/10/debating -mccain.html.

51. Chris Cillizza, "The Nashville Skyline Debate—First Thoughts," *The Fix* (blog), *Washington Post*, October 7, 2008, http://voices.washingtonpost.com /thefix/eye-on-2008/the-nashville-skyline-debate-f.html; Klain, interview.

52. Bob Schieffer, interview by author, March 4, 2014.

53. Stuart Stevens, interview by author, March 18, 2014.

54. Alter, *The Center Holds*, 321–22.

55. Klain, interview.

56. Dan Balz, *Collision 2012: Obama vs. Romney and the Future of Elections in America* (New York: Viking, 2013), 314.

57. Todd S. Purdum, "The Kid Stays in the Picture," *Purdum on Politics* (blog), *Vanity Fair*, October 17, 2012.

58. MSNBC *Hardball*, October 23, 2012; ABC postdebate coverage, October 16, 2012.

59. Frank Bruni, "Obama's Squandered Advantage," *New York Times*, October 27, 2012; Alter, *Center Holds*, 333.

60. Jeff Greenfield, *Oh, Waiter! One Order of Crow: Inside the Strangest Presidential Election Finish in American History* (New York: Putnam, 2001), 198.

61. *Good Morning America*, ABC, October 19, 2000.

62. Evan Thomas and the staff of *Newsweek*, *Election 2004: How Bush Won and What You Can Expect in the Future* (New York: Public Affairs, 2004), 153.

63. Ibid., 158.

64. Adam Nagourney, "Political Memo; For Kerry, a Few Words That May Be Debatable," *New York Times*, October 18, 2004, A14.

65. *Meet the Press*, NBC, October 5, 2008.

66. Moore, *Campaign for President: The Managers Look At '84*, 217–18.

67. *Newsweek* Election Issue, November–December 1992, 88.

68. Ibid., 89.

69. Transcript of "Debates '92: A Symposium," 35.

70. Tom Shales, "McCain's High Horse Meets Obama's High-Mindedness," *Washington Post*, September 27, 2008, C1.

71. *Reliable Sources*, CNN, September 28, 2008.

72. George Lakoff, "A Brief Guide to the Debates," *Huffington Post*, October 2, 2008, http://www.huffingtonpost.com/george-lakoff/a-brief-guide-to-the-deba _b_131178.html.

73. Nessen, *It Sure Looks Different from the Inside*, 262–63.

74. Stephen R. Brydon, "The Two Faces of Jimmy Carter: The Transformation of a Presidential Debater, 1976 and 1980," *Central States Speech Journal* 36 (Fall 1985): 150–51.

75. Drew, *Portrait of an Election*, 435.

76. Cannon, *Reagan*, 295.

77. Richard C. Leone, interview by authors, April 6, 1998.

78. Roger Ailes, *You Are the Message: Secrets of the Master Communicators* (Homewood, Ill.: Dow Jones–Irwin, 1988), 22.

79. Craig Allen Smith and Kathy B. Smith, "The 1984 Reagan–Mondale Presidential Debates," in Friedenberg, *Rhetorical Studies of National Political Debates*, 110.

80. Diana Carlin, interview by author, September 1, 1998.

81. Stanley A. Renshon, *High Hopes: The Clinton Presidency and the Politics of Ambition* (New York: New York University Press, 1996), 106–7.

82. Jonathan Alter, "The Expectations Game," *Newsweek*, September 26, 1988, 17.

83. Dan Payne, "20 Ways to Win Debates," *Boston Globe*, September 26, 2004, D12.

84. James Fallows, "Your Town Hall #2 Debate Wrapup in 3 Points," *Atlantic*, October 7, 2008, http://www.theatlantic.com/technology/archive/2008/10/your-town-hall-2-debate-wrapup-in-3-points/8907/.

85. Samuel Popkin, "Incumbency and Debates in 1996," provided to the author by Popkin.

86. Kevin Sauter, "The 1976 Mondale–Dole Vice Presidential Debate," in Friedenberg, *Rhetorical Studies of National Political Debates*, 59.

87. Margot Hornblower, "Major Debate Impact Held Unlikely," *Washington Post*, October 15, 1976, A7; *NBC Nightly News*, October 15, 1976.

88. James J. Pinkerton, "Instead of Whatever, Dole Needs a Slogan," *New York Newsday*, October 18, 1996, A55.

89. Blake Zeff, "Why It's Impossible to Win a Debate," BuzzFeed, October 1, 2012, http://www.buzzfeed.com/blakezeff/why-its-impossible-to-win-a-debate.

90. ABC postdebate coverage, October 9, 1996; *Today* Show, NBC, October 10, 1996.

91. Stevens, interview.

92. Clinton, *Debating Our Destiny*.

93. Alexis Simendinger and Carl M. Cannon, "Command Performance," *National Journal*, October 16, 2004, 3143.

94. Dan Balz, "Aggressive Underdog vs. Cool Counterpuncher," *Washington Post*, October 16, 2008, A1.

95. Institute of Politics, Harvard University, ed., *Campaign for President: The Managers Look at 2008* (Lanham, Md.: Rowman and Littlefield, 2009), 207–8.

96. *Late Show with David Letterman*, CBS, October 16, 2008.

97. Balz, *Collision 2012*, 310.

98. Richard Wolffe, *The Message: The Reselling of President Obama* (New York: Twelve, 2013), 213.

99. Sigmund Rogich Interview, George H. W. Bush Oral History Project, Miller Center, University of Virginia, March 8–9, 2001, 37.

100. Richard Wolffe, *Renegade: The Making of a President* (New York: Crown, 2009), 190.

101. Thomas et al., *Election 2004*, 153.

102. Mark McKinnon, interview by author, February 27, 2006.

103. Mark Halperin and John Heilemann, *Double Down: Game Change 2012* (New York: Penguin, 2013), 418.

104. Klain, interview.

105. Roger Simon, *Show Time: The American Political Circus and the Race for the White House* (New York: Times Books, 1998), 258.

106. Stevens, interview.

107. Brett O'Donnell, "What to Watch for in the First Presidential Debate," *Daily Beast*, October 3, 2012, http://www.thedailybeast.com/articles/2012/10/03/brett-o-donnell-what-to-watch-for-in-the-first-presidential-debate.html.

108. Klain, interview.

109. James Hoge, interview by author, March 27, 1998.

110. Bob Dole was interviewed by Jim Lehrer on November 10, 1999, for the PBS documentary *Debating Our Destiny*.

111. "Debate Lines," OA/ID 08130, Curt Smith File, White House Office of Speechwriting, Bush Presidential Records, George Bush Presidential Library.

112. Robert Goodwin, interview by author, January 15, 1999.

113. Dan F. Hahn, "The 1992 Carter–Bush–Perot Presidential Debates," in Friedenberg, *Rhetorical Studies of National Political Debates*, 194.

114. Mari Boor Tonn, "Flirting with Perot: Voter Ambivalence About the Third Candidate," in *The 1992 Presidential Debates in Focus*, ed. Diana B. Carlin and Mitchell S. McKinney (Westport, Conn.: Praeger, 1994), 119.

115. Michael Kelly, "Conan the VP," *Washington Post*, October 5, 2000, A35.

116. Germond and Witcover, *Wake Us When It's Over*, 519.

117. Dayle Hardy-Short, "An Insider's View of the Constraints Affecting Geraldine Ferraro's Preparation for the 1984 Vice Presidential Debate," *Speaker and Gavel* 24 (1986): 18.

118. Geraldine Ferraro was interviewed by Jim Lehrer on June 13, 1990, for the PBS documentary *Debating Our Destiny.*

119. Judith S. Trent, "The 1984 Bush–Ferraro Vice Presidential Debate," in Friedenberg, *Rhetorical Studies of National Political Debates,* 128.

120. Germond and Witcover, *Wake Us When It's Over,* 520.

121. David Shribman and Laurie McGinley, "Bush, Ferraro to Air Differences," *Wall Street Journal,* October 11, 1984, 64.

122. Michael J. Robinson, "The Potential of Presidential Debates," *Washington Post,* September 11, 1976, A15.

123. Dan Quayle was interviewed by Jim Lehrer on December 2, 1999, for the PBS documentary *Debating Our Destiny.*

124. Carlin, interview.

125. Kevin Merida, "Straight Man," *Washington Post,* October 19, 2000, C1.

126. James Traub, "Mildly Ambitious," *New York Times Magazine,* June 10, 2001, 61.

127. William Saletan, "Ballot Box; Runners Advance; Edwards Keeps the Democrats' Rally Going," *Slate,* October 6, 2004, http://www.slate.com/articles /news_and_politics/ballot_box/2004/10/runners_advance.html.

128. Klain, interview.

129. John Dickerson, "The Joe Biden Workout," *Slate,* October 12, 2012, http://www.slate.com/articles/news_and_politics/politics/2012/10/vp_debate _joe_biden_tried_to_re_energize_democrats_with_his_attacks_digs.html.

130. James A. Baker 3d, interview by author, September 4, 1998.

131. James Fallows, "An Acquired Taste," *Atlantic Monthly,* July 2000, 33.

132. Paul Begala, "10 Rules for Winning a Debate," CNN.com, October 1, 2008.

133. Alter, *Center Holds,* 323.

134. Deaver, interview.

135. Arthur Miller, "On Politics and the Art of Acting," 30th Jefferson Lecture in the Humanities, Washington, D.C., March 26, 2001, http://www.neh.gov /about/awards/jefferson-lecture/arthur-miller-lecture.

136. Wolffe, *Renegade,* 190.

3. CANDIDATE PREPARATION

1. Joseph I. Lieberman and Hadassah Lieberman, *An Amazing Adventure: Joe and Hadassah's Personal Notes on the 2000 Campaign* (New York: Simon and Schuster, 2003), 146.

2. Sigmund Rogich Interview, George H. W. Bush Oral History Project, Miller Center, University of Virginia, March 8–9, 2001, 92.

3. Ted Sorensen, *Counselor: A Life at the Edge of History* (New York: Harper-Collins, 2008), 189.

4. Christopher Matthews, *Kennedy and Nixon: The Rivalry That Shaped Postwar America* (New York: Simon and Schuster, 1996), 147.

5. David M. Alpern, "The Debates," *Newsweek*, September 27, 1976, 25, 27.

6. Marin Decker, "Carter Credits Redford," *Deseret Morning News*, September 5, 2004.

7. Gerald R. Ford, *A Time to Heal: The Autobiography of Gerald R. Ford* (New York: Harper and Row, 1979), 415.

8. Fay S. Joyce and Joseph Albright, "Carter, Ford Cram for First TV Exam," *Atlanta Constitution*, September 19, 1976, 12A.

9. Stuart Eizenstadt Interview, Jimmy Carter Oral History Project, Miller Center, University of Virginia, January 29–30, 1982, 12.

10. Samuel Popkin, interview by author, October 7, 1998.

11. Hamilton Jordan, *Crisis: The Last Year of the Carter Presidency* (New York: Putnam, 1982), 356; Popkin, interview.

12. *Nightline*, ABC News, October 28, 1980.

13. David Stockman, *The Triumph of Politics: The Inside Story of the Reagan Revolution* (New York: Harper and Row, 1986), 50.

14. David Gergen, *Eyewitness to Power: The Essence of Leadership; Nixon to Clinton* (New York: Simon and Schuster, 2000), 162.

15. Michael Deaver, interview by author, June 17, 1998.

16. Ronald Reagan, *An American Life* (New York: Simon and Schuster, 1990), 328.

17. Nancy Reagan, *My Turn: The Memoirs of Nancy Reagan* (New York: Random House, 1989), 266; Paul Laxalt Interview, Ronald Reagan Oral History Project, Miller Center, University of Virginia, October 9, 2001, 45.

18. *ABC World News Tonight*, October 11, 1984.

19. Lou Cannon, *President Reagan: The Role of a Lifetime* (New York: Simon and Schuster, 1991), 547.

20. Roger Ailes, *You Are the Message: Secrets of the Master Communicators* (Homewood, Ill.: Dow Jones–Irwin, 1988), 22–23.

21. Unedited videotape of the Reagan pep rally can be viewed in the archives of the Ronald Reagan Presidential Library in Simi Valley, California.

22. Deaver, interview.

23. Geraldine Ferraro, *Ferraro: My Story* (New York: Bantam, 1985), 247.

24. Ibid., 250.

25. Ibid., 252–53.

26. Ibid., 248.

27. Dan Quayle, *Standing Firm: A Vice-Presidential Memoir* (New York: Harper-Collins, 1994), 61–62.

3. CANDIDATE PREPARATION / 365

28. Maureen Dowd, "Quayle Gives Up Chance to Study for Bentsen Debate to Discuss It," *New York Times*, October 1, 1988, 8.

29. Quayle, *Standing Firm*, 63.

30. Transcript of "Debating the Debates: Defining Moments in Presidential Campaigns," a symposium presented by the Ronald Reagan Center for Public Affairs, October 15, 1996, 17.

31. Roger Simon, *Show Time: The American Political Circus and the Race for the White House* (New York: Times Books, 1998), 269.

32. Tom Donilon, interview by author, July 14, 1998.

33. Simon, *Show Time*, 252.

34. Clay Mulford, interview by author, August 28, 1998.

35. *NBC Nightly News*, October 5, 1996.

36. Transcript of "Debating the Debates: Defining Moments in Presidential Campaigns," 51–52.

37. Ibid., 227.

38. Ibid.

39. Ibid.

40. Ibid., 259.

41. Kevin Sack, "Gore's Debate 'Advisors' Include Voices from the Campaign Trail," *New York Times*, September 29, 2000, 1.

42. Institute of Politics, Harvard University, ed., *Campaign for President: The Managers Look at 2000* (Hollis, N.H.: Hollis, 2002), 183.

43. Institute of Politics, Harvard University, ed., *Campaign for President: The Managers Look at 2004* (Lanham, Md.: Rowman and Littlefield, 2006), 91.

44. Kathleen Hall Jamieson and Paul Waldman, *Electing the President 2004: The Insiders' View* (Philadelphia: University of Pennsylvania Press, 2006), 122.

45. Gregory Craig, interview with author, May 10, 2006.

46. Robert Draper, *Dead Certain: The Presidency of George W. Bush* (New York: Free Press, 2007), 257.

47. Mark McKinnon, interview by author, February 27, 2006.

48. Sandra McElwaine, "Today's King's Speech Guru," *Daily Beast*, February 26, 2011, http://www.thedailybeast.com/articles/2011/02/26/kings-speech-guru -michael-sheehan-on-helping-presidents-ceos-more.html.

49. Mark Halperin and John Heilemann, *Game Change: Obama and the Clintons, McCain and Palin, and the Race of a Lifetime* (New York: Harper, 2010), 391.

50. Ibid.

51. Amy Chozick, "Biden Prepares for Palin with Eye on Gender Pitfalls," *Wall Street Journal*, October 2, 2008.

52. Patrick Caldwell, "Debate Prep with Joe," *American Prospect*, October 9, 2012, http://prospect.org/article/debate-prep-joe.

53. Dan Balz, *Collision 2012: Obama vs. Romney and the Future of Elections in America* (New York: Viking, 2013), 314.

54. *Newsroom*, CNN, October 11, 2012.

55. Anita Dunn, interview with author, June 24, 2014; Ron Klain, interview with author, February 4, 2014.

56. Klain, interview.

57. John Dickerson, "The Secrets of the 2012 Campaign," *Slate*, December 5, 2012, http://www.slate.com/articles/news_and_politics/politics/2012/12/harvard _s_campaign_decision_makers_conference_barack_obama_and_mitt_romney .html.

58. Folder: "Briefing Materials, League of Women Voters Debate, Manchester, N.H., 14 February 1988," Robert Teeter Collection, box 56, George Bush Presidential Library.

59. Newt Gingrich, "How to Debate President Obama," *Human Events*, September 26, 2012, http://humanevents.com/2012/09/26/gingrich-how-to-debate -obama/.

60. Dick Cheney, *In My Time: A Personal and Political Memoir* (New York: Threshold, 2011), 279.

61. Lou Cannon and Martin Schram, "Campaign Papers Probe Widens; 'Filched' Data Story Laid to Stockman," *Washington Post*, June 30, 1983, A1.

62. Laurence I. Barrett, *Gambling with History: Ronald Reagan in the White House* (Garden City, N.Y.: Doubleday, 1983), 382.

63. "President's News Conference on Foreign and Domestic Matters," *New York Times*, June 29, 1983, A18.

64. James A. Baker III, *"Work Hard, Study . . . and Keep Out of Politics!": Adventures and Lessons from an Unexpected Public Life* (New York: Putnam, 2006), 118.

65. Ibid.

66. Ibid., 119.

67. Mike Allen, "Message Takes a Back Seat to the 'Mole,'" *Washington Post*, September 28, 2000, A1.

68. McKinnon, interview.

4. PREDEBATE NEWS COVERAGE

1. "Century-Apart Rivals Similar," *Chicago Tribune*, September 25, 1960, 9.

2. John Harris, "Jack, Dick Tense as They Clear Decks for Historic TV Encounter Tomorrow," *Boston Globe*, September 25, 1960, 1.

3. Austin C. Wehrwein, "Nominees Agreed on Debate's Value," *New York Times*, September 25, 1960, 52.

4. *New York Times*, September 26, 1960, 66.

5. Marie Torre, "'Great Debate' of 1960 Won't Be One After All," *New York Herald Tribune*, September 16, 1960, 8.

6. *Tonight Show*, NBC, August 25, 1960.

7. "Castro Considers Closing Down U.S. Base by 'International Law,'" *Washington Post*, September 27, 1960, A1.

8. Thomas E. Patterson, *Out of Order* (New York: Knopf, 1993), 82.

9. CBS Radio and MBS Radio, September 26, 1960.

10. Roscoe Drummond, "Studio Brinksmanship," *Boston Globe*, September 24, 1960, 6.

11. Robert J. Donovan, "Nixon, Kennedy to Meet in 2nd Debate Tonight," *Washington Post*, October 7, 1960.

12. Joseph Lelyveld, "Kennedy–Nixon Debates a Key to What '76 Clashes May Hold," *New York Times*, August 30, 1976, 11.

13. Jules Witcover, "The Bottom Line Is Style," *Washington Post*, September 19, 1976, A1.

14. *NBC Nightly News*, September 22, 1976.

15. Elizabeth Drew, "A Reporter in Washington, D.C.," *New Yorker*, January 10, 1977, 54.

16. Jack Kelly, interview by author, March 26, 1998.

17. *NBC Nightly News*, October 6, 1976.

18. *ABC World News Tonight*, October 6, 1976.

19. David S. Broder, "The Final, Crucial Debate," *Washington Post*, October 22, 1976, 1; *ABC World News Tonight*, October 22, 1976; *NBC Nightly News*, October 22, 1976.

20. *This Week*, ABC, October 21, 1984; Howard Rosenberg, "Which Skills Will Win Debate?," *Los Angeles Times*, October 5, 1984, VI-1.

21. Steven Strasser, "And Now, Debate II," *Newsweek*, October 22, 1984, 31.

22. James T. Wooten, "Carter's Aides Expecting Debate to Put People 'Closer to Jimmy,'" *New York Times*, September 23, 1976, 37.

23. Lou Cannon, "Carter Sees Debate 'Tie' as Victory," *Washington Post*, September 4, 1976, 1.

24. *ABC World News Tonight*, October 5, 1976.

25. *CBS Evening News*, September 20, 1980.

26. Lou Cannon and Edward Walsh, "The Debate: A Single Roll of the Dice with White House at Stake," *Washington Post*, October 19, 1980, A5.

27. *ABC World News Tonight*, October 17, 1980.

28. Jack W. Germond and Jules Witcover, *Whose Broad Stripes and Bright Stars? The Trivial Pursuit of the Presidency 1988* (New York: Warner, 1989), 430.

29. Gerald M. Boyd, "Bush Discounts Rise in Jobless Rate," *New York Times*, September 4, 1988, 30.

30. Andrew J. Finke and Todd J. Gillman, "Leading the News: Television Strategies in the 1988 Presidential Campaign," John F. Kennedy School of Government, April 1989, 59.

31. *Inside Politics*, CNN, October 13, 1992.

32. Robin Toner, "2 Campaigns Begin Direct Discussion on Debate Format," *New York Times*, October 1, 1992, A1, A18.

33. *Today*, NBC, September 30, 1996; *Inside Politics*, CNN, September 26, 1996; Adam Nagourney, "Dole Stages a Dress Rehearsal for the Debates," *New York Times*, October 2, 1996, A16.

34. William Goldschlag, "Pardon Bill If He's Ready for Bob Salvo," *New York Daily News*, October 5, 1996, 2; *Live with Regis and Kathie Lee*, October 1, 1996; Gene Gibbons, "Clinton Begins Debate Prep 'Slightly Apprehensive,'" Reuters North American Wire, October 3, 1996.

35. G. Robert Hillman, "Oratorical Question: Who's the Most Formidable Debater?," *Dallas Morning News*, September 28, 2000; Michael Tackett, "Shades of Exaggeration Color Period Before the 1st Match-up," *Chicago Tribune*, October 1, 2000.

36. Katharine Q. Seelye, "At News Conference, Gore Defends Use of Oil Stockpile," *New York Times*, September 23, 2000.

37. Richard L. Berke, "Surprise! Debates May Matter. And Help Bush," *New York Times*, August 27, 2000, IV-4.

38. Institute of Politics, Harvard University, ed., *Campaign for President: The Managers Look at 2000* (Hollis, N.H.: Hollis, 2002), 160–61.

39. Jim Rutenberg, "The Debates," *New York Times*, September 5, 2004, IV-5.

40. *The Daily Show*, Comedy Central, August 24, 2004.

41. Deb Riechmann, "Campaigns Aim to Lower Debate Expectations," Associated Press, September 27, 2004.

42. John Bentley, "McCain Says Obama Is 'Very, Very Good' at Debates," CBSNews.com, September 23, 2008, http://www.cbsnews.com/news/mccain-says-obama-is-very-very-good-at-debates/; Patrick Healy, "Pact on Debates Will Let McCain and Obama Spar," *New York Times*, September 21, 2008.

43. Sarah Kliff, "The View from Wash. U.," *Newsweek*, October 2, 2008, http://www.newsweek.com/view-wash-u-219560; Foon Rhee, "Expectations Game Already Starting for V.P. Debate," Boston.com, September 29, 2008; Associated Press, "Palin Expects Biden to Be a 'Great Debater,'" September 18, 2008.

44. *Face the Nation*, CBS, September 30, 2012.

45. Scott Conroy, "Debate Expectations Are Being Set—With a Wink," RealClear Politics, September 28, 2012, http://www.realclearpolitics.com/articles/2012/09/28/debate_expectations_are_being_set_--_with_a_wink_115601.html.

46. Jim Messina, "Memorandum to Interested Parties," September 20, 2012, http://blogs.suntimes.com/sweet/2012/09/obamas_messina_praising_mitts _.html; Beth Myers, "Memorandum to Interested Parties," September 27, 2012, http://politicalticker.blogs.cnn.com/2012/09/27/first-on-cnn-romney-memo -seeks-to-lower-debate-expectations/; David Axelrod, "Memorandum to Interested Parties," September 28, 2012, https://secure.assets.bostatic.com/pdfs /Axelrod_Memo.pdf.

47. *ABC World News Tonight*, October 11, 1984.

48. "Bush's Wife Assails Ferraro, but Apologizes," *New York Times*, October 9, 1984, A29; Juan Williams and Dale Russakoff, "Bush Sticks to Duties as Debate Approaches," *Washington Post*, October 10, 1984, A4.

49. Geraldine Ferraro, *Ferraro: My Story* (New York: Bantam, 1985), 249.

50. David Shribman and Laurie McGinley, "Bush, Ferraro to Air Differences," *Wall Street Journal*, October 11, 1984, 64; "Ferraro Called 'Too Bitchy,'" *Washington Post*, October 12, 1984, A20.

51. *This Week with David Brinkley*, ABC, October 11, 1992.

52. Patterson, *Out of Order*, 81.

53. Godfrey Sperling Jr., "The Debate—What Carter, Reagan Want to Get from It," *Christian Science Monitor*, October 20, 1980, 12; Lou Cannon and Edward Walsh, "The Debate: A Single Roll of the Dice with White House at Stake," *Washington Post*, October 19, 1980, A5; CBS Debate Coverage, October 28, 1980.

54. Jimmy Carter, *Keeping Faith: Memoirs of a President* (New York: Bantam, 1982), 561.

55. Jack W. Germond and Jules Witcover, *Wake Us When It's Over: Presidential Politics of 1984* (New York: Macmillan, 1985), 497.

56. *NBC Nightly News*, October 5, 1984.

57. E. J. Dionne Jr., "Poll Shows U.S. Voter Optimism Is Helping Bush in the Campaign," *New York Times*, October 13, 1988, 1; Bernard Weinraub, "No Warming Trend, Dukakis Aides Insist," *New York Times*, October 13, 1988, B10.

58. James Fallows, "An Acquired Taste," *Atlantic Monthly*, July 2000, 33–53.

59. Mark McKinnon, interview by author, February 27, 2006.

60. Ceci Connolly, "The Debates; Two Candidates, Two Styles," *Washington Post*, October 2, 2000, A1; *Inside Politics*, CNN, September 29, 2000.

61. Kathleen Hall Jamieson and Paul Waldman, *Electing the President 2000: The Insiders' View* (Philadelphia: University of Pennsylvania Press, 2001), 71.

62. James Fallows, "When George Meets John," *Atlantic Monthly*, July–August 2004, 67.

63. Al Gore, "How to Debate George Bush," *New York Times*, September 29, 2004, A25.

64. *Inside Politics*, CNN, October 8, 2004; *Today* Show, NBC, October 8, 2004.

65. Katharine Q. Seelye, "If They Debate . . . What to Look For?," *The Caucus* (blog), *New York Times*, September 26, 2008, http://thecaucus.blogs.nytimes.com /2008/09/26/if-they-debate-what-to-look-for/.

66. Amy Chozick, "McCain's Town-Hall Prowess Faces Litmus Test in Debate," *Wall Street Journal*, October 6, 2008; Nedra Pickler, "Tonight's Debate Is in McCain's Favorite Style," Associated Press, October 7, 2008.

67. *Good Morning America*, ABC, October 15, 2008; Mark Halperin, "In Final Debate, Can McCain Rattle an Imperturbable Foe?," *Time*, October 15, 2008, http://content.time.com/time/politics/article/0,8599,1850416,00.html.

68. *NBC Nightly News*, October 3, 2012.

69. Chris Cillizza, "At Second Presidential Debate, Pressure Will Be on Obama," *Washington Post*, October 14, 2012, https://www.washingtonpost.com/politics /decision2012/at-second-presidential-debate-pressure-will-be-on-obama/2012 /10/14/e30d46c2-1607-11e2-a55c-39408fbe6a4b_story.html.

70. Beth Fouhy, "Debate Offers Palin, Biden High Risks, Big Rewards," Associated Press, October 1, 2008.

71. Martha T. Moore, "Both VP Hopefuls Have Something to Prove," *USA Today*, October 2, 2008; Dahlia Lithwick, "How to Debate a Girl, and Win," *Slate*, September 5, 2008, http://www.slate.com/articles/news_and_politics/politics /2008/09/how_to_debate_a_girl_and_win.html.

72. Rick Klein, "The Note," ABCNews.com, October 2, 2008, http://abcnews .go.com/Politics/TheNote/story?id=5937827&page=1; Jonathan Martin and Ben Smith, "Vice Presidential Debate: A Barrel of Gaffes?," *Politico*, October 2, 2008, http://www.politico.com/story/2008/10/vice-presidential-debate-a-barrel-of -gaffes-014200.

73. *ABC World News Tonight*, October 11, 1984.

74. Richard W. Stevenson and Randal C. Archibold, "In Battle for No. 2 Spot, Focus Remains at the Top," *New York Times*, October 4, 2004, A22.

75. Jonathan Alter and Eleanor Clift, "The Veep Showdown," *Newsweek*, October 10, 1988, 40.

76. Gerald M. Boyd, "Quayle Getting His Big Chance to Clear Doubts," *New York Times*, October 5, 1988, A30.

77. *Inside Politics*, CNN, October 13, 1992; Tad Devine, "Quayle Can't Lose Tonight," *Washington Post*, October 13, 1992, A21.

78. David Von Drehle, "Punditocracy Faces Dizzying Spin Cycle," *Washington Post*, October 3, 1992, A1.

79. CNN Predebate Special, October 11, 1992.

80. ABC News, *This Week*, October 11, 1992.

81. *Inside Politics*, CNN, October 19, 1992.

82. Ibid., October 13, 1992; *Good Morning America*, ABC, October 13, 1992.

83. *CBS Evening News*, September 23, 1976.

84. Charles T. Royer, ed., *Campaign for President: The Managers Look at '92* (Hollis, N.H.: Hollis, 1994), 252.

85. E. J. Dionne Jr., "Clinton Gets Testy in TV Exchange with Donahue," *Washington Post*, October 7, 1992, A1; Cathleen Decker, "Clinton Returns to Donahue Show—for a Replay of Feisty Exchanges," *Los Angeles Times*, October 7, 1992, A12.

86. Patrick Caldwell, "Debate Prep with Joe," *American Prospect*, October 9, 2012, http://prospect.org/article/debate-prep-joe.

87. *ABC World News Tonight*, September 22, 1976.

88. Ron Nessen, *It Sure Looks Different from the Inside* (Chicago: Playboy Press, 1978), 263.

89. Richard L. Berke, interview by author, September 5, 1998.

90. Robert G. Kaiser, "Carter Winning Gamble on Debates," *Washington Post*, September 18, 1980, A1.

91. Terence Smith, "Presidential Debate Format Set; Camps Differ on Time and Place," *New York Times*, October 21, 1980, A1.

92. *ABC World News Tonight*, October 20, 1980.

93. Vernon Jordan, interview by author, July 11, 2007.

94. Mark Wallace, interview by author, February 28, 2006.

95. Paul Farhi and Mike Allen, "Lots to Debate, Little to Chance," *Washington Post*, September 23, 2004, C1.

96. *ABC World News Tonight*, October 22, 1976.

97. Myles Martel, *Political Campaign Debates: Images, Strategies, and Tactics* (New York: Longman, 1983), 13.

98. *ABC World News Tonight* and *NBC Nightly News*, October 28, 1980.

99. *CBS Evening News*, October 28, 1980.

100. CBS debate coverage, October 7, 1984 and October 21, 1984.

101. *ABC World News Tonight*, October 5, 1988.

102. *McNeil–Lehrer NewsHour*, PBS, October 5, 1988.

103. *ABC World News Tonight*, October 5, 1988.

104. *Face the Nation*, CBS, October 16, 1988.

105. *CBS Evening News* and *ABC World News Tonight*, October 13, 1988.

106. *ABC World News Tonight*, October 16, 1996.

107. *Inside Politics*, CNN, October 2, 2000.

108. *Fox Special Report*, September 30, 2004.

109. *The O'Reilly Factor*, Fox News Channel, September 30, 2004.

110. "Trail Tales: What's That Face?," FOXNews.com, October 1, 2004, http://www.foxnews.com/story/2004/10/01/trail-tales-what-that-face.html.

111. Joshua Micah Marshall, *Talking Points Memo* (blog), October 2, 2004, http://talkingpointsmemo.com/edblog/--97538.

5. THE DEBATERS

1. Walter Mondale, interview by Kevin Sauter, March 31, 1989.

2. *NewsHour with Jim Lehrer*, PBS, October 4, 1996.

3. Erik Barnouw, *The Image Empire: A History of Broadcasting in the United States from 1953* (New York: Oxford University Press, 1970), 160.

4. Harvey Wheeler, "The Great Debates," in Earl Mazo, Malcolm Moos, Hallock Hoffman, and Harvey Wheeler, *The Great Debates* (Santa Barbara, Calif.: Center for the Study of Democratic Institutions, 1962), 18.

5. "Memorandum on Television Debate with Vice President Nixon September 26th," Clark M. Clifford to Senator John F. Kennedy, September 27, 1960, Personal Papers of Robert F. Kennedy, Pre-Administration Political Files 1952–1960, box 36, Kennedy–Nixon Debate folder, John F. Kennedy Presidential Library.

6. Erik Barnouw, *Tube of Plenty: The Evolution of American Television* (New York: Oxford University Press, 1975), 277.

7. Kathleen Hall Jamieson, *Eloquence in an Electronic Age: The Transformation of Political Speechmaking* (New York: Oxford University Press, 1988), 50.

8. Wheeler, "Great Debates," 11.

9. Eugene Patterson, "Kennedy Owes a Debt to TV," *Atlanta Constitution*, October 8, 1960, 4.

10. Wallace Westfeldt, interview by author, March 3, 1998.

11. Gerald Gardner, *All the President's Wits: The Power of Presidential Humor* (New York: Beech Tree, 1986), 157.

12. Elizabeth Drew, "A Reporter in Washington, D.C.," *New Yorker*, January 10, 1977, 56; memorandum, Mike Duval to President Gerald Ford, October 18, 1976, White House Special Files Unit: Presidential Files, box 3, folder "Third Debate: Memos from Duval," Gerald R. Ford Presidential Library; Lloyd Bitzer and Theodore Rueter, *Carter vs. Ford: The Counterfeit Debates of 1976* (Madison: University of Wisconsin Press, 1980), 132.

13. James Gannon, "Our Man Survives the Great Debate, Is Glad It's All Over," *Wall Street Journal*, September 27, 1976, 1; Jules Witcover, *Marathon: The Pursuit of the Presidency 1972–1976* (New York: Viking, 1977), 578.

14. Ron Nessen, *It Sure Looks Different from the Inside* (Chicago: Playboy Press, 1978), 267.

15. Memorandum, Bill Carruthers to Mike Duval, September 20, 1976, Michael Raoul-Duval Papers, box 29, folder "Input—Bill Carruthers," Gerald R. Ford Presidential Library.

16. Memorandum, Dorrance Smith to Mike Duval, September 3, 1976, Michael Raoul-Duval Papers, box 25, folder "Carter Primary Forums," Gerald R. Ford Presidential Library.

17. *CBS Evening News*, September 24, 1976.

18. Richard Steele, "Round Two to Carter," *Newsweek*, October 18, 1976, 21.

19. William Greider, "Last Debate: Substance over Bumbles," *Washington Post*, October 23, 1976, 1.

20. "Words, and Music, in the Debate," *New York Times*, October 30, 1980, A26; Elizabeth Drew, *Portrait of an Election: The 1980 Presidential Campaign* (New York: Simon and Schuster, 1981), 323.

21. David S. Broder, "Carter on Points, but No KO," *Washington Post*, October 29, 1980, A1, A10; Tom Brokaw, interview by author, April 14, 1998.

22. Jack W. Germond and Jules Witcover, *Blue Smoke and Mirrors: How Reagan Won and Why Carter Lost the Election of 1980* (New York: Viking, 1981), 284.

23. David Broder, interview by author, May 12, 1998.

24. Jimmy Carter, *Keeping Faith: Memoirs of a President* (New York: Bantam, 1982), 564–65.

25. William A. Henry III, *Visions of America: How We Saw the 1984 Election* (Boston: Atlantic Monthly Press, 1985), 242.

26. Hugh Sidey, "The Big Fight Syndrome," *Time*, October 29, 1984, 32; John Corry, "A Look at Debate Between Reagan and Mondale," *New York Times*, October 9, 1984, C18.

27. *ABC World News Tonight*, October 8, 1984.

28. Jack W. Germond and Jules Witcover, *Wake Us When It's Over: Presidential Politics of 1984* (New York: Macmillan, 1985), 535.

29. Transcript of "Debating the Debates: Defining Moments in Presidential Campaigns," symposium presented by the Ronald Reagan Center for Public Affairs, October 15, 1996, 41.

30. Bernard Weinraub, "Mondale Farewell," *New York Times*, November 8, 1984, A24.

31. Richard Ben Cramer, *What It Takes: The Way to the White House* (New York: Random House, 1992), 759.

32. William Greider, "Mondale and Dole Better TV Debaters," *Washington Post*, October 16, 1976, A6.

33. Tom Shales, "Round 1: No Big Winner to Speak Of," *Washington Post*, October 7, 1996, C1; ABC postdebate coverage, October 6, 1996.

34. *Today*, NBC, October 17, 1996.

35. Michael Deaver, interview by author, June 17, 1998.

36. Broder, interview.

37. Gil Troy, *See How They Ran: The Changing Role of the Presidential Candidate* (New York: Free Press, 1991), 244.

38. Broder, "Carter on Points, but No KO," A1, A10; John Stacks, "Anatomy of a Landslide," *Time*, November 17, 1980, 31.

39. Germond and Witcover, *Wake Us When It's Over*, 510; Mary McGrory, "A Ghost of His 1980 Self," *Washington Post*, October 9, 1984, A2.

40. Henry, *Visions of America*, 26.

41. Hedrick Smith, "Reagan, Anderson Disagree in Debate on Most Key Issues," *New York Times*, September 22, 1980, 1.

42. *CBS Evening News*, September 20, 1980.

43. Drew, *Portrait of an Election*, 412.

44. George H. W. Bush was interviewed by Jim Lehrer on April 10, 1999, for the PBS documentary *Debating Our Destiny*.

45. Charles T. Royer, ed., *Campaign for President: The Managers Look at '92* (Hollis, N.H.: Hollis, 1994), 258.

46. Ellen Goodman, "A Debate Between Candidates, Not Genders," *Boston Globe*, October 13, 1984, 15.

47. David Hoffman, "Bush Applying Lessons of '84 Ferraro Bout," *Washington Post*, September 24, 1988, A10.

48. George Will, "A National Embarrassment," *Washington Post*, September 27, 1988, A21.

49. "Lectern to Lectern," *Newsweek* Election Issue, November 21, 1988, 140.

50. Michael Kelly, "Clinton Basks in Glow of Easy Lead in Race," *New York Times*, October 13, 1992, A16.

51. *Newsweek* Election Issue, November–December 1992, 91.

52. Monica Crowley, *Nixon Off the Record* (New York: Random House, 1996), 125.

53. Brit Hume, interview by author, May 21, 1998.

54. *CNN Crossfire*, October 9, 1996.

55. Elizabeth Drew, *Campaign Journal: The Political Events of 1983–1984* (New York: Macmillan, 1985), 697.

56. *CNN Crossfire*, October 9, 1996.

57. Robert Healy, "Ferraro Seemed a Natural on TV," *Boston Globe*, October 12, 1984, 1.

58. Peter Goldman and Tony Fuller, *The Quest for the Presidency 1984* (New York: Bantam, 1985), 330–31; William R. Doerner, "Co-Stars on Center Stage," *Time*, October 22, 1984, 30–31.

59. Geraldine Ferraro, *Ferraro: My Story* (New York: Bantam, 1985), 265–66.

60. "Lectern to Lectern," *Newsweek*, November 21, 1988, 124; Christine M. Black and Thomas Oliphant, *All by Myself: The Unmaking of a Presidential Campaign* (Chester, Conn.: Globe Pequot, 1989), 269.

61. David Nyhan, "How Dukakis Is Self-Destructing," *Boston Globe*, October 16, 1988, A31.

62. Kitty Dukakis, *Now You Know* (New York: Simon and Schuster, 1990), 220.

63. David R. Runkel, ed., *Campaign for President: The Managers Look at '88* (Dover, Mass.: Auburn House, 1989), 253–54.

64. Michael Dukakis, interview by author, June 11, 1998.

65. David S. Broder, "JFK's Ghost and the 'Quayle Factor,'" *Washington Post*, October 6, 1988, A1, A32.

66. Warren Weaver, "Bentsen Faces Dual Job in TV Debate Tonight," *New York Times*, October 5, 1988, A30; Jonathan Alter and Eleanor Clift, "The Veep Showdown," *Newsweek*, October 10, 1984, 40; *Today*, NBC, October 5, 1988.

67. NBC postdebate coverage, October 5, 1988.

68. Jack W. Germond and Jules Witcover, *Whose Broad Stripes and Bright Stars? The Trivial Pursuit of the Presidency 1988* (New York: Warner, 1989), 43.

69. Elizabeth Drew, *Election Journal: Political Events of 1987–1988* (New York: William Morrow, 1989), 302.

70. Dan Quayle, *Standing Firm: A Vice-Presidential Memoir* (New York: HarperCollins, 1994), 65; Tom Shales, "Bentsen and Quayle: A Single Point of Light," *Washington Post*, October 6, 1988, C1; Dukakis, interview.

71. Broder, "JFK's Ghost and the 'Quayle Factor,'" A1, A32; Drew, *Election Journal*, 298.

72. George Will, "Never Give a Child a Sword," *Washington Post*, October 6, 1988, A23.

73. Quayle, *Standing Firm*, 65.

74. *This Week with David Brinkley*, ABC, October 6, 1996.

75. Tad Devine, "Quayle Can't Lose Tonight," *Washington Post*, October 13, 1992, A21.

76. R. W. Apple Jr., "Quayle on the Attack," *New York Times*, October 14, 1992, 1.

77. William Safire, "Humans Confront Android," *New York Times*, October 15, 1992, A15.

78. Tom Shales, "The Veep Follies: A Heartbeat Away," *Washington Post*, October 14, 1992, C1.

79. Crowley, *Nixon Off the Record*, 121.

80. Jack W. Germond and Jules Witcover, *Mad as Hell: Revolt at the Ballot Box, 1992* (New York: Warner, 1993), 13–14.

81. Richard L. Berke, "Candidates Cram for First Debate," *New York Times*, October 11, 1992, 1.

82. *Today*, NBC, October 7 1996.

83. Thomas Oliphant, "Another Wipeout," *Boston Globe*, October 17, 1996, A17.

84. Jeffrey Rosen, "Washington Diarist," *New Republic*, November 11, 1996, 62.

85. Elizabeth Kolbert, "Standing Toe to Toe and Slugging It Out on the Air," *New York Times*, October 15, 1992, A11.

86. ABC postdebate coverage, October 13, 1992; "Reaction: Viewers Comment," *Boston Globe*, October 10, 1996, A34; Broder, interview.

87. James Fallows, "An Acquired Taste," *Atlantic Monthly*, July 2000, 33.

88. Michael Kelly, "Conan the VP," *Washington Post*, October 5, 2000, A35.

89. Maureen Dowd, "As the World Churns," *New York Times*, October 15, 2000, IV-17; Jake Tapper, "Paging Mr. Gore," *Salon*, October 12, 2000, http://www.salon.com/2000/10/12/debate_36/.

90. *Good Morning America*, ABC, October 18, 2000.

91. John Heilemann, "The Comeback Kid," *New York*, May 29, 2006, 20.

92. Crowley, *Nixon Off the Record*, 120.

93. ABC postdebate coverage, October 11, 1992; Michael Kelly, "Clinton Basks in Glow of Easy Lead in Race," *New York Times*, October 13, 1992, A16.

94. Brokaw, interview; Tom Shales, "The Debate Goes On . . . and On and On," *Washington Post*, October 16, 1992, D1.

95. John Mashek, interview by author, March 31, 1998; Clay Mulford, interview by author, August 28, 1998.

96. Brokaw, interview.

97. *Newsweek* Election Issue, November–December 1992, 90; Tom Shales, "The Veep Follies: A Heartbeat Away," *Washington Post*, October 14, 1992, C1, C2; Germond and Witcover, *Mad as Hell*, 477.

98. Kolbert, "Standing Toe to Toe," A11.

99. James Stockdale was interviewed by Jim Lehrer on September 4, 1999, for the PBS documentary *Debating Our Destiny*.

100. James Bond Stockdale 2d, "Why Was He There?," *New York Times*, October 17, 1992, A21.

101. *Inside Politics*, CNN, October 14, 1992.

102. Mary McGrory, "'No Surprises' School of Debate," *Washington Post*, October 20, 1992, A2.

103. Broder, interview.

104. Dan Goodgame, "From Savior to Scapegoat," *Time*, October 21, 1996, 37; *Nightline*, ABC, October 13, 1996.

105. *This Week with David Brinkley*, ABC, October 13, 1996.

106. Martin F. Nolan, "Civility Reigns," *Boston Globe*, October 10, 1996, A27; Christopher Buckley, "No Bark, No Bites," *New York Times*, October 11, 1996, A39; ABC postdebate coverage, October 9, 1996.

107. Gregory Craig, interview by author, May 10, 2006.

108. Frank Bruni, *Ambling into History: The Unlikely Odyssey of George W. Bush* (New York: HarperCollins, 2002), 52.

109. James Fallows, "When George Meets John," *Atlantic Monthly*, July–August 2004, 69.

110. Stuart Stevens, *The Big Enchilada: Campaign Adventures with the Cockeyed Optimists from Texas Who Won the Biggest Prize in Politics* (New York: Free Press, 2001), 258.

111. Richard Cohen, "The President Vanishes," *Washington Post*, October 15, 2004, A23.

112. Kevin Merida, "Straight Man," *Washington Post*, October 19, 2000, C1.

113. Bill Nichols and Martin Kasindorf, "Nice Guy vs. the Ice Guy, Tuesday Night in Cleveland," *USA Today*, October 5, 2004, 14A.

114. Anonymous to author, October 5, 2004.

115. "Edwards Woos Another Jury," *Los Angeles Times*, October 6, 2004.

116. Richard Perez-Peña, "The Lieberman Method of Dismantling Opponents: Subtle as a Ton of Brickbats," *New York Times*, September 30, 2000.

117. Jake Tapper, "Joe Lieberman's Blank Slate," *Talk*, November 2001, 162.

118. Joseph I. Lieberman and Hadassah Lieberman, *An Amazing Adventure: Joe and Hadassah's Personal Notes on the 2000 Campaign* (New York: Simon and Schuster, 2003), 160, 162.

119. CNN postdebate coverage, October 5, 2000.

120. Fallows, "When George Meets John," 78.

121. The Kerry–Stephanopoulos exchange took place at an ABC News–sponsored debate in Columbia, South Carolina, May 3, 2003.

122. Matt Bai, "Spoiling (Carefully) for a Fight," *New York Times Magazine*, November 23, 2003, 55.

123. Alessandra Stanley, "Bush Smiles, but Laughter Falls Short," *New York Times*, October 14, 2004, A18.

124. Richard W. Stevenson and Robin Toner, "For Cheney and Edwards, a Night of Sharp Exchanges," *New York Times*, October 6, 2004, 1.

125. Tom Shales, "Cheney Turns on Heat, but Edwards Doesn't Quayle," *Washington Post*, October 6, 2004, C01; Carolyn Jack, "Cheney, Edwards Play Roles Like Pros," *Cleveland Plain Dealer*, October 7, 2004. A10 *David Letterman Show*, CBS, October 6, 2004.

126. NBC postdebate coverage, October 5, 2004.

127. David Remnick, *The Bridge: The Life and Rise of Barack Obama* (New York: Knopf, 2010), 322; J. H. Bowden, "Illinois Primary Debate: Discussion," Democratic Underground, March 4, 2004, http://www.democraticunderground.com/discuss/duboard.php?az=view_all&address=132x435696.

128. Barack Obama, *The Audacity of Hope: Thoughts on Reclaiming the American Dream* (New York: Crown, 2006), 211.

129. "How He Did It," *Newsweek*, November 5, 2008.

130. Ibid.

131. Alessandra Stanley, "Smiles All Around in an Evening of Dueling Niceties," *New York Times*, February 1, 2008, A19, http://www.nytimes.com/2008/02/01/us/politics/01watch.html; Tom Shales, "In Pa. Debate, the Clear Loser Is ABC," *Washington Post*, April 17, 2008.

132. David Brooks, "Thinking About Obama," *New York Times*, October 17, 2008.

133. Maureen Dowd, "Sound, but No Fury," *New York Times*, September 28, 2008, WK 10, http://www.nytimes.com/2008/09/28/opinion/28dowd.html?_r=0.

134. Mary Bruce, "Obama on Romney's Debate Performance: 'Salesmanship,'" ABC News.com, October 9, 2012, http://abcnews.go.com/blogs/politics/2012/10/obama-on-romneys-debate-performance-salesmanship/.

135. Matt Bai, "Obama's Enthusiasm Gap," *The Caucus* (blog), *New York Times*, October 4, 2012, http://thecaucus.blogs.nytimes.com/2012/10/04/obamas-enthusiasm-gap/; *New Yorker*, October 15, 2012.

136. Katharine Q. Seelye, "A Scrappy Fighter, McCain Honed His Debating Style In and Out of Politics," *New York Times*, September 23, 2008.

137. Tom Shales, "A Showdown That Was More of a Letdown," *Washington Post*, October 8, 2008, C1.

138. "The Last Word; The Final Presidential Debate Was the Best so Far," *Economist*, October 16, 2008; John Heilemann, "Obama Nails the Debate Trifecta," *New York*, October 16, 2008, http://nymag.com/daily/intelligencer/2008/10/heilemann_obama_nails_the_deba.html.

139. Mark Leibovich, "Meanwhile, the Other No. 2 Keeps On Punching," *New York Times*, September 20, 2008; McCain–Palin 2008, "Embarrass" web ad, October, 2, 2008, https://www.youtube.com/watch?v=p7RJAnefJKA.

140. Ryan Corsaro, "Biden on Debates, Duty, and His Hair," CBSNews.com, October 13, 2008, http://www.cbsnews.com/news/biden-on-debates-duty-and-his-hair/.

141. Byron Tau, "Biden: I Wasn't Laughing at Paul Ryan," *Politico*, October 17, 2012, http://www.politico.com/blogs/politico44/2012/10/biden-i-wasnt-laughing-at-paul-ryan-138736.

142. Joel Millman, "Palin Proved to Be Formidable Foe in Alaska Debates," *Wall Street Journal*, October 1, 2008.

143. Katharine Q. Seelye, "Past Debates Show a Confident Palin, at Times Fluent but Often Vague," *New York Times*, October 1, 2008; *NBC Nightly News*, October 2, 2008.

144. Libby Copeland, "Shooting from the Hip, with a Smile to Boot," *Washington Post*, October 1, 2008.

145. Maureen Dowd, "Sarah's Pompom Palaver," *New York Times*, October 5, 2008.

146. *Hardball*, MSNBC, July 19, 2012.

147. James Fallows, "Slugfest," *Atlantic*, August 22, 2012, http://www.theatlantic.com/magazine/archive/2012/09/slugfest/309063/.

148. Maggie Haberman, "Santorum Steps into New Debate Role," *Politico*, February 22, 2012, http://www.politico.com/story/2012/02/santorum-steps-into -new-debate-role-073151.

149. *Morning Joe*, MSNBC, October 4, 2012.

150. Robin Abcarian, "Ryan Prepares to Take on His Toughest Debate Opponent Yet," *Los Angeles Times*, October 11, 2012.

151. Ezra Klein, "What I Learned Debating Paul Ryan," *Wonkblog* (blog), *Washington Post*, October 11, 2012, https://www.washingtonpost.com/blogs/ezra -klein/wp/2012/10/11/what-i-learned-debating-paul-ryan/.

152. Juana Summers, "Paul Ryan a Tough Debater, Ex-Rivals Say," Politico .com, October 11, 2012.

153. Jim Acosta, "Ryan Aide Says Magazine Used 'Poor Judgment' Printing Photos," CNN.com, October 11, 2012, http://politicalticker.blogs.cnn.com/2012 /10/11/ryan-aide-says-magazine-used-poor-judgment-printing-photos/.

154. *Anderson Cooper 360 Degrees*, CNN, October 12, 2012.

155. Roger Simon, "Joltin' Joe Biden Wins the Bout," *Politico*, October 12, 2012, http://www.politico.com/story/2012/10/joltin-joe-biden-wins-the-bout -082323.

6. THE QUESTIONERS

1. David S. Broder, *Behind the Front Page: A Candid Look at How the News Is Made* (New York: Simon and Schuster, 1987), 267–68; "Real Presidential Debates," *Washington Post*, September 5, 1984, A19.

2. Jon Margolis, interview by author, March 4, 1998.

3. Peter Jennings, interview by author, May 5, 1998.

4. Jim Lehrer, interview by author, May 11, 1998.

5. Norma Quarles, interview by author, February 23, 1998.

6. Jack White, interview by author, February 24, 1998.

7. Jeff Greenfield, "There's No Debate: The Format Works," *New York Times*, October 13, 1988, A27.

8. Ibid.

9. Mary McGrory, "Politics Without Punditry," *Washington Post*, September 20, 1992, C1.

10. "TV Debate Backstage: Did the Cameras Lie?," *Newsweek*, October 10, 1960, 25.

11. James P. Gannon, "Our Man Survives the Great Debate, Is Glad It's All Over," *Wall Street Journal*, September 27, 1976, 1; Annie Groer, interview by author, March 3, 1998; Andrea Mitchell, interview by author, March 25, 1998.

12. John Mashek, interview by author, March 31, 1998.

13. Elizabeth Drew, interview by author, March 3, 1998.

14. Jennings, interview; Mitchell, interview.

15. Henry Trewhitt, interview by author, March 16, 1998.

16. Richard Nixon, *Six Crises* (Garden City, N.Y.: Doubleday, 1962), 339.

17. Frederick Allen quoted on *CNN Evening News*, October 6, 1988; Brit Hume, interview by author, May 21, 1998.

18. Tom Brokaw, interview by author, April 14, 1998.

19. Jennings, interview.

20. Max Frankel, interview by author, February 25, 1998.

21. Harris Ellis, interview by author, February 25, 1998.

22. Sander Vanocur, interview by author, March 2, 1998.

23. Hal Bruno, interview by author, March 10, 1998.

24. Walter Mears, "A View from the Inside," *Columbia Journalism Review*, January–February 1977, 24.

25. Jack Nelson, interview by author, February 23, 1998.

26. Hume, interview.

27. Brokaw, interview.

28. Walter Mears, interview by author, February 23, 1998.

29. Robert Boyd, interview by author, February 23, 1998.

30. Mitchell, interview.

31. Roger Simon, *Road Show: In America, Anyone Can Become President. It's One of the Risks We Take* (New York: Farrar, Straus and Giroux, 1990), 280–98.

32. Robin Toner, "Dukakis Returns to Stump as Aides Paint Rosy Picture," *New York Times*, October 15, 1988, 9; Walter Shapiro, "Bush Scores a Warm Win," *Time*, October 24, 1988, 18; Bruno, interview.

33. Judy Woodruff, interview by author, March 8, 1998.

34. James Hoge, interview by author, March 27, 1998.

35. Dorothy Ridings, interview by author, April 2, 1998.

36. James A. Baker 3d, interview by author, September 4, 1998; Richard C. Leone, interview by author, April 6, 1998.

37. Tom Shales, "The Debates, Round 1," *Washington Post*, October 8, 1984, D1, D4.

38. Eleanor Randolph, "Three Journalists, Also on the Line," *Washington Post*, September 24, 1988, C1.

39. Jennings, interview.

40. Lehrer, interview.

41. Ibid.

42. Simon, *Road Show*, 283.

43. Janet Brown, interview by author, May 18, 2007.

44. Lehrer, interview. Other quotes about the 1992 and 1996 debates also come from the author's 1998 interview with Lehrer.

45. Lehrer, interview with author, March 20, 2007.

46. Walter Goodman, "A Cool Head at the Eye of the Calm," *New York Times*, November 3, 1996, H37.

47. Richard L. Berke, "Critics Accuse Moderator of Letting Debate Wander," *New York Times*, October 17, 2000, A27.

48. Shafer quoted in Howard Kurtz, "A Picture of Moderation," *Washington Post*, September 29, 2000, C1.

49. Lehrer, 1998 interview.

50. *Reliable Sources*, CNN, September 28, 2008.

51. Richard Kim, "Jim Lehrer Gets Pwned," *Nation*, October 4, 2012, http://www.thenation.com/blog/170351/jim-lehrer-gets-pwned; Peggy Noonan, "Romney Deflates the President," *Wall Street Journal*, October 5, 2012.

52. Jim Lehrer, interview by author, July 15, 2014; Dylan Byers, "Lehrer Says He Was 'Effective,'" *Politico*, October 5, 2012, http://www.politico.com/story/2012/10/exclu-lehrer-says-he-was-effective-082076?o=0.

53. "Moderation of Denver Debate," statement by Commission on Presidential Debates, October 5, 2012, http://www.debates.org/index.php?mact=News,cntnt01,detail,0&cntnt01articleid=44&cntnt01origid=27&cntnt01detailtemplate=newspage&cntnt01returnid=80; Michael McCurry, interview by author, February 5, 2014.

54. Bruno, interview. Other quotes in this section also come from the author's interview with Bruno.

55. Carole Simpson, interview by author, October 25, 1994. Other quotes in this section also come from the author's interview with Simpson.

56. Charles T. Royer, ed., *Campaign for President: The Managers Look at '92* (Hollis, N.H.: Hollis, 1994), 255.

57. Ibid., 254.

58. Leigh Strope, "Shaw Staying Up Studying for Debate," Associated Press, October 5, 2000.

59. Joseph I. Lieberman and Hadassah Lieberman, *An Amazing Adventure: Joe and Hadassah's Personal Notes on the 2000 Campaign* (New York: Simon and Schuster, 2003), 149.

60. Gwen Ifill, interview by author, February 28, 2007. Other quotes in this section about the 2004 vice presidential debate also come from the author's interview with Ifill.

61. Janet Brown, interview by author, February 5, 2014.

62. *Fox and Friends*, Fox News Channel, October 2, 2008.

63. Jim Lehrer, *Tension City: Inside the Presidential Debates* (New York: Random House, 2011), 156.

64. Dylan Byers, "ABC: Daily Caller's Raddatz Inquiry 'Absurd,'" *Politico*, October 9, 2012, http://www.politico.com/blogs/media/2012/10/abc-daily-callers-raddatz-inquiry-absurd-137902.

65. Jeremy W. Peters, "Playing Roles of Referee and, Increasingly, Target During Debates," *New York Times*, October 1, 2012.

66. Dylan Byers, "Candy Crowley: 'I'm Not a Fly on the Wall,'" *Politico*, October 15, 2012, http://www.politico.com/story/2012/10/crowley-im-not-a-fly-on-the-wall-082402.

67. Stuart Stevens, interview by author, March 18, 2014; *The Hugh Hewitt Show*, January 27, 2014.

68. Frank Fahrenkopf Jr., interview by author, March 13, 2014.

69. John Reade, interview by author, May 1, 2014.

70. Jay Rosen, "Ungovernable Reality, not Candy Crowley, Threatens Obama and Romney," *Guardian*, October 16, 2012, http://www.theguardian.com/commentisfree/2012/oct/16/us-presidential-debates-us-elections-2012-candy-crowley-obama-romney.

71. Anita Dunn, interview by author, June 24, 2014.

72. Charles Gibson, interview by author, February 22, 2007.

73. Bob Schieffer, interview by author, March 4, 2014. Other quotes about Schieffer's 2008 and 2012 debates also come from this interview.

74. Bob Schieffer, interview by author, February 28, 2007. Other quotes about Schieffer's debate of 2004 also come from this interview; *Face the Nation*, CBS, October 17, 2004.

75. Robert Goodwin, interview by author, January 15, 1999.

76. James A. Baker 3d, interview by author, April 19, 2007.

77. Monica Crowley, *Nixon Off the Record* (New York: Random House, 1996), 122.

78. Simpson, interview.

79. John B. Judis, "Tonight's Debate: the Tyranny of the Polls," *The Plank* (blog), *New Republic*, October 7, 2012, http://www.newrepublic.com/blog/the-plank/tonights-debate-the-tyranny-the-polls

80. ABC and NBC postdebate coverage, October 15, 1992; "Citizens' Arrest," *Christian Science Monitor*, October 19, 1996, 20.

81. Elizabeth Kolbert, "Bypassing the Press Helps Candidates; Does It Also Serve the Public Interest?," *New York Times*, November 8, 1992, E2.

82. Jake Tapper, "The Two Candidates Share a Podium," *Salon*, October 18, 2000.

83. James Bennet, "In a Disguised Gym, Softballs and Political Drama," *New York Times*, October 9, 2004, A11.

84. NBC postdebate coverage, October 8, 2004.

85. Simpson, interview.

86. Lehrer, 1998 interview.

87. Frank Fahrenkopf Jr., interview by author, May 12, 1998.

7. THE PRODUCTIONS

1. ABC News debate coverage, September 23, 1976.

2. Transcript of "Debating the Debates: Defining Moments in Presidential Campaigns," a symposium presented by the Ronald Reagan Center for Public Affairs, October 15, 1996, 50.

3. Transcript of "Debates '92: A Symposium," presented by the Commission on Presidential Debates, May 9, 1990, 13.

4. Marshall McLuhan was interviewed on NBC's *Today*, September 24, 1976; Joseph Lelyveld, "Focus in the Hall and on the TV Set Differed," *New York Times*, September 25, 1976, 8.

5. *NBC Nightly News*, September 24, 1976.

6. Herbert A. Seltz and Richard D. Yoakam, "Production Diary of the Debates," in *The Great Debates: Carter vs. Ford, 1976*, ed. Sidney Kraus (Bloomington: University of Indiana Press, 1979), 136.

7. Jack Kelly, interview by author, March 26, 1998.

8. Edward M. Fouhy, interview by author, February 27, 1998.

9. Annie Groer, interview by author, March 3, 1998.

10. Edward M. Fouhy, "The Debates: A Winning Miniseries," *Washington Journalism Review*, December 1992, 29.

11. Richard L. Berke, "A Few Tense Moments in the Control Room," *New York Times*, October 15, 1992, A11.

12. Janet Brown, interview by author, March 11, 1998.

13. Fouhy, interview.

14. Transcript of "Debates '92: A Symposium," 34–35.

15. Memorandum of Understanding, 1992, 32–33.

16. Brown, interview.

17. Frank Fahrenkopf Jr., interview by author, May 12, 1998.

18. Mark Sauer, "USD Audience on Its Best Sunday Behavior," *San Diego Union-Tribune*, October 17, 1996, A21.

19. James T. Wooten, "Feeling of Victory Is Sensed by Each Side," *New York Times*, October 7, 1976, 38.

20. Seltz and Yoakam, "Production Diary of the Debates," 139.

21. Brady Williamson, interview by author, November 14, 1998.

22. Ibid.

23. Seltz and Yoakam, "Production Diary of the Debates," 131.

24. Tom Donilon, interview by author, July 14, 1998.

25. Victoria Harian Strella, interview by author, April 2, 1998.

26. Rich Hood and Celeste Hadrick, "Pre-Debate Debate: Candidates' Aides Battle over Lights," *Kansas City Star*, October 21, 1984, 1, 21A.

27. Michael Deaver, interview by author, June 17, 1998.

28. Dudley Clendinen, "Debate Battle Moves to News Shows," *New York Times*, October 23, 1984, A24.

29. Beverly Lindsey, interview by author, April 2, 2007.

30. Janet Brown, interview by author, May 18, 2007.

31. Vernon Jordan, interview by author, July 11, 2007.

32. Lindsey, 2007 interview.

33. Beverly Lindsey, interview by author, December 8, 1998.

34. Maureen Dowd, "Mean and Meaner," *New York Times*, October 20, 1996, IV-5.

35. Memorandum of Understanding, 2004, 25, http://www.gwu.edu/~action/2004/deb04main/debateagreement.pdf.

36. Institute of Politics, Harvard University, ed., *Campaign for President: The Managers Look at 2004* (Lanham, Md.: Rowman and Littlefield, 2006), 157.

37. Chip Colley, interview by author, March 25, 2014.

38. John Dickerson, "The Winner: 'That One,'" *Slate*, October 8, 2008, http://www.slate.com/articles/news_and_politics/politics/2008/10/the_winner_that_one.html.

39. Williamson, interview.

40. Robert Goodwin, interview by author, January 15, 1999.

41. Williamson, interview.

42. Goodwin, interview.

43. Jack W. Germond and Jules Witcover, *Mad as Hell: Revolt at the Ballot Box, 1992* (New York: Warner, 1993), 478.

44. Terry McAuliffe, *What a Party! My Life Among Democrats: Presidents, Candidates, Donors, Activists, Alligators, and Other Wild Animals* (New York: St. Martin's Press, 2007), 360–62.

45. Mary Cheney, *Now It's My Turn: A Daughter's Chronicle of Political Life* (New York: Threshold, 2006), 204.

46. Ibid., 205–6.

47. Williamson, interview.

48. Donilon, interview.

49. Harian Strella, interview.

50. Merriman Smith, "Most Hectic Debate Was Off Camera," *New York World-Telegram*, October 8, 1960, 2.

51. Herbert A. Seltz and Richard D. Yoakam, "Production Diary of the Debates," in *The Great Debates: Background, Perspective, Effects*, ed. Sidney Kraus (Bloomington: Indiana University Press, 1962), 103.

52. J. Leonard Reinsch, *Getting Elected: From Radio and Roosevelt to Television and Reagan* (New York: Hippocrene, 1988), 145.

53. W. H. Lawrence, "Nixon Is 'Shocked' by Kennedy Notes," *New York Times*, October 14, 1960, 22.

54. Memorandum of Understanding, 2012, 3–4, http://thepage.time.com /2012/10/15/the-2012-debates-memorandum-of-understanding-between-the -obama-and-romney-campaigns/.

55. "Hanky or Notes? Did Mitt Cheat?," *Daily Beast*, October 5, 2012, http:// www.thedailybeast.com/cheats/2012/10/05/you-be-the-judge-did-mitt-cheat .html.

56. Seltz and Yoakam, "Production Diary of the Debates," 131.

57. John LiBretto, interview by author, March 17, 1994.

58. Paul Begala, "10 Rules for Winning a Debate," CNN.com, October 1, 2008, http://www.cnn.com/2008/POLITICS/10/01/begala.debate/index.html?iref =24hours.

59. Ibid.; David F. Demarest Junior Interview, George H. W. Bush Oral History Project, Miller Center, University of Virginia, January 28, 2010, 65.

60. Robert Asman, interview by author, March 11, 1998.

61. Colley, interview; John Reade, interview by author, May 1, 2014.

62. *Mitt*, documentary film written and directed by Greg Whiteley, released January 24, 2014, video on demand, Netflix.com.

63. James A. Baker 3d, interview by author, September 4, 1998; Joseph I. Lieberman and Hadassah Lieberman, *An Amazing Adventure: Joe and Hadassah's Personal Notes on the 2000 Campaign* (New York: Simon and Schuster, 2003), 157; Laurie Goldstein, "Bush Uses Religion as Personal and Political Guide," *New York Times*, October 22, 2000.

64. Scott Conroy and Shushannah Walshe, *Sarah from Alaska: The Sudden Rise and Brutal Education of a New Conservative Superstar* (New York: Public Affairs, 2009), 148.

65. Stuart Stevens, *The Big Enchilada: Campaign Adventures with the Cockeyed Optimists from Texas Who Won the Biggest Prize in Politics* (New York: Free Press, 2001), 234.

66. Robert Shrum, *No Excuses: Concessions of a Serial Campaigner* (New York: Simon and Schuster, 2007), 355.

67. *Tonight Show*, NBC, October 5, 2000.

68. Shrum, *No Excuses*, 355.

69. Lawrence Laurent, "ABC Facilities Tonight Just as 'Equal' as Can Be," *Washington Post*, October 13, 1960, B6.

70. John P. Shanley, "Studios on Both Coasts Set Up to Handle Third in TV Debates," *New York Times*, October 14, 1960, 22.

71. David M. Alpern, "The Debates," *Newsweek*, September 27, 1976, 31.

72. Memorandum, William Carruthers to Michael Duval, August 30, 1976, Michael Raoul-Duval Papers, box 29, folder "Input—Bill Carruthers," Gerald R. Ford Presidential Library.

73. Alpern, "Debates," 31.

74. Seltz and Yoakam, "Production Diary of the Debates," 151.

75. Memorandum of Understanding, 1988, 10.

76. John J. O'Connor, "TV: Instant Poll Steals Post-Debate Scene," *New York Times*, October 30, 1980, C26.

77. Todd Rogers and Michael I. Norton, "Presidential Debates: Why Don't They Just Answer the Question?," *Los Angeles Times*, September 22, 2012.

78. George H. W. Bush was interviewed by Jim Lehrer on April 10, 1999, for the PBS documentary *Debating Our Destiny*.

79. LiBretto, interview.

80. Jeremy W. Peters, "Networks Like Split-Screens in Debates, Even if the Candidates Don't," *New York Times*, October 9, 2012.

81. David Bauder, "Networks to Ignore Debate Camera Rules," Associated Press, September 28, 2004.

82. Ron Fournier, "Bush, Kerry Vie to Cement Images," Associated Press, October 1, 2004; Michael Powell, "The Battle, if Not the War, to Kerry; Bush Hit Off-Notes with Debate Viewers," *Washington Post*, October 2, 2004, A1.

83. Mike Allen, "Kerry vs. the Format, Bush vs. His Temper," *Washington Post*, October 1, 2004, A8; Anne E. Kornblut and Patrick Healy, "Debate Provides Bush and Kerry with Fresh Salvos," *Boston Globe*, October 2, 2004, A1; Mark McKinnon, interview by author, February 27, 2006.

84. Alessandra Stanley, "The Choirboy and the Headmaster, and a Face-off Without Fireworks," *New York Times*, October 4, 2012.

85. Harvard University Institute of Politics 2012 Campaign Decision Makers Conference. Excerpted from "Discussions on the General Election, Part 2," audio file recorded November 29, 2012.

86. Camille Ricketts, "Bush's Tailor Unravels Web Rumor," *Seattle Times*, October 9, 2004, A13; Elisabeth Bumiller, "The Mystery of the Bulge in the Jacket," *New York Times*, October 9, 2004, A15.

87. *Meet the Press*, NBC, October 17, 2004; Elisabeth Bumiller, "Talk of Bubble Leads to Battle over Bulge," *New York Times*, October 18, 2004, A14; *Good Morning America*, ABC, October 26, 2004.

88. *Tonight Show*, NBC, October 12, 2004.

89. Kevin Berger, "NASA Photo Analyst: Bush Wore a Device During Debate," *Salon*, October 29, 2004, http://www.salon.com/2004/10/30/bulge_5/.

90. Dave Lindorff, "The Emperor's New Hump," Fairness and Accuracy in Reporting, January 1, 2005, http://fair.org/extra-online-articles/the-emperors -new-hump/.

91. Albert Eisele, "Man the Barricades, It's Bush Again," *The Hill*, November 4, 2004, http://thehill.com/homenews/news/5802-man-the-barricades-its-bush -again.

92. Jim Lehrer, interview by author, May 11, 1998.

93. Fouhy quoted in Berke, "Few Tense Moments in the Control Room," A11.

94. Brown, 1998 interview.

95. Asman, interview.

96. LiBretto, interview.

8. SOCIAL MEDIA AND REAL-TIME REACTIONS

1. Ben Smith, "How Mitt Romney Won the First Debate," BuzzFeed, October 3, 2012, http://www.buzzfeed.com/bensmith/how-mitt-romney-won-the-first -debate#.mhRPq2LWk.

2. Howard Rosenberg, "Perot Pitches, Bush Swings . . . Oops, That's CBS," *Los Angeles Times*, October 12, 1992, A23; Howard Kurtz, "The New Spin on Spin," *Washington Post*, October 8, 1996 A7.

3. Mark Wallace, interview with author, February 28, 2006.

4. Joel Hyatt, "Power to the People," *Presidential Debates Blog*, September 21, 2008, http://presidentialdebateblog.blogspot.com/2008/09/joel-hyatt-of-current -tv-on-debates.html?q=joel+hyatt.

5. Sarah Lai Stirland, "Current TV Hacks the Debates," *Wired*, September 27, 2008, http://www.wired.com/2008/09/current-tv-cras/.

6. Nicholas A. Diakopoulos and David A. Shamma, "Characterizing Debate Performance via Aggregated Twitter Sentiment," *Proceedings of the SIGCHI Conference on Human Factors in Computing Systems* (ACM, 2010); David A. Shamma, Lyndon Kennedy, and Elizabeth F. Churchill, "Tweet the Debates: Understanding Community Annotation of Uncollected Sources," *Proceedings of the First SIGMM Workshop on Social Media* (ACM, 2009).

7. Statistics regarding the number of debate-related tweets in 2012 come from Adam Sharp of Twitter. First Obama/Romney debate: https://blog.twitter .com/2012/dispatch-from-the-denver-debate; vice-presidential debate: https:// blog.twitter.com/2012/recapping-the-vp-debate; second Obama/Romney debate: https://blog.twitter.com/2012/twitter-at-the-town-hall-debate; third Obama/Romney debate: https://blog.twitter.com/2012/the-final-2012-presidential -debate.

8. Ron Klain, interview with author, February 4, 2014. Other quotes from Klain in this chapter also come from the author's interview.

9. Adam Sharp, interview with author, April 9, 2014. Other quotes from Sharp in this chapter also come from the author's interview.

10. Dashiell Bennett, "Twitter Won the Presidential Debate," *The Wire*, Atlantic.com, October 4, 2012, http://www.thewire.com/politics/2012/10/twitter-won-presidential-debate/57593/.

11. Crowdwire findings about use of social media in the 2012 debates are discussed in several posts on the website thecrowdwire.org.

12. Adam Sharp, "Tonight's Town Hall Debate—and You," Twitter.com, October 16, 2012, https://blog.twitter.com/2012/tonights-town-hall-debate-and-you.

13. Michael Roston, "Who Won the Debate? Think Twice About the Answers on Twitter," *The Caucus* (blog), *New York Times*, October 16, 2012, http://thecaucus.blogs.nytimes.com/2012/10/16/who-won-presidential-debate-on-twitter/.

14. Dana Milbank, "Trending on Twitter: Groupthink," *Washington Post*, October 23, 2014.

15. Peter Hamby, "Did Twitter Kill the Boys on the Bus? Searching for a Better Way to Cover a Campaign," Joan Shorenstein Center on the Press, Politics and Public Policy, Discussion Paper Series #D-80, September 2013, 27.

16. "Winning the Media Campaign," Pew Research Center, November 2, 2012, http://www.journalism.org/2012/11/02/winning-media-campaign-2012/.

17. Stephen Kurczy, "Twitter Wins Presidential Debate," *Construction Magazine*, October 5, 2012, http://constructionlitmag.com/politics/election-2012/twitter-wins-presidential-debate/.

18. Zachary Moffatt, interview with author, March 21, 2014.

19. Jeff Maldonado, "65% of Americans Will Use PC, Smartphone, Tablet While Watching the Presidential Debate," Verizon, October 2, 2012, http://forums.verizon.com/t5/Verizon-at-Home/65-of-Americans-Will-Use-PC-Smartphone-Tablet-While-Watching/ba-p/487225.

20. "One-in-Ten 'Dual-Screened' the Presidential Debate," Pew Research Center for the People and the Press, October 11, 2012, http://www.people-press.org/2012/10/11/one-in-ten-dual-screened-the-presidential-debate/.

21. Jenny Xie, "Social Media a Hotbed of Political Debate, Engagement—For the Good?," PBS MediaShift.com, October 29, 2012, http://mediashift.org/2012/10/social-media-a-hotbed-of-political-debate-engagement-for-the-good303/.

22. Moffatt interview, March 21, 2014.

23. Sophie Quinton, "Do Debate Fact-Checkers Matter? Not So Much," *National Journal*, October 15, 2012.

24. Craig Silverman, "Study: Political Journalists Opt for Stenography over Fact Checking During Presidential Debates," Poynter.org, July 16, 2014, http://

www.poynter.org/news/mediawire/259021/study-political-journalists-opt-for
-stenography-over-fact-checking-during-presidential-debates/.

25. Alex Fitzpatrick, "Twitter Dominated Online Chatter About the Presidential Debate," Mashable.com, October 4, 2012, http://mashable.com/2012/10/04/twitter-debate-chatter/#uncaTlioRSqz; and "Second Presidential Debate: Less Twitter, More Facebook," October 17, 2012, Mashable.com, http://mashable.com/2012/10/17/hofstra-debate-twitter-facebook/#PCjgpVZf48qR.

26. Andy Carvin, *Talk of the Nation*, National Public Radio, October 17, 2012.

27. "Live-Giffing the 2012 Debates!," Tumblr press release, October 1, 2012, http://staff.tumblr.com/post/32671284860/live-giffing-the-2012-debates-this-wednesday.

28. Dean Takahashi, "Xbox Live Members Say Obama Won Second Debate," *Games Beat* (blog), VentureBeat.com, October 17, 2012, http://venturebeat.com/2012/10/17/xbox-live-members-say-obama-won-second-debate/; Dean Takahashi, "Obama Wins Again in Final Presidential Debate, Xbox Swing Voters Say," VentureBeat.com, October 23, 2012, http://venturebeat.com/2012/10/23/obama-wins-again-in-final-presidential-debate-xbox-swing-voters-say/.

29. Matt Peckham, "Swing Voters Choose Obama in Final Xbox LIVE debate, but Was Poll Too Distracting?," *Techland* (blog), *Time*, October 23, 2012, http://techland.time.com/2012/10/23/swing-voters-choose-obama-in-final-xbox-live-debate-but-was-poll-too-distracting/.

30. Ken Wheaton, "Want to Get the Most out of Debates? Turn off Social Media," *Advertising Age*, October 15, 2012, http://adage.com/article/viewpoint/debates-turn-social-media/237753/.

9. POSTDEBATE NEWS COVERAGE

1. *Douglas Edwards with the News*, CBS, September 27, 1960.

2. Richard L. Strout, "Not One Slip on Banana Peel!," *Christian Science Monitor*, September 27, 1960, 1; Peter Lisagor, "How Candidates Did in the Big Debate," *Chicago Daily News*, September 27, 1960, 1; Percy Shain, "Candidates Today Must Know Facts, TV Is Too Discerning for Bluffing," *Boston Globe*, September 27, 1960, 9.

3. Richard T. Stout, "Nixon Aides Admit Makeup Job," *Chicago Daily News*, September 30, 1960, 4; "Nixon Says Lost Weight Shows in Face," *Boston Globe*, evening edition, September 27, 1960, 9.

4. Richard T. Stout, "Was Nixon Sabotaged by TV Makeup Artist?," *Chicago Daily News*, September 29, 1960, 1.

5. "TV Debate Backstage: Did the Cameras Lie?," *Newsweek*, October 10, 1960, 25.

6. "Nixon Laments Make-Up in Chat with TV Actor," *New York Times*, October 13, 1960, 27.

7. Russell Baker, *The Good Times* (New York: Morrow, 1989), 326.

8. "How the Battle Shapes Up Now," *U.S. News & World Report*, October 17, 1960, 42.

9. Ralph McGill, "TV vs. Radio in the Great Debate," *Washington Evening Star*, October 1, 1960, A5.

10. "Debate Audience Yields Wide Range of Reaction," *New York Times*, September 27, 1960, 1, 29.

11. "Los Angeles Watches and Listens to the Great Debate," *Los Angeles Times*, September 27, 1960, 3.

12. NBC News debate coverage, September 23, 1976.

13. Mudd and Cronkite both took part in CBS News's postdebate coverage, September 23, 1976.

14. David S. Broder, interview by author, May 12, 1998.

15. David S. Broder, *Behind the Front Page: A Candid Look at How the News Is Made* (New York: Simon and Schuster, 1987), 293.

16. Roger Simon, interview by author, March 14, 2007.

17. James Fallows, interview by author, May 21, 2007.

18. Transcript of "Debates '92: A Symposium," presented by the Commission on Presidential Debates, May 9, 1990, 4.

19. Bob Schieffer, interview by author, November 18, 1998.

20. Blake Zeff, "Why It's Impossible to Win a Debate," BuzzFeed, October 1, 2012, http://www.buzzfeed.com/blakezeff/why-its-impossible-to-win-a-debate.

21. James B. Lemert, William R. Elliott, James M. Bernstein, William L. Rosenberg, and Karl J. Nestvold, *News Verdicts, the Debates, and Presidential Campaigns* (New York: Praeger, 1991), 43, 59.

22. "Winning the Media Campaign 2012," Pew Research Center Project for Excellence in Journalism, November 2, 2012, 6, http://www.journalism.org/2012/11/02/winning-media-campaign-2012/.

23. Dana Milbank, "Reaction Shots May Tell Tale of Debate," *Washington Post*, October 2, 2004, A10.

24. Mark Memmott, "For This Event, the Best Seats Are Often at Home," *USA Today*, October 6, 2004, 10A.

25. Herbert G. Klein, *Making It Perfectly Clear: An Inside Account of Nixon's Love-Hate Relationship with the Media* (Garden City, N.Y.: Doubleday, 1980), 106.

26. W. H. Lawrence, "Neither Nominee Claims a Triumph," *New York Times*, September 27, 1960, 30.

27. Ibid.

28. NBC News postdebate coverage, October 6, 1996.

29. Howard Kurtz, "The New Spin on Spin: Instant Interviews, Polls; Respondents Tended to Side with Their Favorites," *Washington Post*, October 8, 1996, A7.

30. Ron Nessen, *It Sure Looks Different from the Inside* (Chicago: Playboy Press, 1978), 266.

31. Larry Speakes, *Speaking Out: Inside the Reagan White House* (New York: Scribner's, 1980), 55.

32. CBS News postdebate coverage, October 15, 1976.

33. Hal Bruno, interview by author, March 10, 1998.

34. Michael Deaver, interview by author, June 17, 1998.

35. NBC News postdebate coverage, October 11, 1984.

36. Lemert et al., *News Verdicts, the Debates, and Presidential Campaigns*, 69.

37. NBC News postdebate coverage, October 5, 1988.

38. David F. Demarest Jr. Interview, George H. W. Bush Oral History Project, Miller Center, University of Virginia, January 28, 2010, 23.

39. Michael Oreskes, "Both Parties Offer a Spin to the Event," *New York Times*, September 26, 1988, A1, A20.

40. Roger Simon, *Show Time: The American Political Circus and the Race for the White House* (New York: Times Books, 1998), 267–68.

41. Garrett Haake, interview by author, March 18, 2014.

42. Mark Leibovich, *This Town. Two Parties and a Funeral—plus Plenty of Valet Parking!—in America's Gilded Capital* (New York: Penguin, 2013), 269.

43. *ABC World News Tonight*, September 26, 1988.

44. NBC News postdebate coverage, October 7, 1984; E. J. Dionne Jr., "The Debates: Revival for Democrats," *New York Times*, October 7, 1988, B4.

45. *The War Room*, documentary film, directed by Chris Hegedus and D. A. Pennebaker, released December 5, 1993 (USA), Pennebaker Hegedus Films and McEttinger Films.

46. Charles T. Royer, ed., *Campaign for President: The Managers Look at '92* (Hollis, N.H.: Hollis, 1994), 239.

47. Zeke Miller, "4 Ways to Win a Presidential Debate," BuzzFeed, October 3, 2012, http://www.buzzfeed.com/buzzfeedpolitics/4-ways-to-win-a-presidential-debate#.nm55Rn6GZ.

48. Ron Klain, interview by author, February 4, 2014.

49. "The Blooper Heard Round the World," *Time*, October 18, 1976, 13; CBS News and NBC News postdebate coverage, October 6, 1976.

50. Bernard Gwertzman, "Ford Denies Moscow Dominates East Europe; Carter Rebuts Him," *New York Times*, October 7, 1976, 1; Curtis Wilkie, "Aides Celebrate Carter 'Home Run,'" *Boston Globe*, October 7, 1976, 20; David S.

Broder and Lou Cannon, "A Tense, Highly Charged Atmosphere in San Francisco," *Washington Post*, October 7, 1976, A10.

51. *NBC Nightly News*, October 7, 1976.

52. Charles Mohr, "Ford, Trying to Bind Up Wound, Backs Freedom for East Europe," *New York Times*, October 8, 1976, A18; *NBC Nightly News*, October 7, 1976.

53. Charles Mohr, "Ford Makes 2 Attempts to Clarify Statement," *New York Times*, October 9, 1976, 1, 7.

54. Curtis Wilkie, "Ford Admits Error on E. Europe," *Boston Globe*, October 13, 1976, 1.

55. Nessen, *It Sure Looks Different from the Inside*, 272; Gerald Ford, *A Time to Heal: The Autobiography of Gerald R. Ford* (New York: Harper and Row, 1979), 424.

56. Nessen, *It Sure Looks Different from the Inside*, 276.

57. Thomas E. Patterson, *Out of Order* (New York: Knopf, 1993), 156; Nessen, *It Sure Looks Different from the Inside*, 276.

58. Jonathan Moore and Janet Fraser, eds., *Campaign for President: The Managers Look at '76* (Cambridge, Mass.: Ballinger, 1977), 142.

59. Frederick T. Steeper, "Public Response to Gerald Ford's Statements on Eastern Europe in the Second Debate," in *The Presidential Debates: Media, Electoral, and Policy Perspectives*, ed. George F. Bishop, Robert G. Meadow, and Marilyn Jackson-Beeck (New York: Praeger, 1978), 101; Doris Graber, *Processing the News: How People Tame the Information Tide* (New York: Longman, 1984), 264; David Chagall, *The New Kingmakers: An Inside Look at the Powerful Men Behind America's Political Campaigns* (New York: Harcourt Brace Jovanovich, 1981), 108.

60. CBS News and NBC News postdebate coverage, October 7, 1984.

61. Howell Raines, "Reagan and Mondale Debate; Clash on Deficit and Religion," *New York Times*, October 8, 1984, 1; Tom Shales, "The Debates, Round 1," *Washington Post*, October 8, 1984, D1.

62. Rich Jaroslovsky and James M. Perry, "New Question in Race: Is Oldest U.S. President Now Showing His Age?," *Wall Street Journal*, October 9, 1984, 1.

63. David S. Broder, "Reagan's Late-Inning Letdown," *Washington Post*, October 9, 1984, A19.

64. Mark Hertsgaard, *On Bended Knee: The Press and the Reagan Presidency* (New York: Farrar, Straus and Giroux, 1988), 246–47.

65. *ABC World News Tonight*, October 9, 1984.

66. Thomas Rosenstiel, "Debate Aftermath: Media Alter View of Candidates," *Los Angeles Times*, October 14, 1984, 1.

67. *ABC World News Tonight*, October 9, 1984.

68. *NBC Nightly News*, October 10, 1984.

69. Ibid.

70. Steven R. Weisman, "Reagan Criticizes Comments on Age," *New York Times*, October 11, 1984, 1; George Skelton, "Reagan Called 'Alert' in May 18 Medical Report," *Los Angeles Times*, October 11, 1984, 1; *CBS Evening News*, October 10, 1984.

71. Austin Ranney, *The American Elections of 1984* (New York: American Enterprise Institute, 1985), 198–99.

72. Stuart Stevens, *The Big Enchilada: Campaign Adventures with the Cockeyed Optimists from Texas Who Won the Biggest Prize in Politics* (New York: Free Press, 2001), 241.

73. "Press Coverage of the 2000 Presidential Campaign," panel discussion, University of Virginia, November 29, 2000.

74. *Digging the Dirt* aired in the United Kingdom on BBC's *Panorama*, October 22, 2000. Produced by Tom Giles, reported by Peter Marshall, BBC.

75. Martin Lewis, "Unleash All Hell on Al," *Time*, November 5, 2000, http://www.martinlewis.com/column.pl?col=33&cat=time.

76. "GOP's New Battle Cry vs. Gore: Liar! Liar!," *New York Post*, October 5, 2000, 1.

77. Richard Benedetto, "Poll: Bush More Honest, Likeable, Gore Losing Ground After First Debate," *USA Today*, October 10, 2000, 1A.

78. Kathleen Hall Jamieson and Paul Waldman, *The Press Effect: Politicians, Journalists, and the Stories That Shape the Political World* (New York: Oxford University Press, 2003), 56.

79. *Imus in the Morning*, CBS Radio Network, October 10, 2000.

80. Kevin Sack, "Gore Says He Makes Mistakes, but He Does Not Exaggerate," *New York Times*, October 8, 2000.

81. Eric Boehlert, "The Press vs. Al Gore," *Rolling Stone*, November 26, 2001, http://www.freerepublic.com/focus/f-news/579117/posts.

82. "Obama Expected to Win First Presidential Debate," Pew Research Center for the People and the Press, October 2, 2012, http://www.people-press.org /2012/10/02/obama-expected-to-win-first-presidential-debate/; Jeffrey M. Jones, "Romney Narrows Vote Gap After Historic Debate Win," Gallup.com, October 8, 2012, http://www.gallup.com/poll/157907/romney-narrows-vote-gap-historic -debate-win.aspx.

83. Andrew Sullivan, *The Dish* (live-blog), October 3, 2012, http://dish .andrewsullivan.com/2012/10/03/live-blogging-the-first-presidential-debate -2012/.

84. MSNBC and CNN postdebate coverage, October 3, 2012.

85. Fox News Channel and Current TV postdebate coverage, October 3, 2012.

86. Peter Baker and Trip Gabriel, "With Biden Up Next to Debate, Obama's Aides Plot Comeback," *New York Times*, October 7, 2012.

87. Reid J. Epstein, "Obama Makes Fun of His Debate Performance," *Politico*, October 7, 2012, http://www.politico.com/blogs/politico44/2012/10/obama -makes-fun-of-his-debate-performance-137751; Maggie Haberman and Glenn Thrush, "5 Things to Watch at the Debate," *Politico*, October 16, 2012, http:// www.politico.com/story/2012/10/five-things-to-watch-at-the-debate-082438.

88. *Tom Joyner Morning Show*, October 10, 2012; *ABC World News Tonight*, October 10, 2012; Reid J. Epstein, "Obama Makes Fun of His Debate Performance," *Politico*, October 7, 2012, http://www.freerepublic.com/focus/f-news /579117/posts.

89. Richard Wolffe, *The Message: The Reselling of President Obama* (New York: Twelve, 2013), 214; *CBS Evening News*, October 4, 2012.

90. 2012 Campaign Decision Makers Conference, Institute of Politics, John F. Kennedy School of Government, November 29, 2012; Jonathan Alter, *The Center Holds: Obama and His Enemies* (New York: Simon and Schuster, 2013), 329.

91. *CBS Evening News* and ABC News *Nightline*, October 5, 1988; NBC *Today*, *ABC World News Tonight*, *CBS Evening News*, and *NBC Nightly News*, October 6, 1988.

92. *ABC World News Tonight* and *CBS Evening News*, October 6, 1988.

93. Maureen Dowd, "Bush Angrily Insisting He Fully Backs Quayle," *New York Times*, October 9, 1988, 32.

94. *ABC World News Tonight*, October 11, 1988; *CBS Evening News*, October 12, 1988.

95. B. Drummond Ayres, "Quayle, Free of Handlers, Is Going with His Instincts," *New York Times*, October 14, 1988, B11.

96. CNN, November 1, 1988.

97. Roger Simon, *Road Show: In America, Anyone Can Become President. It's One of the Risks We Take* (New York: Farrar, Straus and Giroux, 1990), 296–97.

98. Fox News Channel postdebate coverage, October 13, 2004.

99. Mark Z. Barabak and Michael Finnegan, "Kerry and Bush Wrap Up Debates with New Issues, Familiar Topics," *Los Angeles Times*, October 14, 2004.

100. Michael Laris, "Mention of Gay Daughter a Cheap Trick, Lynne Cheney Says," *Washington Post*, October 14, 2004, A6; Mary Cheney, *Now It's My Turn: A Daughter's Chronicle of Political Life* (New York: Threshold Editions, 2006), 224–25.

101. Cheney, *Now It's My Turn*, 224.

102. Adam Nagourney, "For Kerry, a Few Words That May Be Debatable," *New York Times*, October 18, 2004, A14.

103. ABC News postdebate coverage, October 28, 1980; "Celebrities Name the Winner According to Own Party Labels," *Cleveland Plain Dealer*, October 29, 1980, 8A.

104. *ABC World News Tonight*, October 29, 1980.

105. Dale Russakoff, "Bush Boasts of Kicking 'A Little Ass' at Debate," *Washington Post*, October 13, 1984, A8.

106. Fay S. Joyce, "Bush Is Delighted After His Debate," *New York Times*, October 13, 1984, 9; *NBC Nightly News*, October 12, 1984.

107. George J. Church, "Getting a Second Look," *Time*, October 22, 1984, 26.

10. DEBATES AND VOTERS

1. For a discussion of the ratings in 1960, see Earl Mazo, Malcolm Moos, Hallock Hoffman, and Harvey Wheeler, *The Great Debates* (Santa Barbara, Calif.: Center for the Study of Democratic Institutions, 1962), 4. It bears mention that viewership figures for presidential debates, then as now, are notoriously difficult to pinpoint with precision. As Mazo and his colleagues write, significant disparities existed between ratings figures cited by the broadcast networks in 1960 and those taken by political pollsters. See also Frank Stanton, "A CBS View," in *The Great Debates: Background, Perspective, Effects*, ed. Sidney Kraus (Bloomington: Indiana University Press, 1962), 65–72.

2. Ratings information for presidential debates is culled from various sources, including Nielsen Media Research, contemporaneous news media reports, and the Commission on Presidential Debates.

3. Ratings information for special episodes of TV series and miniseries is culled from various sources, including Nielsen Media Research, *Broadcasting and Cable* magazine, and contemporaneous news media reports.

4. William Safire, "Humans Confront Android," *New York Times*, October 15, 1992, A15.

5. Walter Mondale, interview by Kevin Sauter, March 31, 1989.

6. Stanton, "A CBS View," 69.

7. Walter Goodman, "The Presidential Debate That Wasn't," *New York Times*, September 22, 1992, C18.

8. Norman Cousins, "TV and the Presidency," *Saturday Review*, November 13, 1976, 4.

9. Charles P. Pierce, "The Ghost of Alzheimer's," *Boston Globe*, January 31, 1999, C1.

10. Walter Lippmann, "Today and Tomorrow; The TV Debate," *Washington Post*, September 29, 1960, A23.

11. Richard Severo, "Lawrence E. Spivak, 93, Is Dead; The Originator of 'Meet the Press,'" *New York Times*, March 10, 1994, D21.

12. Henry Allen, "Primate Debate—As the Candidates Face Off, Onlookers Have an Instinctive Reaction," *Washington Post*, October 5, 1996, C1.

13. George Farah, *No Debate: How the Republican and Democratic Parties Secretly Control the Presidential Debates* (New York: Seven Stories, 2004), 14.

14. Elizabeth R. Lamoureux, Heather S. Entrekin, and Mitchell S. McKinney, "Debating the Debates," in *The 1992 Presidential Debates in Focus*, ed. Diana B. Carlin and Mitchell S. McKinney (Westport, Conn.: Praeger, 1994), 58.

15. Robert G. Meadow, "Televised Campaign Debates as Whistle-Stop Speeches," in *Television Coverage of the 1980 Presidential Campaign* , ed. William C. Adams (Norwood, N.J.: Ablex, 1983), 91.

16. Doris Graber, *Mass Media and American Politics* (Washington: CQ, 1997), 257.

17. Kathleen Hall Jamieson and David S. Birdsell, *Presidential Debates: The Challenge of Creating an Informed Electorate* (New York: Oxford University Press, 1988), 127.

18. "Most Voters Say News Media Wants Obama to Win," Pew Research Center for the People and the Press, October 22, 2008.

19. Institute of Politics, Harvard University, ed., *Campaign for President: The Managers Look at 2000* (Hollis, N.H.: Hollis, 2002), 184–85.

20. Diana Carlin, interview by author, September 1, 1998.

21. Lamoureux, Entrekin, and McKinney, "Debating the Debates," 57.

22. Allan Louden, correspondence with author, August 11, 2015.

23. Bill Clinton was interviewed by Jim Lehrer on August 11, 2000, for the PBS documentary *Debating Our Destiny*.

24. Henry Steele Commager, "Washington Would Have Lost a TV Debate," *New York Times Magazine*, October 30, 1960, VI-13.

25. Daniel Boorstin, *The Image: A Guide to Pseudo-Events in America* (New York: Harper and Row, 1964), 43–44.

26. Harvey Wheeler, "The Great Debates," in Mazo et al., *Great Debates*, 15.

27. Lawrie Mifflin, "An Old Hand's View of TV News: Not Good," *New York Times*, March 23, 1998, AR41.

28. Richard Nixon, *RN: The Memoirs of Richard Nixon* (New York: Grossett and Dunlap, 1978), 221.

29. Elizabeth Drew, interview by author, March 3, 1998.

30. Stephen Mills, "Rebuilding the Presidential Debates," *Speaker and Gavel* 24 (1986): 48.

31. Jack W. Germond and Jules Witcover, *Wake Us When It's Over: Presidential Politics of 1984* (New York: Macmillan, 1985), 527.

32. Ronald Brownstein, "Pressure Is on Bush for First Debate," *Los Angeles Times*, October 11, 1992, A1.

33. John Sides and Lynn Vavreck. *The Gamble: Choice and Chance in the 2012 Presidential Election* (Princeton, N.J.: Princeton University Press, 2013), 161.

34. Carlin, interview.

35. David J. Lanoue and Peter R. Schrott, *The Joint Press Conference: The History, Impact, and Prospects of American Presidential Debates* (Westport, Conn.: Greenwood, 1991), 49.

CONCLUSION

1. Gloria Carrasco, "Evo Morales, gran ausente en el primer debate presidencial en Bolivia," CNNEspañol.com, September 20, 2014; "Colombia: Confident President Refuses Debates," *New York Times*, March 29, 2006; Georg Kiesinger information and translation provided by German debate scholar Christoph Bieber of the Universität Duisburg–Essen.

2. The manual can be found on the Jamaica Debates Commission website: http://jamaicadebatescommission.org/wp-content/uploads/2013/08/JDC _Manual.pdf.

3. Kathy Marks, "Whiff of Marijuana Enlivens New Zealand Election Debate," *The Independent* (U.K.), November 24, 1999.

4. Quoted in a lecture by Denise Dresser, professor of political science, Instituto Tecnológico Autónomo de México, delivered at the Center for Latin American Studies, University of California, Berkeley, April 26, 2000.

5. Janet Brown, interview with author, February 4, 2014.

SELECTED BIBLIOGRAPHY

Ailes, Roger. *You Are the Message: Secrets of the Master Communicators*. With Jon Kraushar. Homewood, Ill.: Dow Jones–Irwin, 1988.

Baker, James A., III. *"Work Hard, Study . . . and Keep Out of Politics!": Adventures and Lessons from an Unexpected Public Life*. With Steve Fiffer. New York: Putnam, 2006.

Balz, Dan. *Collision 2012: Obama vs. Romney and the Future of Elections in America*. New York: Viking, 2013.

Balz, Dan, and Haynes Johnson. *The Battle for America 2008: The Story of an Extraordinary Election*. New York: Viking, 2009.

Barrett, Laurence I. *Gambling with History: Ronald Reagan in the White House*. Garden City, N.Y.: Doubleday, 1983.

Bishop, George F., Robert G. Meadow, and Marilyn Jackson-Beeck, eds. *The Presidential Debates: Media, Electoral, and Policy Perspectives*. New York: Praeger, 1978.

Bitzer, Lloyd, and Theodore Rueter. *Carter vs. Ford: The Counterfeit Debates of 1976*. Madison: University of Wisconsin Press, 1980.

Black, Christine M., and Thomas Oliphant. *All by Myself: The Unmaking of a Presidential Campaign*. Chester, Conn.: Globe Pequot, 1989.

Boorstin, Daniel J. *The Image*. New York: Harper and Row, 1964.

Broder, David S. *Behind the Front Page: A Candid Look at How the News Is Made*. New York: Simon and Schuster, 1987.

Brodie, Fawn M. *Richard Nixon: The Shaping of His Character*. New York: Norton, 1981.

Bruni, Frank. *Ambling into History: The Unlikely Odyssey of George W. Bush*. New York: HarperCollins, 2002.

Brydon, Steven R. "The Two Faces of Jimmy Carter: The Transformation of a Presidential Debater, 1976 and 1980." *Central States Speech Journal* 36 (Fall 1985): 138–51.

Bush, George W. *Decision Points*. New York: Crown, 2010.

Cannon, Lou. *President Reagan: The Role of a Lifetime*. New York: Simon and Schuster, 1991.

———. *Reagan*. New York: Putnam, 1982.

Carlin, Diana B., and Mitchell S. McKinney, eds. *The 1992 Presidential Debates in Focus*. Westport, Conn.: Praeger, 1994. [Of particular interest are the chapters by Elizabeth R. Lamoureux, Heather S. Entrekin, and Mitchell S. McKinney; and Mary Boor Tonn.]

Carter, Jimmy. *Keeping Faith: Memoirs of a President*. New York: Bantam, 1982.

Cheney, Dick. *In My Time: A Personal and Political Memoir*. With Liz Cheney. New York: Threshold, 2011.

Commager, Henry Steele. "Washington Would Have Lost a TV Debate." *New York Times Magazine*, October 30, 1960, 79–80.

Corrado, Anthony. "Background Paper." In Twentieth Century Fund Task Force on Presidential Debates, *Let America Decide*. New York: Twentieth Century Foundation, 1995.

Cousins, Norman. "TV and the Presidency." *Saturday Review*, November 13, 1976, 4.

Cramer, Richard Ben. *What It Takes: The Way to the White House*. New York: Random House, 1992.

Crowley, Monica. *Nixon Off the Record*. New York: Random House, 1996.

Drew, Elizabeth. *Campaign Journal: The Political Events of 1983–1984*. New York: Macmillan, 1985.

———. *Election Journal: Political Events of 1987–1988*. New York: William Morrow, 1989.

———. *Portrait of an Election: The 1980 Presidential Campaign*. New York: Simon and Schuster, 1981.

Farah, George. *No Debate: How the Republican and Democratic Parties Secretly Control the Presidential Debates*. New York: Seven Stories, 2004.

Ferraro, Geraldine. *Ferraro: My Story*. New York: Bantam, 1985.

Ford, Gerald. *A Time to Heal: The Autobiography of Gerald R. Ford*. New York: Harper and Row, 1979.

Fouhy, Edward M. "The Debates: A Winning Miniseries." *Washington Journalism Review*, December 1992, 27–29.

Friedenberg, Robert V., ed. *Rhetorical Studies of National Political Debates, 1960–1992*. 2nd ed. Westport, Conn.: Praeger, 1994. [Of particular interest are the chapters by Goodwin Bergquist; Dan F. Hahn; Kevin Sauter; Craig Allen Smith and Kathy B. Smith; and Judith S. Trent.]

Gergen, David. *Eyewitness to Power: The Essence of Leadership; Nixon to Clinton*. New York: Simon and Schuster, 2000.

Germond, Jack W., and Jules Witcover. *Blue Smoke and Mirrors: How Reagan Won and Why Carter Lost the Election of 1980*. New York: Viking, 1981.

———. *Mad as Hell: Revolt at the Ballot Box, 1992*. New York: Warner, 1993.

———. *Wake Us When It's Over: Presidential Politics of 1984*. New York: Macmillan, 1985.

———. *Whose Broad Stripes and Bright Stars? The Trivial Pursuit of the Presidency 1988*. New York: Warner, 1989.

Goldman, Peter, and Tony Fuller. *The Quest for the Presidency 1984*. New York: Bantam, 1985.

Graber, Doris. *Mass Media and American Politics*. Washington, D.C.: CQ, 1997.

———. *Processing the News: How People Tame the Information Tide*. New York: Longman, 1984.

Greenfield, Jeff. *Oh, Waiter! One Order of Crow: Inside the Strangest Presidential Election Finish in American History*. New York: Putnam, 2001.

———. *The Real Campaign: How the Media Missed the Story of the 1980 Campaign*. New York: Summit Books, 1982.

Halberstam, David. "President Video." *Esquire*, June 1976, 94–97, 130–34.

Halperin, Mark, and John Heilemann. *Double Down: Game Change 2012*. New York: Penguin, 2013.

———. *Game Change: Obama and the Clintons, McCain and Palin, and the Race of a Lifetime*. New York: Harper, 2010.

Hamby, Peter. "Did Twitter Kill the Boys on the Bus? Searching for a Better Way to Cover a Campaign." Joan Shorenstein Center on the Press, Politics and Public Policy, Discussion Paper Series no. D-80, September 2013.

Hardy-Short, Dayle. "An Insider's View of the Constraints Affecting Geraldine Ferraro's Preparation for the 1984 Vice Presidential Debate." *Speaker and Gavel* 24 (1986): 8–22.

Hayes, Stephen. *Cheney: The Untold Story of America's Most Powerful and Controversial Vice President*. New York: HarperCollins, 2007.

Henry, William A., III. *Visions of America: How We Saw the 1984 Election*. Boston: Atlantic Monthly Press, 1985.

Hersh, Seymour M. *The Dark Side of Camelot*. Boston: Little, Brown, 1997.

Hertsgaard, Mark. *On Bended Knee: The Press and the Reagan Presidency*. New York: Farrar, Straus and Giroux, 1988.

Institute of Politics, Harvard University, ed. *Campaign for President: The Managers Look at 2000*. Hollis, N.H.: Hollis, 2002.

———. *Campaign for President: The Managers Look at 2004*. Lanham, Md.: Rowman and Littlefield, 2006.

———. *Campaign for President: The Managers Look at 2008*. Lanham, Md.: Rowman and Littlefield, 2009.

Jamieson, Kathleen Hall, ed. *Electing the President, 2008: The Insiders' View.* Philadelphia: University of Pennsylvania Press, 2009.

———. *Eloquence in an Electronic Age: The Transformation of Political Speechmaking.* New York: Oxford University Press, 1988.

Jamieson, Kathleen Hall, and David S. Birdsell. *Presidential Debates: The Challenge of Creating an Informed Electorate.* New York: Oxford University Press, 1988.

Jamieson, Kathleen Hall, and Paul Waldman. *Electing the President 2000: The Insiders' View.* Philadelphia: University of Pennsylvania Press, 2001.

———, eds. *Electing the President 2004: The Insiders' View.* Philadelphia: University of Pennsylvania Press, 2006.

———. *The Press Effect: Politicians, Journalists, and the Stories That Shape the Political World.* New York: Oxford University Press, 2003.

Jordan, Hamilton. *Crisis: The Last Year of the Carter Presidency.* New York: Putnam, 1982.

Klein, Herbert G. *Making It Perfectly Clear: An Inside Account of Nixon's Love-Hate Relationship with the Media.* Garden City, N.Y.: Doubleday, 1980.

Kraus, Sidney, ed. *The Great Debates: Background, Perspective, Effects.* Bloomington: Indiana University Press, 1962. [Of particular interest are the chapters by Douglass Cater; Herbert A. Seltz and Richard D. Yoakam; Robert W. Sarnoff; and Frank Stanton.]

———, ed. *The Great Debates: Carter vs. Ford, 1976.* Bloomington: Indiana University Press, 1979. [Of particular interest is the chapter by Herbert A. Seltz and Richard D. Yoakam.]

———. *Televised Presidential Debates and Public Policy.* Hillsdale, N.J.: Erlbaum, 1988.

Lanoue, David J., and Peter R. Schrott. *The Joint Press Conference: The History, Impact, and Prospects of American Presidential Debates.* Westport, Conn.: Greenwood, 1991.

Lehrer, Jim. *The Last Debate.* New York: Random House, 1995.

———. *Tension City: Inside the Presidential Debates.* New York: Random House, 2011.

Lemert, James B., William R. Elliott, James M. Bernstein, William L. Rosenberg, and Karl J. Nestvold. *News Verdicts, the Debates, and Presidential Campaigns.* New York: Praeger, 1991.

Lieberman, Joseph I., and Hadassah Lieberman. *An Amazing Adventure: Joe and Hadassah's Personal Notes on the 2000 Campaign.* New York: Simon and Schuster, 2003.

Martel, Myles. "Debate Preparations in the Reagan Camp: An Insider's View." *Speaker and Gavel* 18 (Winter 1981): 34–46.

———. *Political Campaign Debates: Images, Strategies, and Tactics.* New York: Longman, 1983.

Matthews, Christopher. *Kennedy and Nixon: The Rivalry That Shaped Postwar America.* New York: Simon and Schuster, 1996.

Mazo, Earl, Malcolm Moos, Hallock Hoffman, and Harvey Wheeler. *The Great Debates*. Santa Barbara, Calif.: Center for the Study of Democratic Institutions, 1962.

McAuliffe, Terry. *What a Party! My Life Among Democrats: Presidents, Candidates, Donors, Activists, Alligators, and Other Wild Animals*. New York: St. Martin's, 2007.

Meadow, Robert G. "Televised Campaign Debates as Whistle-Stop Speeches." In *Television Coverage of the 1980 Presidential Campaign*, ed. William C. Adams, 89–102. Norwood, N.J.: Ablex, 1983.

Mickelson, Sig. *From Whistle Stop to Sound Bite: Four Decades of Politics and Television*. New York: Praeger, 1989.

Mills, Stephen. "Rebuilding the Presidential Debates." *Speaker and Gavel* 24 (1986): 41–51.

Minow, Newton N., J. B. Martin, and Lee M. Mitchell. *Presidential Television*. New York: Basic Books, 1973.

Minow, Newton N., and Clifford M. Sloan. *For Great Debates: A New Plan for Future Presidential TV Debates*. New York: Priority Press, 1987.

Mitchell, Lee M. *With the Nation Watching: Report of the Twentieth Century Fund Task Force*. Lexington, Mass.: Heath, 1979.

Moore, Jonathan, ed. *Campaign for President: The Managers Look at '84*. Dover, Mass.: Auburn House, 1986.

Moore, Jonathan, and Janet Fraser, eds. *Campaign for President: The Managers Look at '76*. Cambridge, Mass.: Ballinger, 1977.

Nessen, Ron. *It Sure Looks Different from the Inside*. Chicago: Playboy Press, 1978.

Nixon, Richard. *RN: The Memoirs of Richard Nixon*. New York: Grossett and Dunlap, 1978.

——. *Six Crises*. Garden City, N.Y.: Doubleday, 1962.

O'Donnell, Kenneth P., and David F. Powers. *Johnny, We Hardly Knew Ye: Memories of John Fitzgerald Kennedy*. With Joe McCarthy. Boston: Little, Brown, 1972.

Palin, Sarah. *Going Rogue: An American Life*. New York: HarperCollins, 2009.

Patterson, Thomas E. *Out of Order*. New York: Knopf, 1993.

Plouffe, David. *The Audacity to Win: The Inside Story and Lessons of Barack Obama's Historic Victory*. New York: Viking, 2009.

Quayle, Dan. *Standing Firm: A Vice-Presidential Memoir*. New York: HarperCollins, 1994.

Ranney, Austin. *The American Elections of 1984*. New York: American Enterprise Institute, 1985.

——, ed. *The Past and Future of Presidential Debates*. Washington, D.C.: American Enterprise Institute, 1979.

Reagan, Ronald. *An American Life*. New York: Simon and Schuster, 1990.

Reinsch, J. Leonard. *Getting Elected: From Radio and Roosevelt to Television and Reagan*. New York: Hippocrene, 1988.

Rove, Karl. *Courage and Consequence: My Life as a Conservative in the Fight*. New York: Simon and Schuster, 2010.

Royer, Charles T., ed. *Campaign for President: The Managers Look at '92*. Hollis, N.H.: Hollis, 1994.

Runkel, David R., ed. *Campaign for President: The Managers Look at '88*. Dover, Mass.: Auburn House, 1989.

Shrum, Robert. *No Excuses: Concessions of a Serial Campaigner*. New York: Simon and Schuster, 2007.

Sides, John and Lynn Vavreck. *The Gamble: Choice and Chance in the 2012 Presidential Election*. Princeton, N.J.: Princeton University Press, 2013.

Simon, Roger. *Road Show: In America, Anyone Can Become President. It's One of the Risks We Take*. New York: Farrar, Straus and Giroux, 1990.

——. *Show Time: The American Political Circus and the Race for the White House*. New York: Times Books, 1998.

Smith, Howard K. *Events Leading Up to My Death: The Life of a Twentieth-Century Reporter*. New York: St. Martin's Press, 1996.

Sorensen, Ted. *Counselor: A Life at the Edge of History*. New York: HarperCollins, 2008.

Speakes, Larry. *Speaking Out: Inside the Reagan White House*. New York: Scribner's, 1980.

Stevens, Stuart. *The Big Enchilada: Campaign Adventures with the Cockeyed Optimists from Texas Who Won the Biggest Prize in Politics*. New York: Free Press, 2001.

Stockman, David. *The Triumph of Politics: The Inside Story of the Reagan Revolution*. New York: Harper and Row, 1986.

Swerdlow, Joel L. *Beyond Debate: A Paper on Televised Presidential Debates*. New York: Twentieth Century Fund, 1984.

——, ed. *Presidential Debates: 1988 and Beyond*. Washington, D.C.: Congressional Quarterly, 1987.

Thomas, Evan, and the Staff of *Newsweek*. *Election 2004: How Bush Won and What You Can Expect in the Future*. New York: Public Affairs, 2004.

Troy, Gil. *See How They Ran: The Changing Role of the Presidential Candidate*. New York: Free Press, 1991.

White, Theodore. *The Making of the President 1960*. New York: Atheneum, 1961.

Witcover, Jules. *Joe Biden: A Life of Trial and Redemption*. New York: William Morrow, 2010.

——. *Marathon: The Pursuit of the Presidency, 1972–1976*. New York: Viking, 1977.

Wolffe, Richard. *The Message: The Reselling of President Obama*. New York: Twelve, 2013.

——. *Renegade: The Making of a President*. New York: Crown, 2009.

INDEX

Academia de las Ciencias y las Artes de Televisión (Spain), 341
Adair, Bill, 287
Ailes, Roger, 56, 76, 84, 97–98, 142
Albright, Madeleine, 98
Allen, Frederic, 210
Allen, Mike, 139
Alter, Jonathan, 65–66, 68, 69–70
Anderson, John, 18, 96, 122, 138, 263–64; performing style, 162–63. *See also* Reagan–Anderson debate
Annenberg Public Policy Center, 287
Apple, R. W., Jr., 170
"Ask George Bush" forums, 42
Asman, Robert, 259, 272
Atwater, Lee, 64, 336–37
audio failure in Ford–Carter debate, 120–21, 240–42, 295–96, 302, 307
Axelrod, David, 67, 80, 267, 318, 319
Ayres, B. Drummond, 320

Bai, Matt, 191
Bailey, Doug, 60
Bailey, Pearl, 245
Baker, James A. 3d, 29, 31, 46, 49, 89, 122–23, 207, 217, 270–71, 296, 305–6; as negotiator for Bush–Cheney campaign, 25, 37–38, 43–44, 138–39, 235; as negotiator for George H. W. Bush, 36, 41–42; as negotiator for Ronald Reagan, 35–36; "Debategate," 111–12
Baker, Russell, 293–94
Balz, Dan, 69, 80, 107
Barbour, Haley, 26–27
Barnes, Fred, 145, 210
Barnouw, Erik, 6, 150
Barrett, Laurence, 111
Bash, Dana, 109
Begala, Paul, 42, 90, 259
Benedetto, Richard, 315

benefits of presidential debates, 330–33
Benenson, Joel, 80
Bennet, James, 237
Bennett, Dashiell, 280
Bentsen, Lloyd, 42, 143, 170; performing style, 168–69; preparation for debates, 52. *See also* Bentsen–Quayle debate
Bentsen–Quayle debate (1988), 42; news coverage, 134, 142–43, 319–20; performance by candidates, 168–70; preparations, 99–100; questioners, 206, 212–13, 215–16; venue, 244–45; "You're no Jack Kennedy," 54–55, 83, 90, 168–70, 213
Berger, Marilyn, 212, 308
Berke, Richard L., 42, 124, 137, 221–22, 243
Berlusconi, Silvio, 340
Bernstein, Elliot, 241–42
Biden, Joseph, 81, 88, 106, 140, 190, 280–81, 289, 319; performing style, 194–96; preparation for debates, 107. *See also* Biden–Palin debate; Biden–Ryan debate
Biden–Palin debate (2008), 58–59; news coverage, 125, 132–33; performance by candidates, 88, 194, 195–96, 197–98; preparations, 106–7; questioners, 72, 229; ratings, 325
Biden–Ryan debate (2012), 88–89, 194, 196, 202–4, 285
Birdsell, David S., 331
Black, Charles, 73–74
Black, Christine M., 57, 167
Blitzer, Wolf, 195
Bluefin Labs, 280
Bode, Ken, 134–35
Boorstin, Daniel, 334
Boxer, Barbara, 107
Boyd, Gerald, 134
Boyd, Robert, 213
Bradley, Bill, 173

Bradley, Ed, 135
Brinkley, David, 241, 295–96, 307
Broder, David S., 54, 58, 120, 156, 161, 168,
170, 173, 178, 300, 311, 312; role of
reporters in debate, 206, 297
Brokaw, Tom, 156, 176, 210, 212, 231, 238,
304, 312, 324
Brooks, David, 191
Brown, Janet, 44, 50, 218, 219, 244, 245, 250,
271, 272, 345
Brown, Pat, 75–76
Bruni, Frank, 69, 180
Bruno, Hal, 176, 212, 215, 223–25, 303
Brydon, Stephen R., 75
Buchanan, Patrick, 24
Buckley, Christopher, 179
Buckley, William F., Jr., 20
Bumiller, Elisabeth, 268
Burton, Bill, 67
Bush, Barbara, 70, 123, 126, 254
Bush, George H.W., 59, 109, 136, 160, 205,
211, 305, 319–20, 323–24, 337; attitude
toward debates, 41, 164, 259; glancing at
watch, 52, 101, 165, 265, 297, 300, 329;
performing style, 64, 84, 164–65, 328;
preparation for debates, 101. *See also*
Bush–Dukakis debates; Bush–Ferraro
debate; "Chicken George"; Clinton–
Bush–Perot debates
Bush, George W., 59, 112–13, 144, 184, 188,
245, 299, 323; allegations of cheating,
267 270; attitude toward debates, 44,
233; debate negotiations, 24–25, 26, 43,
250–51; performing style, 52, 56, 85,
86–87, 91, 179–81, 266–67, 300, 328;
preparation for debates, 102–3, 105, 260,
261; primary debates, 180, 192. *See also*
Bush–Gore debates; Bush–Kerry debates
Bush, Laura, 254
Bush, Prescott, 64
Bush–Dukakis debates (1988), 143, 219,
245–46; debate negotiations, 20–21, 31,
45–46, 49–50; Kitty Dukakis question:
52, 165, 167–68, 214, 227, 263, 321;
news coverage, 122–23, 129–30, 304;
performance by candidates, 57, 164–65,
167–68; questioners, 207, 211, 214–15, 242;
strategy, 64, 73–74
Bush–Ferraro debate (1984), 45; news
coverage, 126, 133, 303, 323–24;
performance by candidates, 164, 166–67;
questioners, 213; strategy, 86–87
Bush–Gore debates (2000), 43, 251;
negotiations, 22–24, 31–32, 37, 44, 46;
news coverage, 124, 130, 313–16;
performance by candidates, 70–71, 78–79,
173, 174–75, 180; questioners, 221–22

Bush–Kerry debates (2004), 254; debate
negotiations, 24–25, 34, 37–38, 43–44,
47–48, 50, 138–39, 251–52; Mary Cheney
reference, 52, 71, 104, 181, 232–33,
321–22; news coverage, 124–25, 130–31,
321–23; performance by candidates, 59,
62, 71, 85–86, 104–5, 180–81, 186–87;
questioners: 231–33, 234, 235, 237–38;
visuals, 266–67

Caddell, Patrick, 19, 60–61, 63–64, 121–22,
128, 163, 353n15
Cahill, Mary Beth, 104, 322
Cameron, Carl, 144–45
Cannon, Lou, 36, 53, 75, 97–98
Capra, Frank, 161
Card, Andrew, 268
Carlin, Diana, 76, 87, 298, 332–33, 338
Carlson, Margaret, 315
Carruthers, William, 93, 258, 262
Carson, Johnny, 18
Carter, Amy, 52, 95 96, 156, 323
Carter, Bill, 23
Carter, Jimmy, 17, 96, 161–62, 210, 246, 337;
Amy Carter reference, 52, 95–96, 156, 323;
debate negotiations, 30–31, 35, 45, 248;
news coverage, 121–22, 128, 140–41,
307–8, 310; performing style, 75, 155–56;
preparation for debates, 63, 93–95,
257–58. *See also* Ford–Carter debates,
Carter–Reagan debate
Carter–Reagan debate (1980), 163, 263–64;
"Debategate," 110–12; debate negotiations,
18–20, 36, 46–47; news coverage, 128, 138,
141, 323; performance by candidates,
156–57, 161–62; preparations, 96–97;
questioners, 211; ratings, 325; strategy, 51,
53–54, 58, 60–61, 63, 75
Carville, James, 73, 165, 317
Casey, William, 111
Castro, Fidel, 116
Cater, Douglass, 41
Chancellor, John, 169, 236–37, 310
Chase, Chevy, 154
Chavez, Hugo, 340
Cheney, Dick, 43, 52, 71, 86–87, 232, 248,
309, 321–22; performing style, 181–83;
preparation for debates, 110, 227. *See also*
Cheney–Edwards debate; Cheney–
Lieberman debate
Cheney, Lynne, 322
Cheney, Mary, 52, 71, 104, 181, 232–33,
254–55, 321–22
Cheney–Edwards debate (2004), 43, 71, 88,
133, 183, 187–88, 228, 254–55, 321
Cheney–Lieberman debate (2000), 50, 87–88,
133, 181–82, 184–85, 227

"Chicken George," 21–22, 23, 36
Chozick, Amy, 131
Christie, Chris, 125
Chromak, Leon, 256
Cillizza, Chris, 67–68, 74, 132
Clark, Helen, 342–43
Clark, Tony, 135
Clifford, Clark, 151
Clinton, Bill, 24, 87, 102, 170, 178, 235, 299; attitude toward debates, 56, 79, 91, 259, 333; debate negotiations, 31, 37, 41–42, 248, 251; in town hall debates, 41–42, 44, 76, 251, 253, 259; news coverage, 136, 144, 301–2; performing style, 56, 57, 76, 79, 90, 154, 171–72, 332, 335; preparation for debates, 100–101, 247–48. *See also* Clinton–Bush–Perot debates (1992); Clinton–Dole debates (1996)
Clinton, Hillary, 70, 107, 123–24, 144, 190, 193, 195, 253, 298, 301
Clinton–Bush–Perot debates (1992), 164, 253; debate negotiations, 21–22, 33, 36–37, 41–42; performance by candidates, 165, 171–72, 175–76, 335–36; preparations, 101, 258–59; questioners, 219–20, 225–27, 236–37; ratings, 325; strategy, 61, 64, 73
Clinton–Dole debates (1996), 60, 65, 201, 254; debate negotiations, 22, 31, 34, 37, 43, 251, 253; news coverage, 123–24, 136, 301–2; performance by candidates, 61–62, 158–60, 172; preparations, 259; questioners, 220–21, 237
CNN, experimental coverage of 1980 debate by, 263–64
Coddington, Mark, 287
Coelho, Tony, 86, 311
Cohen, Richard, 181
College of William and Mary, 242
Colley, Chip, 252, 260
Commager, Henry Steele, 334
Commission on Presidential Debates, 239, 240, 345; format proposals, 41, 43, 44; moderators, 50, 219, 223, 229, 230, 231; production arrangements, 244, 250, 258, 259, 271, 272; sponsorship role, 22–26, 28–34, 35, 37, 330, 341
Compton, Ann, 214
Connally, John, 302
Connolly, Ceci, 130
Conroy, Scott, 260–61
Cooper, Anderson, 200
Corry, John, 157
Couric, Katie, 197, 198
Cousins, Norman, 328
Cox, Archibald, 4, 5
Craig, Gregory, 104, 179–81
Cramer, Richard Ben, 158–59

Cranston, Alan, 142–43
Cronkite, Walter, 3, 128, 291, 296, 303, 307
Crowley, Candy, 72, 229–31, 238, 281, 343
Crowley, Monica, 235
C-SPAN, 172, 183, 238
Cuddy, Amy, 203
Cuomo, Mario, 76
Current TV, 278–79, 283, 317
Cutter, Stephanie, 124

Dale, Billy, 254
Deaver, Michael, 19, 20, 39, 56, 58, 90–91, 97, 98, 249, 303
"Debategate," 110–12
DeKlerk, F. W., 339
Demarest, David, 259, 304
DeParis, George, 268
Devenish, Nicolle, 268
Devine, Tad, 134, 170
DiCaprio, Leonardo, 190
Dickerson, John, 88–89, 252
Digging the Dirt, 314
Diskin, Sonny, 262
Doerner, William R., 166–67
Dole, Bob, 35, 52, 59, 133, 140, 178, 179, 201, 216, 263, 301, 302; attitude toward debates, 77–78; debate negotiations, 31, 248, 251; "Democrat wars" statement, 52, 213, 216; performing style, 65, 77–78, 83–84, 158–59; preparation for debates, 101–2. *See also* Clinton–Dole debates; Dole–Mondale debate
Dole, Elizabeth, 140, 253, 301, 302
Dole–Mondale debate (1976), 40, 65, 87, 140, 157, 158–59, 212, 216, 302–3
Donahue, Phil, 136, 172
Donaldson, Sam, 55, 78, 120–21, 141, 144, 159, 179
Donilon, Thomas, 52, 64, 73, 100–101, 245, 249, 255–56
Donovan, Robert J., 117–18
Dowd, Matthew, 124, 187
Dowd, Maureen, 99, 174, 191, 198, 251
Downey, Thomas, 112
Drew, Elizabeth, 36, 40, 64, 119, 154, 156, 166, 169, 208, 336
Drummond, Roscoe, 117
Dukakis, Kitty, 52, 165, 167–68, 214, 227, 263, 321
Dukakis, Michael, 52, 73, 100, 129–30, 139, 143, 169, 170, 263, 319; debate negotiations, 20–21, 31, 45–46; performing style, 57, 59, 64, 76, 84, 167–68; postdebate interview with Bernard Shaw, 320–21; preparation for debates, 88. *See also* Bush–Dukakis debates
Duncan, Dayton, 123

Dunn, Anita, 29, 108, 231
Duval, Michael, 17, 121–22

early voting, 38–39
Eckart, Dennis, 54–55
Edwards, John, 71, 88, 190, 195, 228, 254–55, 268, 321; performing style, 187–88. *See also* Cheney–Edwards debate
Eisenhower, Dwight D., 15, 16, 152, 209, 211
Eizenstadt, Stuart, 95
Ellis, Harris, 211
Eskew, Carter, 130
Estrich, Susan, 100, 102, 168, 304
Evans, Rowland, 19

Facebook, 275, 288
Face the Nation, 43, 232, 318
Fahrenkopf, Frank J., Jr., 33, 43, 231, 239, 245
Fallows, James, 77, 89, 130–31, 174, 180, 200, 298
Farah, George, 330
Farhi, Paul, 139
Faw, Bob, 163
Federal Communications Commission, 17
Feist, Sam, 265–66
Ferraro, Geraldine, 45, 86–87, 107, 256, 323–24, 328; performing style, 166–67; preparation for debates, 98–99. *See also* Bush–Ferraro debate
Fey, Tina, 198
Field, Sally, 245
Fields, Wayne, 62
Finch, Bob, 81
Fiorentino, Imero, 248
Fisher, Walter, 17
Fitzwater, Marlin, 123
Fleming, Bob, 209
Flowers, Gennifer, 254
focus groups, 276–77
Ford, Betty, 140, 245, 302
Ford, Gerald, 17, 52, 245, 246, 258, 302–3; debate negotiations, 30, 45, 46, 248; Eastern Europe statement, 52, 83, 154, 155, 211, 213, 305, 307–10, 313, 337; performing style, 153–54; preparation for debates, 74, 75, 93, 94, 137. *See also* Ford–Carter debates
Ford–Carter debates (1976), 246, 291, 335; debate negotiations, 30–31; news coverage, 118–20, 121–22, 135, 140, 299, 302–3, 307–10; performance by candidates, 153 154, 155–56, 328; strategy, 17, 43, 45, 48, 60, 74–75; visuals, 262–63. *See also* audio failure in Ford–Carter debate
formats for presidential debates, 41–45, 50, 90, 177–78, 179, 192, 195–96, 197, 203–5; 304. *See also* town hall debates

Fouhy, Beth, 132
Fouhy, Ed, 42, 226, 242, 243, 244, 271
Fournier, Ron, 266
Fox, Michael J., 245
Fox, Vicente, 344
Frankel, Max, 211
Frederick, Pauline, 214
Friedenberg, Robert V., 58
Fuller, Tony, 166

Gallup polling organization, 235, 316
Gannon, James, 154
Genachowski, Julius, 229
Gergen, David, 53, 96–97
Germond, Jack, 36, 86, 158, 171, 176, 254
Gibson, Charles, 86, 190, 197, 198, 227, 231–32
Gingrich, Newt, 110, 145, 200–201
Giscard d'Estaing, Valéry, 77, 343
Gitlin, Todd, 9–10
Giuliani, Rudolph, 192, 195, 200
Goldenson, Leonard, 1
Goldman, Peter, 153
Goldwater, Barry, 16
Goodman, Ellen, 164
Goodman, Walter, 221, 327
Goodwin, Doris Kearns, 150
Goodwin, Robert, 33, 253
Google, 288–89
Gore, Al, 47, 85, 107, 130, 131, 140, 144, 245, 278, 317; performing style, 56, 59, 70–71, 78–79, 85, 91, 173–75, 261, 267, 328; preparation for debates, 103–104, 112, 261; truth issue, 313–16. *See also* Bush–Gore debates; Gore–Kemp debate; Gore–Perot NAFTA debate; Gore–Quayle–Stockdale debate
Gore, Tipper, 245
Gore–Kemp debate (1996), 87, 173, 178–79
Gore–Perot NAFTA debate, 160
Gore–Quayle–Stockdale debate (1992), 47, 123, 170–71, 173, 176–77, 223–24
Grabel, Linda, 79–80
Graber, Doris, 331
Graham, Lindsey, 25–26
Granholm, Jennifer, 107, 137
Greenfield, Jeff, 70, 207, 236
Greenfield, Meg, 170
Greer, Frank, 249–50
Gregory, Bettina, 323
Greider, William, 155–56, 159
Griffin, Tim, 314
Groer, Annie, 207, 208, 242

Haake, Garrett, 305
Haberman, Maggie, 200–201
Hahn, Dan F., 85

Haig, Al, 216
Hair, Princell, 266
Hagerty, James, 16
Halberstam, David, 1, 6, 15
Hall, Leonard, 15
Hall, Marisa, 236
Halperin, Mark, 34, 82, 106, 132
Hamby, Peter, 282
Harian, Victoria, 49, 249, 256
Harris, John, 115
Hastings, Michael, 284
Healy, Robert, 166
Hegedus, Chris, 306
height of presidential debaters, 45–46, 73, 258–59
Heilemann, John, 82, 106, 194
Helmbreck, Valerie, 329–30
Henry, William, 157, 162
Hertsgaard, Mark, 311
Hewitt, Don, 2–4, 6–7, 8, 115, 335
Hilton, Jack, 57
Hoffman, David, 164
Hofstra University, 255
Hoge, James, 83–84, 216
holding rooms, 252–53
Hollande, Francois, 339
Horton, Willie, 73
Huckabee, Mike, 192
Hughes, Karen, 124, 266
Hulu, 289
Hume, Brit, 135, 144–45, 158, 165, 210, 212, 305
humor in presidential debates, 83–86, 159, 162, 175–76, 180, 335–36
Humphrey, Hubert H., 150, 153
Hyatt, Joel, 278

Ifill, Gwen, 72, 198, 228–29
Imus, Don, 315
incumbents as debaters, 15, 16, 17, 19, 20, 22, 24, 38, 44, 46–47, 53, 60–63
influence of presidential debates on voting, 337–38
Instituto Federal Electoral (Mexico), 341

Jagoda, Barry, 262
Jamaica Debates Commission, 341
Jamieson, Bob, 120
Jamieson, Kathleen Hall, 51, 152, 315, 331
Jaroslovsky, Rich, 311
Jarriel, Tom, 137, 141
Jennings, Peter, 206, 208, 211, 217–18
"Joe the Plumber," 80, 193
Johnson, Lyndon, 16, 39, 150, 268, 291
Jordan, Hamilton, 95–96, 308
Jordan, Vernon, 43, 138–39, 250
Joyner, Tom, 318

Judd, Jackie, 142, 320
Judis, John B., 236

Kaiser, Robert G., 138
Kalb, Marvin, 307
Kantor, Mickey, 31, 41, 61
Karl, Jonathan, 144
Keller, Bill, 269
Kelly, Jack, 120, 242
Kelly, Michael, 85, 165, 174, 175
Kemp, Jack, 87, 88, 107, 136, 173, 178–79.
    See also Gore–Kemp debate
Kennedy, Jacqueline, 4–5, 8
Kennedy, John F., 1–11, 15–16, 63, 72, 155, 209, 261, 299; attitude toward debates, 253, 301; debate negotiations, 28, 29, 36, 256–57; performing style, 56, 150–51, 332, 335; pre-presidential debates, 47, 152; preparation for debates, 2, 92, 93; "You're no Jack Kennedy," 52, 54–55, 83, 90, 100, 168–70, 213. See also Kennedy–Nixon debates
Kennedy, Robert F., 160, 256, 301
Kennedy, Ted, 199
Kennedy–Nixon debates (1960), 1–11, 161, 252, 270, 311; critical reaction, 334–35; debate negotiations, 29–30, 39–40, 42–43, 48, 256–57, 343; legacy, 9–11, 93, 293, 339, 345; news coverage, 2–3, 114–19, 122, 140, 291–295, 300–1; origins, 15–17; performance by candidates, 6–7, 150–53; preparations, 2, 92, 93; questioners, 208, 209–10, 211–12; ratings, 325; strategy, 7, 58; visuals, 261–62, 328, 337
Kerrey, Bob, 222
Kerry, John, 52, 56, 62, 66, 105, 108, 144–45, 188, 268; debate negotiations, 28, 248, 250; Mary Cheney reference, 71, 104, 181, 232–33, 321–23; performing style, 56, 76–77, 85–86, 185–87, 266; preparation for debates, 81, 104. See also Bush–Kerry debates
Kerry, Teresa Heinz, 245
Keyes, Alan, 189–90
Khrushchev, Nikita, 4, 116, 152
Kiesinger, Georg, 340
Kiker, Douglas, 118, 295–96
Kim, Richard, 223
King, John, 131
King, Larry, 23, 135, 173
King, Susan, 138
Kinnock, Neil, 194–95
Kirk, Paul G., Jr., 23–24, 34, 235
Kissinger, Henry, 323
Klain, Ron, 44; Biden–Palin debate, 88; Obama–McCain debates, 26–27, 38, 44, 56, 68; Obama–Romney debates, 82, 108, 306–7; social media, 83, 279–80, 284–85, 286, 287

Klein, Ezra, 202
Klein, Herbert G., 9, 15–16, 33, 39, 292, 300
Klein, Joe, 65
Klein, Rick, 133
Knox, Olivier, 318
Kolbert, Elizabeth, 173, 177
Kondracke, Mort, 322
Kraus, Sidney, 43
Kristol, Bill, 178–79
Kurczy, Stephen, 283
Kurtz, Howard, 277, 302

Labastida, Francisco, 344
Lakoff, George, 74
Lanoue, David J., 338
Last Debate, The, 218
Laxalt, Paul, 97
Lazio, Rick, 70
League of Women Voters, 18, 30, 48–49, 159, 217, 248, 249, 256, 258, 262, 264
Leahy, Patrick, 254
Lehrer, Jim, 225, 228, 230; oral history interviews with presidential debaters, 63, 164, 240, 265; performance as moderator, 67, 159, 178, 219–23, 270–71, 281, 343; role of moderator, 206, 217–18, 245; selection as moderator, 50, 227; town hall debates, 237, 239
Lehrer, Kate, 220
Leibovich, Mark, 196, 305
Lelyveld, Joseph, 118, 241
Lemert, James B., 299, 304
Leno, Jay, 58–59, 261
Leone, Richard C., 40, 56, 75–76
Letterman, David, 80, 189
Leubsdorf, Carl, 314
Lewis, Fulton, 117
Lewis, Martin, 315
LiBretto, John, 258–59, 265, 271, 272
Lieberman, Joseph, 87–88, 106, 245, 260; performing style, 184–85; preparation for debates, 92, 227. See also Cheney–Lieberman debate
Limbaugh, Rush, 226
limitations of presidential debates, 333–37
Lincoln, Abraham, 210
Lincoln–Douglas debates, 24, 115, 118
Lindsey, Beverly, 250, 251
Lippmann, Walter, 16, 329
Lisagor, Peter, 292
Lithwick, Dahlia, 133
Lockhart, Joe, 322
Lodge, Henry Cabot, 7, 39, 150
Lotan, Gilad, 282
Lott, Trent, 26
Louden, Allan, 333

Lozano, Yvette, 113
Lugo, Fernando, 340

makeup, use of in debates, 3–4, 83, 120, 153, 261, 292–93, 312–13
Mandela, Nelson, 339
Mankiewicz, Frank, 76
Margolis, Jon, 206, 212
Marshall, Joshua, 145
Martel, Myles, 53
Martin, Jonathan, 133
Mashek, John, 176, 208, 217
Matalin, Mary, 164, 187–88
Matthews, Chris, 69, 317
Mazo, Earl, 16
McAuliffe, Terry, 124–25, 254
McCain, John, 52, 56, 80, 90, 106, 137, 229, 231; attitude toward debates, 259–60; debate negotiations, 25–27, 34, 38, 248; performing style, 59, 66–68, 77, 192–94, 252, 267, preparation for debates, 66, 105. See also Obama–McCain debates
McCarthy, Joseph, 64
McCurry, Mike, 124, 223
McGill, Ralph, 294
McGovern, George, 153
McGrory, Mary, 162, 178, 207
McKinnon, Mark, 82, 105, 113, 267
McLuhan, Marshall, 161, 241
Meacham, Jon, 201
Meadow, Robert G., 331
Meany, George, 83
Mears, Walter, 212, 213
Medvedev, Dmitry, 340
Meet the Press, 23, 43, 72, 94, 102, 268, 329
Mehlman, Ken, 268
Memorandum of Understanding, 247; ban on notes and props, 47, 257; history, 32–35, 138–39; moderators, 49–50, 224–25, 230, 234; production arrangements, 247, 251–52; town hall debates, 44–45; visuals, 263, 266
Merida, Kevin, 88
Messina, Jim, 125
Mickelson, Sig, 4, 7, 29
Miklaszewski, Jim, 159
Milbank, Dana, 282, 300
Miller, Arthur, 91
Miller, Zeke, 306
Millman, Joel, 197
Mills, Stephen, 336
Mitchell, Andrea, 208–9, 214
Mitterand, Francois, 77, 343
moderators of presidential debates, 48–50, 205–6, 212–13, 214–33, 237–39
Moffatt, Zachary, 283–84, 286–87, 288
Mondale, Walter, 20, 72, 140, 149, 162, 166, 210, 308, 311, 313, 328; attitude toward

debates, 326–27; debate negotiations, 36–37, 40, 248–49; performing style, 63–64, 157–58. *See also* Dole–Mondale debate; Reagan–Mondale debates
Moore, Julianne, 106
Moore, Martha T., 133
Morales, Evo, 340
Morris, Dick, 172
Morton, Bruce, 310
Moyers, Bill, 214, 218
Mr. Smith Goes to Washington, 99
Mudd, Roger, 128–29, 142–43, 296, 303–4, 305
Mulford, Clay, 33, 101, 176
Myers, Beth, 109
Myers, Lisa, 78, 172
Myers, Seth, 25

Nader, Ralph, 24
Nelson, Jack, 212
Nelson, Robert M., 269
Nessen, Ron, 74–75, 137, 154–55, 295, 302, 309, 310
Newman, Edwin, 158, 240
Nicholson, Jack, 254
Nixon, Patricia, 5, 9, 52, 292
Nixon, Richard M., 1–11, 15–16, 17, 52, 72, 116, 165, 171, 175, 209–10, 235, 301, 307; attitude toward debates, 15–16, 152, 235, 301, 335; debate negotiations, 28, 29, 36; performing style, 152–53; preparation for debates, 93. *See also* Kennedy–Nixon debates
"Nixopedia," 93
Nolan, Martin F., 179
Noonan, Peggy, 223
Norton, Michael I., 264
notes, use of during debates, 47, 257
Novak, Robert, 19
Nyhan, David, 168

Obama, Barack, 17, 56, 59, 62, 195, 196, 204, 229, 298, 337; attitude toward debates, 190–92, 259–60; debate negotiations, 25–26, 27, 28, 44, 248; "horses and bayonets" reference, 69, 81, 280, 281, 284, 285, 289; performing style, 56, 65–66, 70–71, 74, 80–81, 82, 90, 91, 189–92, 267, 275, 328, 332; preparation for debates, 93, 105, 108–9. *See also* Obama–McCain debates; Obama–Romney debates
Obama–McCain debates (2008), 25–28; debate negotiations, 38, 252; moderator, 222, 231, 232, 238; news coverage, 125, 131–32, 278–79; performance by candidates, 56, 59, 66–68, 90, 191–94, 252; strategy, 74, 80

Obama–Romney debates (2012), 255; debate negotiations, 28, 38; moderator, 222–23, 229–30, 238, 343; news coverage, 125–26, 132, 275, 316–19; performance by candidates, 62–63, 71–72, 82, 90, 191–92, 201–2; preparations, 108–9; social media, 275–76, 280–81, 283, 288–90; strategy, 68–70, 80–81
O'Brien, Shannon, 199
O'Connor, John J., 264
O'Donnell, Brett, 44, 62, 83
O'Donnell, Norah, 131
Oliphant, Pat, 18
Oliphant, Thomas, 57, 167, 172
Olsen, Ted, 107
O'Neill, Tip, 77
on-site debate negotiations, 246–55
O'Reilly, Bill, 145
Oreskes, Michael, 304

Paar, Jack, 1, 116
Packwood, Bob, 99–100
Paley, William, 1
Palin, Sarah, 26, 58–59, 72, 140, 260–61, 299, 317; performing style, 197–98, 336; preparation for debates, 82, 106–7, 137. *See also* Biden–Palin debate
Patterson, Eugene, 153
Patterson, Thomas, 116, 127, 309
Paul, Ron, 192
Payne, Dan, 76
Peckham, Matt, 289
Pennebaker, D. A., 306
Perez-Peña, Richard, 184
Perot, Ross, 22, 84–85, 135, 144, 162, 173, 177, 219–20, 253, 259, 277, 299; performing style, 175–76, 335–36; preparation for debates, 93, 101, 259. *See also* Clinton–Bush–Perot debates
Perry, James M., 311
Perry, Rick, 200
Peters, Jeremy, 230
Pew Research Center, 282, 286, 299, 316, 331
Pfister, Walter, 262
Pickler, Nedra, 131
Pierce, Charles P., 328–29
Pinkerton, James J., 78
Plouffe, David, 27, 318
PolitiFact.com, 287
Polsby, Nelson, 10
Popkin, Sam, 77, 95–96, 337
Portman, Rob, 103, 106
Powell, Jody, 30–31, 36, 135, 296
props, use of during debates, 47, 257
Psaki, Jen, 125
Purdum, Todd S., 69
Putin, Vladimir, 340

Quarles, Norma, 206
Quayle, Dan, 140, 198, 205, 299, 304; in 1988 debate, 210–11, 215–16, 306; in 1992 debate, 42, 47, 87; performing style, 169–70, 328; news coverage, 134, 142–43; preparation for debates, 99–100; "You're no Jack Kennedy," 52, 54–55, 83, 90, 168–70, 213. *See also* Bentsen–Quayle debate; Gore–Quayle–Stockdale debate
Quigley, Joan, 39

Raddatz, Martha, 203–4, 229, 230, 281
Radziwill, Lee, 4
Rafshoon, Gerald, 45
Raines, Howell, 310–11
Ranney, Austin, 60, 313
Rather, Dan, 141–42, 144
ratings for presidential debates, 5, 325–26, 395n1, 395nn2–3
reaction shots, 6–7, 45, 118, 261–67, 300
Reade, John, 231, 260
Reagan, Nancy, 39, 40, 97, 141, 312
Reagan, Ronald, 24, 52, 56, 95, 110–11, 122, 140, 201, 210, 260, 299, 303, 305, 319, 320, 337; age issue, 37, 52, 54, 162, 209, 310–13, 328–29, 336–37; debate negotiations, 28, 31, 35–36, 39, 40, 248–49; performing style, 51, 53–54, 57, 75–76, 90–91, 154, 160–62, 332; preparation for debates, 96–98; 1980 Nashua, New Hampshire, primary debate, 146–47. *See also* Carter–Reagan debate; Reagan–Anderson debate
Reagan–Anderson debate (1980), 18, 40, 141, 161–63, 218
Reagan–Mondale debates (1984), 337; debate negotiations, 36, 40; news coverage, 120–21, 128–29, 141, 303–4, 310–13; performance by candidates, 20, 54, 55, 61, 157–58, 162; questioners, 48–49, 209, 216–17; strategy, 63–64, 72, 75–76
Reasoner, Harry, 240, 307
Reddit, 275
Redford, Robert, 93–94
Reed, Scott, 124
Reinsch, J. Leonard, 43
Remnick, David, 189
Renshon, Stanley, 76
Rhodes, Ben, 109
Rice, Condoleezza, 103
Richards, Ann, 124, 169
Richardson, Bill, 190
Ridings, Dorothy, 49, 217
Roberts, Cokie, 175
Robinson, Michael J., 87, 237
Robison, James, 260
Rockefeller, Nelson, 302
Rockwell, Kelly, 232

Rogers, Ted, 2–4, 6
Rogers, Todd, 264
Rogich, Sigmund, 81, 92
Romney, Mitt, 65–66, 81, 110, 145, 192, 196, 231, 255, 257, 260, 305; Big Bird reference, 81, 276, 280, 281, 284, 289, 318; "binders full of women" reference, 81, 281, 285, 288, 289; performing style, 68, 70–71, 199–202, 267; preparation for debates, 109, 137. *See also* Obama–Romney debates
Rosen, Jay, 32, 231
Rosen, Jeffrey, 172
Rosenberg, Howard, 277
Rosenstiel, Thomas, 312, 316
Routman, Dan, 22
Rove, Karl, 23, 31–32, 37, 66, 124, 266–67, 314, 331–32
Ruge, Daniel, 312
Russert, Tim, 102, 238, 301–2
Rutenberg, Jim, 27
Ryan, Paul, 88–89, 285; performing style, 202–4; preparation for debates, 107. *See also* Biden–Ryan debate

Sabato, Larry, 130
Saddleback Church, 27–28, 193
Safire, William, 171, 326
Saletan, William, 88
Salinger, Pierre, 33
Sallett, Jonathan, 183
Sarkozy, Nicolas, 339
Sarnoff, Robert, 1, 40
Saturday Night Live, 79, 154, 180, 198, 203, 252, 271
Sauter, Kevin, 77
Sawyer, Diane, 49, 318
Scheunemann, Randy, 137
Schieffer, Bob, 68, 71, 93, 143–44, 227–28, 230, 232–33, 298, 307, 321
Schlesinger, Arthur, Jr., 4
Schneider, William, 277
Schorr, Daniel, 263–64
Schrott, Peter R., 338
Schwartz, Tony, 63
Seelye, Katharine Q., 131, 193, 198
Seltz, Herbert A., 30, 246, 248, 263
Shafer, Jack, 222
Shain, Percy, 292
Shales, Tom, 66, 74, 159, 170, 171, 176, 188, 190, 193, 217, 311
Shapiro, Walter, 215
Sharp, Adam, 280, 281, 283, 285
Sharpton, Al, 186
Shaw, Bernard, 41, 214; as moderator of 1988 debate, 52, 100, 165, 167–68, 205, 214–15, 227, 263; as moderator of 2000 vice presidential debate, 50, 182, 227;

postdebate interview with Michael Dukakis, 320–21
Sheehan, Michael, 59, 71, 83, 90, 100, 105
Sherr, Lynn, 133
Shindle, Kate, 198
Shrum, Robert, 32, 38, 104, 252, 261
Sides, John, 337
Sidey, Hugh, 157
Simon, Roger, 37, 101, 203, 297–98, 300, 304–5, 321
Simpson, Carole, 133, 225–27, 229, 235, 239
Six Crises, 9, 209–10
Smith, Aaron, 286
Smith, Ben, 133, 275
Smith, Craig Allen, and Kathy B., 76
Smith, Hedrick, 162–63
Smith, Howard K., 2, 5, 7, 214
Smith, Terence, 138
Sorensen, Theodore, 63, 92
Speakes, Larry, 302
Spielberg, Steven, 190
Spivak, Lawrence, 329
Squier, Robert, 50
Stahl, Lesley, 143, 170, 295–96
Stanley, Alessandra, 187, 190, 267
Stanton, Frank, 4, 115, 327
State of the Union, 161
Steele, Michael, 106
Steele, Richard, 155
Steeper, Fred, 227, 310
Stephanopoulos, George, 37, 64, 66, 132, 136, 185, 190, 306
Stevens, Stuart, 23, 46, 68, 79, 83, 102–3, 109, 230–31, 261, 314
Stewart, Jimmy, 99
Stirland, Sarah Lai, 278
Stockdale, James B., 22, 135; performing style, 176–77; preparation for debate, 93. *See also* Gore–Quayle–Stockdale debate
Stockdale, James Bond 2d, 177
Stockman, David, 53, 96–97, 110–11
Strauss, Robert, 138, 295
Streisand, Barbra, 124
Strout, Richard L., 292
Sullivan, Andrew, 317
Sunlight Foundation, 287

Tapper, Jake, 174, 237
Taylor, Elizabeth, 96
technical checks, predebate, 4, 73, 223–29, 255–60
Teeley, Peter, 126
Teeter, Robert, 310
Thomas, Lowell, 117
Thomason, Harry, 36, 101
Thompson, Fred, 192
Tierney, John, 47–48

Tillotson, Mary, 134
timing lights, 47–48, 250–51
Todd, Chuck, 132, 198
town hall debates, 34, 35, 102, 262, 271, 342; audience participants, 44, 79, 92, 236–39; Bush (George H.W.), 41–42, 52, 165, 205, 265; Bush (George W.), 70, 103, 180, 181, 251–52; Clinton, 41–42, 61, 69, 76. 101, 171, 172, 297, 332; Dole, 159; format, 41–42, 90, 134, 264; Gore, 70–71, 104, 174, 221; Kerry, 86, 186; McCain, 27, 77, 131–32, 193; moderators, 72, 225–27, 229–39, 245; negotiations, 248, 251–52, 253, 258–59; Obama, 69, 108–9, 191–92; Romney, 72, 109, 201, 255; rules, 44–45. *See also individual town hall debates*
Traub, James, 88
Trent, Judith S., 86
Trewhitt, Henry, 209
Treyz, Oliver, 1–2
Troy, Gil, 161
Truman, Harry S, 151, 173
Tumblr, 289
Tumulty, Karen, 47
Twitter, 68, 70, 81, 83, 278–90, 299, 345, 387n7

University of California, Los Angeles, 143, 144, 245
University of Massachusetts, 261
University of Mississippi, 25–26, 244
Univision, 28, 289
Uribe, Alvaro, 340
Usry, Kimberly, 236
Ustream, 289

Van Hollen, Chris, 107
Vanocur, Sander, 209–10, 211, 214
Vavreck, Lynn, 337
Venardos, Lane, 17
venues for presidential debates, 243–46, 261
Verizon, 285–86
vice presidential debates, 86–89. *See also individual vice presidential debates*
Vom Fremd, Mike, 135
Von Drehle, David, 37, 134
Voorhees, Josh, 45
Voorhis, Jerry, 15

Wade, David, 125
Wake Forest University, 245–46
Waldman, Paul, 315
Wallace, George, 153
Wallace, Mark, 43–44, 139, 278
Walshe, Shushannah, 260–61
Walters, Barbara, 120, 212, 214, 216–17, 323
Walthall, Denton, 236

Warner, John, 96
Warner, Margaret, 57, 214
Warren, Charles, 208
Warren, Rick, 27–28, 193
War Room, The, 306
Washington University, 229
Wayne, John, 20
WBBM, 1–8, 140, 225, 305, 351n2, 351n6
Weaver, Warren, 168–69
Weinraub, Bernard, 129
Weld, William, 185
Westfeldt, Wallace, 153
Wheaton, Ken, 290
Wheeler, Harvey, 150–51, 152, 335
White, Jack, 207
White, Theodore, 6, 9
Will, George, 69, 96, 127, 164, 170, 173, 179
Williams, Brian, 195
Williamson, Brady, 247, 248, 252, 255
Wilson, Bill, 6
Wirthlin, Richard, 19, 54, 61

Witcover, Jules, 36, 86, 118, 154, 158, 171, 176, 254
Witt, James Lee, 314
Wolffe, Richard, 81
Woodruff, Judy, 141, 185, 212, 214, 215–16
Woods, Rose Mary, 8–9
Wooten, James, 246, 311–12
Wurzelbacher, Samuel Joseph, 80

Xbox, 275, 289

Yankelovich, Daniel, 161–62
Yellin, Jessica, 222
Yeom, Jaeho, 342
Yoakam, Richard D., 30, 246, 248, 263
YouGov, 289
YouTube, 28, 278, 289, 318, 342

Zeff, Blake, 78, 298
Zelinksy, Aaron, 35
Zimbalist, Efrem, Jr., 293